```
HT
111
.D77
cop. 1
                      12.50
DRUKS
The city in Western
civilization
```

```
HT
111
.D77
cop. 1

DRUKS

THE CITY IN WESTERN CIVILI-
ZATION
```

THE CHICAGO PUBLIC LIBRARY

HILD REGIONAL BRANCH
4546 LINCOLN AVE.
CHICAGO, ILLINOIS 60625

FORM 19

CITIES IN CIVILIZATION

(CITIES IN CIVILIZATION)
THE CITY IN WESTERN CIVILIZATION

Volume I

Herbert Druks Ph. D.
Professor of History
City University of New York

And

Silvio R. Lacetti Ph. D.
Professor of History
Stevens Institute of Technology

ROBERT SPELLER & SONS, PUBLISHERS, INC.
10 EAST 23rd STREET
NEW YORK, N. Y.

© 1971 by Robert Speller & Sons, Publishers, Inc.
10 East 23rd Street
New York, N.Y.

Library of Congress Catalog Card No. 77-149632

FIRST EDITION

SBN 0-8315-0053-0

PRINTED IN THE UNITED STATES OF AMERICA

Table of Contents

I.	From Babel to Jerusalem	1
II.	Greek Urbanism	24
III.	Rome	116
IV.	The Middle Ages	177
V.	The Renaissance City	227
VI.	17th Century Cities	278
VII.	The City and the American Revolution	349
VIII.	Paris in Revolt	361

List of Illustrations

Jerusalem	19
Damascus Gate	20
The Western Wall of the Temple	21
The Via Dolorosa	22
Jaffa	23
The Acropolis	25
The Parthenon	26
The Colosseum	158
View of the Roman Forum	159
The Appian Way	160
Moses	252
St Peter's	253
View of Florence	254
Leonardo's transportation plan	274
Leonardo's church plan	275
Florence	276
St. Mark's Square in Venice	277
Buckingham Palace	316
Lord Mayor's Show	317
House of Parliament	318
Hotel des Invalides	328
Notre Dame	329
Versailles—Hall of Mirrors	336
The USS Constitution	349
Paul Revere's House	350
Bunker Hill	351
Conciergerie	361
Palais Royal	362
Hotel des Invalides	363

The City in Western Civilization

In this late 20th century when city life plays such a vital role in the progress of mankind we ask about the nature of the city. We see that as men gather, a social order is created with certain customs, folkways, mores and laws. In that complex process of social interaction, we see that there likewise develops a network of religion, politics, trade, art and science. And we see that unless the city faces certain basic challenges of survival such as providing for basic health and sanitation needs, transportation, housing, recreation and education, it cannot survive.

There have been many other writings on the city such as Mumford's *City in History* and Toynbee's pictorial *Cities of Destiny* and in their way they have made their contributions to a better understanding of the city, but they have not enabled the people of the city to speak for themselves. You may examine temples, churches, homes, streets, commerce, religion—whatever you wish—but you won't know the city unless you know the people. In these pages we present *The City in Western Civilization* as it appeared to those who lived in the city. In this book we present the testimony of those who lived in the city from ancient times to the late 1700's. The second half of our study will seek to portray the contemporary city from the 1800's to our day. Perhaps after studying the history of the city we may come closer to answering such questions as: What is the city? How do cities come into being? How do our cities differ from those of the past? Does man create the city or does the city create the man?

The goal of this study is to present the reader new perspectives and new understanding of the city as a way of life.

We would like to express our gratitude to the Greek, Israeli and Italian consulates and the national tourist offices of France, Great Britain, Israel and Italy for providing us with pictures of their cities. We would also like to thank Professor Richard Humphrey for his helpfulness and to Oxford University Press for permission to reprint from their English Historical Documents.

I. From Babel to Jerusalem

In Biblical history various references are made to cities. We find the very basic conception of the importance of city life when the people of Babel cry out — "Let us build a city and make a name for ourselves, lest we be forgotten." And we can trace the development of a major cosmopolitan area — Jerusalem. It was King David who established Jerusalem as the capital of Israel. He built his city among the highest mountain peaks in the area and thereby protected it against assault. It was centrally located, a junction on the roads joining Egypt and the Mediterranean shore with Jericho and the area east of Jordan, and linking Shechem and the north with Hebron in the south.

The area was taken over by King David in 1,000 B.C. from its Jebusite defenders. While David founded the new capital it was Solomon who transformed it into a major metropolitan area by constructing a Temple of the Lord atop Mount Moriah, the royal palace nearby and many other structures of grandeur. The period of the First Temple terminated in 587 B.C. when King Nebuchadnesser of Babylon invaded the country. The City fell to the invaders; the Temple was destroyed, and thousands were exiled to Babylon. It was Jeremiah who prophesized the downfall.

Some fifty years later King Cyrus of Persia conquered the Babylonians and granted the Israelites the right to rebuild their City with its Temple. The rebuilding of the Temple marked a resurgence of the people in their own land. Prophet Nehemiah who reached Jerusalem in the middle of the 5th century B.C. set about the task of rebuilding the city's walls to protect it from attack. The Samaritans tried to prevent that reconstruction but they were no match for the dedicated men who had returned. We are told by Nehemiah that everyone had helped build and defend the city. There were to be as many as three quarters of a million people living in this great Metropolitan area and despite many disturbances and invaders it was to remain the center of life for the Israelites.

The Tower of Babel as told in Genesis

CHAPTER XI.

1 And the whole earth was of one language, and of one kind of words.

2 And it came to pass, as they journeyed toward the east, that they found a plain in the land of Shinar, and they dwelt there.

3 And they said to one another, Go to, let us make bricks, and burn them thoroughly. And thus, the brick served them for stone, and slime served them for mortar.

4 And they said, Go to, let us build ourselves a city, and a tower, the top of which may reach unto heaven; and let us make ourselves a name, lest we be scattered abroad upon the face of the whole earth.

5 And the Lord came down to see the city and the tower which the children of man were building.

6 And the Lord said, Behold, it is one people, and they have all one language, and this is the first thing they undertake to do; and now shall they not be restrained in all which they have imagined to do?

7 Go to, let us go down, and confound there their language, that they may not understand one another's speech.

8 So the Lord scattered them abroad from there over the face of all the earth; and they left off to build the city.

9 Therefore is the name of it called Babel, because the Lord did there confound the language of all the earth; and from there did the Lord scatter them abroad over the face of all the earth.

Jerusalem as the Capital (Kings I)

CHAPTER V.

1 ¶Then came all the tribes of Israel to David unto Hebron, and spoke, saying, Behold us, thy bone and thy flesh are we;

2 Already yesterday, and even before, when Saul was king over us, thou wast the one that led out and brought in Israel:

¶ And the Lord said to thee, Thou shalt indeed feed my people Israel, and thou shalt be a chief over Israel.

3 Thus came all the elders of Israel to the king unto Hebron;

and King David made a covenant with them in Hebron before the Lord: and they anointed David as king over Israel.

4 ¶Thirty years was David old when he became king, (and) forty years he reigned.

5 In Hebron he reigned over Judah seven years and six months: and in Jerusalem he reigned thirty and three years over all Israel and Judah.

6 And the king and his men went to Jerusalem against the Jebusites, the inhabitants of the land; who said unto David, as followeth, Thou shalt not come in hither, except thou (first) remove away the blind and the lame: meaning, David cannot come in hither.

7 Nevertheless David captured the strong-hold of Zion; the same is the city of David.

8 And David said on that day, Whosoever will smite the Jebusites, and reach the aqueduct and the lame and the blind, that are hateful to David's soul,—Wherefore people usually say, The blind and the lame shall not come into the house.

9 And David dwelt in the fort, and he called it "The City of David." And David built (it) round about from the Millo and inward.

10 And David went on, and became greater and greater, and the Lord the God of hosts was with him.

11 ¶And Hiram the king of Tyre sent messengers to David, and cedar-trees, and carpenters, and stone-masons; and they built a house for David.

And Solomon Built the Temple (Kings I)

V.

17 Thou well knowest of David my father, that he was not able to build a house unto the name of the Lord his God, on account of the war wherewith his enemies encompassed him until the Lord had put them under the soles of his feet.

18 But now hath the Lord my God given me rest on every side, there is neither adversary nor evil hinderance.

19 And, behold, I purpose to build a house unto the name of the Lord my God, as the Lord hath spoken unto David my father, saying, Thy son, whom I will place in thy room upon thy throne, he it is that shall build the house unto my name.

20 And now command thou that they hew me cedar-trees out of Lebanon; and my servants shall be with thy servants; and the wages of thy servants will I give unto thee in accordance with all that thou wilt say; for thou well knowest that there is not among us a man that hath the skill to hew timber like unto the Zidonians

21 ¶And it came to pass, when Hiram heard the words of Solomon, that he rejoiced greatly; and he said, Blessed be the Lord this day, who hath given unto David a wise son over this numerous people.

22 And Hiram sent to Solomon, saying, I have heard what thou hast sent to me for: I will gladly execute all thy desire in respect of timber of cedar, and in respect of timber of fir.

23 My servants shall bring them down from the Lebanon unto the sea: and I will convey them by sea in floats unto the place of which thou wilt send me word, and I will cause them to be taken apart there, and thou shalt take them away; and thou shalt accomplish my desire, in giving the food for my household.

24 So Hiram gave Solomon cedar-trees and fir-trees, all his desire.

25 And Solomon gave Hiram twenty thousand kors of wheat as provision for his household, and twenty kors of beaten oil: thus did Solomon give to Hiram year by year.

26 ¶And the Lord gave wisdom unto Solomon, as he had spoken to him; and there was peace between Hiram and Solomon; and they made a covenant with each other.

27 And king Solomon raised a levy out of all Israel; and the levy was thirty thousand men.

28 And he sent them into the Lebanon, ten thousand in each month by turns; one month they used to be in the Lebanon, two months at home: and Adoniram was over the levy.

29 ¶And there belonged to Solomon seventy thousand bearers of burdens, and eighty thousand stone-cutters in the mountains.

30 Besides the chiefs who were appointed by Solomon over the work, three thousand and three hundred, who ruled over the people that wrought on the work.

31 And when the king commanded, they quarried out great stones, heavy stones, to lay the foundation of the house, and hewn stones.

32 And the builders of Solomon, and the builders of Hiram, and

the Giblites hewed them; and so they prepared the wood and the stones to build the house.

VI.

1 ¶And it came to pass, in the four hundred and eightieth year after the going forth of the children of Israel out of the land of Egypt, in the fourth year, in the month Ziv, which is the second month, of the reign of Solomon over Israel, that he built the house unto the Lord.

2 And the house which king Solomon built unto the Lord, was sixty cubits in length, and twenty in breadth, and thirty cubits in height.

3 And the porch before the temple of the house, was twenty cubits in length, in front of the breadth of the house; and ten cubits in breadth at the east side of the house.

4 And he made for the house windows wide without and narrow within.

5 And he built on the wall of the house a gallery round about, on the walls of the house round about, of the temple and of the most holy place: and he made side-chambers round about.

6 The nethermost gallery was five cubits in breadth, and the middle was six cubits in breadth, and the third was seven cubits in breadth; for projections had he made to the house round about on the outside, so as to fasten nothing in the walls of the house.

7 And the house, when it was in building, was built of entire stones as they had been prepared at the quarry: so that neither hammer, nor axe, nor any tool of iron was heard in the house, while it was in building.

8 The door for the middle (gallery) sidechamber was in the right side of the house: and with winding stairs they went up into the middle chamber, and out of the middle into the third.

9 So he built the house, and finished it; and covered the house with hollow tiles, and with boards of cedar.

10 And he built the gallery against all the house, (each) five cubits in height; and it was fastened on to the house with timber of cedar.

11 ¶And the word of the Lord came to Solomon, saying,

12 This house which thou art building—if thou wilt walk in my statutes, and execute my ordinances, and keep all my command-

ments to walk in them: then will I perform my word with thee, which I have spoken unto David thy father.

13 And I will dwell in the midst of the children of Israel, and I will not forsake my people Israel.

14 ¶So did Solomon build the house, and finish it.

15 And he built the walls of the house within with boards of cedar; from the floor of the house to where the walls touched the ceiling did he overlay it on the inside with wood; and he overlaid the floor of the house with boards of fir.

16 And he built the twenty cubits on the lower side of the house with boards of cedar, from the floor to the battlements; and he built it within, for the debir, for the holy of holies.

17 And the house, that is, the temple before it, was forty cubits long.

18 And the cedar on the house within was carved with colocynths and opening flowers; all was cedar, no stone was seen.

19 And the debir in the house within did he prepare, to set therein the ark of the covenant of the Lord.

20 And the interior of the debir was twenty cubits in length, and twenty cubits in breadth, and twenty cubits was its height: and he overlaid it with pure gold; and he overlaid the altar with cedarwood.

21 And Solomon overlaid the house within with pure gold: and he barred by means of chains of gold the front of the debir; and he overlaid it with gold.

22 And the whole house he overlaid with gold, until all the house was finished: also the whole altar that was before the debir did he overlay with gold.

23 And within the debir he made two cherubims of oleaster-wood, each ten cubits high.

24 And five cubits was the one wing of the cherub, and five cubits the other wing of the cherub: (there were) ten cubits from the uttermost part of the one wing unto the uttermost part of the other.

25 And the other cherub was also ten cubits: both the cherubim were of one measure and one form.

26 The height of the one cherub was ten cubits, and so that of the other cherub.

27 And he set the cherubim within the innermost part of the house: and they spread forth the wings of the cherubim, so that the

wing of the one touched the one wall, and the wing of the other cherub touched the other wall; and their wings toward the middle of the house touched one another.

28 And he overlaid the cherubim with gold.

29 And on all the wall of the house round about he carved figures of cherubim and palm-trees and opening flowers, in the debir and in the temple.

30 And the floor of the house he overlaid with gold for the debir and for the temple.

31 And for the entrance of the debir he made doors of oleaster-wood: the lintel with the side-posts forming five sides.

32 And also upon the two doors of oleaster-wood he carved figures of cherubim and palm-trees and opening flowers, and overlaid them with gold, and spread the gold, by beating, upon the cherubim, and upon the palm-trees.

33 So also made he for the entrance of the temple door-posts of oleaster-wood in shape of a square;

34 And two doors of fir-wood: the one door having two leaves which were folding, and the other door having two leaves which were folding.

35 And he carved thereon cherubim, and palm-trees and opening flowers: and he overlaid them with gold fitting upon the carved work.

36 And he built the inner court of three rows of hewn stone, and one row of cedar beams.

37 In the fourth year was the foundation of the house of the Lord laid, in the month Ziv;

38 And in the eleventh year, in the month Bul, which is the eighth month, was the house finished throughout all its parts, and according to all its requirements. So was he building it seven years.

VII.

1 But his own house was Solomon building thirteen years, and then he finished all his house.

2 He built also the house of the forest of Lebanon: a hundred cubits was its length, and fifty cubits was its breadth, and thirty cubits was its height, upon four rows of cedar pillars, with cedar beams upon the pillars.

3 And it was covered with cedar above over the beams, that lay on the forty-five pillars, fifteen in a row.

4 And there were window-spaces in three rows, and windows were opposite each other in three ranks.

5 And all the entrances and door-posts formed a square in shape: and windows were opposite windows in three ranks.

6 And he made a porch of pillars: fifty cubits was its length, and thirty cubits its breadth; and the porch was before them; and the other pillars with an entablature before them.

7 Then he made a porch for the throne where he might judge, the porch of judgment: and it was covered with cedar from one side of the floor to the other.

8 And his house where he dwelt in another court within the porch, was of the like work: and Solomon made also a house for Pharaoh's daughter, whom he had taken for wife, like unto this porch.

9 All these were of heavy stones, hewn after a fixed measure, sawed with the saw inside and outside, even from the foundation unto the coping, and from the outside unto the great court.

10 And the foundation was of heavy stones, large stones, stones of ten cubits, and stones of eight cubits.

11 And above were heavy stones, hewn after a fixed measure, and cedars.

12 And the great court round about was of three rows of hewn stones, and one row of cedar beams, both for the inner court of the house of the Lord, and for the porch of the house.

13 ¶ And king Solomon sent and fetched Hiram out of Tyre.

14 He was the son of a widow of the tribe of Naphtali, and his father was a man of Tyre, a worker in copper: and he was filled with wisdom, and understanding, and knowledge, to make every work in copper; and he came to king Solomon, and did all his work.

15 And he cast two pillars of copper, eighteen cubits was the height of the one pillar; and a line of twelve cubits did encompass the second pillar.

16 And he made two capitals, to set upon the tops of the pillars, of molten copper; five cubits was the height of the one capital, and five cubits was the height of the other capital;

17 And nets of checker-work, and wreaths of chain-work, for

the capitals which were upon the top of the pillars; seven for the one capital, and seven for the other capital.

18 And he made the pillars, so that two rows of pomegranates were round about upon the one net-work, to cover the capitals that were upon the top: and the same he made for the other capital.

19 And the capitals, that were upon the top of the pillars, furnished with lily-work, (as) those in the porch, were four cubits.

20 And the capitals upon the two pillars rose also above, close by the rounding which was on the side of the network: and the pomegranates were two hundred, in rows round about, upon either capital.

21 And he set up the pillars for the porch of the temple; and he set up the right pillar, and called its name Yachin; and he set up the left pillar, and called its name Boaz.

22 And upon the top of the pillars there was lily-work: and so was finished the work of the pillars.

23 ¶ And he made the molten sea, ten cubits from the one brim to the other, rounded all about, and it was five cubits in height: and a line of thirty cubits did encompass it round about.

24 And colocynth-shaped knobs were under its brim round about encompassing it, ten in a cubit, encircling the sea round about: the colocynths were in two rows, and were cast (with it) when it was cast.

25 It was standing upon twelve oxen, three looking toward the north, and three looking toward the west, and three looking toward the south, and three looking toward the east; and the sea was resting above upon them, and all their hinder parts were inward.

26 And its thickness was a hand's breadth, and its brim was wrought like the brim of a cup, with lily-buds: it could contain two thousand baths.

27 ¶ And he made ten bases of copper: four cubits was the length of each one base, and four cubits its breadth, and three cubits its height.

28 And this was the workmanship of the bases: They had borders, and the borders were between the corner ledges;

29 And on the borders that were between the ledges were lions, oxen, and cherubim; and upon the corner ledges it was thus also above; and likewise beneath the lions and oxen were pendant wreaths of plated work.

30 And every base had four copper wheels, and axles of copper; and its four corners had undersetters; under the laver were the undersetters cast on; at the side of each were pendants.

31 And its mouth was within the capital and above a cubit in height; but the mouth of this was rounded after the work of the base, a cubit and a half cubit; and also upon its mouth were carvings; and their borders were square, not rounded.

32 And the four wheels were under the borders; and the axletrees of the wheels were joined to the base: and the height of each one wheel was a cubit and a half cubit.

33 And the workmanship of the wheels was like the workmanship of a chariot-wheel: their axletrees, and their naves, and their felloes, and their spokes, were all cast.

34 And there were four undersetters to the four corners of each one base; the undersetters were of one piece with the base itself.

35 And on the top of the base was a rounded compass of half a cubit high: and on the top of the base were its side-ledges; and its borders were of one piece with itself.

36 And he engraved on the plates of its side-ledges and on its borders, cherubim, lions, and palm-trees: and in the open space of every one were pendant wreaths round about.

37 After this manner did he make the ten bases: one casting, one measure, one form, was there for all of them.

38 ¶ Then made he ten lavers of copper; forty baths could each one laver contain; every laver was four cubits: each one laver was upon each one base of the ten bases.

39 And he put the bases, five on the right side of the house, and five on the left side of the house: and the sea he set on the right side of the house eastward opposite the south.

40 ¶ And Hiram made the lavers, and shovels, and the basins; so Hiram made an end of doing all the work that he made for king Solomon for the house of the Lord.

41 The two pillars, and the two bowl-shaped capitals that were on the top of the two pillars; and the two networks, to cover the two bowl-shaped capitals which were upon the top of the pillars;

42 And the four hundred pomegranates for the two networks, two rows of pomegranates for each one net-work, to cover the two bowl-shaped capitals that were upon the front of the pillars;

43 And the ten bases, and the ten lavers upon the bases;

44 And the one sea, and the twelve oxen under the sea;

45 And the pots, and the shovels, and the basins; and all these vessels, which Hiram had made for king Solomon for the house of the Lord, were of polished copper.

46 In the plain of Jordan did the king cast them, in the clay-ground between Succoth and Zarethan.

47 And Solomon set down all the vessels (unweighed), because they were exceedingly many: the weight of the copper was not inquired into.

48 And Solomon made all the vessels that pertained unto the house of the Lord: The altar of gold, and the table whereupon the show-bread was, of gold,

49 And the candlesticks, five on the right side, and five on the left, before the debir, of pure gold, with the flowers, and the lamps, and the tongs of gold,

50 And the bowls, and the knives, and the basins, and the spoons, and the censers of pure gold; and the hinges, for the doors of the inner house, for the holy of holies, for the doors of the house, and for the temple, (were) of gold.

51 ¶ and so was ended all the work that king Solomon made for the house of the Lord: and Solomon brought in the things sanctified by David his father, the silver, and the gold, and the vessels, (and) he placed (these) in the treasuries of the house of the Lord.

CHAPTER VIII.

1 ¶ Then did Solomon assemble, the elders of Israel, and all the heads of the tribes, the princes of the divisions of the children of Israel, unto king Solomon in Jerusalem, to bring up the ark of the covenant of the Lord out of the city of David, which is Zion.

2 And all the men of Israel assembled themselves unto king Solomon at the feast in the month Ethanim, which is the seventh month.

3 And all the elders of Israel came, and the priests took up the ark.

4 And they brought up the ark of the Lord and the tabernacle of the congregation, and all the holy vessels that were in the tabernacle: even these did the priests and the Levites bring up.

5 And king Solomon, and all the congregation of Israel, that

were assembled unto him, were with him before the ark, sacrificing sheep and oxen, that could not be told nor numbered for multitude.

6 And the priests brought in the ark of the covenant of the Lord unto its place, into the debir of the house, into the most holy place, under the wings of the cherubim.

7 For the cherubim spread forth their wings over the place of the ark, and the cherubim covered the ark and its staves from above.

8 And they had made the staves so long, that the ends of the staves were seen out in the holy place in the front of the debir, but they were not seen without; and they have remained there until this day.

9 There was nothing in the ark save the two tables of stone, which Moses had placed therin at Horeb, where the Lord made a covenant with the children of Israel, when they came out of the land of Egypt.

Prophet Jeremiah Castigated the Way of Life in Jerusalem, and Prophesized the City's Destruction

1 ¶ Roam about through the streets of Jerusalem; and see now, and notice, and search in its broad places, if ye can find one man, if there be one that executeth justice, that searcheth for truth: and I will pardon it.

2 And though they say, "As the Lord liveth!" surely they only swear to a falsehood.

3 O Lord, are not thy eyes (directed) to the truth? thou didst strike them, but they felt it not; thou didst make an end of them, (yet) they refused to accept correction: they made their faces harder than a rock, they refused to return.

4 Yet I myself thought, Oh these are but poor; they are foolish; for they knew not the way of the Lord, the ordinance of their God.

5 I had better go unto the great men, and let me speak with them; for these surely know the way of the Lord, the ordinance of their God; but these altogether have broken the yoke, burst the bands.

6 Therefore slayeth them the lion out of the forest, the wolf of the deserts wasteth them, the leopard lieth in wait against their cities: every one that cometh out thence shall be torn in pieces; be-

cause many are their transgressions, very numerous are their backslidings.

7 How shall I for this pardon thee? thy children have forsaken me, and sworn by those that are not gods: when I had fed them to the full, they then committed adultery, and assembled themselves by troops in the harlot's house.

8 As robust horses they rose by times in the morning: every one neighed after the wife of his neighbor.

9 Shall I not for these things inflict punishment? saith the Lord: and shall on a nation such as this my soul not be avenged?

10 ¶ Scale ye her walls, and destroy; but make not a full end: remove her young shoots; for they are not the Lord's.

11 For the house of Israel and the house of Judah have dealt very treacherously against me, saith the Lord.

12 They have denied the Lord, and said, "He existeth not; nor will evil come over us; and the sword and famine shall we not see.

13 And the prophets shall become wind, and the word is not in them:" thus shall it be done unto them.

14 ¶ Therefore thus hath said the Lord the God of hosts, Because ye speak this word, behold, I will make my words in thy mouth to be a fire, and this people wood, and it shall devour them.

15 Lo, I will bring over you a nation from afar, O house of Israel, saith the Lord: It is a mighty nation, it is a most ancient nation, a nation whose language thou wilt not know, and thou wilt not understand what they speak.

16 Their quiver is as an open sepulchre: they are all mighty men.

17 And they shall consume thy harvest, and thy bread; they shall consume thy sons and thy daughters; they shall consume thy flocks and thy herds; they shall consume thy vines and thy fig--trees; they shall depopulate thy fortified cities, those wherein thou trustedst, with the sword.

18 Nevertheless even in those days, saith the Lord, will I not make a full end of you.

19 And it shall come to pass, when ye will say, For what reason hath the Lord our God done all these things unto us? that thou shalt say unto them, In the same manner as ye have forsaken me, and served strange gods in your land, so shall ye serve strangers in a land that is not yours.

20 ¶ Announce this in the house of Jacob, and publish it in Judah saying,

21 Do now hear this, O sottish people, who have no heart; who have eyes, and see not; who have ears, and hear not;

22 Will ye not fear me? saith the Lord; will ye not tremble at my presence, who have placed the sand as a bound for the sea by an everlasting law, which it can never pass over? and though the waves thereof be upheaved, yet can they not prevail; though they roar, yet can they not pass over it.

23 But this people hath a stubborn and rebellious heart: they have departed (from the right) and have gone their way.

24 And they have not said in their heart, Let us now fear the Lord our God, that giveth rain, the early and the latter rain, in its season: the appointed weeks of the harvest doth he ever preserve for us.

25 Your iniquities have turned away these things, and your sins have withholden what is good from you.

26 For there are found among my people wicked men: they lie in wait, as he that layeth snares; they set a trap, they catch men.

27 As a coop is full of birds, so are their houses full of deceit: therefore are they become great, and grown rich.

28 They are grown fat, they are stout; yea, they surpass even the deeds of the wicked: they pronounce no (just) sentence, the sentence of the fatherless, that they might prosper; and the cause of the needy do they not judge.

29 Shall I not for these things inflict punishment? saith the Lord: or shall on a nation such as this my soul not be avenged?

30 ¶ An astonishing and horrible thing is committed in the land.

Prophet Nehemiah Described the Rebuilding of Jerusalem

Chapter II.

1 ¶ And it came to pass in the month Nissan, in the twentieth year of king Artaxerxes, that wine (stood) before him and I took up the wine, and gave it unto the king. But I had never been sad in his presence.

2 Then said the king unto me, Why is thy countenance sad, see-

ing thou art not sick? this is nothing but an illness of heart. Then was I very greatly afraid.

3 And I said unto the king, May the king live for ever: why should not my countenance be sad, when the city, the place of my fathers' sepulchres, lieth ruined, and her gates are consumed by fire?

4 Then said the king unto me, For what then dost thou make request? Then did I pray to the God of heaven.

5 And I said unto the king, If it seem good to the king, and if thy servant might be pleasing in thy presence, (I desire) that thou wouldst send me unto Judah, unto the city of my fathers' sepulchres, that I may build it.

6 And the king said unto me, while the queen was sitting beside him, When is thy journey to be undertaken? and when wilt thou return? So it pleased the king to let me go; and I indicated to him a time.

7 And I said unto the king, If it seem good to the king, let letters be given unto me for the governors beyond the river, that they may convey me over till the time that I come into Judah;

8 Also a letter unto Assaph the keeper of the king's forests, that he may give me timber to make beams for the gates of the fortress which appertaineth to the house, and for the wall of the city, and for the house that I shall move into. And the king gave (them) to me, according to the good hand of my God upon me.

9 And (so) came I to the governors beyond the river, and I gave them the king's letters. Now the king had sent with me captains of the army and horsemen.

10 ¶ When Sanballat the Choronite, and Tobiyah the servant, the 'Ammonite, heard of it, it displeased them exceedingly, that there was come a man to seek the welfare of the children of Israel.

11 So came I to Jerusalem, and remained there three days.

12 Then arose I in the night, I and some few men with me but I had not told any man what my God had put in my heart to do for Jerusalem: nor was there any beast with me, save the beast on which I rode.

13 And I went out through the gate of the valley by night even toward the direction of the dragon-well, and to the dung gate; and I was viewing the walls of Jerusalem, which were broken down, and the gates wherof were consumed by fire.

14 Then passed I on to the gate of the fountain, and to the king's pool; but there was no space for the beast that was under me to pass through.

15 Then went I up through the valley in the night and I was viewing the wall, and I returned and entered through the gate of the valley, and so returned home.

16 And the rulers knew not whither I was gone, or what I was doing: nor had I as yet told it to the Jews, and to the priests, and to the nobles, and to the rulers, and to the rest of the superintendents of the work.

17 Then said I unto them, Ye see the misery in which we are, how Jerusalem lieth in ruins, and its gates are burnt with fire: come, and let us build up the wall of Jerusalem, that we may no more be for a reproach.

18 And I told them of the hand of my God, which was good upon me, as also the king's words which he had spoken unto me. And they said, We will rise up and build. So they strengthened their hands for the good work.

19 ¶ But when Sanballat the Choronite, and Tobiyah the servant, the Ammonite, and Geshem the Arabian, heard it, they laughed us to scorn, and despised us, and said, What is this thing that ye are doing? are ye rebelling against the king?

20 And I returned them an answer, and said unto them, The God of heaven will indeed give us prosperity, and we his servant will truly rise up and build, but ye have no portion, nor right, nor memorial, in Jerusalem.

IV.

1 And it came to pass, when Sanballat and Tobiyah, and the Arabians, and the Ammonites, and the Ashdodities, heard that the walls of Jerusalem were restored, and that the breaches began to be closed up, that it displeased them greatly.

2 And they conspired all of them together to come to fight against Jerusalem, and to do it an injury.

3 But we prayed unto our God, and set a watch over them day and night, because of the others.

4 And Judah said, the strength of the bearers of the burden is failing and there is much rubbish; and we are not able to build on the wall.

5 And our adversaries said, "They shall not know, nor see, until we come in the midst of them, and slay them, and so stop the work."

6 And it came to pass, when the Jews who dwelt near them came, that they said unto us ten times, "From all places whence ye may return home — they intend to come — over us."

7 I placed therefore on the lower parts of the place on the naked rocks behind the walls —there I placed the people after their families with their swords, their spears, and their bows.

8 And I looked (about), and rose up, and said unto the nobles, and to the rulers, and to the rest of the people, Be not afraid of them: think on the Lord, the great and terrible, and fight for your brethren, your sons, and your daughters, your wives and your houses.

9 And it came to pass, that, when our enemies heard that it was known unto us, God frustrated their counsel: and we returned, all of us, to the wall, every one unto his work.

10 And it came to pass from that day forth, that the half of my young men wrought at the work, while the other half of them were holding spears, the shields, and the bows, and coats of mail. . . .

11 Those that built on the wall, and those that bore burdens, with those that loaded — every one with one of his hands wrought on the work, and with the other hand held a weapon.

CHAPTER VII.

1 ¶ And it came to pass, when the wall was built, that I set up the doors; and then were appointed the gatekeepers and the singers and the (other) Levites (to their offices).

2 And I gave my brother Chanai, and Chauanyah the commander of the fortress, charge over Jerusalem; for he was esteemed a faithful man, and one that feared God these many days.

3 And I said unto them, The gates of Jerusalem must not be opened until the sun be hot; and while ye stand by, let them shut the doors, and do ye bar them; and station watches of the inhabitants of Jerusalem, every one in his watch, and every one opposite to his house.

4 But the city was roomy in space and large: while the people therein were few, and the houses were not yet built.

CHAPTER XI.

1 And the rulers of the people dwelt at Jerusalem: and the rest of the people cast lots, to bring one of every ten to dwell in Jerusalem the holy city, and the nine parts to (remain) in the (other) cities.

2 And the people blessed all the men, that offered themselves voluntarily to dwell at Jerusalem.

3 ¶ Now these are the chiefs of the province that dwelt in Jerusalem; but in the cities of Judah dwelt every one in his possession in their cities, (to wit,) Israel, the priests, and the Levites, and the temple-servants, and the children of Solomon's servants.

Jerusalem

Damascus Gate
This entrance leads to the old city of Jerusalem. On the skyline are the twin domes of the Church of the Holy Sepulchre.

The Western Wall of the Temple

The Via Dolorosa
The Way of the Cross is a narrow street in the Old City of Jerusalem connecting the Roman Judgement Hall and the Church of the Holy Sepulchre. The roadway follows the route taken by Jesus on his way to Calvary.

Jaffa
The port of Jaffa, sister to Tel Aviv, is one of the oldest ports in the world. According to the Bible it is the port from which Jonah set sail.

II. Greek Urbanism

Home of one of the first Western cultures, Greece gave rise to an urban form at once vital and profound. Yet, in the end, the brilliance of Greek promise was overshadowed by the glaring weaknesses of city life as the wars between Athens and Sparta sapped the vitality of a people.

Our witnesses present both the grandeur and grimness of Greek urbanism. The high-flown praises of Athens in Pericles' Funeral Oration is contrasted with Thucydides' relation of the horrors of plague-beseiged Athens and the breakdown in fundamental social and human relations during one of the many revolutions which rocked Greek city-states. The plans of finely tuned intellects like Aristotle and Xenophon failed of implementation in an age characterized by a dualism between the free and the expoloited, between natural civic growth and rampant imperialism.

Notwithstanding the decline of Hellenic Greece, its cities and its civilization provided a promise and a testament to both the possible and the desirable. Men in contemporary Western cities have not entirely lost sight of this perspective.

The Athens of Thucydides

Thucydides' *History of the Peloponnesian War* is not only the classic story of diplomacy and war, it is the story of a people and their way of life. In the following selection from Pericles' Funeral Oration delivered in 432 B.C. one can see that the city symbolized life itself for the Greek citizen.

In Praise of Athens

Many of those who have spoken before me on these occasions, have commended the author of that law which we are now obeying, for having instituted an oration to the honour of those who sacrifice their lives in fighting for their country. For my part, I

GREEK URBANISM

The Acropolis

The Parthenon
The Parthenon was the main temple of the Acropolis. It was built to house a gold and ivory statue of Athena, the goddess of war and wisdom.

think it sufficient, for men who have approved their virtue in action, by action to be honoured for it—by such as you see the public gratitude now performing about this funeral; and that the virtues of many ought not to be endangered by the management of any one person, when their credit must precariously depend on his oration, which may be good and may be bad. Difficult indeed it is, judiciously to handle a subject where even probable truth will hardly gain assent. The hearer, enlightened by a long acquaintance, and warm in his affection, may quickly pronounce every thing unfavourably expressed, in respect to what he wishes and what he knows,—whilst the stranger pronounceth all exaggerated through envy of those deeds which he is conscious are above his own achievement. For the praises bestowed upon others, are then only to be endured, when men imagine they can do those feats they hear to have been done: they envy what they cannot equal, and immediately pronounce it false. Yet, as this solemnity hath received its sanction from the authority of our ancestors, it is my duty also to obey the law, and to endeavour to procure, as far as I am able, the good will and approbation of all my audience.

I shall therefore begin first with our forefathers, since both justice and decency require we should on this occasion bestow on them an honourable remembrance. In this our country they kept themselves always firmly settled, and through their valour handed it down free to every since-succeeding generation. Worthy indeed of praise are they, and yet more worthy are our immediate fathers? since, enlarging their own inheritance into the extensive empire which we now possess, they bequeathed that their work of toil to us their sons. Yet even these successes, we ourselves here present, we who are yet in the strength and vigour of our days, have noble improved, and have made such provisions for this our Athens, that now it is all-sufficient in itself to answer every exigence of war and of peace. I mean not here to recite those martial exploits by which these ends were accomplished, or the resolute defences we ourselves and our fathers have made against the formidable invasions of Barbarians and Greeks—your own knowledge of these will excuse the long detail. But by what methods we have risen to this height of glory and power, by what polity and by what conduct we are thus aggrandized, I shall first endeavor to show; and then proceed to the praise of the deceased. These, in my opinion, can be no impertinent topics on this occasion? the discussion of them must be beneficial to this numerous company of Athenians and of strangers.

We are happy in a form of government which cannot envy the laws of our neighbours;—for it hath served as a model to others, but is original at Athens. And this our form, as committed not to the few, but to the whole body of the people, is called a democracy. How different soever in a private capacity, we all' enjoy the same general equality our laws are fitted to preserve; and superior honours just as we excel. The public administration is not confined to a particular family, but is attainable only by merit. Poverty is not a hindrance since whoever is able to serve his country, meets with no obstacle to preferment from his first obscurity. The offices of the state we go through without obstructions from one another; and live together in the mutual endearments of private life without suspicions; not angry with a neighbour for following the bent of his own humour, nor putting on that countenance of discontent, which pains though it cannot punish—so that in private life we converse without diffidence or damage, whilst we dare not on any account offend against the public, through the reverence we bear to the magistrates and the laws, chiefly to those enacted for redress on the injured, and to those unwritten, a breach of which is allowed disgrace. Our laws have further provided for the mind most frequent intermissions of care by the appointment of public recreations and sacrifices throughout the year, elegantly performed with a peculiar pomp, the daily delight of which is a charm that puts melancholy to flight. The grandeur of this our Athens causeth the produce of the whole earth to be imported here, by which we reap a familiar enjoyment, not more of the delicacies of our own growth, than of those of other nations.

In the affairs of war we excel those of our enemies, who adhere to methods opposite to our own. For we lay open Athens to general resort, nor ever drive any stranger from us whom either improvement or curiosity hath brought amongst us, lest any enemy should hurt us by seeing what is never concealed. We place not so great a confidence in the preparatives and artifices of war, as in the native warmth of our souls impelling us to action. In point of education, the youth of some people are inured by a course of laborious exercise, to support toil and exercise like men; notwithstanding our easy and elegant way of life, face all the dangers of war as intrepidly as they. This may be proved by facts. since the Lacedaemonians never invade our territories barely with their own, but with the united strength of all their confederates. But, when we invade the dominions of our neighbours, for the most part we conquer without difficulty in an enemy's country those who fight in defence of their own habitations. The strength of our whole force no enemy yet hath ever experienced, because it is divided by our naval expeditions, or engaged in the different quarters of our service by land. But if any where they engage and defeat a small party of our forces, they boastingly give it out a total defeat? and if they are beat, they were certainly overpowered by our united strength. What though from a state of inactivity rather than laborious exercise, or with a natural rather than an acquired valour we learn to encounter danger?—this good at least we receive from it, that we never droop under the apprehension of possible misfortunes, and when we hazard the danger, are found no less courageous than those who are continually inured to it. In these respects our whole community deserves justly to be admired, and in many we have yet to mention.

In our manner of living we show an elegance tempered with frugality, and we cultivate philosophy without enervating the mind. We display our wealth in the season of beneficence, and not in the navity of discourse. A confession of poverty is disgrace to no man, no effort to avoid it is disgrace indeed. There is visibly in the same persons an attention to their own private concerns and those of the public; and in others engaged in the labours of life, there is a competent skill in the affairs of government. For we are the only people who think him that does not meddle in state-affairs—not indolent, but good for nothing. And yet we pass the soundest judgments, and are quick at catching the right apprehensions of things, not thinking that words are prejudicial to actions, but rather the not being duly prepared by previous debate, before we are obliged to proceed to execution. Herein consists our distinguishing excellence, that in the hour of action we show the greatest courage, and yet debate beforehand the expediency of our measures. The courage of others is the result of ignorance; deliberation makes them cowards. And those undoubtedly must be owned to have the greatest souls, who most acutely sensible of the miseries of war and the sweets of peace, are not hence in the least deterred from facing danger.

In acts of beneficence, further, we differ from the many. We preserve friends not by receiving but by conferring obligations. For he who does a kindness hath the advantage over him who by the law of gratitude becomes a debtor to his benefactor. The person obliged is compelled to act the more insipid part, conscious that a return of kindness is merely a payment and not an obligation. And we alone are splendidly beneficent to others, not so much from interested motives, as for the credit of pure liberality. I shall sum up what yet remains by only adding— that our Athens in general is the school of Greece; and, that every single Athenian amongst us is excellently formed, by his personal qualification, for all the various scenes of active life, acting with a most graceful demeanor, and a most ready habit of despatch.

That I have not on this occasion made use of a pomp of words, but the truth of facts, that height to which by such a conduct this state hath risen, is an undeniable proof. For we are now the only people of the world who are found by experience to be greater than in report— the only people who, repelling the attacks of an invading enemy, exempts their defeat from the blush of indignation, and to their tributaries yields no discontent, as if subject to men unworthy to command. That we deserve our power, we need no evidence to manifest. We have great and signal proofs of this, which entitle us to the admiration of the present and future ages. We want no Homer to be the herald of our praise; no poet to deck off a history with the charms of verse, where the opinion of exploits must suffer by a strict relation. Every sea has been opened by our fleets, and every land hath been penetrated by our armies, which have every where left behind them eternal monuments of our enmity and our friendship.

In the just defence of such a state these victims of their own valour, scorning the ruin threatened to it, have valiantly fought and bravely died. And every one of those who survive is ready, I am persuaded, to sacrifice life in such a cause. And for this reason have I enlarged so much on national points, to give the clearest proof that in the present war we have more at stake than men whose public advantages are not so valuable, and to illustrate by actual evidence, how great a commendation is due to them who are now my subject, and the greatest part of which they have already received. For the encomiums with which I have celebrated the state, have been earned for it by the bravery of these, and of men like these. And such compliments might be thought too high and exaggerated, if passed on any Grecians but them alone. The fatal period to which these gallant souls are now reduced, is the surest evidence of their merit—an evidence begun in their lives and completed in their deaths. For it is a debt of justice to pay superior honours to men, who have devoted their lives in fighting for their country, though inferior to others in every virtue but that of valour. Their last service effaceth all former demerits,—it extends to the public; their private demeanors reached only to a few. Yet not one of these was at all induced to shrink from danger, through fondness of those delights which the peaceful affluent life bestows,—not one was the less lavish of his life, through that flattering hope attendant upon want, that poverty at length might be exchanged for affluence. One passion there was in their minds much stronger than these,—the desire of vengeance on their enemies. Regarding this as the most honourable prize of danger, they boldly rushed towards the mark, to glut revenge, and then to satisfy those secondary passions. The uncertain event, they had already secured in hope; what their eyes showed plainly must be done, they trusted their own valour to accomplish, thinking it more glorious to defend themselves and die in the attempt, than to yield and live. From the reproach of cowardice indeed they fled, but presented their bodies to the shock of battle; when, insensible of fear, but triumphing in hope, in the doubtful charge they instantly dropped—and thus discharged the duty which brave men owe to their country.

As for you, who now survive them—it is your business to pray for a better fate—but, to think it your duty also to preserve the same spirit and warmth of courage against your enemies; not judging of the expediency of this from a mere harangue—where any man indulging a flow of words may tell you, what you yourselves know as well as he, how many advantages there are in fighting valiantly against your enemies—but, rather, making the daily-increasing grandeur of this community the object of your thoughts, and growing quite enamoured of it. And when it really appears great to your apprehensions, think again, that this grandeur was acquired by brave and valiant men; by men who knew their duty, and in the moments of action were sensible of shame; who, whenever their attempts were unsuccessful, thought it dishonour their country should stand in need of any thing their valour could do for it, and so made it the most glorious present. Bestowing thus their lives on the public, they have every one received a praise that will never decay, a sepulchre that will always be most illustrious— not that in which their bones lie mouldering, but that in which their frame is preserved, to be on every occasion, when honour is the employ of either word or act, eternally remembered. This whole earth is the sepulchre of illustrious men: nor is it the inscription on the columns in their native soil alone that show their merit, but the memorial of them, better than all inscriptions, in every foreign nation, reposited more durable in universal remembrance than on their own tomb. From this very moment, emulating these noble patterns, placing your happiness in liberty, and liberty in valour, be prepared to encounter all the dangers of war. For, to be lavish of life is not so noble in those whom misfortunes have reduced to misery and despair, as in men who hazard the loss of a comfortable subsistence, and the enjoyment of all the blessings this world affords, by an unsuccessful enterprise. Adversity, after a series of ease and affluence, sinks deeper into the heart of a man of spirit, than the stroke of death insensibly received in the vigour of life and public hope.

For this reason, the parents of those who are now gone, whoever of them may be attending here, I do not bewail,—I shall rather comfort. It is well known to what unhappy accidents they were liable from the moment of their birth; and, that happiness belongs to men who have reached the most glorious period of life, as these now have who are to you the source of sorrow,—these, whose life hath received its ample measure, happy in its continuance, and equally happy in its conclusion. I know it in truth a difficult task, to fix comfort in those breasts, which will have frequent remembrances in seeing the happiness of others, of what they once themselves enjoyed. And sorrow flows not from the absence of those good things we have never yet experienced, but from the loss of those to which we have been accustomed. They who are not yet by age exempted from issue, should be comforted in the hope of having more. The children yet to be born will be a private benefit to some, in causing them to forget such as no longer are, and will be a double benefit to their country in preventing its desolation, and providing for its security.

To you, the sons and the brothers of the deceased, whatever number of you are here, a field of hardy contention is opened. For him who no longer is, every one is ready to commend, so that to whatever height you push your deserts, you will scarce ever be thought to equal, but to be somewhat inferior to these. Envy will exert itself against a competitor, whilst life remains: but when death stops the competition, affection will applaud without restraint.

If after this it be expected from me to say any thing to you who are now reduced to a state of widowhood, about female virtue, I shall express it all in one short admonition;—It is your greatest glory not to be deficient in the virtue peculiar to your sex, and to give the men as little handle as possible to talk of your behaviour, whether well or ill.

I have now discharged the province allotted me by the laws, and said what I thought most pertinent to this assembly. Our departed friends have by facts been already honoured. Their children from this day till they arrive at manhood shall be educated at the public expense of the state which hath appointed so beneficial a meed for these and all future relics of the public contests. For wherever the greatest rewards are proposed for virtue, there the best of patriots are ever to be found.—Now, let every one respectively indulge the decent grief for his departed friends, and then retire.

Such was the manner of the public funeral solemnized this winter, and with the end of which, the first year of this war was also ended.

Revolt in the Cities

At the same time that there was a great deal of love and devotion to the city there often was political rivalry and dissension. Thucydides portrayed this instability that contributed to the disintegration of the city-states.

> The Corcyreans were now embroiled in a sedition, excited by the return of the prisoners, whom the Corinthians had taken in the naval engagements of Epidamnus. They had obtained their release, as was publicly given out, for the sum of eighty talents, for the payment of which their former friends at Corinth had joined in a security; but, in fact, for a secret promise they had made the Corinthians, to put Corcyra into their hands. To fulfil their engagements

they tampered with every single Corcyrean in order to bring about a revolt from the Athenians. An Athenian and Corinthian ship arrived at the same time with ambassadors on board. These were admitted together to an audience, at which the Corcyreans decreed "to maintain their alliance with the Athenians according to treaty,—but to be friends to the Peloponnesians as in preceding times." Pythias, who at that time was at the head of the people, entertained and lodged the Athenians without the public warrant. And therefore against him the accomplices prefer an accusation, as plotting how to subject Corcyra to Athenian slavery. Pythias being acquitted, in his turn exhibits a charge against five of the most considerable of their number, for having cut pales in the sacred grove of Jupiter and Alcinus. The fine for every pale was by law a stater. Being condemned to pay the whole, they fled into the temples and sat down as supplicants, in hope to obtain a mitigation of their fine, which was quite exorbitant. Pythias, who was also strong in the senate, gets a fresh order to have it levied in all the rigour of law. Thus debarred of any legal redress, and conscious further that Pythias, so long as he continued in the senate, would prevail upon the people to declare those their friends and those their foes who were so to Athens,— they rise up from the sanctuary, and seizing daggers rush suddenly into the senate-house, where they stab Pythias and others both senators and private persons, to the number of sixty. Some few indeed who were the adherents of Pythias, saved themselves on board the Athenian vessels which yet lay in the harbour.

After this bold assassination, they summoned the Corcyreans to assemble immediately, where they justified their proceedings "as most highly for the public good, and the only expedient of preventing Athenian slavery;"—advising them "for the future to receive neither of the rival parties, unless they came peacefully in a single vessel; if in more to declare them enemies;" and in conclusion they forced the ratification of whatever they had proposed. They also instantly despatch ambassadors to Athens, representing the necessity they lay under to act as they had done, and to persuade those who had fled for refuge thither, not to rush into such measures as might hurt the welfare of their country, from a dread of the miseries which might thence ensue.

When these ambassadors were arrived at Athens, the Athenians laid them and all their adherents under an arrest as enemies to the state, and sent them prisoners to Aegina.

In the meantime, those of the Corcyreans who had thus seized the government, animated by the arrival of a Corinthian trireme and a Lacedaemonian embassy, attack the people and overpower them in battle. The people, by favour of the night which approached, fly to the citadel and more elevated parts of the city, where they drew up together and secured their posts; they also got possession of the Hyllaic harbour. But their opponents seized the forum, where most of their own houses were situated, and the harbour which points towards the forum and the continent.

The day following they skirmished a little with their missive weapons, and both parties sent out detachments into the fields, to invite the concurrence of the slaves, upon a promise of their freedom. A majority of slaves came in to the assistance of the people, and the other party got eight hundred auxiliaries from the continent.

After one day's respite they come again to blows. The people get the better now, by the advantage of their strong posts and their numbers. The women with notable boldness assisted in the combat, by throwing tiles from the tops of the houses, and sustaining the tumult beyond their sex. About the close of the evening, the few were forced to fly, and then, apprehensive lest the people should rush down upon, and so at a shout seize the dock and put them to the sword, in order to stop their passage they set fire to the houses all round the forum and to such as were adjacent, sparing neither their own nor those of their enemies. The large effects of the merchants were consumed in the flames, and the whole city was in danger of being reduced to ashes, had a gale of wind arose to drive the flame that way. This put a stop to the contest, and brought on a cessasation, when both sides applied themselves to strict guard for the night. The Corinthian vessel, after this victory on the side of the people, stole privately away; and many of the auxiliaries, who crept off unperceived, repassed to the opposite shore.

The day following, Nicostratus the son of Diotrephes, who commanded the Athenian squadron, comes up to their assistance with his twelve sail from Naupactus and five hundred heavy-armed Messenians. He forthwith negotiated an accommodation, and persuades them to make up the affair with one another, by instantly condemning the ten principal authors of the sedition (who immediately fled), and permitting all others to continue in the city, upon articles signed between both parties and the Athenians—"To have the same friends and the same foes." Having so far carried his point, he was intent on immediate departure. But the managers for the people made him a proposal, to leave five ships of his squadron with them, to deter the enemy from any fresh commotion, which should be replaced by five of their own, which they would instantly man to attend him on his station. With this proposal he complied; and they named distinctly the mariners, who to a man were of the opposite party. Affrighted at this as a pretext to convey them to Athens, they sit down in the temple of Diosuri. Nicostratus endeavoured to raise them up and to cheer their despondency. Yet all he could say was unavailing; and the people ran again to arms, pretending that such a refusal to put to sea was a plain proof, that their intentions were insincere throughout. Then they rifled their houses of all the arms they could find; and some of them who fell into their hands had immediately been butchered, if Nicostratus had not interposed.

A second party, terrified at these proceedings, take their seats also as suppliants in the temple of Juno. The number of these was not less than four hundred. The people, grown now apprehensive of some fatal turn, persuade them to leave their sanctuary; and having prevailed, transport them into that island which faceth the temple of Juno, whither every thing needful for their sustenance was carefully sent them.

/ / /

Great was the tumult now at Corcyra: they were afraid of the malcontents within, and the hostile fleet approaching the city. They got sixty ships immediately on float, and each so fast as it was manned advanced to meet the foe. The Athenians indeed proposed to put out first to sea themselves; and that the Corcyreans should afterwards come out and join them, when they had got all their ships together. But, as they advanced in a struggling manner towards the

Note: Three / / / indicate that material has been deleted from the beginning or middle of the selection.

Four / / / / indicate omission from the end of selection.

enemy, two ships went directly over to them; and on board others the mariners were at blows with one another. In short, there was no manner of order in any of their motions. The Lacedaemonians, perceiving how it was, with twenty of their ships drew up to engage the Corcyreans, and opposed the remainder to the twelve Athenian, two of which were only the Salaminian and the Paralus.

The Corcyreans, who charged in this disorderly manner, and with few ships in a line, were on their side terribly distressed; while the Athenians, fearing lest the other, vastly superior in number, might quite surround their little squadron, would not venture to attack them when altogether, nor to break upon the middle of the enemy's line; but, assaulting them towards one of the extremities, sink one of their ships. Upon this, the Peloponnesians having formed a circle, the Athenians sailed round and round, and endeavoured to break their order. Those who pursued the Corcyreans perceiving this, and fearing what had happened formerly at Naupactus, steered away from thence to support their own squadron. And now, with their whole embodied strength, they designed to pour upon the Athenians. They, having already shifted the helm, fell gradually away. They were desirous to favour the flight of the Corcyreans beyond the possibility of a chase, and so they fell off entirely at their own leisure, keeping the enemy in their front still ranged in order. Such was this engagement, which at the setting of the sun was quite ended.

The Corcyreans were afraid lest the enemy, in prosecution of their victory, should immediately assault the city, or take up the persons in the island, or by some other method attempt to distress them. For this reason, they removed the prisoners again from the island, into the temple of Juno, and applied themselves to guard the city. But the enemy, though victorious at sea, durst not think of proceeding to attack the city; but satisfied with taking thirteen ships belonging to the Corcyreans, they returned to the main, from whence they had sallied to the engagement. The next day also, they refrained from making any attempt upon the city, where the disorder and consternation were as great as ever. Brasidas is reported urgently to have pressed it upon Alcidas, but in the council of war it was quite overruled. They landed however at cape Leucymne, and plundered the country.

The Corcyrean people, whose fears were still suggesting that they should be attacked by the enemy's fleet, had conferred with the suppliants and others about the only means to preserve the city. And some of them they persuaded to join in navigating their ships; for by some means or other they had again manned thirty, expecting every moment the enemy's approach. But the Peloponnesians continued the ravage of their fields only till noon, and then repassed to their former stations. Yet before the dawn of the succeeding day they saw sixty lights held up, to denote an equal number of Athenian ships advancing from Leucas. The Athenians, advertised of the sedition and the course of the fleet under Alcidas against Corcyra, had sent away this reinforcement under the command of Eurymedon the son of Thucles. Upon this the Peloponnesians, whilst yet it was night, crept homewards along the shore, and carrying their vessels over the isthmus of Leucas, lest they should be discovered in going round it, are safely retreated within their own confines.

When the Corcyreans had discovered the approach of the Athenian reinforcement, and the departure of the enemy, they received the Messenians within their walls, who till now had lodged without; and, having ordered the ships which they had manned to come about into the Hyllaic harbour, whilst they were going about in pursuance of this order, they put all the adverse faction whom they found to the sword. Those further, who had taken on in the ships at their persuasion, they threw into the sea and then retired. They afterwards went to Juno's temple, and persuaded a party of suppliants there, to the amount of fifty, to undergo a judicial trial, in which they were all condemned to die. The majority of suppliants, who refused to hear such persuasion, no sooner saw the fate of their brethren, than they either slew one another within the temple, or hung themselves up upon the trees within its verge: each finding some expedient for his own despatch. During those seven days that Eurymedon with his reinforcement continued at Corcyra, the people of that city extended the massacre to all whom they judged their enemies. The crime on which they justified their proceedings, was their attempt to overturn the democracy.

Some perished merely through private enmity; some for the sums they had lent, by the hands of the borrowers. Every kind of death was here exhibited. Every dreadful act usual in a sedition, and more than usual, was perpetrated now. For fathers slew their children, some were dragged from altars; and some were butchered at them. And a number of persons immured in the temple of Bacchus were starved to death. So cruel was the progress of the sedition, and so excessively cruel did it appear, because the first of so black a nature that ever happened. But afterwards the contagion spread, one may say, through the whole extent of Greece, when factions raged in every city, the popular demagogues contending for the Athenians, the aspiring few for the Lacedaemonians. In peace, it is true, they were void of all pretext, of all opportunity to invite these rivals. But now, amidst declared hostilities, and the quest of alliance to afflict their enemies and add an increase of strength to themselves, opportunities were easily found by such as were fond of innovations to introduce the side they favoured. The consequence of this was sedition in cities, with all its numerous and tragical incidents. Such were now, and such things ever will be, so long as human nature continues the same; but under greater or less aggravations and diversified in circumstances, according to the several vicissitudes of conjunctures, which shall happen to occur. In the seasons of peace and affluence, communities as well as individuals have their tempers under better regulation, because not liable to that violence which flows from necessity. But war, which snatcheth from them their daily subsistence, is the teacher of violence, and assimilates the passions of men to their present condition.

By these means were cities harassed with seditions. And those to whose fate the later commotions fell, through inquiry what had happened in such instances before, grew enormously ambitious to suppress the machination of others, both in policy of attempts and extravagance of revenge. Even words lost now their former significance, since to palliate actions they were quite distorted. For truly, what before was brutal courage, began to be esteemed that fortitude which becomes a human and sociable creature; prudent consideration, to be specious cowardice; modesty, the disguise of effeminacy; and being wise in every thing, to be good for nothing. The hot fiery temper was adjudged the exertion of true manly valour; cautious and calm deliberation, to be a plausible pretext for intended knavery. He who boiled with indignation was undoubtedly trusty; who presumed to contradict was ever suspected. He who succeeded in a roguish scheme was wise, and he who suspected such practices in others, was still a more able genius. But was he provident enough, so as never to be in need of such base expedients; he was one that would not stand to his engagements, and most shamefully awed by his foes. In short, he who could prevent another in executing villany, or could persuade a well-designing person to it, was sure to be applauded.

Men now, who were allied in blood, were less valued or caressed, than such as were connected by voluntary combination; since the latter, unscrupulous and uninquisitive, were more ready to embark in any scheme whatever. For now associations were not formed for such mutual advantage as is consistent with, but for the execution of such rapines as are contrary to human laws. In mutual trust they persisted, not out of any regard to religious obligation, but from the bond of communicated guilt. To the fair and honest proposals of adversaries, they hearkened indeed when such by active strength could control them, but never through candid ingenuity. Revenge upon another was a more valued possession than never to have suffered injury. Oaths, if ever made for present reconciliation, had a temporary force, so long as neither knew how to break them; but never when either party had power to abet their violation. He who, at inviting opportunity, durst first incur the perjury, if the adversary was off his guard, executed his rancour with higher spirit than from enmity open and avowed. Such a step was thought most secure; and, because he had thus surpassed in guile, it was certainly extolled as a master-piece of cunning. Large is the number of villains, and such obtain more easily the reputation of dexterity than their dupes can that of goodness the latter are apt to blush; the former most impudently triumph.

The source of all these evils is a thirst of power, in consequence either of rapacious or ambitious passions. The mind, when actuated by such, is ever ready to engage in party-feuds. For the men of large influence in communities avowing on both sides a specious cause, some standing up for the just equality of the popular, others for the fair decorum of the aristocratical government, by artful sounds, embarrassed those communities for their own private lucre. Both sides, intent on victory, carried on the contention with the keenest spirit. They most daringly projected, and then regularly executed, the most dreadful machinations. Their revenge was not limited by justice or the public welfare; it aimed at more ample satisfaction. Either side constantly measured it by such retailiation as was judged the sweetest, either by a capital condemnation through an iniquitous sentence, or by earning the victory with their own hands, in which they were always ready to glut the present rancour of their hearts. And hence it was, that the pious and upright conduct was on both sides disregarded. And when any point of great importance was before them, to carry it by specious collusive oratory was the greatest enhancement of their credit. Yet all this while, the moderate members of such communities, either hated because they would not meddle, or envied for such obnoxious conduct, fell victims to both.

Seditions in this manner introduced every species of outrageous wickedness into the Grecian manners. Sincerity, which is most frequently to be found in generous tempers, was laughed out of countenance and for ever vanished. It was become the universal practice, to keep up a constant enmity of intention against one another, and never to believe. No promise was strong enough, no oath sufficiently solemn, to banish such mutual diffidence. Those who excelled in shrewd consideration resigned all hope of any lasting security, and stood ever on their guard against whom it was impossible for them to trust. But persons of meaner understandings took more effectual means for their preservation. Living in constant apprehensions, from their own inferiority and the craft of their opponents, lest by words they should be over-reached, or that such subtile heads might execute their treacheries upon them unawares, they boldly seized the present moment, and at once despatched the men they dreaded; who, presuming too much on their own penetration, and that it was superflous to aim a blow at those whom they could at any time supplant by cunning, despised them so far as to neglect a proper guard, and so contributed to their own destruction.

Many such daring outrages were now by way of precedent committed at Corcyra; nay, all whatever, that men, who are wreaking revenge upon such as before were their masters, and had exerted their superiority with savageness more than humanity, can in turn retaliate upon them, were executed there.—Some joined in these acts of violence to procure a discharge from their former poverty; but the greater number, through a passionate desire to seize the property of their neighbours: or, though they were not lured by the lust of rapine, but engaged in the contest upon fair and open views, yet hurried to wild extravagence through mad and undisciplined anger, they proceeded to cruel acts, and with inexorable fury. The whole order of human life was for a season confounded in this city. The human temper, too apt to transgress in spite of laws, and now having gained the ascendant over law, seemed pleased with exhibiting this public manifestation, that it was too weak for anger, too strong for justice, and an enemy to all superiority. Men could not otherwise have awarded the preference to revenge over righteous duty, and to lucre over that habit of justice in which envy never yet had power to annoy them. But more than this, when the point of view is revenge upon others, men haughtily make precedents against themselves, by infringing those laws which are binding by the ties of nature, and from which alone any hope of safety can be extracted for themselves in a plunge of misery, precluding thus all possibility of redress, should they be reduced in some future extremity to make the same appeal.

And thus the Corcyreans continued to execute the rage of such cruel passions, upon the heads of one another, within the precincts of their own city, of which this was the first example in Greece, till Eurymedon with the Athenian fleet under his command put out again to sea.

But, after his departure, they who by flight had preserved their lives, to the number of about five hundred, having seized their forts upon the opposite shore, got possession of their own land, on that side the water. Putting out hence, they plundered the Corcyreans in the island, and made such havoc that a violent famine ensued the city. They further sent a deputation to Lacedaemon and Corinth, to negotiate the means of their restoration. But nothing of this kind succeeding, they got together afterwards a body of auxiliaries and transports, and so passed over to the island of Corcyra, to the amount of six hundred men. Having now set fire to their transports, to preclude every other expedient but gaining firm footing where now they were, they marched up to the mountain Istone, and having fortified themselves there, made cruel work with those in the city, and were masters of the country round about.

/ / /

In the beginning of the winter the plague broke out a second time at Athens, not that during this whole interval of time it had wholly ceased, though its rage had very much abated. But now the mortality began again, and continued not less than a year: but the former had raged for the space of two. There was nothing which lay upon the Athenians so hard as this, or so much impared their strength. It appeared from the muster-rolls, that there perished four thousand and four hundred of those citizens who wore the heavy armour, and three hundred of the horsemen. The number of the lower people that died was not to be computed.—There happened at the same time many earthquakes; at Athens; in Euboea; amongst the Boeotians, and especially at the Boeotian Orchomenus.

2

/ / / /

The Plague in Athens as Thucydides Saw It

In the very beginning of summer, the Peloponnesians and allies, with two-thirds of their forces, made an incursion as before into Attica, under the command of Archidamus son of Zeuxidamus, king of the Lacedaemonians, and having formed their camp, ravaged the country.

They had not been many days in Attica, before a sickness began first to appear amongst the Athenians, such as was reported to have raged before this in other parts, as about Lemnos and other places. Yet a plague so great as this, and so dreadful a calamity, in human memory could not be paralleled. The physicians at first could administer no relief, through utter ignorance; nay, they died the faster, the closer their attendance on the sick, and all human art was totally unavailing. Whatever supplications were offered in the temples, whatever recourse to oracles and religious rites, all were insignificant; at last, expedients of this nature they totally relinquished, overpowered by calamity. It broke out first, as it is said, in that part of Aethiopia which borders upon Egypt; it afterwards spread into Egypt and Libya, and into great part of the king's dominions, and from thence it on a sudden fell on the city of the Athenians. The contagion showed itself first in the Piraeus, which occasioned a report that the Peloponnesians had caused poison to be thrown into the wells, for as yet there were no fountains there. After this it spread into the upper city, and then the mortality very much increased. Let every one, physician or not, freely declare his own sentiments about it; let him assign any credible account of its rise, or the causes strong enough in his opinion to introduce so terrible a scene—I shall only relate what it actually was; and as, from an information in all its symptoms, none may be quite at a loss about it, if ever it should happen again, I shall give an exact detail of them; having been sick of it myself, and seen many others afflicted with it.

This very year, as is universally allowed, had been more than any other remarkably free from common disorders; or, whatever diseases had seized the body, they ended at length in this. But those who enjoyed the most perfect health were suddenly, without any apparent cause, seized at first with head-aches extremely violent, with inflammations, and fiery redness in the eyes. Within—the throat and tongue began instantly to be red as blood; the breath was drawn with difficulty and had a noisome smell. The symptoms that succeeded these were sneezing and hoarseness; and not long after, the malady descended to the breast, with a violent cough: but when once settled in the stomach, it excited vomitings, in which was thrown up all that matter physicians call discharges of bile, attended with excessive torture. A great part of the infected were subject to such violent hiccups without any discharge, as brought upon them a strong convulsion, to some but of a short, to others of a very long continuance. The body, to the outward touch, was neither exceeding hot, nor of a pallid hue, but reddish, livid, marked all over with little pustules and sores. Yet inwardly it was scorched with such excessive heat, that it could not bear the lightest covering or the finest linen upon it, but must be left quite naked. They longed for nothing so much as to be plunging into cold water; and many of those who were not properly attended, threw themselves into wells, hurried by a thirst not to be extinguished; and whether they drank much or little, their torment still continued the same. The restlessness of their bodies, and an utter inability of composing themselves by sleep, never abated for a moment. And the body, so long as the distemper continued in its height, had no visible waste, but withstood its rage to a miracle, so that most of them perished within nine or seven days, by the heat that scorched their vitals, though their strength was not exhausted; or, if they continued longer, the distemper fell into the belly, causing violent ulcerations in the bowels, accompanied with an incessant flux, by which many, reduced to an excessive weakness, were carried off. For the malady beginning in the head, and settling first there, sunk afterwards gradually down the whole body. And whoever got safe through all its most dangerous stages, yet the extremities of their bodies still retained the marks of its violence. For it shot down into their privy-members, into their fingers and toes, by losing which they escaped with life. Some there were who lost their eyes; and some who, being quite recovered, had at once totally lost all memory, and quite forgot not only their most intimate friends, but even their own selves. For as this distemper was in general virulent beyond expression, and its every part more grievous than had yet fallen to the lot of human nature, so in one particular instance, it appeared to be none of the natural infirmities of man, since the birds and the beasts that prey on human flesh either never approached the dead bodies, of which many lay about uninterred; or certainly perished if they ever tasted. One proof of this is the total disappearance then of such birds, for not one was to be seen, either in any other place, or about any one of the carcases. But the dogs, because of their familiarity with man, afforded a more notorious proof of this event.

The nature of this pestilential disorder was in general—for I have purposely omitted its many varied appearances, or the circumstances particular to some of the infected in contradiction to others—such as hath been described. None of the common maladies incident to human nature prevailed at that time; or whatever disorder any where appeared, it ended in this. Some died merely for want of care; and some, with all the care that could possibly be taken; nor was any one medicine discovered, from whence could be promised any certain relief, since that which gave ease to one was prejudicial to another. Whatever difference there was in bodies, in point of strength or in point of weakness, it availed nothing; all were equally swept away before it, in spite of regular diet and studied prescriptions. Yet the most affecting circumstances of this calamity were—that dejection of mind, which constantly attended the first attack; for the mind sinking at once into despair, they the sooner gave themselves up without a struggle—and that mutual tenderness, in taking care of one another, which communicated the infection, and made them drop like sheep. This latter case caused the mortality to be so great. For if fear withheld them from going near one another, they died for want of help, so that many houses became quite desolate for want of needful attendance; and if they ventured, they were gone. This was most frequently the case of the kind and compassionate. Such persons were ashamed, out of a selfish concern for themselves, entirely to abandon their friends, when their menial servants, no longer able to endure the groans and lamentations of the dying, had been compelled to fly from such a weight of calamity. But those especially, who had safely gone through it, took pity on the dying and the sick, because they knew by experience what it really was, and were now secure in themselves; for it never seized any one a second time so as to be mortal. Such were looked upon as quite happy by others, and were themselves at first overjoyed in their late escape, and the groundless hope that hereafter no distemper would prove fatal to them. Beside this reigning calamity, the general removal from the country into the city was a heavy grievance, more particularly to those who had been necessitated to come thither. For as they had no houses, but dwelled all the summer season in booths, where there was scarce room to breathe, the pestilence destroyed with the utmost disorder, so that they lay together in heaps, the dying upon the dead, and the dead upon the dying. Some were tumbling one over another in the public streets, or lay expiring round about every fountain, whither they had crept to assuage their immoderate thirst. The temples, in which they had erected tents for their reception, were full of the bodies of those who had expired there. For in a calamity so outrageously violent, and universal despair, things sacred and holy had quite lost their distinction. Nay, all regulations observed before in matters of sepulture were quite confounded, since every one buried wherever he could find a place. Some, whose sepulchres were already filled by the numbers which had perished in their own families, were shamefully compelled to seize those of others. They surprised on a sudden the piles which others had built for their own friends, and burned their dead upon them; and some, whilst one body was burning on a pile, tossed another body they had dragged thither upon it, and went their way.

Thus did the pestilence give their first rise to those iniquitous acts which prevailed more and more in Athens. For every one was now more easily induced openly to do what for decency they did only covertly before. They saw the strange mutability of outward condition, the rich untimely cut off, and their wealth pouring suddenly on the indigent and necessitous; so that they thought it prudent to catch hold of speedy enjoyments and quick gusts of pleasure; persuaded that their bodies and their wealth might be their own merely for the day. Not any one continued resolute enough to form any honest or generous design, when so uncertain whether he should live to effect it. Whatever he knew could improve the pleasure or satisfaction of the present moment, that he determined to be honour and interest. Reverence of the gods or the laws of society laid no restraints upon them; either judging that piety and impiety were things quite indifferent, since they saw that all men perished alike; or, throwing away every apprehension of being called to account for their enormities, since justice might be prevented by death; or rather, as the heaviest of judgments to which man could be doomed, was already hanging over their heads, snatching this interval of life for pleasure, before it fell.

With such a weight of calamity were the Athenians at this time on all sides oppressed. Their city was one scene of death, and the adjacent country of ruin and devastation. In this their affliction they called to mind, as was likely they should, the following prediction, which persons of the greatest age informed them had been formerly made:

> Two heavy judgments will at once befall,
> A Doric war without, a plague within your wall.

There had indeed been a dispute before, whether their ancestors in this prediction read $\lambda οιμος$ a plague, or $\lambda ιμος$ a famine. Yet in their present circumstances all with probability agreed that $\lambda οιμος$ a plague, was the right: for they adapted the interpretation to what they now suffered.—But in my sentiments, should they ever again be engaged in a Doric war, and a famine happen at the same time, they will have recourse with equal probability to the other interpretation. It was further remembered by those who knew of the oracle given to the Lacedaemonians, that when they inquired of the god, "whether they should engage in this war," his answer was, that—"if they carried it on with all their strength, they should be victorious, and he himself would fight on their side;"—and therefore they concluded that what now befell was the completion of the oracle. The pestilence broke out immediately upon the irruption of the Peloponnesians, and never extended itself to Peloponnesus, a circumstance which ought to be related. It raged the most, and for the longest time, in Athens, but afterwards spread into the other towns, especially the most populous. And this is an exact account of the plague.

The Peloponnesians, after they had ravaged the inland parts, extended their devastations to those which are called The Coast, as far as Mount Laurium, where the Athenians had silvermines. And here they first ravaged the part which looks towards Peloponnesus, and afterwards that which lies towards Euboea and Andros. But Pericles, who was then in the command, persisted in the same opinion as before in the former incursion, that "the Athenians ought not to march out against them." Yet, whilst the enemy was up in the country, before they had advanced as far as the coast, he had equipped a fleet of a hundred ships to invade Peloponnesus: and when every thing was ready, he put to sea. On board these ships he had embarked four thousand heavy-armed Athenians; and in vessels for transporting horse, now first fitted up for this service out of old ships, three hundred horsemen. The Chians and the Lesbians joined in the expedition with fifty sail. At the very time this fleet went to sea from Athens, they left the Peloponnesians on the coast of Attica. When they were arrived before Epidaurus, a city of Peloponnesus, they ravaged great part of the country about it, and making an assault on the city itself, had some hopes of taking it, but did not succeed. Leaving Epidaurus, they ravaged the country about Troexene, Halias, and Hermione; all these places are situated on the sea-coast of Peloponnesus. But sailing hence, they came before Prasiae, a fort of Laconia, situated upon the sea, around which they laid the country waste; and having taken the fort by assault, demolished it. After these performances they returned home, and found the Peloponnesians no longer in Attica, but retired within their own dominions.

The whole space of time that the Peloponnesians were upon the lands of the Athenians, and the Athenians employed in their sea expedition, the plague was making havoc both in the troops of the

Athenians, and within the city. This occasioned a report that the Peloponnesians, for fear of the infection, as having been informed by deserters that it raged in the city, and been witnesses themselves of their frequent interments, retired out of their territory with some precipitation. Yet they persevered in this incursion longer than they had ever done before, and had made the whole country one continued devastation; for the time of their continuance in Attica was about forty days. **3**

Xenophon's Athens

In the following selections Xenophon (430-355 B.C.) Greek historian and philosopher records some of the general feelings and attitudes on work and labor in the city of Athens.

Work and Labor Attitudes in Athens

He (Socrates) had two ways of dealing with the difficulties of his friends; where ignorance was the cause, he tried to meet the trouble by a dose of common sense; or where want and poverty were to blame, by teaching them that they should assist one another according to their ability; and here I may mention certain incidents which occurred within my own knowledge. How, for instance, he chanced upon Aristarchus wearing the look of one who suffered from a fit of the "sullens," and thus accosted him:—

SOCRATES. You seem to have some trouble on your mind, Aristarchus; if so, you should share it with your friends. Perhaps together we might lighten the weight of it a little.

ARISTARCHUS. Yes, Socrates, I am in sore straits indeed. Ever since the party strife declared itself in the city, what with the rush of people to Peiraeus and the wholesale banishments, I have been fairly at the mercy of my poor female relatives. Sisters, nieces, cousins, they all come flocking to me for protection. I have fourteen free-born souls, I tell you, under my single roof, and how are we to live? We can get nothing out of the soil—that is in the hands of the enemy; nothing from my house property, for there is scarcely a living soul left in the city; my furniture? no one will buy it; money? there is none to be borrowed—you would have a better chance to find it by looking for it on the road than to borrow it from a banker. Yes, Socrates, to stand by and see one's relatives die of hunger is hard indeed, and yet to feed so many at such a pinch impossible.

After he had listened to the story Socrates asked: How comes it that Ceramon, with so many mouths to feed, not only contrives to furnish himself and them with the necessaries of life, but to realize a handsome surplus, whilst you being in like plight are afraid that you will one and all perish of starvation for want of the necessaries of life?

A. Why, bless you, do you not see he has only slaves and I have free-born souls to feed?

S. And which should you say were the better human beings, the free-born members of your household or Ceramon's slaves?

A. The free souls under my roof without a doubt.

S. Is it not a shame, then that he with his baser folk to back him should be in easy circumstances, while you and your far superior household are in difficulties?

A. To be sure it is, when he has only a set of handicraftsmen to feed, and I my liberally-educated household.

S. What is a handicraftsman? Does not the term apply to all who can make any sort of useful product or commodity?

A. Certainly.

S. Barley-meal is a useful product, is it not?

A. Preeminently so.

S. And loaves of bread?

A. No less.

S. Well, and what do you say to cloaks for men and for women-tunics, mantles, vests?

A. Yes, they are all highly useful commodities.

S. Then your household do not know how to make any of them.

A. On the contrary, I believe they can make them all.

S. Then you are not aware that by means of the manufacture of one of these alone-his barley-meal store—Nausicydes not only maintains himself and his domestics, but many pigs and cattle besides and realizes such large profits that he frequently contributes to the state benevolences; while there is Cyrebus, again, who out of a bread factory, more than maintains the whole of his establishment, and lives in the lap of luxury; and Demeas of Collytus gets a livelihood out of a cloak business, and Menon as a mantle-maker;

and thus more than half the Megarians maintain themselves by the making of vests.

A. Bless me, yes! They have got a set of barbarian fellows, whom they purchase and keep, to manufacture by forced labor whatever takes their fancy. My kinswomen, I tell you, are free-born ladies.

S. Then, on the ground that they are free-born and your kinswomen, you think they ought to do nothing but eat and sleep? Or is it your opinion that people who live in this way—I speak of free-born people in general—lead happier lives, and are more to be congratulated, than those who give their time and attention to such useful arts of life as they are skilled in? Is this what you see in the world, that for the purpose of learning what it is well to know, and of recollecting the lessons taught, or with a view to health and strength of body, or for the sake of acquiring and preserving all that gives life its charm, idleness and inattention are found to be helpful, whilst work and study are simply a dead loss? Pray, when those relatives of yours were taught what you tell me they know, did they learn it as barren information which they would never turn to practical account, or on the contrary, as something with which they were to be seriously concerned some day, and from which they were to reap solid advantage? Do human beings in general attain to well-tempered manhood by a course of idling, or by carefully attending to what will be of use? Which will help a man the more to grow in justice and uprightness, to be up and doing, or to sit with folded hands revolving the ways and means of existence? As things now stand, if I am not mistaken, there is no love lost between you. You cannot help feeling that they are costly to you, and they must see that you find them a burden. This is a perilous state of affairs, in which hatred and bitterness have every prospect of increasing whilst the preexisting bond of affection is likely to be snapped.

But now, if you will only allow them free scope for their energies, when you come to see how useful they can be, you will grow quite fond of them, and they, when they perceive that they can please you, will cling to their benefactor warmly. Thus, with the memory of former kindnesses gratitude will increase; you will in consequence be knit in closer bonds of love and domesticity. If, indeed, they were called upon to do any shameful work, let them choose death rather than that; but now they know, it would seem, the very arts and accomplishments which are regarded as the loveliest and the most suitable for women; and the things which we know, any of us, are just those which we can best perform, that is to say, with ease and expedition, it is a joy to do them, and the result is beautiful. Do not hesitate then, to initiate you friends in what will bring advantage to them and you alike; probably they will gladly respond to your summons.

A. Well, upon my word, I like so well what you say, Socrates, that though hitherto I have not been disposed to borrow, knowing that when I had spent what I got I should not be in a condition to repay, I think I can now bring myself to do so in order to raise a fund for these works.

Thereupon a capital was provided; wools were purchased; the goodman's relatives set to work, and even whilst they breakfasted they worked, and on and on till work was ended and they supped. Smiles took the place of frowns; they no longer looked askance with suspicion, but full into each other's eyes with happiness. They loved their kinsman for his kindness to them. He became attached to them as helpmates; and the end of it all was, he came to Socrates and told him with delight how matters fared; "and now," he added, "they tax me with being the only drone in the house, who sit and eat the bread of idleness."

To which Socrates replied: Why do you not tell them the fable of the dog? Once on a time, so goes the story, when beasts could speak, the sheep said to their master, "What a marvel is this, master, that to us, your own sheep, who provide you with fleeces and lambs and cheese, you give nothing, save only what we may nibble off earth's bosom; but with this dog of yours, who provides you with nothing of the sort, you share the very meat out of your mouth." When the dog heard these words, he answered promptly, "Ay, in good sooth, for is it not I who keep you safe and sound, you sheep, so that you are not stolen by man nor harried by wolves; since, if I did not keep watch over you, you would not be able so much as to graze afield, fearing to be destroyed." And, so says the tale, the sheep had to admit that the dog was rightly preferred to themselves in honor. And so do you tell your flock yonder that like the dog in the fable you are their guardian and overseer, and it is thanks to you that they are protected from evil and evildoers, so that they work their work and live their lives in blissful security.

8. At another time chancing upon an old friend (Eutherus) whom he had not seen for a long while, he greeted him thus:—

Soc. What quarter of the world do you hail from, Eutherus?

EUTHERUS. From abroad, just before the close of the war; but at present from the city itself. You see, since we have been denuded of our possessions across the frontier, and my father left me nothing in Attica, I must needs bide at home, and provide myself with the necessaries of life by means of bodily toil, which seems preferable to begging from another, especially as I have no security on which to raise a loan.

S. And how long do you expect your body to be equal to providing the necessaries of life for hire?

E. Goodness knows, Socrates—not for long.

S. And when you find yourself an old man, expenses will not diminish and yet no one will care to pay you for the labor of your hands.

E. That is true.

S. Would it not be better then to apply yourself at once to such work as will stand you in good stead when you are old—that is, address yourself to some large proprietor who needs an assistant in managing his estate? By superintending his works, helping to get in his crops, and guarding his property in general, you will be a benefit to the estate and be benefited in return.

E. I could not endure the yoke of slavery, Socrates!

S. And yet the heads of departments in a state are not regarded as adopting the badge of slavery because they manage the public property, but as having attained a higher dignity of freedom rather.

E. In a word, Socrates, the idea of being held to account to another is not at all to my taste.

S. And yet, Eutherus, it would be hard to find a work which did not involve some liability to account: in fact it is difficult to do anything without some mistake or other, and no less difficult, if you should succeed in doing it immaculately, to escape all unfriendly criticism. I wonder now whether you will find it easy to get through your present occupations entirely without reproach. No? Let me tell you what you should do. You should avoid censorious persons and attach yourself to the considerate and kindhearted, and in all your affairs accept with good grace what you can and decline what you feel you cannot do. Whatever it be, do it heart and soul, and make it your finest work. There lies the method at once to silence fault-finders and to minister help to your own difficulties. Life will flow smoothly, risks will be diminished, provision against old age secured.

4

Xenophon—in one of the first documents of its kind—analyzed various economic and city planning problems of Athens.

The Soil

1. I AM always of opinion that of whatever character governors are, of a similar character also are the governments which they conduct. But as some of those who rule at Athens have been said to know what is just, no less than other men, but have declared that they are compelled, through the poverty of the common people, to act with somewhat of injustice towards the allied cities, I have in consequence set myself to consider whether the citizens may by any means be maintained from the resources of their own country, from which it is most just that they should be maintained, thinking that, if this should be the case, remedy would at once be afforded for their wants, and for the jealousy which they incur from the other Greeks.

2. As I revolved in my mind what I observed, it readily appeared to me that the country is well qualified by nature to afford very large revenues; and in order that it may be understood that I say this with truth, I will first of all give an account of the natural resources of Attica. 3. That the seasons in it are extremely mild, the products of the soil testify; for such as will not even grow in many countries bear fruit in perfection in Attica. And as the land is most productive, so likewise is the sea that surrounds the land; and whatever fruits the gods afford in their several seasons begin in this country earliest, and cease latest. 4. Nor is the land superior only in things that grow up and decay annually, but has also permanent advantages; for stone is supplied from it in abundance, from which the most magnificent temples, the most beautiful altars, and the finest statues of the gods are made, and in which many both Greeks and barbarians desire to participate. 5. There

are indeed portions of the soil which, though sown, will not produce fruit, but which, if they are penetrated by digging, will support many more people than if they produced corn, as, doubtless by divine dispensation, they contain silver beneath the surface; and though there are many states lying near, both by land and by sea, not even the smallest vein of silver is found to extend into any one of them.   6. A person might not unreasonably suppose that the state is situated in the centre, not only of Greece, but of the whole inhabited world; for the further people are from it, the more severe cold or heat do they experience; and whatever travelers would pass from one end of Greece to the other, must all either sail by Athens, or pass it by land, as the centre of their circle.   7. Though it is not surrounded by water, it nevertheless attracts to itself like an island, with the aid of every wind, whatever it requires, and sends away whatever it desires to export; for it has sea on each side of it. By land, too, it receives many kinds of merchandise, as it is joined to the continent.   8. To many states, moreover, barbarians who dwell on their borders cause annoyance; but states border on the Athenians which are themselves at a distance from the barbarians.

The Athenians Sought to Attract Foreigners to Their Shores

1. OF all these advantages, I think that the land is itself, as I said, the cause; and if to the blessings bestowed by nature there be joined, in the first place, an attention to the interests of strangers sojourning in it, (for that source of revenue appears to me to be one of the best, since strangers, while they maintain themselves, and confer great benefits on the states in which they live, receive no pension from the public, but pay the tax imposed on aliens,) such attention would seem to me likely to be of the utmost benefit;   2. especially if we relieve them at the same time from such impositions as, while they are of no benefit to the state, appear to cast on them a mark of dishonour, and if we exempt them likewise from taking the field as heavy-armed infantry along with the citizens; for the danger which they incur is great, and it is a great trouble to them to be away from their trades and families.   3. The state would also be much more benefited, if the citizens stood by the side of one another in the field, than if, as is the case at present,

Lydians, and Syrians, and Phrygians, and other barbarians from every nation be amalgamated with them. 4. In addition, too, to the good attendant on the exemption of strangers from joining the army, it would be an honour to the country for the Athenians to be seen to trust to themselves in the field of battle rather than to foreigners. 5. While we give a share, moreover, to foreigners of other privileges which it is proper to share with them, we should be likely in my opinion, if we gave them admission also into the cavalry, to render them better disposed towards us, and to increase the strength and greatness of our country. 6. Besides, as there are within the walls many pieces of ground for building, vacant of houses, I think that if the state were to allow them to become the property of those who might build upon them, and who on applying for them, might seem to be deserving, a greater number of respectable persons would by that means become desirous of a settlement at Athens. 7. If we should institute an order of guardians of foreigners, also, as we have one of guardians of orphans, and some honour should be conferred on such of them as should bring in the greatest number of foreigners, such a plan would make the foreigners more contented under us, and, as is likely, all who have no residence in any other city would eagerly seek a settlement at Athens, and would thus increase the public revenue.

As Cities in our Time Athens Sought to Attract Business and Trade

1. IN proof that the city is extremely pleasant and lucrative as a place of trade, I will mention the following particulars. In the first place, it has the finest and safest harbours for vessels, where navigators may moor and rest in case of a storm. 2. In the next place, merchants, in most other cities, must barter one commodity for another; for the inhabitants use money that will not pass beyond the limits of the country; but at Athens, while there is abundance of goods, such as people require, for exportation, still, if merchants do not wish to barter, they may carry off an excellent freight by taking away our silver, for wherever they dispose of it, they will always gain more than its original value.

3. If we should propose rewards, however, for the judges of the tribunal of commerce, to be given to such as should decide points of controversy with the greatest justice and expedition, so that per-

sons who wished to sail might not be detained, a still larger number of people would by that means be brought to trade with us, and with greater pleasure.   4. It would be for our advantage and credit also, that such merchants and shipowners as are found to benefit the state by bringing to it vessels and merchandise of great account should be honoured with seats of distinction on public occasions, and sometimes invited to entertainments; for, being treated with such respect, they would hasten to return to us, as to friends, for the sake, not merely of gain, but of honour.   5. The more people settled among us and visited us, the greater quantity of merchandise, it is evident, would be imported, exported, and sold, and the more gain would be secured, and tribute received.   6. To effect such augmentations of the revenue, it is not necessary for us to be at any cost but that of philanthropic ordinances and careful superintendence.

For securing whatever other revenues seem likely to come in to us, I know that there will be need of a fund.   7. Yet I am not without hope that the citizens will readily contribute for this purpose, when I reflect how much the state contributed at the period when it assisted the Arcadians under the command of Lysistratus, and how much under that of Hegesilaus.   8. I know also that galleys have often been sent out at great expense, galleys which were built when it was uncertain whether the result of the expedition would be for better or worse, though it was very certain that the contributors would never receive back what they had paid or even recover any portion of it.   9. But at present the citizens can acquire no gains so creditable as those from what they may contribute for this fund; for to him whose contribution shall be ten minae, about the fifth part will return as interest from the fleet, as he will receive three oboli a day; and to him whose contribution shall be five minae, there will be a return of more than the third.   10. The most of the Athenians, assuredly, will receive annually more than they have contributed; for those who contribute a mina will have an income of almost two minae, and will have it in the city, being an income, too, that appears the safest and most durable of human things.   11. I think, too, for my own part, that if the benefactors to our state were to have their names enrolled for transmission to posterity, many foreigners would give us their contributions, as well as some whole cities, through a desire for such enrolment. I should expect also that kings and other sovereign princes and satraps would feel a desire to participate in so gratifying an acknowledgment.

12. When a fund is established, it will be for the honour and interest of the state to build lodging-houses, in addition to those at present existing round the harbours, for the accommodation of seamen; and it would be well, also, to build others for merchants, in places convenient for buying and selling, as well as public houses of entertainment for all that come to the city.   13. If, moreover, houses and shops were to be erected for retail dealers, at the Peiraeeus and in the city, they would not only be an ornament to the city, but a great accession of income would be derived from them.   14. It seems to me, likewise, proper to try whether it be possible for the state, as it possesses public war-galleys, to have also public vessels for conveying merchandise, and to let them out for hire, upon persons giving security for them, as is the case with other things belonging to the public; for if this should appear practicable, a large income might be derived from that source.

Silver Mining in Athens

1. SHOULD our silver mines, too, be managed as they ought to be, I consider that great profits might be drawn from them, in addition to our other revenues. To those who do not know their value, I should wish to make it known; for, when you know this, you will be the better enabled to form plans for arrangements respecting them.   2. That they were wrought in very ancient times is well known to all; for assuredly no one attempts to specify at what time they began to be formed. But though the earth containing silver has been so long dug and cast up, consider how small a portion the heaps which have been thrown out are of the hills that remain still in their natural state, and that contain silver underneath them.   3. Nor does the space of ground that is dug for silver appear to be at all diminished, but to be perpetually extended in a wider circuit; and during the time that the greatest number of men were in the mines, no one was ever in want of occupation, but there was always more work than enough for the hands employed.

4. At the present time, too, no one of those who have slaves in the mines is diminishing the number of them, but is indeed contin-

ually adding to it as many as he can; for when but few are engaged in digging and searching, little treasure is found; but when many are employed, a far greater quantity of silver ore is discovered; so that in this occupation alone, of all those that I know, no one envies those that extend their operations.   5. All persons that have farms would be able to say how many yokes of oxen, and how many workmen, would be sufficient for their land; and if they send into the fields more than are necessary, they consider it a loss; but in the mining operations for silver, they say that all are constantly in want of workman.   6. For the consequence is not the same in this case as it is when there are numbers of workers in brass, and when, as articles made of brass then necessarily become cheap, the workmen are ruined, nor is it the same as when there are excessive numbers of blacksmiths; or as when there is abundance of corn and wine, and when, as the fruits of the earth are cheap, agriculture become unprofitable, so that many farmers, quitting their occupation of tilling the ground, betake themselves to the employments of merchants, or inn-keepers, or bankers; but, in regard to the silver mines, the more silver ore is found, and the more silver is extracted, the greater is the number that devote themselves to mining.   7. Of furniture, when people have got enough of it for their houses, they do not much care for buying additional supplies; but nobody has ever yet had so much silver as not to desire an increase of it; and if people have a superabundance, they hoard it, and are not less delighted with doing so than with putting it to use.   8. When communities, too, are in the most flourishing condition, people have very great use for money, for the men are ready to be at expense for beautiful arms, or fine horses, or magnificent houses or furniture; and the women are eager for expensive dresses and golden ornaments.   9. When communities, on the other hand, are in distress, whether from scarcity of corn or from the effects of war, they are still more in want of money, as the land lies uncultivated, both for purchasing provisions and for paying auxiliary troops.

10. If any one should say that gold is not less useful for such purposes than silver, I do not dispute the truth of the assertion; but I am aware at the same time that gold, if it shows itself in great quantities, becomes much less valuable, and renders silver of a higher price.   11. These remarks I have made with a view that

we should send with confidence as many workmen as possible into the silver mines, and should with confidence continue our operations in them, fully trusting that the silver ore is not going to fail, and that silver will never lose its value. 12. The state, however, appears to me to have known this long before I knew it; for it allows any foreigner that pleases to work in the mines, on paying the same duty as the citizens.

13. But that I may make the subjects still more clear with reference to the maintenance of the citizens, I will state how the mines may be managed so as to be most beneficial to the country. For what I am going to say, however, I do not desire to court admiration, as if I had found out something difficult to be discovered; for part of what I shall state we all at present see before us, and the condition of things in times past, we hear, was of an exactly similar character. 14. But we cannot but feel surprised that the state, when it sees many private individuals enriching themselves from its resources, does not imitate their proceedings; for we heard long ago, indeed, at least such of us attended to these matters, that Nicias the son of Niceratus kept a thousand men employed in the silver mines, whom he let on hire to Sosias of Thrace, on condition that he should give him for each an obolus a-day, free of all charges; and this number he always supplied undiminished. Hipponicus also had six hundred slaves let out at the same rate, which brought him in a clear mina a-day; Philemonides had three hundred, which brought him half a mina; and others had other complements of slaves, according, I suppose, to their respective resources. 16. But why should I dwell upon former times, when there are numbers of men in the mines let out in the same manner at present? 17. And if what I propose be carried into effect, the only new point in it would be, that as private individuals, by the possession of slaves, have secured themselves a constant revenue, so the state should possess public slaves, to the number of three for each Athenian citizen.

18. Whether what I propose is practicable, let him who chooses, after considering every point of it, pronounce a judgment. As to the price for slaves, it is evident that the state can procure it better than private individuals. It is easy for the senate to issue a proclamation that he who will may bring his slaves, and then to buy all that are brought. 19. When they are bought, why should not any

person be as willing to hire slaves from the state as from a private individual, if he is to have them on the same terms? At least they hire from the state consecrated grounds, and temples, and houses, and farm the public taxes. 20. That the slaves purchased for the public may be kept safe, the state may require sureties from those who hire them, as they require them from those who farm the taxes; and it is indeed much easier for him who farms a tax to defraud the public than for him who hires slaves. 21. For how can any one identify the public money that is embezzled, when private money is exactly like it; but as for slaves, when they are marked with the public mark, and when a penalty is denounced against him who sells or exports them, how could any one steal them? So far, therefore, it will appear to be possible for the state to acquire and to preserve slaves.

22. But if any one doubts whether, after a great number of workmen have been procured, a great number of persons will also present themselves to hire them, let him be of good courage, reflecting that many of those who already possess slaves will still hire those belonging to the public, (for there is plenty of work to employ them), and that many of those engaged in the works are growing old, while there are many others, both Athenians and foreigners, who would neither be able nor willing to engage in corporeal labour, but who would gladly gain a subsistence by applying their minds to the superintendence of the business. 23. If at first, then, a thousand two hundred slaves be collected, it is probable that, with the income from that number a complement of not less than six thousand might in five or six years be obtained; and if, of this number, each brings in a clear obolus, the profit will be sixty talents a year. 24. If of those sixty talents twenty be devoted to the purchase of more slaves, the state will be at liberty to use the other forty for whatever other purpose it may think proper; and then the number of ten thousand slaves is made up, the yearly revenue from them will be a hundred talents.

25. That the state will receive even a far greater profit than this, those will agree with me in thinking, who remember, if there are any that still remember, how great a height the income from the slaves reached before the occurrences at Deceleia. The fact, also, that, though innumerable workmen have been perpetually employed in the mines, their present condition is not at all different

from that in which our forefathers remember them to have been, affords me additional support for this supposition. 26. Indeed, all that is now done in the mines testifies that there can never be a greater number of slaves there than the works require; for those who are employed in digging find no limit to the depth or ramifications of their works. 27. To cut in a new direction is assuredly not less practicable now than it was formerly; nor can any one say, from certain knowledge, whether there is more silver ore in the parts which have been opened than is to be found in those which are undisturbed. 28. Why then, some one may ask, do not many make new cuttings now, as of old? It is because those engaged about the mines are now poorer; for it was but lately that they began to be wrought again; and great risk is incurred by a person commencing new operations; for he indeed that finds a profitable field of labour becomes rich, but he who does not find one loses all that he has expended; and into such risk the men of the present day are by no means willing to run.

30. I think, however, that I am able to give some advice with regard to this difficulty also and to show how new operations may be conducted with the greatest safety. There are ten tribes at Athens, and if to each of these the state should assign an equal number of slaves, and the tribes should all make new cuttings, sharing their fortune in common, then, if but one tribe should make any useful discovery, it would point out something profitable to the whole;

31 but if two, or three, or four, or half the number should make some discovery, it is plain that the works would be more profitable in proportion; and that they should all fail is contrary to all the experience of past times. 32. It is possible also for private individuals to unite and share their fortunes together, and thus to venture with greater safety; and you need entertain no apprehensions either that the public company thus constituted will injure the private adventurers, or that the private adventurers will inconvenience the public company; but as allies in the field of battle, the greater the number in which they meet, render one another proportionately stronger, so the greater the number that are employed in the mines, the more gain will they acquire and bring to the state.

33. I have now stated how I think that public matters may be arranged, so that sufficient maintenance may be secured from our common resources for the whole body of the Athenian people.

34. If any of us, considering that there will be need of vast funds for all these works, think that sufficient money will never be contributed, let them not be cast down through that apprehension.   35. For there is no necessity that all these things should be done at once, or else no profit will result from them; but whatever buildings are erected, or ships constructed, or slaves purchased, the proceedings will straightway be attended with profit.   36. It is indeed more advantageous that such things should be done gradually than that they should all be done at once; for if we were to build all together, we should do our work at greater cost and with less efficiency than if we were to build by degrees; and if we were to get a vast number of slaves at once, we should be compelled to buy them in worse condition and at a higher price.   37. Proceeding however according to our ability, we may continue any operations that have been well planned, and if any error has been committed, we may take care not to repeat it.   38. Besides, if everything were to be done at once, it would be necessary for us to procure means for everything at the same time; but if part be done now, and part deferred, the incoming revenue may assist in obtaining what is necessary for future proceedings.

39. But as to that which appears to everybody most to be apprehended, I mean that, if the state purchase an extraordinary number of slaves, the works may be overstocked, we may feel quite free from that apprehension, if we do not send into the mines every year a greater number than the operations require.   40. Thus it appears to me that the way in which it is easiest to pursue these plans is also that in which it is best. But if, again, you think that, on account of the contributions made during the present war, you are unable to contribute anything further, you must, whatever sum of money the taxes brought in before the peace, conduct the administration with that exact sum during the next year, and whatever additional sum they may bring, through peace having taken place, through attention being paid to the sojourners and merchants, through more commodities being imported and exported in consequence of a greater number of people resorting to us, and through the sale of goods being increased at the harbour, you must take that sum and appropriate it in such a way that the revenues may be advanced to the utmost.   41. If, however, any feel apprehensive that this course, if war occur, will prove ineffectual, let them consider

that, even if war should break out, it will be far more formidable to those who attack us than to our state. 42. For what acquisition would be more useful for war than a great number of people, since they would be able to man many of the public vessels, while many of them also, serving for the public on land, would offer a powerful resistance to the enemy, provided that we do but treat them well?

43. I consider, too, that even if war takes place, it is possible to prevent our mines from being abandoned; for there is, we know, a fortress near the mines at Anaphylstus, on the sea towards the south, and another at Thoricus, on the sea towards the north; and these two are distant from each other about sixty furlongs. 44. If, then, a third fort should be built between those on the summit of Besa, the workmen might then retire into some one of all these fortresses, and if they should see an enemy approaching, it would be but a short distance for each to retreat to a place of safety. 45. Should even an overpowering number of enemies come, they would, doubtless, if they found corn, or wine, or cattle, without the works, carry them off; but if they even occupied the mining ground, of what more would they possess themselves than a heap of stones? 46. But how, indeed, could our enemies ever make an inroad on our mines, for the city of Megara, which is nearest to them is distant much more than five hundred stadia; and Thebes, which is the nearest city after Megara, is distant much more than six hundred. 47. If they should advance upon the mines, then, from any part in that direction, they will be under the necessity of passing by the city of Athens; and if they come in small numbers, it is probable that they will be cut off by the cavalry and the guards of the frontier; while it is difficult to imagine that they will march out with a large force, leaving their own country unguarded; for the city of Athens would be much nearer to their cities, than they themselves would be when they are at the mines. 48. But, even if they should come in great force, how could they stay, when they would have no provisions? since, should they go out to get provisions in small parties, there would be danger both to those who went out for provisions, and to those who remained behind to fight; and, if their whole force went out foraging on every occasion, they would be besieged rather than besiegers.

49. Not only the profit from the slaves, then, would increase the

resources of the city, but, as a vast number of people would collect about the mines, there would also arise a great income from the market held there, from the rent of the public buildings around the mines, from the furnaces, and from all other sources of that kind. 50. Our city, too, if it be thus supported, will become extremely populous, and land about the mines will grow as valuable to those who possess it there as to those who have it around Athens. 51. Should all indeed be done that I have proposed, I maintain that the state will not only be better supplied with money, but will be more quiet and orderly, and better prepared for war.

/ / /

Peace Can Bring Prosperity to the City

1. But if it appears evident, that, if the full revenues from the state are to be collected, there must be peace, is it not proper for us also to appoint guardians of peace? for such an office, if established, would render the city more agreeable for all men to visit, and more frequented. 2. Should any persons imagine, however, that if our state continues to maintain peace, it will be less powerful, and esteemed, and celebrated through Greece, such persons, in my opinion, entertain an unreasonable apprehension; for those states, assuredly, are most prosperous, which have remained at peace for the longest period; and of all states Athens is the best adapted by nature for flourishing during peace. 3. Who, indeed, if the city were in the enjoyment of peace, would not be eager to resort to it, and shipowners and merchants most of all? Would not those who have plenty of corn, and ordinary wine, and wine of the sweetest kind, and olive oil, and cattle, flock to us, as well as those who can make profit by their ingenuity and by money-lending? 4. Where would artificers, too, and sophists, and philosophers, and poets, and such as study their works, and such as desire to witness sacrifices, or religious ceremonies worthy of being seen and heard, and such as desire to make a quick sale or purchase of many commodities, obtain their objects better than at Athens? 5. If no one can answer in the negative to these questions, and yet some, who desire to recover the supreme dominion for our state, think that that end would be effected better by war than by

peace, let them contemplate, first of all, the Persian invasion, and consider whether it was by force of arms or by good offices to the Greeks that we attained the head of the naval confederacy, and the management of the treasury of Greece. 6. Besides, when our state, from being thought to exercise its power too tyrannically, was deprived of its supremacy, were we not then also, after we abstained from encroachment again made rulers of the fleet by the unanimous consent of the islanders; 7. Did not the Thebans, in consideration of the benefits which they had received, allow the Athenians to lead them? Even the Lacedaemonians, not from being forced, but from having been assisted by us, allowed the Athenians to settle matters as they pleased respecting the supreme command. 8. And at the present time, through the disturbances prevailing in Greece, it seems to me that an opportunity has offered itself to our city to attach the Greeks to it again without difficulty, without danger, and without expense; for we may endeavour to reconcile the states that are at war with one another, and we may try also to unite such as are divided into factions. 9. If you should make it evident, too, not by forming warlike confederacies, but by sending embassies throughout Greece, that you are anxious for the temple at Delphi to be free as it was formerly, I think it would not be at all surprising if you would find all the Greeks ready to agree, and to form confederacies and alliances with you, against those who sought to gain the mastery over the Delphic temple when the Phocians relinquished it. 10. If you indicate, moreover, that you are desirous that peace should prevail over the whole land and sea, I consider that all the Greeks, next to the security of their own countries, would pray for the preservation of Athens.

11. But if any one still thinks that war is more conducive to the wealth of our city than peace, I know not by what means this point can be better decided, than by considering what effect events that occurred in former times produced on our city. 12. For he will find that in days of old vast sums of money were brought into the city during peace, and that the whole of it was expended during war; and he will learn, if he gives his attention to the subject, that, in the present day, many branches of the revenue are deficient in consequence of the war, and that the money from those which have been productive has been spent on many urgent requisitions of every kind; but that now, when peace is established at sea, the reve-

nues are increasing, and that the citizens are at liberty to make whatever use of them they please.

13. If any one should ask me this question, "Do you mean that, even if any power should unjustly attack our state, we must maintain peace with that power?" I should not say that I had any such intention; but I may safely assert, that we shall retaliate on any aggressors with far greater facility, if we can show that none of our people does wrong to any one; for then our enemies will not have a single supporter.

Xenophon Summed Up the Advantages That Would Arise From the Proposed Plans

1. IF, then of all that has been said, nothing appears impossible or even difficult, and if, in case that what I propose be effected, we shall secure increased attachment from the Greeks in general, dwell in greater security, and be distinguished with greater honour,—if the common people will have plenty of provisions, and the rich be eased of the expenses for war,—if, as abundance increases, we shall celebrate our festivals with greater magnificence than at present, shall repair our temples, rebuild our walls and docks, and restore their civil rights to the priests, the senate, the magistrates, and the cavalry, is it not proper that we should proceed to execute these plans as soon as possible, that, even in our days, we may see our country flourishing in security? 2. Should we resolve on pursuing these measures, I should recommend that we should send to Dodona and Delphi to inquire of the gods whether it will be better and more advantageous for the state, for the present time and for posterity, thus to regulate itself. 13. If the gods should give their assent to the proccedings, I should say that we ought then to ask which of the gods we should propitiate in order to execute our designs in the best and most efficient manner; and whichever of the deities they name in their reply, it will be proper to seek favourable omens from them by sacrifices, and then to commence our operations; for if our undertakings are begun with the support of the gods, it is likely that the results from them will lead continually to that which is still better and more advantageous for the state. 5

The Ideal State

Aristotle (384-322 B.C.) Greek philosopher was a student of Plato from 366 to 347 B.C. and the tutor of Alexander the Great from 343 to 336 B.C. His talents and genius were far reaching and his works included *Organon* (treatises on logic) *Metaphysics, Physics, On the Heavens, History of Animals, On the Soul, Poetics* and in the following selections we find him discussing the *Politics and Economics* of the city-state.

He spoke of an ideal city state taking into account such factors as law and order, size of population, area, occupations, defense, communication and trade.

How Many People in a City?

As what has already been said finishes the preface of this subject, and as we have considered at large the nature of other states, it now remains that I should first say what ought to be the form laid down as that of the state which is in accordance with our idea; for no good state can exist without a proportionate supply of what is necessary. Many things therefore ought to be obviously laid down as objects desirable, . . . I mean, relative to the number of citizens and the extent of the territory. For as other artificers, such as the weaver and the shipwright, ought to have such materials as are fit for their work, (since in proportion as they are better, by so much superior will the work itself necessarily be;) so also ought the legislator and politician to endeavour to procure proper materials for the business they have in hand. Now the first instrument of the politician is the number of the people; he should therefore know how many and what they naturally ought to be; in like manner as to the country, how large and of what kind it ought to be. Most persons think that it is necessary for a city to be large in order to be happy; but even should this be true, still they cannot tell what is a large one, and what a small one. For they estimate its greatness according to the multitude of its inhabitants; but they ought rather to look to its strength than to its numbers. For a state has a certain object in view, so that the state which is most able in itself to accomplish this end, this we ought to consider the greatest; as a person might say that Hippocrates was a greater physician, though not a greater man, than one who was taller than him in person. But even if it were proper to determine the strength of the city from the number of the inhabitants, it should never be inferred from the multitude in general who may happen to be in it—(for in a city there must necessarily be many slaves, sojourners, and foreigners)—but from those who are really part of the state, and properly constitute the members of it. A multitude of these is indeed a proof that the city is large, but where a large number of mechanics dwell, and but few soldiers, such a state cannot be great; for a great city and a populous one are not the same thing. This too is evident from the fact that it is very difficult, if not impossible, properly to govern a very numerous body of men; for of all the states which appear well governed, we find not one where the rights of a citizen are laid open to the entire multitude. And this is also made evident by proof from the nature of the thing; for as law is a certain order, so good law is of course a certain good order; but too large a multitude is incapable of this. For this is in very truth the prerogative of that Divine Power which comprehends the universe. Not but that, as quantity and greatness are usually essential to beauty, the perfection of a city consists in its being large, if only consistent with that order already mentioned. But still there is a determinate size to all cities, as well as every thing else, whether animals, plants, or machines; for each of these have their proper powers, if they are neither too little nor too large; but when they have not their due growth, or are badly constructed,—(as a ship a span long is not properly a ship, nor one of two furlongs length, but only when it is of a fit size; for either from its smallness or from its largeness, it will make all sailing hopeless;)—so it is with a city. One that is too small has not in itself the power of self-defence, but this power is essential to a city: one that is too large is capable of self-defence in what is necessary, in the same way as a nation, but then it is not a city; for it will be very difficult to find a form of government for it. For who would choose to be the general of such an unwieldy multitude, or who could be their herald but a Stentor? The first thing therefore necessary is, that a city should consist of the lowest numbers which will be sufficient to enable the inhabitants to live happily in their political community. And it follows, that the more the inhabitants exceed that necessary number, the greater will the city be. But, as we have already said, this must not be without bounds; but what is the proper limit of the excess, experience will easily show, and this experience is to be collected from the actions both of the governors and the governed. Now, as it belongs to the first to direct the inferior magistrates and to act as judges, it follows that they can neither determine causes with justice, nor issue their orders with propriety, without they know the characters of their fellow-citizens: so that whenever this happens to be impossible in these two particulars, the state must of necessity be badly managed; for in both of them it is unjust to determine too hastily, and without proper knowledge, which must evidently be the case where the number of the citizens is too many. Besides, it is more easy for strangers and sojourners to assume the rights of citizens, as they will easily escape detection owing to the greatness of the multitude. It is evident then, that the best boundary for a city is that wherein the numbers are the greatest possible, that they may be the better able to be sufficient in themselves, while they are not too large to be under the eye of the magistrates. And thus let us determine the extent of a city.

Geographic and Climatic Considerations

The above may readily be applied to a country; for as to what soil it should have, it is clear that every one will praise it in proportion as it is sufficient in itself. For which purpose such a country must of necessity supply its inhabitants with all the necessaries of life; for it is the having these in plenty, without any want, which makes them content. As to its extent, it should be such as may enable the inhabitants to live at their ease with freedom and temperance. Whether we have done right or wrong in fixing this limit to the territory, shall be considered more minutely hereafter, when we come particularly to inquire into property, and as to the amount of fortune requisite, and how and in what manner a man ought to employ it. For many doubts are started as to this question, while men strive to bring it on either side to an excess, the one of severity, the other of indulgence. What the situation of the country should be, is not difficult to determine; but in some particulars respecting this point, we ought to be advised by those who are skilful in military affairs. It should be difficult of access to an enemy, but easy of egress to the inhabitants; and, as we said that the number of inhabitants ought to be such as can come under the eye of the magistrate, so should it be with the country; for by that means the country is easily defended. As to the position of the city, if one could place it to one's wish, it ought to lie well both for sea and land. One situation which it ought to have has been already mentioned; for it should be so placed as easily to give assistance to all parts, and also to receive the necessaries of life from every quarter; as also it should be accessible for the carriage of wood, or any other materials of the like kind which may happen to be in the country.

But with respect to placing a city in communication with the sea, there are some who have many doubts whether it is serviceable or hurtful to well-regulated states; for they say, that it becomes the resort of persons brought up under a different system of government, and so is far from serviceable to the state, towards the preservation of law and the increase of population; for a multitude of merchants must necessarily arise from trading backwards and forwards upon the seas, which will hinder the city from being well governed. But if this inconvenience does not arise, it is evident that it is better both for safety, and also for the acquisition of the necessaries of life, that both the city and the country should be near the sea. For in order to bear up against wars, it is necessary to be able to bring up forces both by land and by sea; and in order to damage the invaders, if it is not possible to do so both ways, still either course is available if they possess both. It is also necessary for them to import from abroad what does not grow in their own country, and to export the superfluous productions; for a city ought to traffic to supply its own wants, and not the wants of others: for those who themselves furnish an open market for every one, do it for the sake of gain; but as to the city which ought not to take part in this ambitious trading, it ought not to encourage the growth of such a mart. Now, as we see that many places and cities have docks and harbours lying very convenient for the city, while those who frequent them have no communication with the citadel, and yet they are not too far off, but are surrounded by walls and other such-like fortifications, it is evident, that if any good arises from such an intercourse, the city will perceive it, but if any thing hurtful, it will be easy to restrain it by a law; declaring and deputing who ought to have a trading intercourse with each other, and who ought not. As to a naval power, it is by no means doubtful that it is necessary to have one to a certain degree; and this not only for the sake of the city itself, but also because it may be necessary to appear formidable to some of the neighbouring states, or to be able to assist them as well by sea as by land. But in order to know how great that power should be, we must look into the condition of the state, and if it shall show such vigour as to enable her to take the lead of other communites, it is necessary that her force should correspond with her actions. As for that multitude of people which arises around a maritime power, they are by no means necessary to a state, nor ought they to make a part of the citizens. For the mariners and infantry who have the chief command at sea, are freemen, and upon these depends a naval engagement. But when there are many of the surrounding inhabitants and husbandmen, there they will always have a number of sailors: as we now see happens to some states; at Heraclea, for instance, where they man many triremes, though the extent of their city is much more easily measured than some others. And thus let it suffice that we have determined concerning the country, the port, the city, the sea, and a maritime power: as to the number of the citizens, we have already said what the limit ought to be.

We now proceed to point out of what natural disposition the citizens ought to be: but this surely any one would easily perceive who casts his eye over those states of Greece which bear a high repute, and indeed over all the habitable world, as it is divided among the nations. Those who live in cold countries, as the north of Europe, are full of courage, but wanting in understanding and in art; therefore they remain free for a long time; but, not being versed in the political science, they cannot reduce their neighbours under their power. But the Asiatics, whose understandings are quick, and who are conversant in the arts, are deficient in courage; and therefore they continue to be always conquered, and the slaves of others. But the Greeks, placed as it were between these two parts, partake of the nature of both, so as to be at the same time both courageous and intellectual; for which reason Greece continues free, and governed in the best manner possible, and capable of commanding the whole world, could it be combined into one system of policy. The races of the Greeks have the very same difference among themselves: for part of them possess but one of these qualities, whereas in the other they are both happily blended together. Hence it is evident, that those persons ought to be both intelligent and courageous who will be readily obedient to a legislator, whose object is virtue.—As to what some persons say, that the military must be friendly towards those whom they know, but severe towards those whom they know not, it is courage which makes any one lovely; for that is the faculty of the soul on account of which we most admire. As a proof of this, our resentment rises higher against our friends and acquaintance than against those whom we know not: for which reason Archilochus, properly accusing his friends, addresses the irascible part of his soul, and says, "Art thou not strangled by these friends?" The spirit of freedom and command also is inherited by all who are of this disposition; for courage is commanding and invincible. It also is not right for any one to say, that you should be severe to those you know not; for this behaviour is proper for no one: nor are those who are of a noble disposition harsh in their manners, excepting only towards injurers; and when they are particularly so, it is, as has been already said, against their friends, when they think they have injured them. And this is agreeable to reason: for when those who think they ought to receive a favour from any one do not receive it, beside the injury done them, they consider what they are deprived of. Hence the saying,

"Cruel the wars of brethren are;"

and this,

"Those who have greatly loved do greatly hate."

And thus we have nearly determined how many the members of a state ought to be, and what their natural disposition; as also how large, and of what sort, their country should be; and I say "nearly," because we ought not to require the same accuracy in matters of reasoning as in those which are the objects of the senses.

The Needs of a City

As in other naturally constituted bodies, those things are not admitted to be parts of them without which the whole would not exist; so also it is evident, that in a political state every thing that is necessary thereunto is not to be considered as a part of it, nor of any other community, from whence one genus is made. For one thing ought to be common and the same to the community, whether they partake of it equally or unequally, as, for instance, food, land, or the like; but when one thing is for the benefit of one person, and another for the benefit of another, in this there is nothing like a community, excepting that one makes it and the other uses it. As, for instance, between any instrument employed in making any work, and the workmen, as there is nothing common between the house and the builder, but the art of the builder is employed on the house. Thus property is necessary for states, but property is no part of the state, though many species of it have life; but a city is a community of equals, for the purpose of enjoying the best life possible. But happiness is the best: and this consists in the perfect practice of virtuous energies. As, therefore, some persons have great, others little or no share in this, it is evident, that this is the cause of the difference which exists between the different cities and communities there are to be found; for while each of these seeks after what is best by various and different means, they give rise to different modes of living and different forms of government. We are now to consider what those things are without which a city cannot possibly exist; for what we call parts of the city must of necessity be inherent in it. And this we shall more plainly understand, if we know the number of things necessary to a city. First, the inhabitants must have food: secondly, arts, for many instruments are necessary in life: thirdly, arms, for it is necessary that the community should have an armed force within themselves, both to support their government against the disaffected of themselves, and also to defend it from those who seek to attack it from without: fourthly, a certain revenue, as well for the internal necessities of the state, as for the business of war: fifthly, and indeed chief of all, the care of the service of the gods: sixthly in order, but most necessary of all, a court to determine both civil and criminal causes. These things are matters which are absolutely required, so to speak, in every state; for a city is a number of people, not accidentally met together, but with a purpose of insuring to themselves sufficient independency and self-protection; and if any thing necessary for these purposes is wanting, it is impossible that in such a situation these ends can be obtained. It is necessary therefore that a city should be composed with reference to these various trades; for this purpose a proper number of husbandmen are necessary to procure food; as also artificers and soldiers, and rich men, and priests, and judges, to determine what is necessary and beneficial.

Having determined thus far, it remains that we consider whether all ought to share these different employments; (for it is possible for the same persons always to be husbandmen, artificers, judges, or counsellors;) or whether different persons ought to be appointed to each of those employments which we have already mentioned; or whether some of them should be appropriated to particular persons, and others common to all. But this does not take place in every state; for, as we have already said, it is possible that all may be shared by all, or not by all, but only by some; and this makes one government to differ from another: for in democracies the whole community partakes of every thing, but in oligarchies it is different.

Variety of Jobs and Occupations

Since we are inquiring what is the best government possible, and as it is admitted to be that in which the citizens are happy, and that, as we have already said, it is impossible to obtain happiness without virtue; it follows, that in the best governed states, where the citizens are really men of intrinsic and not relative goodness, none of them should be permitted to exercise any low mechanical employment or traffic, as being ignoble and destructive to virtue: neither should they who are destined for office be husbandmen; for leisure is necessary in order to improve in virtue, and to perform the duty which they owe to the state. But since the soldiery, and the senate which consults, and the judge who decides on matters of law, are evidently necessary to the community, shall they be allotted to different persons, or shall they both be given to the same person? This too is clear: for in some cases the same persons may execute them, in others they should be different; for where the different employments require different abilities, as when practical wisdom is wanting for one, but energy for the other, there they should be allotted to different persons. But where it is evidently impossible that those who are able to do violence and to impede matters, should always be under command, there these different employments should be trusted to one person; for those who have arms in their hands have it in their option whether the supreme power shall remain or no. It remains, then, that we should intrust the government to these two parties; but not at the same time, but as nature directs; what requires energy, to the young; what requires practical wisdom, to the old. Thus each will be allotted the part for which they are fit according to their different merits. It is also necessary that the landed property should belong to these men; for it is necessary that the citizens should be rich, and these are the men proper for citizens; for no low mechanic ought to be admitted to the rights of a citizen, nor any other sort of people, whose employment is not productive of virtue. This is evident from our first principlé; for to be happy it is necessary to be virtuous; and no one should say that a city is happy so long as he considers only one part of its citizens, but he must look to the whole body. It is evident, therefore, that the landed property should belong to these, though it may be necessary for them to have for husbandmen, either slaves, barbarians, or servants. There remains of the classes of the people already enumerated, one only, that of the priests; for these evidently compose a rank by themselves; for the priests are by no means to be reckoned amongst the husbandmen or the mechanics; for it is fitting that the gods should be reverenced by the citizens. And since the citizens have been divided into two orders, namely, the military and the council, and since it is proper to offer due worship to the gods, and since it is necessary that those who are employed in their service should have nothing else to do, let those who are ripe in years be set aside for the business of the priesthood. We have now shown what is necessary to the existence of a city, and of what parts it consists; and that husbandmen, mechanics, and the class of mercenary servants are necessary to a city; but that the parts of it are the soldiery and the councillors. Each of these also is separated from the other; the one indeed always, but the other only in part.

It seems neither now nor very lately to have become known to those philosophers who have made politics their study, that a city ought to be divided by families into different orders of men; and that the husbandmen and soldiers should be kept separate from each other; a custom which is even to this day preserved in Egypt and in Crete also; Sesostris having founded it in Egypt, Minos in Crete. The common meals seem also to have been an ancient regulation, and to have been established in Crete during the reign of Minos, and in a still more remote period in Italy. For it is said by those who are the best versed in the annals of the people who dwell there, that one Italus was king of Aenotria, and that from him the people changed their names, and were called Italians instead of Aenotrians, and that part of Europe was called Italy, which is bounded by the Scylletic gulf on the one side, and the Lametic on the other, the distance between which is about half a day's journey. Now this Italus, as they relate, made husbandmen of the Aenotrians, who were formerly shepherds, and gave them other laws, and especially was the first who established the common meals; for which reason some of his descendants still use them, and observe some of his laws. The Opici inhabit that part which lies towards the Tyrrhenian Sea, who both now are and formerly were called Ausonians. The Chaonians inhabited the part toward Iapygia and the Ionian Sea, which is called the Syrtis. These Chaonians were descended from the Aenotrians. Hence arose the custom of common meals, but the separation of the citizens into different families came from Egypt: for the reign of Sesostris is of much higher antiquity than that of Minos. As we ought to think that most other things were often found out in a long time, nay, times without number—(for reason teaches us that want would make men first invent that which was necessary, and, when that was obtained, then those things which were requisite for the conveniencies and ornament of life)—so should we conclude the same with respect to a political state. But every thing in Egypt is a proof of the great antiquity of these customs; for the people of Egypt seem to be the most ancient of all others, and yet they have acquired laws and political order. We should therefore make a proper use of what is told us concerning states, and endeavour to find out what others have omitted. We have already said, that the landed property ought to belong to the military and those who partake of the government of the state; and that therefore the husbandmen should be a separate order of people; and how large, and of what nature, the country ought to be. We will therefore first treat of the division of the land, and of the husbandmen, how many, and of what sort they ought to be; since we by no means hold that property ought to be common, as some persons have said, but only by way of friendship it should be made common, so as to let no citizen want subsistence. As to common meals, it is in general agreed that they are proper in well-regulated cities; but on account of what reasons we also approve of them shall be mentioned hereafter. They are things of which all the citizens ought to partake; but it will not be easy for the poor, out of what is their own, to contribute as much as is enjoined, and to supply their own house besides. The expense also of religious worship should be defrayed by the whole state. Of necessity therefore the land ought to be divided into two parts, one of which should belong to the community in general, the other to the individuals separately. Each of these parts should again be subdivided into two: and half of that which belongs to the public should be appropriated to maintain the worship of the gods, the other half to support the common meals. Half of that which belongs to the individuals should be at the extremity of the country, the other half near the city; so that these two portions being allotted to each person, all would partake of land in both places, which would be both equal and right; and induce them to act more in concert in any war with their neighbours. For when the land is not divided in this manner, one party neglects the inroads of the enemy on the borders, the other makes it a matter of too much consequence, and more than is fair. For which reason, in some places there is a law, which forbids the inhabitants of the borders to have any vote in council when they are debating upon a war made against them, as their private interest might prevent their voting impartially. Thus, therefore, the country ought to be divided, and for the reasons before mentioned. But those who are to act as husbandmen, if choice be allowed, should by all means be slaves, nor all of the same nation, nor men of any spirit: for thus they will probably be industrious in their business, and safe from attempting any novelties. Next to these, barbarian servants are to be preferred, similar in natural disposition to those we have already mentioned. Of these, some who are to cultivate the private property of the individual, should belong to that individual, and those who are to cultivate the public territory should belong to the public. In what manner these slaves ought to be used, and for what reason it is very proper that they should have liberty held out to them as a reward for their services, we will mention hereafter.

Air, Water, Housing and Defense

We have already mentioned, that the city should communicate

both with the continent and the sea, and with the adjoining territory equally, as much as possible. There are these four things of which we should be particularly desirous in the position of the city with respect to itself. In the first place, as to health, as the first thing necessary. Now a city which fronts the east and receives the winds which blow from thence is esteemed most healthful; next to this a northern position is to be preferred, as best in winter. It should next be contrived, that it may have a proper situation for the business of government, and for defence in war; that in war the citizens may have easy access to it, but that it may be difficult of access to the enemy, and hardly to be taken. In the next place, that there may be a suitable supply of water and rivers near at hand; but if those cannot be found, very large and immense cisterns must be prepared to save rain water, so that there may be no want of it when cut off from the country in time of war. And as great care should be taken of the health of the inhabitants, the first thing to be attended to is that the city should have a good situation and a good position; the second is, that they may have good water to drink, and this must not be taken care of as a secondary matter. For what we chiefly and most frequently use for the support of the body, must principally contribute to its health; and this is the influence which the air and water naturally have. For this reason, in all wise governments, the water ought to be appropriated to different purposes if they are not equally good; and, if there is not a plenty of both kinds of water, that which is to drink should be separated from that which is for other uses. As to fortified places, what is suitable to some governments is not equally suited to all; as, for instance, a lofty citadel is proper for a monarchy and an oligarchy, but a city built upon a plain suits a democracy; neither of these for an aristocracy, but rather many strong places. As to the form of private houses, those are thought to be best, and most useful for their different purposes, which are separate from each other, and built in the modern manner, after the plan of Hippodamus. But for safety in time of war, on the contrary, they should be built as they formerly were; for they were such that strangers could not easily find their way out of them, and the method of access to them such as an enemy who assailed them could with difficulty find. A city, therefore, should have both these sorts of buildings; and this may easily be contrived, if any one will so regulate them as the planters do their rows of vines; not making the buildings throughout the city detached, but only in some parts of it; for thus elegance and safety will be equally consulted.

With respect to walls, those who say that a courageous people ought not to have any, form their ideas from antiquated notions; particularly, as we may see those cities which pride themselves herein confuted by facts. It is indeed disreputable for those who are equal, or nearly equal, to the enemy, to endeavour to save themselves by taking refuge within their walls; but since it is possible, and very often happens, that those who make the attack are too powerful for the courage of those few who oppose them to resist, if they would be saved, and not encounter much suffering and insolence, it must be thought the part of a good soldier to make the fortification of the walls such as to give the best protection, more especially since so many missile weapons and machines have been ingeniously invented to besiege cities. Indeed to neglect surrounding a city with a wall would be similar to choosing a country which is easy of access to an enemy, or levelling the eminences of it; or as though an individual should not have a wall to his house, as if those who dwelt in it were likely to be cowards. Nor should this be left out of our account, that those who have a city surrounded with walls, may act both ways, either as if it had, or as if it had not; but where it has not, they cannot do this. If this be true, not only is it necessary to have walls, but care must be taken that they may be a proper ornament to the city, as well as a defence in time of war, not only according to the old methods, but also according to modern improvements. For as those who make offensive war seek by what means they can gain advantages over their adversaries, so for those who are upon the defensive, some means have been already found out, and others they ought scientifically to devise, in order to defend themselves; for people seldom attempt to attack those who are well prepared.

And as it is necessary that the citizens in general should eat at public tables, and as it is necessary that the walls should have bulwarks and towers at proper distances, it is evident that the nature of the case demands that they prepare some of the public tables in the towers. And these indeed any one could arrange for this purpose ornamentally. But the temples for public worship, and the hall for the public tables of the chief magistrates, ought to be built in proper places, and contiguous, except those temples which the law or the oracle from the god orders to be separate from all other buildings. And the site of these should be so conspicuous, that they may have an eminence which will give them the advantage of distinction, and this, too, near that part of the city which is best fortified. Adjoining to this place there ought to be a large square, like that which they call in Thessaly the square of freedom, in which nothing is permitted to be bought or sold; into which no low mechanic or husbandman, or any such person, should be permitted to enter, unless commanded by the magistrates. It will also be an ornament to this place, if the gymnastic exercises of the elders are performed in it. For it is proper that for the performance of these exercises the citizens should be divided into distinct classes, according to their ages, and that the young persons should have proper officers to be with them, and that the seniors should be with the magistrates; for the presence of the magistrates before their eyes would greatly inspire true modesty and ingenuous fear. There ought to be another square separate from this, for buying and selling, which should be so situated as to be commodious for the reception of goods both by sea and by land. As the citizens may be divided into magistrates and priests, it is proper that the public tables of the priests should be in buildings near the temples. Those of the magistrates who preside over contracts, indictments, and such like, and also over the markets and the public streets, should be near the square, or some public way, I mean the square where things are bought and sold; for we intend the other for those who are at leisure, and this for necessary business.

/ / /

The Nature of Government

All the discourses of Socrates, then, contain much which is highly wrought and ingenious, new and curious; but it may probably be hard to say that all their contents are true. For now, with respect to the numbers just mentioned, it must not be concealed that he would want the country of Babylonia, or some other like it of immeasurable extent, to support five thousand idle persons, besides another and much greater number of women and servants to attend them. It is true that a man may sketch out an ideal state as he pleases, but yet it ought to be something possible. It is said that when a legislator frames his laws, he should have two things in view, the country and the people. He will also do well to add to this some regard to the neighbouring states, if he intends that his community should maintain any political intercourse with them; for it is necessary that they should employ not only those weapons of war which are adapted to their own land, but those which suit foreign countries also; for even granting that no one chooses this life either in public or private, yet, nevertheless, there is occasion for the people to be formidable to their enemies, not only when they invade their country, but also when they retire out of it. It should also be considered, whether the quantity of property may not be settled in a different manner, and better too, by more clearly defining it; for he says that it ought to be large enough for every one to live moderately, as if any one had said "enough to live well," which is the most vague expression. Besides, a man may live moderately and miserably at the same time; he had therefore better have laid it down, that they should live both moderately and liberally; for unless these two conspire, luxury will follow on the one course, and wretchedness on the other; since these two habits of living are the only ones which regard the employment of our substance; for it is not possible for a man to be mild and courageous in the use of his fortune; but he may be prudent and liberal; so that these uses are the only ones necessarily connected with property. It is also absurd to render property equal, and not to provide for the number of the citizens, but to leave the increase of population uncertain; as if it would regulate itself according to the number of women who should happen to be childless, let that be what it may, because this seems now to take place in other states. But the case of necessity would not happen with the same certainty in such a state which he proposes, as in those which now exist; for in these no one actually wants, as the property is divided amongst the whole body, be its numbers what they will; but as it could not then be divided, the supernumeraries, whether they are many or few, must needs have nothing at all. But one would suppose that it is even more necessary than the regulation of property, to provide, as to the increase of numbers, that not more than a certain number should become parents; and to determine this number by calculating the chances of those children who will die, and of those women who will be barren; and to neglect this, as is done in several states, is to bring certain poverty on the citizens; and poverty is the cause of sedition and evil. Now Pheidon the Corinthian, one of the oldest of legislators, thought that the families and number of citizens ought to continue the same; although it should happen that all at the first have allotments disproportionate to their numbers. In Plato's Laws it is however different; and we must mention hereafter what we think would be best in these particulars. He has also neglected in this same book of Laws to point out how the governors are to be distinguished from the governed; for he says, that as of one sort of wool the warp ought to be made, and of another the woof, so ought the governors to be in regard to those who are governed. But since he admits that all their property may be increased fivefold, why should he not allow the same increase to the country to some extent? He ought also to consider whether his allotment of houses will be useful to the community, for he has appointed two houses to each person, separate from each other; but it is inconvenient for a person to regulate two houses. And his whole system of government claims to be neither a democracy nor an oligarchy, but something between both, which is generally called a polity, for it is to be composed of men-at-arms. If Plato intended to frame a state, in which more than in any other every thing should be common, he has certainly given it a right name; but if he intended it to be the next in perfection to the best theoretic state, it is not so; for perhaps some persons will give the preference to the Lacedaemonian form of government, or some other which may more nearly approximate to an aristocracy. Now some persons say, that the most perfect government should be one composed of all others blended together, for which reason they commend that of Lacedaemon; for some say, that this is composed of an oligarchy, a monarchy, and a democracy; their kings representing the monarchical part, their gerusia the oligarchical; and that in the ephoralty may be found the democratical element, as they are taken from the body of the people. But others assert, that the ephors have absolute power, and that it is their common meals and daily course of life, in which the democratic form is represented. It is also said in this treatise of Laws, that the best form of government must be one composed of a democracy and a tyranny; though such a mixture no one would allow to be any government at all, or, if it is, the worst possible. Those, on the other hand, propose what is much better, who blend many governments together; for the most perfect is that which is formed of many parts. But now this polity (of Plato's) shows no traces of a monarchy, but only of an oligarchy and democracy; and it seems rather to incline towards an oligarchy, as is evident from the appointment of the magistrates; for to choose them by lot, is common to both; but the fact that men of fortune must necessarily be members of the assembly, and elect the magistrates, and take part in the management of other public affairs, while the rest are passed over, this makes the state incline to an oligarchy; as does the endeavouring that the greater part of the rich may be in office, and that the rank of their appointments may correspond with their fortunes. The oligarchic principle prevails also in the choice of their senate; the manner of electing which is favourable also to an oligarchy; for all are obliged to vote for senators out of the first class, afterwards for the same number out of the second, and then out of the third; but this compulsory voting does not extend to all of the third and fourth classes, but only the first and second classes out of the entire four. By this means, he says, he ought to show an equal number of each rank elected: but he is mistaken; for the majority will always consist of the first rank, and the most considerate people; and for this reason, that many of the commonalty, not being obliged to it, will not attend the elections. From hence it is evident, that such a state will not consist of a democracy and a monarchy, as well as from what we shall say when we come particularly to consider this form of government.

Danger also will arise from the manner of choosing the senate, when those who are elected themselves are afterwards to elect others; for, if a certain number choose to combine together, though not very considerable, the election will always fall according to their pleasure. Such are the points on which Plato touches, concerning his form of government, in his book of Laws.

6

Aristotle on the Regulation of Property and Planning

In his *Politics* Aristotle presented suggestions aimed at revitalizing the city. In the following selection he evaluated some of the theories on property regulation and crime prevalent in 4th century B.C. Greece.

Property and the State

There are some who think that the first object of government should be to regulate well every thing relating to property; for they say, that herein lies the source of all seditions whatsoever. For this reason, Phaleas the Chalcedonian was the first who proposed this plan, that the fortunes of the citizens should be equal. This he thought was not difficult to accomplish when a community was first settled, but that it was of much difficulty in states which had been long established; but yet that an equality might possibly be effected as follows: namely, that the rich should give marriage portions but never receive any, while the poor should always receive but never give them.

But Plato, in his treatise of Laws, thinks that a difference in circumstances should be permitted to a certain degree; but that no citizen should be allowed to possess more than five times as much as the lowest income, as we have already mentioned. But one thing ought not to escape the notice of legislators who would establish this principle, though now they are apt to overlook it; that while they regulate the quantity of property belonging to each individual, they ought also to regulate the number of his children; for if the number of his family exceed the allotted quantity of property, the law must necessarily be repealed; and yet, apart from such a repeal, it will have the bad effect of reducing many from wealth to poverty; so difficult is it for innovators not to fall into such mistakes. That an equality of goods has some force to strengthen political society, seems to have been determined by some of the ancients; for Solon made a law to this effect; and also among certain others there is a law restraining persons from possessing as much land as they please. And upon the same principle there are laws which forbid men to sell their property, (as among the Locrians,) unless they can prove that some notorious misfortune has befallen them. They were also to preserve their ancient patrimony; and this custom being broken through among the Leucadians, made their government too democratic; for by that means it was no longer necessary to be possessed of a certain fortune, in order to step into the magistracy. But it is possible that an equality of goods is established, and yet that this may be either too great, when it tends to luxurious living, or too little, when it obliges them to live hard. Hence it is evident, that it is not enough for the legislator to establish an equality of circumstances, but he must aim at a proper medium. Besides, if any one should so regulate property, as that there should be a moderate sufficiency for all, it would be of no use; for it is of more consequence that the citizens should entertain a similarity of feelings than an equality of property; but this can never be, unless they are properly educated under the direction of the laws. But probably Phaleas may say, that this is what he himself mentions; for he thinks that states ought to possess an equality of these two things, property and education. But he should have said particularly what education he intended; nor is it of any service to have this one and the same for all; for this education may be one and the same, and yet such as will make the citizens over-greedy to grasp after honours, or riches, or both. Besides, not only an inequality of possessions, but also one of honours, occasions seditions, though in a contrary way in either case; for the vulgar will be seditious if there be an equality of goods, but those of more elevated sentiments, if there is an equality of honours; whence it is said,

"When good and bad do equal honours share."
Homer, Il. ix. 319.

For men are not guilty of crimes for necessaries only,—(for which they think an equality of goods would be a sufficient remedy, as they would then have no occasion to steal for cold or hunger,)—but that they may enjoy what they desire, and not wish for it in vain; for if their desires extend beyond the common necessaries of life, they will do any injustice to gratify them; and not only so, but, if they feel a desire, they will do the same to enjoy pleasures free from pain. What remedy then shall we find for these three disorders? For the first, let every one have a moderate subsistence, and labour for his living. For the second, let him practise temperance; and thirdly, let those who wish for pleasure through themselves, seek for it only in philosophy; for all other pleasures want the assistance of man. Men, then, are guilty of the greatest crimes from ambition, and not from necessity; no one, for instance, aims at being a tyrant, to keep him from the cold; hence great honour is due to him who kills not a thief, but a tyrant, so that form of polity which Phaleas establishes, would only be salutary to prevent little crimes. He is also very desirous to establish such rules as will tend to better the internal policy of his state; but he ought also to have done the same with respect to its neighbours, and all foreign nations; for it is necessary that every government should be well appointed as to its military force; but of this he has said nothing. So also with respect to property; it ought not only to be adapted to the exigencies of the state, but also to such dangers as may arise from without. Thus it should not be so great as to tempt those that are near and more powerful to invade it, while those who possess it are not able to drive out the invaders, nor so little as that the state should not be able to go to war with those who are quite equal to itself; of this too he has determined nothing; but it ought not to be forgotten that some amount of resources is advantageous to a state. Perhaps, then, the proper boundary is this; not to possess enough to make it worth while for a more powerful neighbour to attack you, any more than those who have not so much as yourself. Thus when Autophradatus proposed to besiege Atarneus, Eubulus advised him to consider what time it would require to take the city, and then to calculate the expenses of that period; for that he would be willing for a less sum at once to quit Atarneus: his saying this made Aurophradatus reflect upon the business, and give over the siege. There is, indeed, some advantage in an equality of goods, to prevent seditions amongst the citizens; and yet, to say the truth, it is no very great one; for men of great abilities will be likely to feel hurt at not being reckoned at their proper worth, and hence they will very often appear ready for commotion and sedition. For the wickedness of mankind is insatiable. For though at first two obols might be sufficient pay, yet when once it is become customary, they continually want something more, until they set no limits to their expectations; for it is the nature of our desires to be boundless, and many live only to gratify them. But for this purpose, the first object is not so much to establish an equality of fortune, as to prevent those who are of a good disposition from desiring more than their own, and those who are of a bad one from being able to acquire it; and this may be done if they are kept in an inferior station, and not exposed to injustice. Nor has he treated well one of the equality of goods; for he has extended his regulation only to land, whereas a man's substance consists not only in this, but also in slaves, cattle, money, and all that variety of things which fall under the name of chattels. Now there must be either an equality established in all these, or some certain general rule, or they must be left entirely at large. It appears too by his laws, that he intends to establish his state on a small scale, as all the artificers are to belong to the public, and will add nothing to the complement of citizens; but if all those who are to be employed upon public works are to be public slaves, it should be done in the same manner as it is at Epidamnus, and as Diophantus formerly regulated it at Athens. From these particulars any one may nearly judge whether Phaleas has said well or ill as to his community.

Law and Order

But Hippodamus, the son of Euryphon, a Milesian, the same who contrived the art of laying out towns, . . . planned his state to consist of ten thousand persons, and divided into three parts, one consisting of artisans, the second of husbandmen, and the third of the military order; he also divided the lands into three parts, allotting one to sacred purposes, another to the public, and the third to individuals. The first of these was to supply what was necessary for the established worship of the gods; the second was to be allotted to the support of the soldiery; and the third was to be the property of the husbandmen. He thought also that there need only be three sorts of laws, for there are only three matters on account of which actions can be brought, namely, assault, trespass, or death. He ordered also that there should be one final court of appeal, into which all causes were to be removed which seemed to have been unjustly determined elsewhere; and this court he composed out of a body of elders chosen for that purpose. He thought also that they should not pass sentence by votes; but that every one should bring with him a tablet, on which he should write that he found the party guilty, if such was the case, but that, in case of an acquittal, he should bring a plain tablet, but if he acquitted him of one part of the indictment, but not of the other, he should express that also on the tablet; for he disapproved of the custom already established by law, as obliging the judges to be guilty of perjury if they determined positively on the one side or the other. He also made a law, that those should be rewarded who devised any thing for the good of the city, and that the children of those who fell in battle should be educated at the public expense: this law had never up to that time been proposed by any other legislator, though it is at present in use at Athens as well as in other cities. Further, he would have the magistrates all chosen out of the people; (meaning by the people the three parts before spoken of;) and that those who were so elected, should be the particular guardians of what belonged to the public, to strangers, and to orphans. These are the principal parts and most worthy of notice in the plan of Hippodamus. But some persons might doubt the propriety of his dividing the citizens into three parts; for the artisans, the husbandmen, and soldiery, all are to have a share in the community, while the husbandmen are to have no arms, and the artisans neither arms nor land, which would in a manner render them slaves to the soldiery. It is also impossible that they should all partake of all the posts of honour; for the generals and the guardians of the state must necessarily be appointed out of the soldiery, and indeed, so to say, the most honourable magistrates; but if the others have not their share in the government, how can they be expected to be friendly disposed towards it? But it is necessary that the soldiery should be superior to the other two parts, and this will not be effected unless they are very numerous; and if they are so, why should the community consist of any other members, and have a right to elect the magistrates? Besides, of what use are the husbandmen to this community? Artisans, it is true, are necessary, for these every city wants, and they can live off their business as in all other states. If the husbandmen indeed furnished the soldiery with provisions, they would be properly part of the community; but these are supposed to have their private property, and to cultivate it for their own use. Moreover, if the soldiery are themselves to cultivate that common land which is appropriated for their support, there will be no distinction between the soldier and the husbandman, which the legislator intended there should be; and if there should be any others besides those who cultivate their own private property, and the military, there will be a fourth order in the state, which has no share in it, and will always be alien from it. But further, if any one should propose that the same persons should cultivate their own lands and the public land also, then there would be a deficiency of provisions to supply two families, as the lands would not immediately yield enough for themselves and the soldiers also; all these things, then, involve great confusion. Neither is his method of determining causes a good one, when he would have the judge, in deciding, split the case which comes simply before him, and thus, instead of being a judge, become an arbitrator. Now in matters of arbitration, this is possible to a number of individuals; (for they confer together upon the business that is before them;) but when a cause is brought before judges it is not so; but on the contrary, the majority of legislators take care that the judges shall not communicate their sentiments to each other. Besides, what can prevent confusion in the decision, when one judge thinks a fine should be inflicted, but not so great an one as that which the suitor thinks fit; the latter proposing twenty minae, while the judge imposes ten, or be it more or less, another four, and another five? It is evident then that in this manner they will differ from each other, some giving the whole damages sued for, and others nothing; and if so, how shall the determinations of their votes be settled? Besides, nothing compels a judge to perjure himself who simply acquits or condemns, if the action is fairly and justly brought; for he who acquits the party, does not say that he ought not to pay any fine at all, but that he ought not to pay a fine of twenty minae. But he that condemns him is guilty of perjury, if he sentences him to pay twenty minae, while he believes the damages ought not to be so high. But with respect to the honours which he proposes to bestow on those who devise any thing which is useful to the community, this, though all very pleasing to the ear, is not safe for the legislator to settle, for it would occasion informers, and, it may be, commotions too in the state. And this proposal of his gives rise also to a further conjecture and inquiry; for some persons doubt whether it is useful or hurtful to alter the established laws of any country, if even it be for the better; for which reason one cannot immediately accede to what is here said, since it is not advantageous to alter them. We know indeed, that it is possible to propose a remodelling of both the laws and government as a common good; and since we have mentioned this subject, it may be very proper to enter into a few particulars concerning it; for it contains some difficulties, as we have already said, and it may appear better to alter them, for it has been found useful in other sciences at all events so to do. Thus the science of physics is extended beyond its ancient bounds; so is the gymnastic, and indeed all other arts and faculties; and hence, since the political science must be held to be one of them, it is clear that the same thing will necessarily hold good in its respect. And it may also be affirmed that experience itself gives a proof of this; for the ancient laws are too simple and barbarous; for example, the Greeks used to wear armour in common, and to buy their wives of each other. And indeed all the remains of the old laws which we have, are very simple; for instance, a law in Cyme relative to murder, by which if any one, in prosecuting another for murder, can produce a certain number of witnesses to it of his own relations, the accused person is to be held guilty of the crime. But, in a word, all persons ought to endeavour to follow what is right, and not what is established; and it is probable that the first of the human race, whether they sprung out of the earth, or were saved from some general calamity, were much in the same state as the vulgar and unlearned now, as is affirmed of the aborigines; so that it would be absurd to continue in the paractice of their rules. Nor is it moreover right to permit written laws always to remain unaltered; for as in all other sciences, so in politics, it is impossible that every thing should be expressed in writing with perfect exactness; for when we commit a thing to writing we must use general terms; but in every action there is something particular to itself, which these may not comprehend; and hence it is evident, that certain laws will at certain times admit of alterations. But if we consider this matter in another point of view, it will appear to be one which requires great caution; for when the advantage proposed is trifling, as the accustoming the people easily to abolish their laws is a bad thing, it is evidently better to pass over some faults on the part of both the legislator and the magistrates; for the alterations will not be productive of so much good, as a habit of disobeying the magistrates will be of harm. Besides, the instance brought from the arts is fallacious; for it is not the same thing to alter the one as to the other. For a law derives from custom all its power to enforce obedience, and this requires long time to establish; so that to make it an easy matter to pass from the established laws to other new ones, is to weaken the power of laws. And besides, if the laws are to be altered, are they all to be altered, and in every government or not? and shall it be the pleasure of any chance person, or of whom? Now all these particulars make a great difference; for which reason let us at present drop this inquiry, for it better suits some other occasion.

Citizenship

After what has been said, it follows that we should consider, whether the virtue of a good man is the same as that of a valuable citizen, or different from it; and since this point ought to have a particular inquiry, we must first give in a general outline the virtue of a good citizen. For as a sailor is one of those who make up a community, this also we say of a citizen; although the province of one sailor may be different from that of another,—(for one is a rower, another a steersman, a third a boatswain, and so on, each having their several denominations.)— it is evident, that though the most accurate description of any one good sailor must refer to his peculiar abilities, still there is some common description which will apply to the whole crew; for the safety of the ship is the common business of all of them, as this is the point at which each sailor aims. So also with respect to citizens, although different from each other, yet they have one common care, the safety of the community; for the state is a community: and for this reason, the virtue of a citizen has necessarily a reference to the state. But since there are different kinds of governments, it is evident, that those actions which constitute the virtue of an excellent citizen will not always be the same, and hence that it cannot be perfect; but we call a man good when he is of perfect virtue; and hence it follows, that a man who is an excellent citizen may not possess that virtue which constitutes a good man. Those who are doubtful concerning this same question as to the best polity, may follow up the matter in another way; for if it is impossible that a state should consist entirely of excellent citizens, (while it is necessary that every one should do well in his calling, in which consists his excellence, and as it is impossible that all the citizens should be upon the same level,) it is impossible that the virtue of a citizen and a good man should be the same. For all should possess the virtue of an excellent citizen, for from hence necessarily arises the perfection of the state; but that every one should possess the virtue of a good man is impossible, if it is not necessary that all the citizens in a well-regulated state should be virtuous. Besides, as a state is composed of dissimilar parts, as an animal is of life and body; the soul, of reason and appetite; a family, of a man and his wife; property, of a master and a slave; in the same manner, as a state is composed of all these, and of many other very different parts, it necessarily follows, that the virtue of all the citizens cannot be the same; as the business of the leader of a chorus is different from that of a dancer. From all these proofs it is evident that the virtues of a citizen cannot be one and the same. But do we never find those virtues united which constitute a good man and an excellent citizen? for we say that such a one is an excellent magistrate, and a prudent and good man, but prudence is necessary to all who engage in public affairs. Nay, some persons affirm, that the education of those who are intended to command, should from the beginning be different from other citizens; as is shown by those who instruct the children of kings in riding and warlike exercises; and thus Euripides says,

"No showy arts be mine,
But what the state requires;"

as if there were some education peculiar to a ruler. But since the virtues of a good man and a good magistrate may be the same, and since a citizen is one who obeys the magistrate, it follows that the virtue of the one cannot in general be the same as the virtue of the other, although it may be true of some particular citizen; for the virtue of the magistrate must be different from the virtue of the citizen. For this reason Jason declared, that were he no longer king, he should pine away with regret, as not knowing how to live a private man. But it is a great recommendation to know how to command as well as to obey; and to do both these things well is the virtue of an accomplished citizen. Since then the virtue of a good man consists in being able to command, but that of a good citizen renders him equally fit for either post, they are not both equally praiseworthy. It appears then, that both he who commands and he who obeys should each of them learn their separate business, and not the same; but that the citizen should be master of and take part in both these, as any one may see from the fact that in a family government there is no occasion for the master to know how to perform the necessary offices, but rather to enjoy the labour of others; for to do the other is a servile part. I mean by the other, the performance of the family business of the slave.

There are many sorts of slaves, for their employments are various; one of these are the handicraftsmen, who, as their name imports, get their living by the labour of their hands; and amongst these all mechanics are included. For which reasons such workmen in some states were not formerly admitted into any share in the government, till at length democracies were established: it is not therefore proper for any man of honour, or any citizen, or any one who engages in public affairs, to learn these servile employments, without they have occasion for them for their own use; for otherwise the distinction between a master and a slave would be lost. But there is a government of another sort, in which men govern those who are their equals in rank and freemen; this we call a political government, in which men learn to command, but first submitting to obey; just as a good general of horse, or a commander-in-chief, must acquire a knowledge of his duty, by having been long under the command of another, and having served in command of a rank and a troop; for well is it said, that no one knows how to command, who has not himself been under command of another. The virtues of each are indeed different, but a good citizen must know how to be able to command and to obey; he ought also to know in what manner freemen ought to govern and be governed. Both too belong to the good man, even though the temperance and justice of him who commands is different in kind from that of another; for it is evident that the virtue of a good citizen cannot be the same when he is under command or free, (as justice, for instance,) but must be of a different species in either of these different situations, as the temperance and courage of a man and a woman are different from each other; for a man would appear a coward, who had only that courage which would be graceful in a woman, and a woman would be thought a chatterer, who should take as large a part in the conversation as would become a man of consequence. The domestic employments of each of them are also different; it is the man's business to acquire a subsistence, the woman's to take care of it. But practical wisdom is a virtue peculiar to those who govern, while all others seem to belong in common to both parties. But practical wisdom does not concern the governed, but only to entertain just notions; the latter indeed are like flute-makers, while he who governs is the musician who plays on the flutes. And thus much to show whether the virtue of a good man and an excellent citizen is the same, or if it is different, and also how far it is the same, and how far different.

But with respect to the citizens there is a doubt remaining, whether those only are truly so who are allowed a share in the government, or whether mechanics also are to be considered as such. For if those who are not permitted to rule are to be reckoned among them, it is impossible that the virtue of all the citizens should be the same; (for these also are citizens) and if none of them are admitted to be citizens, where shall they be ranked? for they are neither sojourners, nor foreigners. Or shall we say that no absurdity will arise from their not being citizens, as neither the slaves nor the freedmen consist of those above mentioned? This is certainly true, that all are not citizens who are necessary to the existence of a state, as boys are not citizens in the same manner that men are, for the former are perfectly so, the latter under some conditions; for they are citizens, though imperfect ones. In former times indeed, among some people, the mechanics and foreigners were slaves; and for this reason many of them are so now; and indeed the best-regulated states will not permit a mechanic to be a citizen; but if it be allowed them, we cannot then attribute the virtue which we have described to every citizen or freeman, but to those only who are disengaged from servile offices. Now those who are employed in such things by one person, are slaves; those who do them for money, are mechanics and hired servants; and hence it is evident on the least reflection what is their situation, for what I have said is self-evident, and fully explains the matter. Since the number of communities is very great, it follows necessarily that there will be many different sorts of citizens, particularly of those who are governed by others; so that in one state it may be necessary to admit mechanics and hired servants to be citizens, but in others it may be impossible; as particularly in an aristocracy, and where honours are bestowed on virtue and merit; for it is impossible for one who lives the life of a mechanic or hired servant to practise a life of virtue. In oligarchies also hired servants are not admitted to be citizens; because there a man's right to bear any office is regulated by the size of his fortune; but mechanics are admitted, for the majority of citizens are very rich. There was a law at Thebes, that no one could have a share in the government, till he had been ten years out of trade. In many states the law invites strangers to accept the freedom of the city; and in some democracies the son of a free-woman is himself free. The same is also observed in many others with respect to natural children; but it is through want of citizens regularly born that they admit such; for these laws are always made in consequence of a scarcity of inhabitants; so, as their numbers increase, they first deprive the children of a male or female slave of this privilege, next the child of a freewoman, and last of all, they will admit none but those whose fathers and mothers were both free. From this it is clear that there are many sorts of citizens, and that he who shares the honours of the state may be called a complete citizen. Thus Achilles, in Homer, complains of Agamemnon's treating him

"like some unhonoured stranger;"

for he who shares not in the honours of a state, is as it were a stranger, or sojourner; and whenever such a thing as this is concealed, it is for the sake of deceiving the inhabitants. From what has been said then, it is plain whether we must lay down the virtue of a good man and an excellent citizen to be the same or different; for we find that in some states it is the same, in others not, and also that this is not true of each citizen, but of those only who take the lead, or are capable of taking the lead, in public affairs, either alone or in conjunction with others.

Who Should Govern?

There may also be a doubt as to who should possess the supreme power of the state. Shall it be the majority, or the wealthy, or a number of proper persons, or one better than the rest, or a tyrant? But whichever of these we prefer, some difficulty will arise. For what? if the poor, because they are the majority, may divide among themselves what belongs to the rich, is not this unjust? In sooth, by heaven, it will have been judged just enough by the multitude when they gain the supreme power. What therefore is the extremity of injustice, if this is not? Again, if the many seize into their own hands every thing which belongs to the few, it is evident that the state will be at an end. But virtue never tends to destroy what is itself virtuous; nor can what is right be the ruin of the state. Therefore such a law can never be right; nor can the acts of a tyrant ever be wrong, for of necessity they must all be just; for, from his unlimited power, he compels every one to obey his command, as the multitude oppress the rich. Is it right then that the rich and few should have the supreme power? and what if they be guilty of the same rapine, and plunder the possessions of the majority, will this be just? It will be the same as in the other case; but it is evident that all things of this sort are wrong and unjust. Well, then, suppose that those of the better sort shall have the supreme power, must not then all the other citizens live unhonoured, without sharing the offices of the state? for the offices of a state we call honours, and if one set of men are always in power, it is evident that the rest must be without honours. Then, will it be better that the supreme power be in the hands of that one person who is fittest for it? but by this means the power will be still more confined, for a greater number than before will continue unhonoured. But some one may say, that, in short, it is wrong that man should have the supreme power rather than the law, as his soul is subject to so many passions. But if this law appoints an aristocracy, or a democracy, how will it help us in our present doubts? for those things will happen which we have already mentioned.

On other particulars, then, let us treat hereafter: And as to the fact that the supreme power ought to be lodged with the many, rather than with those of the better sort, who are few, there would seem to be some doubt, though also some truth as well. Now, though each individual of the many may himself be unfit for the supreme power, yet, when these many are joined together, it is possible that they may be better qualified for it, than the others; and this not separately, but as a collective body. So the public suppers exceed those which are given at one person's private expense: for, as they are many, each person brings in his share of virtue and wisdom; and thus, coming together, they are like one man made up of a multitude, with many feet, many hands, and many senses. Thus is it with respect to the character and understanding. And for this reason the many are the best judges of music and poetry; for some understand one part, some another, and all collectively the whole. And in this particular men of consequence differ from each of the many; as they say those who are beautiful differ from those who are not so, and as fine pictures excel any natural objects, by collecting into one the several beautiful parts which were dispersed among different originals, although the separate parts of individuals, as the eye or any other part, may be handsomer than in the picture. But it is not clear whether it is possible that this distinction should exist between every people and general assembly, and some few men of consequence; but, by heaven, doubtless it is clear enough that, with respect to a few, it is impossible; since the same conclusion might be applied even to brutes: and indeed, so to say, wherein do some men differ from brutes? But nothing prevents what I have said being true of the people in some states. The doubt, then, which we have lately proposed, with that which is its consequence, may be settled in this manner; it is necessary that the freemen and the bulk of the people should have absolute power in some things; but these are such as are not men of property, nor have they any reputation for virtue. And so it is not safe to trust them with the first offices in the state, both on account of their injustice and their ignorance; from the one of which they are likely to do what is wrong, from the other to make mistakes. And yet it is dangerous to allow them no power or share in the government; for when there are many poor people who are excluded from office, the state must necessarily have very many enemies in it. It remains, then, that they should have a place in the public assemblies, and in determining causes. And for this reason Socrates and some other legislators give them the power of electing the officers of the state, and also of inquiring into their conduct after their term of office, but do not allow them to act as magistrates by themselves. For the multitude, when they are collected together, have all of them sufficient understanding for these purposes, and by mixing among those of higher rank are serviceable to the state; as some things which alone are improper for food, when mixed with others, make the whole more wholesome than a few of them would be; though each individual is unfit to form a judgment by himself. But there is a difficulty attending this form of government; for it seems that the same person, who himself was capable of curing any one who was then sick, must be the best judge who to employ as a physician; but such a one must be himself a physician. And the same holds true in every other practice and art: and as a physician ought to give an account of his practice to physicians, so ought it to be in other arts. But physicians are of three sorts; the first makes up the medicines; the second prescribes; the third understand the science, but never practises it. Now these three distinctions may be found in those who understand all other arts; and we have no less opinion of their judgment who are only instructed in the principles of the art, than of those who practise it. And with respect to elections the same would seem to hold true; for to elect a proper person in any line, is the business of those who are skilled in it; as in geometry, it is the part of geometricians, and of steersmen in the art of steering. But even if some individuals do know something of particular arts and works, they do not know more than the professors of them; so that, even upon this principle, neither the election of magistrates, nor the censure of their conduct, should be intrusted to the many. But possibly much that has been here said may not be right; for, to resume the argument lately used, if the people are not very brutal indeed, although we allow that each individual knows less of these affairs than those who have given particular attention to them, yet when they come together they will know them better, or at least not worse: besides, in some particular arts it is not the workman only who is the best judge, as in those the works of which are understood by those who do not profess them. Thus he who builds a house is not the only judge of it, (for the master of the family who inhabits it is a better one;) thus also a steersman is a better judge of a tiller than he who made it, and he who gives an entertainment than the cook. What has been said seems a sufficient solution of this difficulty; but there is another that follows: for it seems absurd that greater power in the state should be lodged with the bad than with the good. Now the power of election and censure are of the very utmost consequence, and this, as has been said, in some states they intrust to the people; for the general assembly is the supreme court of all. And yet they have a voice in this court, and deliberate on all public affairs, and try all causes, without any objection to the meanness of their circumstances, and at any age: but their quaestors, generals, and other great officers of state are taken from men of high condition. This difficulty, then, may be solved upon the same principle; and here too may be right. For the power is not in the man who is member of the assembly or council, but in the assembly itself, and in the council and people, of which each individual of the whole community forms a part, as senator, adviser, or judge. And for this reason it is very right that the many should have the greatest powers in their own hands; for the people, the council, and the judges are composed of them, and the property of all these collectively is more than the property of any person, or of a few who fill the great offices of the state: and thus let us determine these points.

But the first question that we stated shows nothing besides so plainly, as that the supreme power should be lodged in laws duly made, and that the magistrate, or magistrates, (either one or more,) should be authorized to determine those cases on which the laws cannot define particularly; as it is impossible for them, in general language, to explain themselves upon every thing that may arise. But what these laws are, which are established upon the best foundations, has not been yet explained, but still remains a matter of some question: but the laws of every state will necessarily be like the state itself, either trifling or excellent, just or unjust; for it is evident, that the laws which are framed, must correspond to the institution of the government; and, if so, it is plain, that a well-formed government will have good laws, a bad one, bad ones.

Since in every art and science the end aimed at is always good, the great good is particularly the end of that which is the most excellent of all, and this is the political science: the political good is justice; for this, in other words, is the interest of all. Now, it is the common opinion, that justice is a certain equality; and up to a certain point men agree with the teaching of philosophers, when they lay down definitions of morals: for they say what is just, and to whom; and that equals ought to receive equals; but we should know how to determine of what things there is equality, and of what there is an inequality; and in this there is some difficulty, which calls for the philosophy of the writer on morals. Some persons will probably say that the offices of state ought unequally to be given according to every particular excellence of each citizen, if there is no other difference between them and the rest of the community, but they are in every respect else alike: for to persons who differ from each other, justice is one thing and that which is according to worth is another. But if this is admitted to be true, complexion, or height, or any such advantage will be made by the superiors a means of grasping for a great share of the public rights. But, surely, this is evidently absurd; as is clear from the other arts and sciences; for with respect to musicians who are equal in their art, the best flute is not to be given to those who are of the best family, for they will play never the better for that, but the best instrument ought to be given to him who is the best artist. But if what is now said does not make this clear, we will explain it still further: if there should be any one who is a very excellent player on the flute, but very deficient in family and beauty, (though each of these are, more valuable endowments than a skill in music, and excel this art in a higher degree than that player excels others,) yet the best flutes ought to be given to him; for the superiority in beauty and fortune should have a reference to the business in hand; but these have none. Moreover, according to this reasoning, every possible excellence might be brought into comparison with every other; for if some bodily strength might dispute the point with riches or liberty, even any amount of strength might do it; so that if one person excelled in size more than another did in virtue, and if, in short, bodily size was a thing more excellent than virtue, all things must then admit of a comparison with each other. For if such a size is greater than virtue by so much, it is evident that another size must be equal to it. Since, however, this is impossible, it is plain that it would be contrary to common sense to dispute a right to any office in the state according to every point of superiority whatsoever: for if one set of persons be slow, and another swift, neither are the one better qualified, nor the other worse, on that account; though in the gymnastic races a difference in these particulars will gain the prize, but a pretension to offices of state should be founded on those qualifications which are part of itself. And for this reason, men of family, independence, and fortune, with great propriety contend with each other for office; for those who hold office ought to be persons of independence and property: for a state can no more consist of all poor men, than it can of all slaves. But although such persons are requisite, it is evident that there is an equal need of justice and military valour. For without justice and valour, no state can be supported; just as without the former class a state cannot exist, and without the latter it cannot be well governed. **7**

Alexandria

When the Greeks expanded from city-states to empire they exported their concept of the city. Alexandria, Egypt became one of the chief centers of that Hellenistic experience and Theocritus, a Greek poet of the 3rd century B.C., pictured every day life of Alexandria in his *Idyl*. His description reminds us of bargain day shopping or a Monday morning commuters' crush.

Ye gods, what a crowd! How on earth are we ever to get through this coil? They are like ants that no one can measure or number. Many a good deed have you done, Ptolemy; since your father joined the immortals, there's never a malefactor to spoil the passerby, creeping on him in Egyptian fashion—O, the tricks those perfect rascals used to play. Birds of a feather, ill jesters, scoundrels all! Dear Gorgo, what will become of us; Here come the king's war-horses! My dear man, don't trample on me. Look, the bay's rearing, see, what temper! Eunoe, you fool-hardy girl, will you never keep out of the way? The beast will kill the man that's leading him. What a good thing it is for me that my brat stays safe at home.

G. Courage, Praxinoe. We are safe behind them, now, and they have gone to their positions.

P. There! I begin to be myself again. Ever since I was a child I have feared nothing so much as horses and the chilly snake. Come along, the huge mob is overflowing us.

G. *(to an old woman)*. Are you from the Court, mother?

OLD WOMAN. I am, my child.

P. Is it easy to get there?

OLD W. The Achaeans got into Troy by trying, my prettiest lady. Trying will do everything in the long run.

G. The old wife has spoken her oracles, and off she goes.

P. Women know everything, yes, and how Zeus married Hera!

G. See Praxinoe, what a crowd there is about the doors.

P. Monstrous, Gorgo! Give me your hand, and you, Eunoe, catch hold of Eutychis; never lose hold of her, for fear lest you get lost! Let us all go in together; Eunoe, clutch tight to me. O how tiresome, Gorgo, my muslin veil is torn in two already! For heaven's sake, sir, if you ever wish to be fortunate, take care of my shawl!

STRANGER. I can hardly help myself, but for all that I will be as careful as I can.

P. How close-packed the mob is, they hustle like a herd of swine.

S. Courage, lady, all is well with us now.

P. Both this year and forever may all be well with you, my dear sir, for your care of us. A good kind man! We're letting Eunoe get jammed—come, wretched girl, push your way through. This is the way. We are all on the right side of the door, quoth the bridegroom, when he had shut himself in with his bride.

G. Do come here, Praxinoe. Look first at these embroideries. How light and how lovely! You will call them the garments of the gods.

P. Lady Athene, what spinning-women wrought them, what painters designed these drawings, so true they are? How natural they stand and move, like living creatures, not patterns woven. What a clever thing is man! Ah, and himself, Adonis, how beautiful to behold he lies on his silver couch, with the first down on his cheeks, the thrice-beloved Adonis—Adonis beloved even among the dead.

STRANGER II. You weariful women, do cease your endless cooing talk! They bore one to death with their eternal broad vowels!

G. Indeed! And where may this person come from? What is it to you if we are chatterboxes! Give orders to your servants, sir. Do you pretend to command ladies of Syracuse; If you must know, we are Corinthians by descent, like Bellerophon himself, and we speak Peloponnesian. Dorian women may lawfully speak Doric, I presume?

P. Lady Persephone, never may we have more than one master. I am not afraid of *your* putting me on short commons.

G. Hush, hush, Praxinoe—the Argive woman's daughter, the great singer, is beginning the *Adonis;* she that won the prize last year for dirge-singing. I am sure she will give us something lovely; see, she is preluding with her airs and graces.

G. Praxinoe, the woman is cleverer than we fancied! Happy woman to know so much, thrice happy to have so sweet a voice. Well, all the same, it is time to be making for home. Diocleides has not had his dinner, and the man is all vinegar. Don't venture near him when he is kept waiting for dinner. Farewell, beloved Adonis, may you find us glad at your next coming! 8

Social Reform in the Third Century B. C.

As with almost all cities so with the Greek cities there was need for reform. Plutarch (46-120 A.D.) a Greek biographer who wrote *Parallel Lives* described attempts at reform undertaken by Agis and Kleomenes.

Life of Agis

After the desire for silver and gold had penetrated into Sparta, the acquisition of wealth produced greed and meanness, while the use and enjoyment of riches was followed by luxury, effeminacy, and extravagance. Thus it fell out that Sparta lost her high and honoured position in Greece, and remained in obscurity and disgrace until the reign of Agis and Leonidas.

On the other hand, the goodness of heart and intellectual power of Agis proved so greatly superior not only to that of Leonidas, but of every king since Agesilaus the Great, that before he arrived at his twentieth year, in spite of his having been brought up in the greatest luxury by his mother Agesistrata and his grandmother Archidamia, the two richest women in Sparta, he abjured all frivolous indulgence, laid aside all personal ornament, avoided extravagance of every kind, prided himself on practising the old Laconian habits of dress, food, and bathing, and was wont to say that he would not care to be king unless he could use his position to restore the ancient customs and discipline of his country.

The corruption of the Lacedaemonians began at the time when, after having overthrown the Athenian empire, they were able to satiate themselves with the possession of gold and silver. Nevertheless, as the number of houses instituted by Lykurgus was still maintained, and each father still transmitted his estate to his son, the original equal division of property continued to exist and preserved the state from disorder. But a certain powerful and self-willed man, named Epitadeus, who was one of the Ephors, having quarrelled with his son, proposed a rhetra permitting a man to give his house and land to whomsoever he pleased, either during his life, or by his will after his death. This man proposed the law in order to gratify his own private grudge; but the other Spartans through covetousness eagerly confirmed it, and ruined the admirable constitution of Lykurgus. They now began to acquire land without limit, as the powerful men kept their relatives out of their rightful inheritance; and as the wealth of the country soon got into the hands of a few, the city became impoverished, and the rich began to be viewed with dislike and hatred. There were left at that time no more than seven hundred Spartans, and of these about one hundred possessed an inheritance in land, while the rest, without money, and excluded from all the privileges of citizenship, fought in a languid and spiritless fashion in the wars, and were ever on the watch for some opportunity to subvert the existing condition of the affairs at home.

Agis, therefore, thinking that it would be an honourable enterprise, as indeed it was, to restore these citizens to the state and to re-establish equality for all, began to sound the people themselves as to their opinion about such a measure. The younger men quickly rallied round him, and, with an enthusiasm which he had hardly counted upon, began to make ready for the contest; but most of the elder men, who had become more thoroughly tainted by the prevailing corruption, feared to be brought back to the discipline of Lykurgus as much as a runaway slave fears to be brought back to his master, and they bitterly reviled Agis when he lamented over the condition of affairs and sighed for the ancient glories of Sparta. His enthusiastic aspirations, however, were sympathised with by Lysander the son of Libys, Mandrokleidas the son of Ekphanes, and Agesilaus. Lysander was the most influential of all the Spartans, while Mandrokleidas was thought to be the ablest politician in Greece, as he could both plot with subtlety and execute with boldness. Agesilaus was the uncle of King Agis and a fluent speaker, but of a weak and covetous disposition. It was commonly supposed that he was stirred to action by the influence of his son Hippomedon, who had gained great glory in the ward and was exceedingly popular among the younger citizens; but what really determined him to join the reformers was the amount of his debts, which he hoped would be wiped out by a revolution. As soon as Agis had won over this important adherent, he began to try to bring over his mother to his views, who was Agesilaus's sister, and who, from the number of her friends, debtors, and dependants, was very powerful in the state, and took a large share in the management of public affairs.

When she first heard of Agis's designs she was much startled, and dissuaded the youth from an enterprise which she thought neither practicable nor desirable. However, when Agesilaus pointed out to her what a notable design it was, and how greatly to the advantage of all, while the young king himself besought his mother to part with her wealth in order to gain him glory, arguing that he could not vie with other kings in riches, as the servants of Persian satraps, and the very slaves of the intendants of Ptolemy and Seleukus possessed more money than all the kings that ever reigned in Sparta; but that, if he could prove himself superior to those vanities of his temperance, simplicity of life, and true greatness of mind, and could succeed in restoring equality among his fellow-countrymen, he would be honoured and renowned as a truly great king. By this means the youth entirely changed his mother's mind, and so fired her with his own ambition, as if by an inspiration from heaven, that she began to encourage Agis and urge him on, and invited her friends to join them, while she also communicated their design to the other women, because she knew that the Lacedaemonians were in all things ruled by their women, and that they had more power in the state than the men possessed in their private households. Most of the wealth of Lacedaemon had fallen into female hands at this time, and this fact proved a great hindrance to the accomplishment of Agis's schemes of reform; for the women offered a vehement opposition to him, not merely through a vulgar love for their idolised luxury, but also because they saw that they would lose all the influence and power which they derived from their wealth. They betook themselves to Leonidas, and besought him, as being the elder man, to restrain Agis, and check the development of his designs. Leonidas was willing enough to assist the richer class, but he feared the people, who were eager for reform, and would not openly oppose Agis, although he endeavoured secretly to ruin his scheme, and to prejudice the Ephors against him, by imputing to him the design of hiring the poor to make him despot with the plunder of the rich, and insinuating that by his redistribution of lands and remission of debts he meant to obtain more adherents for himself instead of more citizens for Sparta.

In spite of all this, Agis contrived to get Lysander appointed one of the Ephors, and immediately brought him to propose a rhetra before the Gerusia, or Senate, the main points of which were that all debts should be cancelled; that the land should be divided, that between the valley of Pellene and Mount Taygetus, Malea, and Sellasia into four thousand five hundred lots, and the outlying districts into fifteen thousand: that the latter district should be distributed among the Perioeki of military age, and the former among the pure Spartans: that the number of these should be made up by an extension of the franchise to Perioeki or even foreigners of free birth, liberal education, and fitting personal qualifications: and that these citizens should be divided into fifteen companies some of four hundred, and some of two hundred, for the public meals, and should conform in every respect to the discipline of their forefathers.

When this rhetra was proposed, as the Senate could not agree whether it should become law, Lysander convoked a popular assembly and himself addressed the people. Mandrokleidas and Agesilaus also besought them not to allow a few selfish voluptuaries to destroy the glorious name of Sparta, but to remember the ancient oracles, warning them against the sin of covetousness, which would prove the ruin of Sparta, and also of the responses which they had recently received from the oracle of Pasiphae. The temple and oracle of Pasiphae at Thalamae was of peculiar sanctity. Pasiphae is said by some writers to have been one of the daughters of Atlas, and to have become the mother of Ammon by Zeus, while others say that Kassandra the daughter of Priam died there, and was called Pasiphae because her prophecies were plain to all men. Phylarchus again tells us that Daphne the daughter of Amyklas, while endeavouring to escape from the violence of Apollo, was transformed into the laurel, which bears her name, and was honoured by the god and endowed by him with the gift of prophecy. Be this as it may, the oracular responses which were brought from this shrine bade the Spartans all become equal according as Lykurgus had originally ordained. After these speeches had been delivered, King Agis himself came forward, and after a few introductory words, said that he was giving the strongest possible pledges of his loyalty to the new constitution; for he declared his intention of surrendering to the state, before any one else, his own property, consisting of a vast extent of land, both arable and pasture, besides six thousand talents of money; and he assured the people that his mother and her friends, the richest people in Sparta, would do the same.

The people were astounded at the magnanimity of the youth, and were filled with joy, thinking that at last, after an interval of three hundred years, there had appeared a king worthy of Sparta.

Leonidas, on the other hand, opposed him as vigorously as he could, reflecting that he would be forced to follow his example, and divest himself of all his property, and that Agis, not he, would get the credit of the act. He therefore inquired of Agis whether he thought Lykurgus to have been a just and well-meaning man. Receiving an affirmative reply, he again demanded, "Where, then, do we find that Lykurgus approved of the cancelling of debts, or of the admission of foreigners to the franchise, seeing that he did not think that the state could prosper without a periodical expulsion of foreigners?" To this Agis answered, that it was not to be wondered at if Leonidas, who had lived in a foreign country, and had a family by the daughter of a Persian satrap, should be ignorant that Lykurgus, together with coined money, had banished borrowing and lending from Sparta, and that he had no hatred for foreigners, but only for those whose profession and mode of life made them unfit to associate with his countrymen. These men Lykurgus expelled, not from any hatred of their persons, but because he feared that their manners and habits would infect the citizens with a love of luxury, effeminacy, and avarice. Terpander, Thales, and Pherekydes were all foreigners, but, since they sang and taught what Lykurgus approved, they lived in Sparta, and were treated with especial honour. "Do you," asked he, "praise Ekprepus, who when Ephor cut off with a hatchet the two additional strings which Phrynis the musician had added to the original seven strings of the lyre, and those who cut the same strings off the harp of Timotheus, and yet do you blame us when we are endeavouring to get rid of luxury, extravagance, and frivolity, just as if those great men did not merely mean thereby to guard against vain refinements of music, which would lead to the introduction of extravagant and licentious manners, and cause the city to be at discord and variance with itself?"

After this the people espoused the cause of Agis, while the rich begged Leonidas not to desert them, and by their entreaties prevailed upon the senators, who had the power of originating all laws, to throw out the rhetra by a majority of only one vote. Lysander, who was still one of the Ephors, now proceeded to attack Leonidas, by means of a certain ancient law, which forbade any descendant of Herakles to beget children by a foreign wife, and which bade the Spartans put to death any citizen who left his country to dwell in a foreign land. He instructed his adherents to revive the memory of this law, and threaten Leonidas with its penalties, while he himself with the other Ephors watched for the sign from heaven. This ceremony is conducted as follows:—Every ninth year the Ephors choose a clear moonless night, and sit in silence watching the heavens. If a star shoots across the sky, they conclude that the kings must have committed some act of impiety, and they suspend them from their office, until they were absolved by a favourable oracle from Delphi or Olympia. Lysander now declared that he had beheld this sign, and impeached Leonidas, bringing forward witnesses to prove that he had two children born to him by an Asiatic wife, the daughter of one of the lieutenants of Seleukus, and that having quarrelled with his wife and become hated by her he had unexpectedly returned home, and in default of a direct heir, had succeeded to the throne. At the same time Lysander urged Kleombrotus, the son-in-law of Leonidas, who was also of the royal family, to claim the throne for himself. Leonidas, terrified at this, took sanctuary in the temple of Athena of the Brazen House, and was joined there by his daughter, who left her husband Kleombrotus. When the trial came on, Leonidas did not appear in court, he was removed from the throne, and Kleombrotus was appointed in his stead.

At this crisis Lysander was forced to lay down his office, as the year for which he had been elected had expired. The Ephors at once took Leonidas under their protection, restored him to the throne, and impeached Lysander and Mandrokleidas as the authors of illegal measures in the cancelling of debts and the redistribution of the land. As these men were now in danger of their lives, they prevailed upon the two kings to act together and overrule the decision of the Ephors; for this, they declared, was the ancient rule of the constitution, that if the kings were at variance, the Ephors were entitled to support the one whom they judged to be in the right against the other, but their function was merely to act as arbitrators and judges between the kings when they disagreed, and not to interfere with them when they were of one mind. Both the kings agreed to act upon this advice, and came with their friends into the assembly, turned the Ephors out of their chairs of office, and elected others in their room, one of whom was Agesilaus. They now armed many of the younger citizens, released the prisoners, and terrified their opponents by threatening a general massacre. No one, however, was killed by them; for although Agesilaus desired to kill Leonidas, and when he withdrew from Sparta to Tegea, sent men to waylay and murder him on the road, Agis, hearing of his intention, sent others on whom he could rely, who escorted Leonidas safely as far as Tegea.

Thus far all had gone well, and no one remained to hinder the accomplishment of the reforms; but now Agesilaus alone upset and ruined the whole of this noble and truly Spartan scheme by his detestable vice of covetousness. He possessed a large quantity of the best land in the country, and also owed a great sum of money, and as he desired neither to pay his debts nor to part with his land, he persuaded Agis that it would be too revolutionary a proceeding to carry both measures at once, and that the moneyed class were first propitiated by the cancelling of debts, they would afterwards be inclined to submit quietly to the redistribution of lands. Lysander and the rest were deceived by Agesilaus into consenting to this, and they brought all the written securities for money which had been given by debtors, which are called by them *klaria,* into the market-place, collected them into one heap, and burned them. As the flames rose up, the rich and those who had lent money went away in great distress, but Agesilaus, as if exulting at their misfortune, declared that he had never seen a brighter blaze or a purer fire. As the people at once demanded the division of the land, and called upon the kings to distribute it among them, Agesilaus put them off with various excuses, and managed to spin out the time till Agis was sent out of the country on military service.

Life of Kleomenes

/ / /

Kleomenes became inspired with fresh confidence, and was convinced that if he only were allowed undisputed management he would easily conquer the Achaeans. He explained to his step-father Megistonous that the time had at length come for the abolition of the Ephors, the redistribution of property, and the establishment of equality among the citizens, after which Sparta might again aspire to recover her ancient ascendancy in Greece. Megistonous agreed, and communicated his intentions to two or three of his friends. It chanced that at this time one of the Ephors who was sleeping in the temple of Pasiphae dreamed an extraordinary dream, that in the place where the Ephors sat for the dispatch of business he saw four chairs removed, and one alone remaining, while as he wondered he heard a voice from the shrine say "This is best for Sparta." When the Ephor related this dream to Kleomenes, he was at first much alarmed, and feared that the man had conceived some suspicion of his designs, but finding that he was really in earnest recovered his confidence. Taking with him all those citizens whom he suspected to be opposed to his enterprise, he captured Heraea and Alsaea, cities belonging to the Achaean league, revictualled Orchomenus, and threatened Martinea. By long marches and counter-marches he so wearied the Lacedaemonians that at last at their own request he left the greater part of them in Arcadia, while he with the mercenaries returned to Sparta. During his homeward march he revealed his intentions to those whom he considered to be most devoted to his person, and regulated his march so as to be able to fall upon the Ephors while they were at their evening meal.

When he drew near to the city, he sent Eurykleidas into the dining-room of the Ephors, on the pretence of bringing a message from the army. After Eurykleidas followed Phoebis and Therukion, two of the foster-brothers of Kleomenes, called *mothakes* by the Lacedaemonians, with a few soldiers. While Eurykleidas was parleying with the Ephors, these men rushed in with drawn swords and cut them down. The president, Agylaeus, fell at the first blow and appeared to be dead, but contrived to crawl out of the building unobserved into a small temple, sacred to Fear, the door of which was usually closed, but which then chanced to be open. In this he took refuge and shut the door. The other four were slain, and some few persons, not more than ten, who came to assist them. No one who remained quiet was put to death, nor was any one prevented from leaving the city. Even Agylaeus, when he came out of his sanctuary on the following day, was not molested.

The Lacedaemonians have temples dedicated not only to Fear, but to Death, and Laughter, and the like. They honour Fear, not as a malevolent divinity to be shunned, but because they think that the constitutions of states are mainly upheld by Fear. For this reason, Aristotle tells us that the Ephors, when they enter upon their office, issue a proclamation ordering the citizens to shave the moustache and obey the laws, that the laws might not be hard upon them. The injunction about shaving the moustache is inserted, I imagine, in order to accustom the young to obedience even in the most trivial matters. It seems to me that the ancient Spartans did not regard bravery as consisting in the absence of fear, but in the fear of shame and dread of dishonour; for those who fear the laws most are the bravest in battle; and those who most fear disgrace care least for their own personal safety. The poet was right who said

> "Where there is fear, is reverence too;"

and Homer makes Helen call Priam

> "My father-in-law dear,
> Whom most of all I reverence and fear,"

while he speaks of the Greek army as obeying

> "Its chief's commands in silence and with fear."

Human nature, indeed, leads most men to reverence those whom they fear; and this is why the Lacedaemonians placed the temple of Fear close to the dining-hall of the Ephors, because they invested that office with almost royal authority.

On the following morning Kleomenes published a list containing the names of eighty citizens, whom he required to leave the country, and removed the chairs of the Ephors, except one, which he intended to occupy himself. He now convoked an assembly, and made a speech justifying his recent acts. In the time of Lykurgus, he said, the kings and the senate shared between them the supreme authority in the State; and for a long time the government was carried on in this manner without any alteration being required, until, during the long wars with Messene, as the kings had no leisure to attend to public affairs, they chose some of their friends to sit as judges in their stead, and these persons acted at first merely as the servants of the kings, but gradually got all power into their own hands, and thus insensibly established a new power in the State. A proof of the truth of this is to be found in the custom which still prevails, that when the Ephors send for the king, he refuses to attend at the first and second summons, but rises and goes to them at the third. Asteropus, who first consolidated the power of the Ephors, and raised it to the highest point, flourished in comparatively recent times, many generations after the original establishment of the office. If, he went on to say, the Ephors would have behaved with moderation, it would have been better to allow them to remain in existence; but when they began to use their ill-gotten power to destroy the constitution of Sparta, when they banished one king, put another to death without trial, and kept down by terror all those who wished for the introduction of the noblest and most admirable reforms, they could no longer be borne. Had he been able without shedding a drop of blood to drive out of Lacedaemon all those foreign pests of luxury, extravagance, debt, money-lending, and those two more ancient evils, poverty and riches, he should have accounted himself the most fortunate of kings, because, like a skilful physician, he had painlessly performed so important an operation upon his country: as it was, the use of force was sanctioned by the example of Lykurgus, who, though only a private man, appeared in arms in the market-place, and so terrified King Charilaus, that he fled for refuge to the altar of Athena. He, however, being an honest and patriotic man, soon joined Lykurgus, and acquiesced in the reforms which he introduced, while the acts of Lykurgus prove that it is hard to effect a revolution without armed force, of which he declared that he had made a most sparing use, and had only put out of the way those who were opposed to the best interests of Lacedaemon. He announced to the rest of the citizens that the land should be divided among them, that they should be relieved from all their debts, and that all resident aliens should be submitted to an examination, in order that the best of them might be selected to become full citizens of Sparta, and to help to defend the city from falling a prey to Altolians and Illyrians for want of men to defend her.

After this he himself first threw his inheritance into the common stock, and his example was followed by his father-in-law Megistonous, his friends, and the rest of the citizens. The land was now divided, and one lot was assigned to each of those whom he had banished, all of whom he said it was his intention to bring back as soon as order was restored. He recruited the numbers of the citizens by the admission of the most eligible of the Perioeki to the franchise, and organised them into a body of thousand heavy armed infantry, whom he taught to use the sarissa, or Macedonian pike which was grasped with both hands, instead of the spear, and to sling their shields by a strap instead of using a handle. He next turned his attention to the education and discipline of the youth, in which task he was assisted by Sphaerus. The gymnasia and the common meals were soon re-established, and the citizens, for the most part willingly, resumed their simple Laconian habits of living. Kleomenes, fearing to be called a despot, appointed his own brother, Eukleidas, as his colleague. Then for the first time were two kings of the same family seen at once in Sparta.

As Kleomenes perceived that Aratus and the Achaeans thought that while Sparta was passing through so perilous a crisis her troops were not likely to leave the country, he thought that it would be both a spirited and a useful act to display the enthusiasm of his army to the enemy. He invaded the territory of Megalopolis, carried off a large booty, and laid waste a large extent of country. Finding a company of players on their road from Messene, he took them prisoners, caused a theatre to be erected in the enemy's country, and offered them forty minae for a performance for one day, at which he himself attended as a spectator, not that he cared for the performance, but because he wished to mock at his enemies, and to show by this studied insult the enormous superiority of which he was conscious. At this period his was the only army, Greek or foreign, which was not attended by actors, jugglers, dancing-girls, and singers; but he kept it free from all licentiousness and buffoonery, as the younger men were nearly always being practised in martial exercises, while the elders acted as their instructors; and when they were at leisure they amused themselves with witty retorts and sententious Laconian pleasantries.

In everything Kleomenes himself acted as their teacher, and example, offering his own simple, frugal life, so entirely free from vulgar superfluities, as a model of sobriety for them all to copy, and this added greatly to his influence in Greece. For when men attended the courts of the other kings of that period they were not so much impressed by their wealth and lavish expenditure as they were disgusted by their arrogant, overbearing manners; but when they met Kleomenes, who was every inch a king, and saw that he wore no purple robes, did not lounge on couches and litters, and was not surrounded by a crowd of messengers, door-keepers, and secretaries, so as to be difficult of access, but that he himself, dressed in plain clothes, came and shook them by the hand, and conversed with them in a kindly and encouraging tone, they were completely fascinated and charmed by him, and declared that he alone was a true descendant of Herakles. **9**

III. Rome

The history of Roman urbanism provides us with an illustration of the successes and failures of city life centered about the pursuit of power. The documents reveal the stormy history of the early city, the difficulties of the later republic, and the seeming triumph of the empire in maintaining the basis of urban life. Yet, the testimony reveals that as Roman civilization marched toward the goal of the mastery of power, and while it was largely successful in its quest, its very success was mocked by a host of problems which proved insoluble and were in part created by unrestrained force. Numerous eyewitness accounts reflect the dissatisfaction and helpless groping for meaning in a life too regimented, perhaps too ordered.

Comparisons are often drawn between Roman civilization and modern American civilization. In both instances, the centralization of overbearing power contrasted with urban blight and misery.

Early Rome

Revolt of the Debtors

In his *The History of Rome,* Livy (59 B.C.-17 A.D.) presented us with one of the earliest descriptions of a populous that rejected the ruling classes and demanded that those who reaped the advantages of war also face its dangers.

> After the defeat of the Auruncans, the people of Rome, victorious in so many wars within a few days, were looking to the consul to fulfil his promises, and to the senate to keep their word, when Appius, both from his natural pride, and in order to undermine the credit of his colleague, issued a decree concerning borrowed money in the harshest possible terms. From this time, both those who had been formerly in confinement were delivered up to their creditors, and others also were taken into custody. Whenever this happened to any soldier, he appealed to the other consul. A crowd gathered

about Servilius: they threw his promises in his teeth, severally upbraiding him with their services in war, and the scars they had received. They called upon him either to lay the matter before the senate, or, as consul, to assist his fellow-citizens, as commander, his soldiers. These remonstrances affected the consul, but the situation of affairs obliged him to act in a shuffling manner: so completely had not only his colleague, but the whole of the patrician party, enthusiastically taken up the opposite cause. And thus, by playing a middle part, he neither escaped the odium of the people, nor gained the favour of the senators. The patricians looked upon him as wanting in energy and a popularity-hunting consul, the people, as deceitful: and it soon became evident that he had become as unpopular as Appius himself. A dispute had arisen between the consuls, as to which of them should dedicate the Temple of Mercury. The senate referred the matter from themselves to the people, and ordained that, to whichever of them the task of dedication should be intrusted by order of the people, he should preside over the markets, establish a guild of merchants, and perform the ceremonies in presence of the Pontifex Maximus. The people intrusted the dedication of the temple to Marcus Laetorius, a centurion of the first rank, which, as would be clear to all, was done not so much out of respect to a person on whom an office above his rank had been conferred, as to affront the consuls. Upon this one of the consuls particularly, and the senators, were highly incensed: however, the people had gained fresh courage, and proceeded in quite a different manner to what they had at first intended. For when they despaired of redress from the consuls and senate, whenever they saw a debtor led into court, they rushed together from all quarters. Neither could the decree of the consul be heard distinctly for the noise and shouting, nor, when he had pronounced the degree, did any one obey it. Violence was the order of the day, and apprehension and danger in regard to personal liberty was entirely transferred from the debtors to the creditors, who were individually maltreated by the crowd before the very eyes of the consul. In addition, the dread of the Sabine war spread, and when a levy was decreed, nobody gave in his name: Appius was enraged, and bitterly inveighed against the self-seeking conduct of his colleague, in that he, by the inactivity he displayed to win the favour of the people, was betraying the republic, and, besides not having enforced justice in the matter of debt, likewise neglected even to hold a levy, in obedience to the decree of the senate. Yet he declared that the commonwealth was not entirely deserted, nor the consular authority altogether degraded: that he, alone and unaided, would vindicate both his own dignity and that of the senators. When day by day the mob, emboldened by license, stood round him, he commanded a noted ringleader of the seditious outbreaks to be arrested. He, as he was being dragged off by the lictors, appealed to the people; nor would the consul have allowed the appeal, because there was no doubt regarding the decision of the people, had not his obstinacy been with difficulty overcome, rather by the advice and influence of the leading men, than by the clamours of the people; with such a superabundance of courage was he endowed to support the weight of public odium. The evil gained ground daily, not only by open clamours, but, what was far more dangerous, by secession and by secret conferences. At length the consuls, so odious to the commons, resigned office, Servilius liked by neither party, Appius highly esteemed by the senators.

Then Alus Verginius and Titus Vetusius entered on the consulship. Upon this the commons, uncertain what sort of consuls they were likely to have, held nightly meetings, some of them upon the Esquiline, and others upon the Aventine, lest, when assembled in the forum, they should be thrown into confusion by being obliged to adopt hasty resolutions, and proceed inconsiderately and at haphazard. The consuls, judging this proceeding to be of dangerous tendency, as it really was, laid the matter before the senate. But, when it was laid before them, they could not get them to consult upon it regularly; it was received with an uproar on all sides, and by the indignant shouts of the fathers, at the thought that the consuls threw on the senate the odium for that which should have been carried out by consular authority. Assuredly, if there were real magistrates in the republic, there would have been no council at Rome, but a public one. As it was, the republic was divided and split into a thousand senate-houses and assemblies, some meetings being held on the Esquiline, others on the Aventine. One man, like Appius Claudius—for such a one was of more value than a consul—would have dispersed those private meetings in a moment. When the consuls, thus rebuked, asked them what it was that they desired them to do, declaring that they would carry it out with as much energy and vigour as the senators wished, the latter issued a decree that they should push on the levy as briskly as possible, declaring that the people had become insolent from want of employment. When the senate had been dismissed, the consuls assembled the tribunal and summoned the younger men by name. When none of them answered to his name, the people, crowding round after the manner of a general assembly, declared that the people could no longer be imposed on: that they should never enlist one single soldier unless the engagement made publicly with the people were fulfilled: that liberty must be restored to each before arms should be given, that so they might fight for their country and fellow-citizens, and not for lords and masters. The consuls understood the orders of the senate, but saw none of those who talked so big within the walls of the senate-house present themselves to share the odium they would incur. In fact, a desperate contest with the commons seemed at hand. Therefore, before they had recourse to extremities, they thought it advisable to consult the senate a second time. Then indeed all the younger senators almost flew to the chairs of the consuls, commanding them to resign the consulate, and lay aside an office which they lacked the courage to support.

Both plans having been sufficiently made proof of, the consuls at length said: "Conscript fathers, that you may not say that you have not been forewarned, know that a great disturbance is at hand. We demand that those who accuse us most loudly of cowardice, shall assist us when holding the levy; we will proceed according to the resolution of the most intrepid among you, since it so pleases you." Returning to their tribunal, they purposely commanded one of the leaders of the disturbance, who were in sight, to be summoned by name. When he stood without saying a word, and a number of men stood round him in a ring, to present violence being offered, the consuls sent a lictor to seize him, but he was thrust back by the people. Then, indeed, those of the fathers who attended the consuls, exclaiming against it as an intolerable insult, hurried down from the tribunal to assist the lictor, But when the violence of the people was turned from the lictor, who had merely been prevented from arresting the man, against the fathers, the riot was quelled by the interposition of the consuls, during which, however, without the use of stones or weapons, there was more noise and angry words than actual injury inflicted. The senate, summoned in a tumultuous manner, was consulted in a manner still more tumultuous, those who had been beaten demanding an inquiry, and the most violent of them attempting to carry their point, not so much by votes as by clamor and bustle. At length, when their passion had subsided, and the consuls reproached them that there was no more presence of mind in the senate than in the forum, the matter began to be considered in order. Three different opinions were held. Publius Verginius was against extending relief to all. He voted that they should consider only those who, relying on the promise of Publius Servilius the consul, had served in the war against the Volscians, Auruncans, and Sabines. Titus Larcius was of opinion, that it was not now a fitting time for services only to be rewarded: that all the people were overwhelmed with debt, and that a stop could not be put to the evil, unless measures were adopted for the benefit of all: nay, further, if the condition of different parties were different, discord would thereby rather be inflamed than healed. Appius Claudius, being naturally of a hard disposition, and further infuriated by the hatred of the commons on the one hand, and the praises of the senators on the other, insisted that such frequent riots were caused not by distress, but by too much freedom: that the people were rather insolent than violent: that this mischief, in fact, took its rise from the right of appeal; since threats, not authority, was all that remained to the consuls, while permission was given to appeal to those who were accomplices in the crime. "Come," added he, "let us create a dictator from whom there lies no appeal, and this madness, which has set everything ablaze, will immediately subside. Then let me see the man who will dare to strike a lictor, when he shall know that that person, whose authority he has insulted, has sole and absolute power to flog and behead him."

/ / /

Fear then seized the senators lest, if the army were disbanded, secret meetings and conspiracies would be renewed; accordingly, although the levy had been held by the dictator, yet, supposing that, as they had sworn obedience to the consuls, the soldiers were bound by their oath, they ordered the legions to be led out of the city, under the pretext of hostilities having been renewed by the Aequans. By this course of action the sedition was accelerated. And indeed it is said that it was at first contemplated to put the consuls to death, that the legions might be discharged from their oath: but that, being afterward informed that no religious obligation could be rendered void by a criminal act, they, by the advice of one Sicinius, retired, without the orders of the consuls, to the Sacred Mount, beyond the river Anio, three miles from the city: this account is more commonly adopted than that which Piso has given, that the secession was made to the Aventine. There, without any leader, their camp being fortified with a rampart and trench, remaining quiet, taking nothing but what was necessary for subsistence, they remained for several days, neither molested nor molesting. Great was the panic in the city, and through mutual fear all was in suspense. The people, left by their fellows in the city, dreaded the violence of the senators: the senators dreaded the people who remained in the city, not feeling sure whether they preferred them to stay or depart. On the other hand, how long would the multitude which had seceded, remain quiet? what would be the consequences hereafter, if, in the meantime, any foreign war should break out? they certainly considered there was no hope left, save in the concord of the citizens: that this must be restored to the state at any price. Under these circumstances it was resolved that Agrippa Menenius, an eloquent man, and a favourite with the people, because he was sprung from them, should be sent to negotiate with them. Being admitted into the camp, he is said to have simply related to them the following story in an old-fashioned and unpolished style: "At the time when the parts of the human body did not, as now, all agree together, but the several members had each their own counsel, and their own language, the other parts were indignant that, while everything was provided for the gratification of the belly by their labour and service, the belly, resting calmly in their midst, did nothing but enjoy the pleasures afforded it. They accordingly entered into a conspiracy, that neither should the hands convey food to the mouth, nor the mouth receive it when presented, nor the teeth have anything to chew: while desiring, under the influence of this indignation, to starve out the belly, the individual members themselves and the entire body were reduced to the last degree of emaciation. Thence it became apparent that the office of the belly as well was no idle one; that it did not receive more nourishment than it supplied, sending, as it did, to all parts of the body that blood from which we derive life and vigour, distributed equally through the veins when perfected by the digestion of the food." By drawing a comparison from this, how like was the internal sedition of the body to the resentment of the people against the senators, he succeeded in persuading the minds of the multitude.

Then the question of reconciliation began to be discussed, and a compromise was effected on certain conditions: that the commons should have magistrates of their own, whose persons should be inviolable, who should have the power of rendering assistance against the consuls, and that no patrician should be permitted to hold that office. Accordingly, two tribunes of the commons were created, Gaius Licinius and Lucius Albinus. These created three colleagues for themselves. It is clear that among these was Sicinius, the ringleader of the sedition; with respect to the other two, there is less agreement who they were. There are some who say that only two tribunes were elected on the Sacred Mount, and that there the lex sacrata was passed.

During the secession of the commons, Spurius Cassius and Postumus Cominius entered on the consulship. During their consulate, a treaty was concluded with the Latin states. To ratify this, one of the consuls remained at Rome: the other, who was sent to take command in the Volscian war, routed and put to flight the Volscians of Antium, and pursuing them till they had been driven into the town of Longula, took possession of the walls. Next he took Polusca, also a city of the Volscians: he then attacked Corioli with great violence. There was at that time in the camp, among the young nobles, Gnaeus Marcius, a youth distinguished both for intelligence and courage, who was afterward surnamed Coriolanus. While the Roman army was besieging Corioli, devoting all its attention to the townspeople, who were kept shut up within the walls, and there was no apprehension of attack threatening from without, the Volscian legions, setting out from Antium, suddenly attacked them, and the enemy sallied forth at the same time from the town. Marcius at that time happened to be on guard. He, with a chosen body of men, not only beat back the attack of those who had sallied forth, but boldly rushed in through the open gate, and, having cut down all who were in the part of the city nearest to it, and hastily seized some blazing torches, threw them into the houses adjoining the wall.

The men of Rome were not grudging in the award of their due praise to the women, so truly did they live without disparaging the merit of others: a temple was built, and dedicated to female Fortune, to serve also as a record of the event.

The Volscians afterward returned, having been joined by the Aequans, into Roman territory: the latter, however, would no longer have Attius Tullius as their leader; hence from a dispute, whether the Volscians or the Aequans should give the general to the allied army, a quarrel, and afterward a furious battle, broke out. Therein the good fortune of the Roman people destroyed the two armies of the enemy, by a contest no less ruinous than obstinate. Titus Sicinius and Gaius Aquilius were made consuls. The Volscians fell to Sicinius as his province; the Hernicans—for they, too, were in arms—to Aquilius. That year the Hernicans were completely defeated; they met and parted with the Volscians without any advantage being gained on either side.

Spurius Cassius and Proculus Verginius were next made consuls; a treaty was concluded with the Hernicans; two thirds of their land were taken from them: of this the consul Cassius proposed to distribute one half among the Latins, the other half among the commons. To this donation he desired to add a considerable portion of land, which, though public property, he alleged was possessed by private individuals. This proceeding alarmed several of the senators, the actual possessors, at the danger that threatened their property; the senators moreover felt anxiety on public grounds, fearing that the consul by his donation was establishing an influence dangerous to liberty. Then, for the first time, an agrarian law was proposed, which from that time down to the memory of our own days has never been discussed without the greatest civil disturbances. The other consul opposed the donation, supported by the senators, nor, indeed, were all the commons opposed to him: they had at first begun to feel disgust that this gift had been extended from the citizens to the allies, and thus rendered common: in the next place they frequently heard the consul Verginius in the assemblies as it were prophesying, that the gift of his colleague was pestilential: that those lands were sure to bring slavery to those who received them: that the way was being paved to a throne. Else why was it that the allies were thus included, and the Latin nation? What was the object of a third of the land that had been taken being restored to the Hernicans, so lately their enemies, except that those nations might have Cassius for their leader instead of Coriolanus? The dissuader and opposer of the agrarian law now began to be popular. Both consuls then vied with each other in humouring the commons. Verginius said that he would suffer the lands to be assigned, provided they were assigned to no one but a Roman citizen. Cassius, because in the agrarian donation he sought popularity among the allies, and was therefore lowered in the estimation of his countrymen, commanded, in order that by another gift he might win the affections of the citizens, that the money received for the Sicilian corn should be refunded to the people. That, however, the people spurned as nothing else than a ready money bribe for regal authority: so uncomprisingly were his gifts rejected, as if there was abundance of everything, in consequence of their inveterate suspicion that he was aiming at sovereign power. As soon as he went out of office, it is certain that he was condemned and put to death. There are some who represent that his father was the person who carried out the punishment: that he, having tried the case at home, scourged him and put him to death, and consecrated his son's property to Ceres; that out of this a statue was set up and inscribed, "Presented out of the property of the Cassian family." In some authors I find it stated, which is more probable, that a day was assigned him to stand his trial for high treason, by the quaestors, Caeso Fabius and Lucius Valerius, and that he was condemned by the decision of the people; that his house was demolished by a public decree: this is the spot where there is now an open space before the Temple of Tellus. However, whether the trial was held in private or public, he was condemned in the consulship of Servius Cornelius and Quintus Fabius.

The resentment of the people against Cassius was not lasting. The charm of the agrarian law, now that its proposer was removed, of itself entered their minds: and their desire of it was further kindled by the meanness of the senators, who after the Volscians and Aequans had been completely defeated in that year, defrauded the soldiers of their share of the booty; whatever was taken from the enemy, was sold by the consul Fabius, and the proceeds lodged in the public treasury. All who bore the name of Fabius became odious to the commons on account of the last consul: the patricians, however, succeeded in getting Caeso Fabius elected consul with Lucius Aemilius. The commons, still further aggravated at this, provoked war abroad by exciting disturbance at home; in consequence of the war civil dissensions were then discontinued. Patricians and commons uniting, under the command of Aemilius, overcame the Volscians and Aequans, who renewed hostilities, in a successful engagement. The retreat, however, destroyed more of the enemy than the battle; so perseveringly did the cavalry pursue them when routed. During the same year, on the ides of July, the Temple of Castor was dedicated: it had been vowed during the Latin war in the dictatorship of Postumius: his son, who was elected duumvir for that special purpose, dedicated it.

In that year, also, the minds of the people were excited by the allurements of the agrarian law. The tribunes of the people endeavoured to enhance their authority, in itself agreeable to the people, by promoting a popular law. The patricians, considering that there was enough and more than enough frenzy in the multitude without any additional incitement, viewed with horror largesses and all inducements to ill-considered action: the patricians found in the consuls most energetic abettors in resistance. That portion of the commonwealth therefore prevailed; and not for the moment only, but for the coming year also they succeeded in securing the election of Marcus Fabius, Caeso's brother, as consul, and one still more detested by the commons for his persecution of Spurius Cassius—namely, Lucius Valerius. In that year also there was a contest with the tribunes. The law came to nothing, and the supporters of the law proved to be mere boasters, by their frequent promises of a gift that was never granted. The Fabian name was thenceforward held in high repute, after three successive consulates, and all as it were uniformly tested in contending with the tribunes; accordingly, the honour remained for a considerable time in that family, as being right well placed. A war with Veii was then begun: the Volscians also renewed hostilities; but, while their strength was almost more than sufficient for foreign wars, they only abused it by contending among themselves. In addition to the distracted state of the public mind prodigies from heaven increased the general alarm, exhibiting almost daily threats in the city and in the country, and the soothsayers, being consulted by the state and by private individuals, declared, at one time by means of entrails, at another by birds, that there was no other cause for the deity having been roused to anger, save that the ceremonies of religion were not duly performed. These terrors, however, terminated in this, that Oppia, a vestal virgin, being found guilty of a breach of chastity, suffered punishment.

Quintus Fabius and Gaius Julius were next elected consuls. During this year the dissension at home was not abated, while the war abroad was more desperate. The Aequans took up arms: the Veientines also invaded and plundered the Roman territory: as the anxiety about these wars increased, Caeso Fabius and Spurius Furius were appointed consuls. The Aequans were laying siege to Ortona, a Latin city. The Veientines, now sated with plunder, threatened to besiege Rome itself. These terrors, which ought to have assuaged the feelings of the commons, increased them still further: and the people resumed the practice of declining military service, not of their own accord, as before, but Spurius Licinius, a tribune of the people, thinking that the time had come for forcing the agrarian law on the patricians by extreme necessity, had undertaken the task of obstructing the military preparations. However, all the odium against the tribunician power was directed against the author of this proceeding: and even his own colleagues rose up against him as vigorously as the consuls; and by their assistance the consuls held the levy. An army was raised for the two wars simultaneously; one was intrusted to Fabius to be led against the Veientines, the other to Furius to operate against the Aequans. In regard to the latter, indeed, nothing took place worthy of mention. **10**

Party Strife in Rome

Livy presented us with one of the perennial problems of cities—Party strife.

> The day of trial was now at hand, and it was evident that people in general considered that their liberty depended on the condemnation of Caeso: then, at length being forced to do so, he solicited the commons individually, though with a strong feeling of indignation; his relatives and the principal men of the state attended him. Titus Quinctius Capitilinus, who had been thrice consul, recounting many splendid achievements of his own, and of his family, de-

clared that neither in the Quinctian family, nor in the Roman state, had there ever appeared such a promising genius displaying such early valour. That he himself was the first under whom he had served, that he had often in his sight fought against the enemy. Spurius Furius declared that Caeso, having been sent to him by Quinctius Capitolinus, had come to his aid when in the midst of danger; that there was no single individual by whose exertions he considered the common weal had been more effectually re-established. Lucius Lucretius, the consul of the preceding year, in the full splendour of recent glory, shared his own meritorious services with Caeso; he recounted his battles, detailed his distinguished exploits, both in expeditions and in pitched battle; he recommended and advised them to choose rather that a youth so distinguished, endowed with all the advantages of nature and fortune, and one who would prove the greatest support of whatsoever state he should visit, should continue to be a fellow-citizen of their own, rather than become the citizen of a foreign state: that with respect to those qualities which gave offence in him, hotheadedness and overboldness, they were such as increasing years removed more and more every day: that was lacking, prudence, increased day by day: that as his faults declined, and his virtues ripened, they should allow so distinguished a man to grow old in the state. Among these his father, Lucius Quinctius, who bore the surname of Cincinnatus, without dwelling too often on his services, so as not to heighten public hatred, but soliciting pardon for his youthful errors, implored them to forgive his son for his sake, who had not given offence to any either by word or deed. But while some, through respect or fear, turned away from his entreaties, others, by the harshness of their answer, complaining that they and their friends had been ill-treated, made no secret of what their decision would be.

Independently of the general odium, one charge in particular bore heavily on the accused; that Marcus Volscius Fictor, who some years before had been tribune of the people, had come forward to bear testimony: that not long after the pestilence had raged in the city, he had fallen in with a party of young men rioting in the Subura; that a scuffle had taken place: and that his elder brother, not yet perfectly recovered from his illness, had been knocked down by Caeso with a blow of his fist: that he had been carried home half dead in the arms of some bystanders, and that he was ready to declare that he had died from the blow: and that he had not been permitted by the consuls of former years to obtain redress for such an atrocious affair. In consequence of Volscius vociferating these charges, the people became so excited that Caeso was near being killed through the violence of the crowd. Verginius ordered him to be seized and dragged off to prison. The patricians opposed force to force. Titus Quinctius exclaimed that a person for whom a day of trial for a capital offence had been appointed, and whose trial was now close at hand, ought not to be outraged before he was condemned, and without a hearing. The tribune replied that he would not inflict punishment on him before he was condemned: that he would, however, keep him in prison until the day of trial, that the Roman people might have an opportunity of inflicting punishment on one who had killed a man. The tribunes being appealed to, got themselves out of the difficulty in regard to their prerogative of rendering aid, by a resolution that adopted a middle course: they forbade his being thrown into confinement, and declared it to be their wish that the accused should be brought to trial, and that a sum of money should be promised to the people, in case he should not appear. How large a sum of money ought to be promised was a matter of doubt: the decision was accordingly referred to the senate. The accused was detained in public custody until the patricians should be consulted: it was decided that bail should be given: they bound each surety in the sum of three thousand asses; how many sureties should be given was left to the tribunes; they fixed the number at ten: on this number of sureties the prosecutor admitted the accused to bail. He was the first who gave public sureties. Being discharged from the forum, he went the following night into exile among the Tuscans. When on the day of trial it was pleaded that he had withdrawn into voluntary exile, nevertheless, at a meeting of the comitia under the presidency of Verginius, his colleagues, when appealed to, dismissed the assembly: the fine was rigorously exacted from his father, so that, having sold all his effects, he lived for a considerable time in an out-of-the-way cottage on the other side of the Tiber, as if in exile.

  This trial and the proposal of the law gave full employment to the state: in regard to foreign wars there was peace. When the tribunes, as if victorious, imagined that the law was all but passed owing to the dismay of the patricians at the banishment of Caeso, and in fact, as far as regarded the seniors of the patricians, they had relinquished all share in the administration of the commonwealth, the juniors, more especially those who were the intimate friends of Caeso, redoubled their resentful feelings against the commons, and did not allow their spirits to fail; but the greatest improvement was made in this particular, that they tempered their animosity by a certain degree of moderation. The first time when, after Caeso's banishment, the law began to be brought forward, these, arrayed and well prepared, with a numerous body of clients, so attacked the tribunes, as soon as they afforded a pretext for it by attempting to remove them, that no one individual carried home from thence a greater share than another, either of glory or ill-will, but the people complained that in place of one Caeso a thousand had arisen. During the days that intervened, when the tribunes took no proceedings regarding the law, nothing could be more mild or peaceable than those same persons; they saluted the plebians courteously, entered into conversation with them, and invited them home: they attended them in the forum, and suffered the tribunes themselves to hold the rest of their meetings without interruption: they were never discourteous to any one either in public or in private, except on occasions when the matter of the law began to be agitated. In other respects the young men were popular. And not only did the tribunes transact all their other affairs without disturbance, but they were even re-elected for the following year. Without even an offensive expression, much less any violence being employed, but by soothing and carefully managing the commons the young patricians gradually rendered them tractable. By these artifices the law was evaded through the entire year.

The consuls Gaius Claudius, the son of Appius, and Publius Valerius Publicola, took over the government from their predecessors in a more tranquil condition. The next year had brought with it nothing new: thoughts about carrying the law, or submitting to it, engrossed the attention of the state. The more the younger patricians strove to insinuate themselves into favour with the plebeians, the more strenuously did the tribunes strive on the other hand to render them suspicious in the eyes of the commons by alleging that a conspiracy had been formed; that Caeso was in Rome; that plans had been concerted for assassinating the tribunes, for butchering the commons. That the commission assigned by the elder members of the patricians was, that the young men should abolish the tribunician power from the state, and the form of government should be the same as it had been before the occupation of the Sacred Mount. At the same time a war from the Volscians and Aequans, which had now become a fixed and almost regular occurrence every year, was apprehended, and another evil nearer home started up unexpectedly. Exiles and slaves, to the number of two thousand five hundred, seized the Capitol and citadel during the night, under the command of Appius Herdonius, a Sabine. Those who refused to join the conspiracy and take up arms with them, were immediately massacred in the citadel: others, during the disturbance, fled in headlong panic down to the forum: the cries, "To arms!" and "The enemy are in the city!" were heard alternately. The consuls neither dared to arm the commons, nor to suffer them to remain unarmed; uncertain what sudden calamity had assailed the city, whether from without or within, whether arising from the hatred of the commons or the treachery of the slaves: they tried to quiet the disturbances, and while trying to do so they sometimes aroused them; for the populace, panic-stricken and terrified, could not be directed by authority. They gave out arms, however, but not indiscriminately; only so that, as it was yet uncertain who the enemy were, there might be a protection sufficiently reliable to meet all emergencies. The remainder of the night they passed in posting guards in suitable places throughout the city, anxious and uncertain who the enemy were, and how great their number. Daylight subsequently disclosed the war and its leader. Appius Herdonius summoned the slaves to liberty from the Capitol, saying, that he had espoused the cause of all the most unfortunate, in order to bring back to their country those who had been exiled and driven out by wrong, and to remove the grievous yoke from the slaves: that he had rather that were done under the authority of the Roman people. If there were no hope in that quarter, he would rouse the Volscians and Aequans, and would try even the most desperate remedies.

The whole affair now began to be clearer to the patricians and consuls; besides the news, however, which was officially announced, they dreaded lest this might be a scheme of the Veientines or Sabines; and, further, as there were so many of the enemy in the city, lest the Sabine and Etruscan troops might presently come up according to a concerted plan, and their inveterate enemies, the Volscians and Aequans should come, not to ravage their territories, as before, but even to the gates of the city, as being already in part taken. Many various were their fears, the most prominent among which was their dread of the slaves, lest each should harbour an enemy in his own house, one whom it was neither sufficiently safe to trust, nor, by distrusting, to pronounce unworthy of confidence, lest he might prove a more deadly foe. And it scarcely seemed that the evil could be resisted by harmony: no one had any fear of tribunes or commons, while other troubles so predominated and threatened to swamp the state: that fear seemed an evil of a mild nature, and one that always arose during the cessation of other ills, and then appeared to be lulled to rest by external alarm. Yet at the present time that, almost more than anything else, weighed heavily on their sinking fortunes: for such madness took possession of the tribunes, that they contended that not war, but an empty appearance of war, had taken possession of the Capitol, to divert the people's minds from attending to the law: that these friends and clients of the patricians would depart in deeper silence than they had come, if they once perceived that, by the law being passed, they had raised these tumults in vain. They then held a meeting for passing the law, having called away the people from arms. In the meantime, the consuls convened the senate, another dread presenting itself by the action of the tribunes, greater than that which the nightly foe had occasioned.

When it was announced that the men were laying aside their arms, and quitting their posts, Publius Valerius, while his colleague still detained the senate, hastened from the senate-house, and went thence into the meeting-place to the tribunes. "What is all this," said he, "O tribunes? Are you determined to overthrow the commonwealth under the guidance and auspices of Appius Herdonius? Has he been so successful in corrupting you, he who, by his authority, has not even influenced your slaves? When the enemy is over our heads, is it your pleasure that we should give up our arms, and laws be proposed?" Then, directing his words to the populace: "If, Quirites, no concern for your city, or for yourselves, moves you, at least revere the gods of your country, now made captive by the enemy. Jupiter, best and greatest, Queen Juno, and Minerva, and the other gods and goddesses, are being besieged; a camp of slaves now holds possession of the tutelary gods of the state. Does this seem to you the behaviour of a state in its senses? Such a crowd of enemies is not only within the walls, but in the citadel, commanding the forum and senate-house: in the meanwhile meetings are being held in the forum, the senate is in the senate-house: just as when tranquility prevails, the senator gives his opinion, the other Romans their votes. Does it not behoove all patricians and plebeians, consuls, tribunes, gods, and men of all classes, to bring aid with arms in their hands, to hurry into the Capitol, to liberate and restore to peace that most august residence of Jupiter, best and greatest? O Father Romulus! do thou inspire thy progeny with that determination of thine, by which thou didst formerly recover from these same Sabines this citadel, when captured by gold. Order them to pursue this same path, which thou, as leader, and thy army, pursued. Lo! I, as consul, will be the first to follow thee and thy footsteps, as far as I, a mortal, can follow a god." Then, in concluding his speech, he said that he was ready to take up arms, that he summoned every citizen of Rome to arms; if any one should oppose, that he, heedless of the consular authority, the tribunician power, and the devoting laws, would consider him as an enemy, whoever and wheresoever he might be, in the Capitol, or in the forum. Let the tribunes order arms to be taken up against Publius Valerius the consul, since they forbade it against Appius Herdonius; that he would dare to act in the case of the tribunes, as the founder of his family had dared to act in the case of the kings. It was now clear that matters would come to violent extremities, and that a quarrel among Romans would be exhibited to the enemy. The law, however, could neither be carried, nor could the consul proceed to the Capitol. Night put an end to the struggle that had been begun; the tribunes yielded to the night, dreading the arms of the consuls. When the ringleaders of the disturbances had been removed, the patricians went about among the commons, and, mingling in their meetings, spread statements suited to the occasion: they advised them to take heed into what danger they were bringing the commonwealth: that the contest was not one between patricians and commons, but that patricians and commons together, the fortress of the city, the temples of the gods, the guardian gods of the state and of private families, were being delivered up to the enemy. While these measures were being taken in the forum for the purpose of appeasing the disturbances, the consuls in the meantime had retired to visit the gates and the walls, fearing that the Sabines or the Veientine enemy might bestir themselves.

During the same night, messengers reached Tusculum with news of the capture of the citadel, the seizure of the Capitol, and also of the generally disturbed condition of the city. Lucius Mamilius was at that time dictator at Tusculum; he, having immediately convoked the senate and introduced the messengers, earnestly advised, that they should not wait until ambassadors came from Rome, suing for assistance; that the danger itself and importance of the crisis, the gods of allies, and the good faith of treaties, demanded it; that the gods would never afford them a like opportunity of obliging so powerful a state and so near a neighbour. It was resolved that assistance should be sent: the young men were enrolled, and arms given them. On their way to Rome at break of day, at a distance they exhibited the appearance of enemies. The Aequans or Volscians were thought to be coming. Then, after the groundless alarm was removed, they were admitted into the city, and descended in a body into the forum. There Publius Valerius, having left his colleague with the guards of the gates, was now drawing up his forces in order of battle. The great influence of the man produced an effect on the people, when he declared that, when the Capitol was recovered, and the city restored to peace, if they allowed themselves to be convinced what hidden guile was contained in the law proposed by the tribunes, he, mindful of his ancestors, mindful of his surname, and remembering that the duty of protecting the people had been handed down to him as hereditary by his ancestors, would offer no obstruction to the meeting of the people. Following him, as their leader, in spite of the fruitless opposition of the tribunes, they marched up the ascent of the Capitoline Hill. The Tusculan troops also joined them. Allies and citizens vied with each other as to which of them should appropriate to themselves the honour of recovering the citadel. Each leader encouraged his own men. Then the enemy began to be alarmed, and placed no dependence on anything but their position. While they were in this state of alarm, the Romans and allies advanced to attack them. They had already burst into the porch of the temple, when Publius Valerius was slain while cheering on the fight at the head of his men. Publius Volumnius, a man of consular rank, saw him falling.

Having directed his men to cover the body, he himself rushed forward to take the place and duty of the consul. Owing to their excitement and impetuosity, this great misfortune passed unnoticed by the soldiers; they conquered before they perceived that they were fighting without a leader. Many of the exiles defiled the temple with their blood; many were taken prisoners: Herdonius was slain. Thus the Capitol was recovered. With respect to the prisoners, punishment was inflicted on each according to his station, as he was a freeman or a slave. The Tusculans received the thanks of the Romans: the Capitol was cleansed and purified. The commons are stated to have thrown every man a farthing into the consul's house, that he might be buried with more splendid obsequies.

Order being thus established, the tribunes then urged the patricians to fulfil the promise given by Publius Valerius; they pressed on Claudius to free the shade of his colleague from breach of faith, and to allow the matter of the law to proceed. The consul asserted that he would not suffer the discussion of the law to proceed, until he had appointed a colleague to assist him. These disputes lasted until the time of the elections for the substitution of a consul. In the month of December, by the most strenuous exertions of the patricians, Lucius Quinctius Cincinnatus, Caeso's father, was elected consul, to enter upon office without delay. The commons were dismayed at being about to have for consul a man incensed against them, powerful by the support of the patricians, by his own merit, and by reason of his three sons, not one of whom was inferior to Caeso in greatness of spirit, while they were his superiors in the exercise of prudence and moderation, whenever occasion required. When he entered upon office, in his frequent harangues from the tribunal, he was not more vehement in restraining the commons than in reproving the senate, owing to the listlessness of which body the tribunes of the commons, now become a standing institution, exercised regal authority, by means of their readiness of speech and prosecutions, not as if in a republic of the Roman people, but as if in an ill-regulated household. That with his son Caeso, valour, constancy, all the splendid qualifications of youth in war and in peace, had been driven and exiled from the city of Rome: that talkative and turbulent men, sowers of discord, twice and even thrice re-elected tribunes by the vilest intrigues, lived in the enjoyment of regal irresponsibility. "Does that Aulus Verginius," said he, "deserve less punishment than Appius Herdonius, because he was not in the Capitol? considerably more, by Hercules, if any one will look at the matter fairly. Herdonius, if nothing else, by avowing himself an enemy, thereby as good as gave you notice to take up arms: this man, by denying the existence of war, took arms out of your hands, and exposed you defenceless to the attack of slaves and exiles. And did you—I will speak with all due respect for Gaius Claudius and Publius Valerius, now no more—did you decide to advance against the Capitoline Hill before you expelled those enemies from the forum? I feel ashamed in the sight of gods and men. When the enemy were in the citadel, in the Capitol, when the leader of the exiles and slaves, after profaning everything, took up his residence in the shrine of Jupiter, best and greatest, arms were taken up at Tusculum sooner than at Rome. It was a matter of doubt whether Lucius Mamilius, the Tusculan leader, or Publius Valerius and Gaius Claudius, the consuls, recovered the Roman citadel, and we, who formerly did not suffer the Latins to touch arms, not even in their own defence, when they had the enemy on their very frontiers, should have been taken and destroyed now, had not the Latins taken up arms of their own accord, Tribunes, is this bringing aid to the commons, to expose them in a defenceless state to be butchered by the enemy? I suppose, if any one, even the humblest individual of your commons—which portion you have as it were broken off from the rest of the state, and created a country and a commonwealth of your own—if any one of these were to bring you word that his house was beset by an armed band of slaves, you would think that assistance should be afforded him: was then Jupiter, best and greatest, when hemmed in by the arms of exiles and of slaves, deserving of no human aid? And do these persons claim to be considered sacred and inviolable, to whom the gods themselves are neither sacred nor inviolable? Well but, loaded as you are with crimes against both gods and men, you proclaim that you will pass your law this year. Verily then, on the day I was created consul, it was a disastrous act of the state, much more so even than the day when Publius Valerius the consul fell, if you shall pass it. Now, first of all," said he, "Quirites, it is the intention of myself and of my colleague to march the legions against the Volscians and the Aequans. I know not by what fatality we find the gods more propitious when we are at war than in peace. How great the danger from those states would have been, had they known that the Capitol was besieged by exiles, it is better to conjecture from what is past, than to learn by actual experience."

The consul's harangue had a great effect on the commons: the patricians, recovering their spirits, believed the state re-established. The other consul, a more ardent partner than promoter of a measure, readily allowing his colleague to take the lead in measures of such importance, claimed to himself his share of the consular duty in carrying these measures into execution. Then the tribunes, mocking these declarations as empty, went on to ask how the consuls were going to lead out an army, seeing that no one would allow them to hold a levy? "But," replied Quinctius, "we have no need of a levy, since, at the time Publius Valerius gave arms to the commons to recover the Capitol, they all took an oath to him, that they would assemble at the command of the consul, and would not depart without his permission. We therefore publish an order that all of you, who have sworn, attend tomorrow under arms at the Lake Regillus." The tribunes then began to quibble, and wanted to absolve the people from their obligation, asserting that Quinctius was a private person at the time when they were bound by the oath. But that disregard of the gods, which possesses the present generation, had not yet gained ground: nor did every one accommodate oaths and laws to his own purposes, by interpreting them as it suited him, but rather adapted his own conduct to them. Wherefore the tribunes, as there was no hope of obstructing the matter, attempted to delay the departure of the army the more earnestly on this account, because a report had gone out, both that the augurs had been ordered to attend at the Lake Regillus, and that a place was to be consecrated, where business might be transacted with the people by auspices: and whatever had been passed at Rome by tribunician violence, might be repealed there in the assembly. That all would order what the consuls desired: for that there was no appeal at a greater distance than a mile from the city: and that the tribunes, if they should come there, would, like the rest of the Quirites, be subjected to the consular authority. This alarmed them: but the greatest anxiety which affected their minds was because Quinctius frequently declared that he would not hold an election of consuls. That the malady of the state was not of an ordinary nature, so that it could be stopped by the ordinary remedies. That the commonwealth required a dictator, so that whoever attempted to disturb the condition of the state, might feel that from the dictatorship there was no appeal.

The senate was assembled in the Capitol. Thither the tribunes came with the commons in a state of great consternation: the multitude, with loud clamours, implored the protection, now of the consuls, now of the patricians: nor could they move the consul from his determination, until the tribunes promised that they would submit to the authority of the senate. Then, on the consul's laying before them the demands of the tribunes and commons, decrees of the senate were passed: that neither should the tribunes propose the law during that year, nor should the consuls lead out the army from the city—that, for the future, the senate decided that it was against the interests of the commonwealth that the same magistrates should be continued and the same tribunes be reappointed. The consuls conformed to the authority of the senate: the tribunes were reappointed, notwithstanding the remonstrances of the consuls. The patricians also, that they might not yield to the commons in any particular, themselves proposed to re-elect Lucius Quinctius consul. No address of the consul was delivered with greater warmth during the entire year. "Can I be surprised," said he, "If your authority with the people is held in contempt, O conscript fathers? it is you yourselves who are weakening it. Forsooth, because the commons have violated a decree of the senate, by reappointing their magistrates, you yourselves also wish it to be violated, that you may not be outdone by the populace in rashness; as if greater power in the state consisted in the possession of greater inconstancy and liberty of action; for it is certainly more inconstant and greater folly to render null and void one's own decrees and resolutions, than those of others. Do you, O conscript fathers, imitate the unthinking multitude; and do you, who should be an example to others, prefer to transgress by the example of others, rather than that others should act rightly by yours, provided only I do not imitate the tribunes, nor allow myself to be declared consul, contrary to the decree of the senate. But as for you, Gaius Claudius, I recommend that you, as well as myself, restrain the Roman people from this licentious spirit, and that you be persuaded of this, as far as I am concerned, that I shall take it in such a spirit, that I shall not consider that my attainment of office has been obstructed by you, but that the glory of having declined the honour has been augmented, and the odium, which would threaten me if it were continued, lessened." Thereupon they issued this order jointly: That no one should support the election of Lucius Quinctius as consul: if any one should do so, that they would not allow the vote. **11**

The Later Republic

Citizen Responsibilities

Cicero, Marcus Tullius or Tully (106-43 B.C.) Roman orator, politician, and philosopher who was executed by the Triumvirate for his opposition to certain state practices wrote in his treatise *On Duties* on the question of a citizen's responsibilities.

> The private individual ought first, in private relations, to live on fair and equal terms with his fellow citizens, with a spirit neither servile and groveling nor yet domineering; and second, in matters pertaining to the state, to labor for her peace and honor; for such a man we are accustomed to esteem and call a good citizen. As for the foreigner or resident alien, it is his duty to attend strictly to his own concerns, not to pry into other people's business, and under no circumstances to meddle in the politics of a country not his own. . . .
>
> The man in administrative office, however, must make it his first care that everyone shall have what belongs to him and that private citizens shall suffer no invasion of their property rights by act of the state. It was a ruinous policy that Philippus proposed when in his tribuneship be introduced his agrarian bill. However, when his law was rejected, he took his defeat with good grace and displayed extraordinary moderation. But in his public speeches on the measure he often played the demagogue, and particularly viciously when he said that there were not in the entire state two thousand people who owned any property. That speech deserves unqualified condemnation, for it favored an equal distribution of property; and what more ruinous policy than that could be conceived? For the chief purpose of the establishment of constitutional state and municipal governments was that individual property rights might be secured. For although it was by nature's guidance that men were

drawn together into communities, it was in the hope of safeguarding their possessions that they sought the protection of cities.

The administration should also put forth every effort to prevent the levying of a property tax, and to this end precautions should be taken long in advance. Such a tax was often levied in the time of our forefathers on account of the depleted state of their treasury and their incessant wars.

But they who pose a friend of the people, and who for that reason either attempt to have agrarian laws passed in order that the occupants may be driven out of their established places, or propose that money loaned should be remitted to the borrowers—these are undermining the foundations of the commonwealth. First of all, they are destroying harmony, which cannot exist when money is taken away from one party and bestowed upon another; and second, they do away with equity, which is utterly subverted if the rights of property are not respected. For as I said above, it is the peculiar function of the state and the city to guarantee every man the free and untroubled control of his own particular. . . .the part of a good citizen, not to divide the interests of the citizens but to unite all on the basis of impartial justice. "Let them live in their neighbor's house rent-free." Why so? In order that, when I have bought, built, kept up, and spent my money on a place, you may without my consent enjoy what belongs to me? What else is that but to rob one man of what belongs to him and give to another what does not belong to him? And what is the meaning of an abolition of debts, except that you buy a farm with my money? You have the farm, and I have not my money.

We must, therefore, take measures that there shall be no indebtedness of a nature to endanger the public safety. It is a menace that can be averted in many ways; but should a serious debt situation arise, we are not to allow the rich to lose their property while the debtors profit by what is their neighbors'. For there is nothing that upholds a government more powerfully than its credit; and it can have no credit unless the payment of debts is enforced by law. Never were measures for the repudiation of debts more strenuously agitated than in my consulship. Men of every sort and rank attempted with arms and armies to bring it about. But I opposed them with such energy that this plague was wholly eradicated from the body politic. Indebtedness was never greater, yet debts were never liquidated more easily or more fully; for the hope of defrauding the creditor was cut off and payment was enforced by law. . . .

Those, then, whose office it is to look after the interests of the state will refrain from that form of liberality which robs one man to enrich another. Above all they will use their best endeavors that everyone shall be protected in the possession of his own property by the fair administration of the law and the courts, that the poorer classes shall not be oppressed because of their helplessness, and that envy shall not stand in the way of the rich to prevent them from keeping or recovering possession of what is theirs. **12**

Unrest in Rome

Roman historian Sallust (86-34 B.C.) in his *Catalina* described the Romans as prosperous but still very unhappy and miserable. This description might well apply to some city dwellers of our own time.

> At no other time has the condition of imperial Rome, as it seems to me, been more pitiable. The whole world, from the rising of the sun to its setting, subdued by her arms, rendered obedience to her; at home there was peace and an abundance of wealth, which mortal men deem the chiefest of blessings. Yet there were citizens who from sheer perversity were bent upon their own ruin and that of their country. For in spite of the two decrees of the senate not one man of all that great number was led by the promised reward to betray the conspiracy, and not a single one deserted Catiline's camp; such was the potency of the malady which like a plague had infected the minds of a great many citizens.
>
> This insanity was not confined to those who were implicated in the plot, but the whole body of the commons through desire for change favored the designs of Catiline. In this very particular they seemed to act as the populace usually does; for in every community those who have no means envy the good, exalt the base, hate what is old and established, long for something new, and from disgust with their own lot desire a general upheaval. Amid turmoil and rebellion they maintain themselves without difficulty, since poverty is easily provided for and can suffer no loss. But the city populace in particular acted with desperation for many reasons. To begin with, all who were easily conspicuous for their shamelessness and impu-

dence, those, too, who had squandered their patrimony in riotous living, finally all whom disgrace or crime had forced to leave home, had all flowed into Rome as into a cesspool. Many, too, who recalled Sulla's victory, when they saw common soldiers risen to the rank of senator, and others become so rich that they feasted and lived like kings, hoped each for himself for like fruits of victory if he took the field. Besides this, the young men who had maintained a wretched existence by manual labor in the country, tempted by public and private doles, had come to prefer idleness in the city to their unprofitable toil; these, like all the others, battened on the public ills. Therefore it is not surprising that men who were beggars and without character, with illimitable hopes, should respect their country as little as they did themselves. Moreover, those to whom Sulla's victory had meant the proscription of their parents, loss of property, and curtailment of their rights, looked forward in a similar spirit to the outcome of a war. Finally, all who belonged to another party than that of the senate preferred to see the government overthrown rather than be out of power themselves. Such then was the evil which after many years had returned upon the state.

For after the tribunician power has been restored in the consulship of Gnaeus Pompey and Marcus Crassus, various young men, whose age and disposition made them aggressive, attained that high authority; they thereupon began to excite the commons by attacks upon the senate and then to inflame their passions still more by doles and promises, thus making themselves conspicuous and influential. Against these men the greater part of the nobles strove with might and main, ostensibly in behalf of the senate but really for their own aggrandizement. For to tell the truth in a few words, after that time all who took part in politics used specious pretexts, some maintaining that they were defending the rights of the commons, others that they were upholding the prestige of the senate; but under pretense of the public welfare each in reality was striving for personal power. Such men showed neither self restraint nor moderation in their strife, and both parties used their victory ruthlessly. When, however, Gnaeus Pompey had been dispatched to wage war against the pirates and against Mithridates, the power of the commons was lessened, while that of the few increased. These possessed the magistracies, the provinces, and everything else; being themselves rich and secure against attack, they lived without fear and by resort to the courts terrified the others, in order that they might manage the commons with less friction under their magistracy. But as soon as the political situation became doubtful and offered hope of revolution, then the old controversy aroused their passions anew.

13
The Theory of Republican Administration as Presented by Cicero

Cicero wrote in his *Laws* of the theoretical basis of the Republic. As with contemporary society the theory was far different from the practice.

> Commands shall be just, and the citizens shall obey them dutifully and without protest. Upon the disobedient or guilty citizen the magistrate shall use compulsion by means of fines, imprisonment, or lashing, unless an equal or higher authority or the people, to which the citizens shall have the right of appeal, forbids it. After the magistrate has made judicial examination and pronounced sentence, there shall be a trial before the people for the final determination of the fine or other penalty. There shall be no appeal from decisions of the commander in the field; while a magistrate is waging war his commands shall be valid and binding.
>
> There shall be minor magistrates with partial authority, who shall be assigned to special functions. In the army they shall command those over whom they are placed, and be their tribunes; in the city they shall be custodians of public moneys; they shall have charge of the confinement of criminals; they shall inflict capital punishment; they shall coin bronze, silver, and gold money; they shall decide lawsuits; they shall do whatsoever the senate decrees.
>
> There shall also be aediles, who shall be caretakers of the city, of the markets, and of the traditional games. This magistracy shall be their first step in the advancement to higher office.
>
> Censors shall make a list of the citizens, recording their ages, families, and slaves and other property. They shall have charge of the temples, streets, and aqueducts within the city, and of the public treasury and the revenues. They shall make a division of the citizens into tribes, and other divisions according to wealth, age, and class. They shall enroll the recruits for the cavalry and infantry; they shall prohibit celibacy; they shall regulate the morals of the people; they shall allow no one guilty of dishonorable conduct to

remain in the senate. They shall be two in number and shall hold office for five years. The other magistrates shall hold office for one year. The office of censor shall never be vacant.

The administrator of justice, who shall decide or direct the decision of civil cases, shall be called praetor, he shall be the guardian of the civil law. There shall be as many praetors, with equal powers, as the senate shall decree or the people command.

There shall be two magistrates with royal powers. Since they precede, judge, and consult, from these functions they shall be called praetors, judges, and consuls. In the field they shall hold the supreme military power and shall be subject to no one. The safety of the people shall be their highest law.

No one shall hold the same office a second time except after an interval of ten years. They shall observe the age limits for the several offices, as fixed by the law on the subject.

But when a serious war or civil dissensions arise, one man shall hold, for not longer than six months, the power which ordinarily belongs to the two consuls, if the senate shall so decree. And after being appointed under favorable auspices, he shall be master of the people. He shall have an assistant to command the cavalry, whose rank shall be equal to that of the administrator of justice.

But when there are neither consuls nor a master of the people, there shall be no other magistrates, and the auspices shall be in the hands of the senate, which shall appoint one of its number to conduct the election of consuls in the customary manner.

Officials with and without *imperium* and ambassadors shall leave the city when the senate shall so decree or the people so command; they shall wage just wars justly; they shall spare the allies; they shall hold themselves and their subordinates in check; they shall increase the national renown; they shall return home with honor.

No one shall be made an ambassador for the purpose of attending to his own personal affairs.

The ten officials whom the plebeians shall elect to protect them from violence shall be their tribunes. Their prohibitions and resolutions passed by the plebeians under their presidency shall be binding. Their persons shall be inviolable. They shall not leave the plebeians without tribunes.

All magistrates shall possess the right of taking the auspices, and the judicial power. The senate shall consist of those who have held magistracies. Its decrees shall be binding. But in case an equal or higher authority than the presiding officer shall veto a decree of the senate, it shall nevertheless be written out and preserved.

The senatorial order shall be free from dishonor, and shall be a model for the rest of the citizens.

When elective, judicial, and legislative acts of the people are performed by vote, the people shall enjoy freedom of the ballot, but shall reveal their votes to *optimates*.

But if any acts of administration shall be necessary in addition to those done by the regular magistrates, the people shall elect officials to perform them, and give them the authority to do so.

Consuls, praetors, masters of the people, masters of the horse, and those officials whom the senate shall appoint to conduct the election of consuls shall have the right to preside over meetings of the people and the senate. The tribunes chosen by the plebeians shall have the right to preside over the senate and shall also refer whatever is necessary to the plebeians.

Moderation shall be preserved in meetings of the people and the senate.

A senator's absence from a meeting of the senate shall be either for cause or culpable. A senator shall speak in his turn and at moderate length. He shall be conversant with public affairs.

No violence shall be used at meetings of the people. An equal or higher authority than the presiding officer shall have the greater power. But the presiding officer shall be responsible for any disorder which may occur. He who vetoes a bad measure shall be deemed a citizen of distinguished service.

Presiding officers shall observe the auspices and obey the state augur. They shall see that bills, after being read, are filed among the archives in the state treasury. They shall not take the people's vote on more than one question at a time. They shall instruct the people in regard to the matter in hand, and allow them to be instructed by other magistrates and by private citizens.

No law of personal exception shall be proposed. Cases in which the penalty is death or loss of citizenship shall be tried only before the greatest assembly and by those whom the censors have enrolled among the citizens.

No one shall give or receive a present, either during a candidacy or during or after a term of office.

The punishment for violation of any of these laws shall fit the offense.

The censors shall have charge of the official text of the laws. When officials go out of office, they shall report their official acts to censors but shall not receive exemption from prosecution thereby.

Imperial Rome

Public Works of Augustus

Suetonius (circa 120) Roman biographer wrote in his *Life of Augustus* of city planning and public works projects undertaken by Emperor Augustus.

> Publike works he built very many whereof the chiefe and principal was his Forum or stately Hall of Justice, together with the temple of Mars the Revenger: the temple of Apollo in Palatium; the Temple likewise of Jupiter the Thunderer, in the Capitol. The reason why he built the said Forum, was the multitude of men and their suites: which because it would not suffice, seemed to have need of a third also. And therefore with great speed erected it was for that publike use, even before the temple of Mars was finished. And expressly provided it was by law, that in it publike causes should be determined apart, and choosing of Judges (or Juries) by it selfe. The temple of Mars hee had vowed unto him, in the Philippian warre which hee tooke in hand for the revenge of his fathers death. He ordained therefore by an Act, that heere the Senate should be consulted with, as touching warres and triumphs: that from hence those Pretours or Governours who were to goe into their provinces should be honorably attended and brought onward on their way: and that hither they should bring the ensignes and ornaments of triumph, who returned with victorie. The temple of Apollo he reared in that part of the Palatine house, which being smitten with lightning was by that God required, as the Soothsayers out of their learning had pronounced: hereto was adjoyned a gallerie, with a librarie of Latine and Greeke In which temple, he was wont in his old age both to sit oftentimes in counsaile with the senate, and also to over-see and review the Decuries of the Judges. He consecrated the temple unto Jupiter the Thunderer, upon occasion that he escaped a daunger, what time as in his Cantabrian ex-

pedition, as he travailed by night, a flash of lightning glaunced upon his licter, and strucke his servant stone dead, that went with a light before. Some works also he made under other folkes names, to wit his nephew, his wife and sister; as the Gallerie and stately Pallace of Lucius and Caius: likewise the Gallerie or Porches of Livia and Octavia: the Theatre also of Marcellus. Moreover divers other principall persons hee oftentimes exhorted to adorne and beutifie the City, every man according to his ability either by erecting new monuments, or else by repairing and furnishing the old. By which meanes many an Aedifice was by many a man built: as namely the temple of Hercules and the Muses by Marcus Philippus: the temple of Diana by L. Cornificius: the Court of Liberty by Asinius Pollio: a temple of Saturne by Manatius Plancus: a Theatre by Cornelius Balbus; and an Amphitheatre by Statillus Taurus: but many and those very goodly monuments by M. Agrippa.

The whole space of the City he devided into wards and streetes. He ordained, that as Magistrates or Aldermen yeerely by lot should keepe and governe the former: so their should be Maisters or Constables elected out of the Commons of every streete, to looke unto the other. Against skarefires he devised night-watches and watchmen. To keepe downe Inundations and Deluges, he enlarged and cleansed the channel of the River Tiberis, which in times past was full of rammell and the ruines of houses, and so by that meanes narrow and choaked. And that the Avenues on every side to the City might be more passable, he tooke in hand himselfe to repair the high way or Cawsie Flaminia, so farre as to Ariminnum: and the rest he committed to sundry men who had triumphed, for to pave; and the charges thereof to be defraied out of the money raised of spoiles and sackage. The sacred Churches and Chappels decayed and ruinate by continuance of time, or consumed by fire he reedified: and those together with the rest hee adorned with most rich oblations: as who brought into the Cell, or Tabernacle of Jupiter Capitolinus at one Donation, 16000 pound weight of gold, besides pretious stones valued at 50 millions of Sesterces.

In number, varietie, and magnificence of solemne shewes exhibited unto the people he went beyond all men. Hee reporteth of himselfe that he set foorth plaies and games in his owne name foure and twentie times: and for other magistrates who either were absent or not sufficient to beare the charges, three and twentie times.

Divers times, he exhibited plaies by everie streete, and those uppon many stages, and acted by plaiers skilfull in all languages not in the Common forum onely, nor in the ordinarie Amphitheater, but also in the cirque. In the enclosure called Septa, he never represented any sportes but the baiting and coursing of wild beasts and the shewes of champions-sight; having built woodden scaffolds and seates for the nonce in Mars field. In like manner, he made the shew of a Navall battaile about the River Tiberis, have digged of purpose a spacious hollow pit within the ground, even there whereas now is to be seene the grove of the Caesars. On which dayes he bestowed warders in diverse places of the citie, for feare it might be endangered by sturdie theeves and robbers, taking their vantage, that so few remained at home in their houses. In the Cirque he brought forth to doe their devoir, Charioters, Runners, and killers of savage beasts: otherwhiles out of the noblest young gentlemen of all the Cittie. As for the warlike Riding or Turnament called Troie, he exhibited it oftenest of all other, making choyse of boys to perform it, as well bigger as smaller: supposing it a matter of antiquitie: a decent and honorable maner besides, that the towardly disposition and proofe of noble bloud should thus be seene and knowne. In this solemnitie and sport, he rewarded C. Nonius Asprenas weakened by a fall from his horse, with a wreath or chaine of gold, and permitted both himselfe and also his posteritie to beare the surname of Torquatus. But afterwards he gave over the representation of such pastimes, by occasion that Asinius Pollio the Oratour, made a grievous and invidious complaint in the Senate house, of the fall that Aeserninus his nephew tooke, who likewise had thereby broken his legge. To the performance of his stage plaies also and shews of sworde fight, he employed some times even the Gentlemen and knights of Rome: but it was before he was inhibited by vertue of an Act of the Senate. For after it verily, he exhibited no more, save onely a youth called L. Itius, borne of worshipful parentage, onely for a shew: that being a dwarfe not two foote high, and weighing 17 l'. yet he had an exceeding great voice. One day of the sword fight that he set forth, he brought in for to behould the solemnitie, even through the midst of the Shew place, the Parthians hostages who then were newly sent (to Rome) and placed them in the second ranke or row of seates above himselfe. His manner was moreover, before the usuall daies of such spectacles and solemne sights, and at other times, if any strang and new thing were brought over unto him, and worthie to be knowne, to bring it abroad for to be seene upon extraordinary daies, and in any place whatsoever. As for example, a Rhinoceros within the empaled or railed enclosure called Septa: a Tigre upon the stage: and a Serpent 50 cubits long, within the Hall Comitium. It fortuned that during the Great Circeian games which he had vowed before, he fell sicke: whereby he lay in his litter and so devoutly attended upon the sacred chariots called Thensae. Againe, it happened at the beginning of those plaies, which he set out when he dedicated the temple of Marcellus, that his curule chaire became unjoincted, and thereby he fel upon his back: also at the games of his nephewes when the people their assembled were mightily troubled and astonied, for feare that the Theater would fall: seeing that by no means he could hold them in, nor cause them to take heart againe, he removed out of his owne place, and sat him downe in that part thereof which was most suspected. The most confuse and licentious manner of beholding such spectacles, hee reformed and brought into order,; mooved thereto, by the wrong done to a Senatour, whom at Puteoli in a frequent assemble sittings at their right solemne Games, noe man had received to him and vouchsafed a rowne.

Hereupon when a decree of the Senate was passed, That so often as in any place there was ought exhibited publikely to be seene, the first ranke or course of Seates should be kept cleere and wholly for Senatours: he forbad the Embassadour of free nations and confederats to sit at Rome within the *Orchestra*: because he had found, that even some of their libertines kind were sent in embassage. The soldiers hee severed from the other people. To maried men that were commoners, he assigned several rewes by themselves. To Noble mens children under age his own quarter: and to their teachers and governers the next thereto. He made an Act also, that not one of the base Commons wearing blacke and sullied gownes should sit so neere as the midst of the Theatre. As for women he would not allow them to behold so much, as the sword Fencers, (who customarily in the time past were to be seene of all indifferently) but from some higher loft above the rest, sitting there by themselves. To the Vestall Nunnes he graunted a place a part from the rest within the Theatre, and the same just over against the Pretours Tribunall.

Howbeit from the Solemnitie of Champions-shew, he banished all the female sex: so farre forth, as that during the Pontificiall Games, he put of a couple of them who were called for to enter in to combat, untill the morrow morning. And made proclamation, that his will and pleasure was, That no woman should come into the Theatre before the fift hower of the day.

Himself behelde the Circeian Games, for the most part from the upper lofts and lodging of his friendes and freedmen, sometime out of the Pulvinar, sitting there with his wife onely and children. From these shewes and sights he would be absent many houres together, and otherwhiles whole dayes: but first having craved leave of the people, and recommended those unto them, who should sitte as presidentes of those Games in his turne. But so often as he was at them, he did nothing els but intend the same: either to avoide the rumor and speech of men, whereby his father Caesar (as he said himselfe) was commonly taxed, namely for that in beholding those solemnities he used betweene whiles mind to read letters and petitions, yea and to write backe againe: or els uppon an earnest desire and delight he had, in seeing such pastimes, his pleasure and contentment wherein, he never dissimuled, but oftentimes frankely professed. And therefore he proposed and gave of his owne at the games of prise and plaies even of other men, Coronets and rewards, both many in number, and also of great worth: neither was he present at any of these Greek games and solemnities, but he honored everie one of the Actors and provers of Maisteries therein according to their deserts. But moste affectionately of all other he loved to see the Champions at fist fight: and the Latines especially; not those onely who by lawfull calling were professed, and by order allowed (and even those he was wont to match with Greeks) but such also as out of the common sort of townes-men, fell together by the eares pell mell in the narrow streets, and though they had no skill at all of fight, yet could lay on load, and offend their concurrents one way or other. In summe, all those in generall, who had any hand in those publike games or set them forward any way, he deigned good rewards and had a speciall respect of them. The priviledges of Champions he both maintained entier, and also amplified. As for sword fencers he would not suffer them to enter into the lists, unlesse they might be discharged of that profession, in case they became victours. The power to chastice Actours and plaieers at all times and in everie place (granted unto the Magistrates by aunciet law) he tooke from them, save onely during the plaies and uppon the stage. Howbeit he examined streightly neverthelesse at all times either the matches or combats of Champions called *Xystici*, or the fights of sword fencers. For the licentiousnesse of stage plaiers he so repressed, that when he had for certaine found out, that Stephanio, an actor of Romaine playes had a mans wife waiting upon him shorne and rounded in manner of a boy, he confined and sent him away as banished: but well beaten first with rods through all the three Theatres. And Hylas the Pantomime at the complaint made of him by the Pretour, he skourged openly in the Court yard before his house: and excluded no man from the sight thereof: yea and he banished Pylades out of the Cittie of Rome and Italie, because he had pointed with his finger at a Spectatour who hissed him out of the stage, and so made him to be knowne.

Having in this manner ordred the Cittie and administred the civile affaires therein, he made Italie populous and much frequented with Colonies to the number of 28, brought thither and planted by him; yea he furnished the same with publike workes and revenues in many places. He equalled it also after a sort, and in some part with the verie Cittie of Rome in priviledges and estimation: by devising a new kind of Suffrages which the decurions or elders of Colonies gave every one in their owne Towneshippe, as touching Majestrates to bee created in Rome, and sent under their hands and seales to the City against the day of the Solemne Elections. And to the end, there should not want in any place either honest and worshipfull inhabitants, or issue of the multitude; looke who made suite to serve as men of armes on horse-backe upon the publique commendation of any towneship whatsoever, those hee enrolled and advanced unto the degree of Gentlemen. But to as many of the Commoners as could by goode evidence prove unto him as hee visited the Countries and Regions of Italy, that they had sonnes and daughters he distributed a thousand sesterces a piece, for every child they had. **15**

Nero's Fire

Tacitus (55-117 A.D.) Roman historian described Nero's fire of 64 A.D., and the rebuilding of Rome.

And now came a calamitous fire—whether it was accidental or purposely contrived by the Emperor, remains uncertain: for on this point authorities are divided—more violent and destructive than any that ever befell our city. It began in that part of the Circus which adjoins the Palatine and Caelian hills. Breaking out in shops full of inflammable merchandise, it took hold and gathered strength at once; and being fanned by the wind soon embraced the entire length of the Circus, where there were no mansions with protective walls, no temple-enclosures, nor anything else to arrest its course. Furiously the destroying flames swept on, first over the level ground, then up the heights, then again plunging into the hollows, with a rapidity which outstripped all efforts to cope with them, the ancient city lending itself to their progress by its narrow tortuous streets and its misshapen blocks of buildings. The shrieks of panic-stricken women; the weakness of the aged, and the helplessness of the young; the efforts of some to save themselves, of others to help their neighbours; the hurrying of those who dragged their sick along, the lingering of those who waited for them—all made up a scene of inextricable confusion.

Many persons, while looking behind them, were enveloped from the front or from the side, or having escaped to the nearest place of safety, found this too in possession of the flames, and even places which they had thought beyond their reach in the same plight with the rest. At last, not knowing where to turn, or what to avoid, they poured into the roads or threw themselves down in the fields: some having lost their all, not having even food for the day; others, though with means of escape open to them, preferred to perish for love of the dear ones whom they could not save. And none dared to check the flames; for there were many who threatened and forced back those who would extinguish them, while others openly flung in torches, saying that *they had their orders;*—whether it really was so, or only that they wanted to plunder undisturbed.

At this moment Nero was at Antium. He did not return to the city until the flames were approaching the mansion which he had built to connect the Palatine with the Gardens of Maecenas; nor could they be stopped until the whole Palatine; including the palace and everything around it, had been consumed. Nero assigned the Campus Martius and the Agrippa monuments for the relief of the fugitive and houseless multitude. He threw open his own gardens also, and put up temporary buildings for the accommodation of the destitute; he brought up provisions from Ostia and the neighbouring towns; and he reduced the price of corn to three sesterces the peck. But popular as these measures were, they aroused no gratitude; for a rumour had got abroad that at the moment when the city was in flames Nero had mounted upon a stage in his own house, and by way of likening modern calamities to ancient, had sung the tale of the sack of Troy.

Not until the sixth day was the fire got under, at the foot of the Esquiline hill, by demolishing a vast extent of buildings, so as to present nothing but the ground, and as it were the open sky, to its continued fury. But scarcely had the alarm subsided, or the populace recovered from their despair, when it burst out again in the more open parts of the city; and though here the loss of life was less, the destruction of temples and porticoes of pleasaunce was still more complete. And the scandal attending this new fire was the greater that it broke out in property owned by Tigellinus, in the Aemilian quarter; the general belief being that Nero had the ambition to build a new city to be called after his own name. For of the fourteen regions into which Rome was divided only four remained intact. Three were burnt to the ground; in the other seven, nothing remained save a few fragments of ruined and half-burnt houses.

To count up the number of mansions, of tenements, and of temples that were destroyed would be no easy matter. Among the oldest of the sacred buildings burnt was that dedicated by Servius Tullius to the Moon, and the Great Altar and fane raised by Evander to the Present Hercules. The temple vowed by Romulus to Jupiter, the Stayer of flight; the Royal Palace of Numa; the Temple of Vesta, with the Household Gods of the Roman people, were all destroyed; added to these were the treasures won in numerous battles, and masterpieces of Greek art, as well as ancient and genuine monuments of Roman genius which were remembered by the older generation amid all the splendour of the restored city, and which could never be replaced. Some noted that the 19th of July, the day on which the fire began, was also the day on which the Senonian Gauls had taken and burnt the city; others were so curious in their calculations as to discover that the two burnings were separated from one another by exactly the same number of years, of months, and of days.

Nero profited by the ruin of his country to errect a palace in which the marvels were not to be gold and jewels, the usual and common-place objects of luxury, so much as lawns and lakes and mock-wildernesses, with woods on one side and open glades and vistas on the other. His engineers and masters-of-works were Severus and Celer; men who had the ingenuity and the impudence to fool away the resources of the Empire in the attempt to provide by Art what Nature had pronounced impossible.

For these men undertook to dig a navigable canal, along the rocky shore and over the hills, all the way from Lake Avernus to the mouths of the Tiber. There was no other water for supplying such a canal than that of the Pontine marshes; and even if practicable, the labour would have been prodigious, and no object served. But Nero had a thirst for the incredible, and traces of his vain attempt to excavate the heights adjoining Lake Avernus are to be seen to this day.

The parts of the city unoccupied by Nero's palace were not built over without divisions, or indiscriminately, as after the Gallic fire, but in blocks of regular dimensions, with broad streets between. A limit was placed to the height of houses; open spaces were left; and colonnades were added to protect the fronts of tenements, Nero undertaking to build these at his own cost, and to hand over the building sites, cleared of rubbish, to the proprietors. He offered premiums also, in proportion to the rank and means of owners, on condition of mansions or tenements being completed within a given time; and he assigned the marshes at Ostia for the reception of the rubbish, which was taken down the Tiber in the same vessels which had brought up the corn. Certain parts of the houses were to be built without beams, and of solid stone, Gabian or Alban, those stones being impervious to fire. Then as water had often been improperly intercepted by individuals, inspectors were appointed to secure a more abundant supply, and over a larger area, for public use; owners were required to keep appliances for quenching fire in some open place; party walls were forbidden, and every house had to be enclosed within walls of its own.

These useful provisions added greatly to the appearance of the new city; and yet there were not wanting persons who thought that the plan of the old city was more conducive to health, as the narrow streets and high roofs were a protection against the rays of the sun, which now beat down with double fierceness upon broad and shadeless thoroughfares.

Such were the measures suggested by human counsels; after which means were taken to propitiate the Gods. The Sibylline books were consulted, and prayers were offered, as prescribed by them, to Vulcan, to Ceres, and to Proserpine. Juno was supplicated by the matrons, in the Capitol first, and afterwards at the nearest point upon the sea, from which water was drawn to sprinkle the temple and image of the Goddess; banquets to the Goddesses and all-night festivals were celebrated by married women.

But neither human aid, nor imperial bounty, nor atoning-offerings to the Gods, could remove the sinister suspicion that the fire had been brought about by Nero's order. To put an end therefore to this rumour, he shifted the charge on to others, and inflicted the most cruel tortures upon a body of men detested for their abominations, and popularly known by the name of Christians. This name came from one Christus, who was put to death in the reign of Tiberius by the Procurator Pontius Pilate; but though checked for the time, the detestable superstition broke out again, not in Judaea only, where the mischief began, but even in Rome, where every horrible and shameful iniquity, from every quarter of the world, pours in and finds a welcome.

16

Juvenal's View of Rome.

From Juvenal (1st-2nd century A.D.) Roman poet we learn of the frailities and excesses of Rome's populous.

What, are the services of the poor man, what are his good offices worth here, if he takes pains to hurry in his toga before daybreak, when a praetor is urging on his lictor and bidding him go with all speed, since the childless matrons have been long awake, for fear his colleague be beforehand in paying his morning respects to Albina and Modia? Here the son of freeborn parents walks on the left of a rich man's slave; another gives to Calvina or Catiena, to enjoy her favors once and again, as much as tribunes in the legion receive; but you, [poor man], when the face of a dress harlot pleases you, hesitate and are doubtful. . . .'How many salves does he keep? How many *iugera* of land does he possess? How numerous and how large are the dishes at his dinners?' The credence accorded a man is in proportion to the amount of money he keeps in his strong box. . . . Why add that this same poor man furnished everybody with material and occasions for jest, if his cloak is dirty and torn, if his toga is a trifle shabby and one of his shoes shows a break in the leather, or if more than one tear reveals the coarse, recently applied thread where the rent has been sewn together? There is nothing about unhappy poverty that is crueler than this, that it makes and Bruges in the Low Countries, and Beauvais and Arras, were celebrated for their not easily do those emerge from obscurity whose noble qualities are cramped by domestic poverty. But at Rome the attempt is still harder for them; a great price must be paid for a wretched lodging, a great price for slaves' keep, a great price for a modest little dinner. A man is ashamed to dine off earthenware. . . . Here splendor of dress is carried beyond people's means; here something more than is enough is occasionally borrowed from another man's strongbox. This vice is common to all of us; here all of us live in a state of pretentious poverty.

We inhabit a city supported to a great extent by slender props; for in this way the bailiff saves the houses from falling. And when he has plastered over the gaping hole of an old crack, he bids us sleep securely, with ruin overhanging us. The place to live in is where there are no fires, no noctural alarms. . . . Already your third story is smoking; you yourself know nothing about it; for if the alarm begins from the bottom of the stairs, the last man to know there is a fire will be the one who is protected from the rain only by the roof tiles, where the gentle doves lay their eggs. . . . A wretched man has lost the little he had; but the crowning point of his misery is this, that though he is naked and begging for scraps, no one will help him with food, no one with the shelter of a roof. If the great house of Asturicus has been destroyed, we have the matrons and nobles in mourning, the praetor adjourns his court; then we groan over the accidents of the city, then we detest fires. The fire is still burning, and already someone runs up to make a present of marble, to contribute to the expenses of rebuilding. One will contribute nude white statues, another some masterpieces of Euphranor or Polyclitus; some lady will give antique ornaments of

Asiatic gods; another man, books and bookcases and a statue of Minerva to put among them; another, a bushel of silver plate. Persicus, most sumptuous of childless men, replaces what is lost by choicer and more numerous objects and is in fact with reason suspected of having himself set fire to his own house.

Many a sick man dies here from want of sleep, the sickness itself having been produced by undigested food clinging to the fevered stomach. For what rented lodgings allow of sleep? It takes great wealth to sleep in the city. Hence the origin of the disease. The passage of carriages in the narrow winding streets, and the abuse of the drivers of the blocked teams would rob even [the heaviest sleepers] of sleep.

If a social duty calls him, the rich man will be carried through the yielding crowd and will speed over their heads on his huge Liburnian litter bearers; he will read on his way, or write, or even sleep inside, for a litter with closed windows induces sleep. Yet he will arrive before us. We in our hurry are impeded by the wave in front, while the multitude which follows us presses on our back in dense array; one strikes me with his elbow, another with a hard pole, one knocks a beam against my head, another a wine jar. My legs are sticky with mud; before long I am trodden on all sides by large feet.

Observe now the different and varied dangers of the night. What a height it is to the lofty roofs, from which a tile brains you, and how often cracked and broken utensils fall from windows—with what a weight they mark and damage the pavement when they strike it! You may well be accounted remiss and improvident about sudden accidents if you go out to supper without making a will. There are just so many fatal chances as there are wakeful windows open at night when you are passing by. Hope, then, and carry this pitiable prayer about with you, that they may be content merely to empty broad wash basins over you. The drunken and insolent fellow who has not chanced to fall on someone suffers tortures. . . . But though heated with wine, he keeps clear of the man whom the scarlet cloak, the very long train of attendants, the many torches, and the bronze lamp point out as one to be avoided. Me, whom the moon or the brief light of a candle whose wick I regulate and adjust is wont to escort home, he despises. Mark the preliminaries of the wretched brawl, if brawl it be, where you strike and I alone am beaten. He stands facing you, and orders you to stand; you must obey, for what are you to do when a madman forces you, and moreover one stronger than yourself? . . . It is all one whether you try to say anything or draw back in silence. They beat you in either case; then in anger they make you post bail. This is the liberty of a poor man: after being beaten, he prays, and after being thrashed with fisticuffs he entreats, to be allowed to retire,from the scene with a few teeth left him. Nor yet are such things all you have to fear, for there will not be wanting one to plunder you after the houses are shut, and all the shops everywhere are quiet, their shutters closed fast with bolts. **17**

Justinian's Code

Many historians of Rome have observed that the declining urban base of the Empire was one of the most important factors in Rome's collapse. Documents of the 4th century A.D. are replete with descriptions of dying municipalities. Clearly during the later days of the Empire Romans preferred to escape rather than face their responsibilities in the cities. The Emperors Diocletian (245-313) and Justinian (483-565) sought to keep city government in operation in view of the wholesale flight of the middle classes from their duties, and the following selections from Justinian's Code shows an attempt to codify various city functions.

> Municipal duties of a personal character are: representation of a municipality, that is, becoming a public advocate; assignment to taking the census or registering property; secretaryships; camel transport; commissioner of food supply and the like, of public lands, of grain procurement, of water supply; horse races in the circus; paving of public streets; grain storehouse; heating of public baths; distribution of food supply; and other duties similar to these.
>
> The governor of the province shall see to it that the compulsory public services and offices in the municipalities are imposed fairly and in rotation according to age and rank, in accordance with the gradation of public services and offices long ago established, so that

THE CITY IN WESTERN CIVILIZATION

The Colosseum
This arena was begun under Vespasian in 72 and finished by Titus in the year 80. It was located near the southeast end of the Forum and was in the center of town. Its four stories held some 50,000 spectators and covered nearly six acres. The basement held compartments for the gladiators and wild beasts, and it provided space for a network of water and drainage pipes which could flood the arena and transform it into a lake. The wall surrounding the arena was fifteen feet high.

View of the Roman Forum
The Roman Forum was a market and meeting place of ancient Rome. Down to Julius Ceasar's time it was the main plaza inside the city limits. It encompassed such public buildings as the Basilica Aemilia, the Curia—meeting place of the Senate—and the open-air law court.

The Appian Way
Begun by Appius Claudius Caecus in 312 B.C. it is the oldest of Rome's southern roads. Since its original gravel it has been covered with various substances including lava and stone. The road—though narrow by modern standards—is still in use today.

the men and resources of municipalities are not inconsiderately ruined by frequent oppression of the same persons.

The care of constructing or rebuilding a public work in a municipality is a compulsory public service from which a father of five living children is excused; and if this service is forcibly imposed, this fact does not deprive him of the exemption that he has from other public services. The excusing of those with insufficient resources who are nominated to public services or offices is not permanent but temporary. For if a hoped-for increase comes to one's property by honorable means, when his turn comes an evaluation is to be made to determine whether he is suitable for the services for which he was chosen. . . . A person who is responsible for public services to his municipality and submits his name for military service for the purpose of avoiding the municipal burden cannot make the condition of his community worse.

The prefect of the city has jurisdiction over all offenses whatsoever not only those committed inside the city but also those outside the city in Italy, according to a rescript of the deified Emperor Severus addressed to Fabius Cilo, prefect of the city. He shall hear complaints against masters by slaves who have sought asylum at sacred images or have been purchased with their own money for the purpose of being manumitted. He shall also hear the complaints of needy patrons concerning their freedmen, especially if they declare that they are ill and wish to be supported by their freedmen. The authority to relegate and deport persons to an island designated by the emperor is vested in him.

The same rescript begins as follows: "Inasmuch as we have entrusted our city to your care," therefore any offense committed within the city is held to be under the jurisdiction of the prefect of the city; and likewise any offense committed within a hundred miles is under the jurisdiction of the prefect of the city; an offense committed beyond the hundredth milestone is outside the purview of the prefect of the city. . . .

Maintenance of the public peace and of order at the spectacles is also held to be under the jurisdiction of the prefect of the city; and indeed he should also have soldiers stationed at various points for the purpose of maintaining the public peace and to report to him whatever occurs anywhere. The prefect of the city can debar anyone from the city, as well as from any one of the official districts [of

Rome] and can debar him from a business or profession or from the practice of law or from the Forum, either temporarily or permanently. He can also debar him from the spectacles. . . .

The deified Severus declared in a rescript that those who are accused of having held unlawful assemblies must be prosecuted before the prefect of the city. . . .

Augustus held that the protection of the public security belonged to no one more than to the emperor, and that no one else was equal to the task; accordingly, he stationed seven cohorts in suitable places, so that each cohort protected two districts of the city; in command of the cohorts were tribunes, and at the head of all was an official . . . called the prefect of the night patrol.

The prefect of the night patrol tries incendiaries, housebreakers, thieves, robbers, and harborers of criminals, unless the individual is so vicious and notorious that he is turned over to the prefect of the city. And since fires are generally caused by the negligence of occupants, he either punishes with beating those who have been unduly careless in the use of fire, or he suspends the sentence of beating and issues a severe reprimand.

Housebreaking is generally committed in apartment houses and in warehouses where men deposit the most valuable part of their property, when either a storeroom or a closet or a money box is broken into; in which case the guards are generally punished. The deified Antoninus stated this in a rescript to Erucius Clarus, saying that if warehouses are broken into he can examine by torture the slaves guarding them, even if some of them may belong to the emperor himself.

It should be noted that the prefect of the night patrol must be on duty the entire night, and should make his rounds equipped with water buckets and axes. He must notify all residents to exercise care that no fire occur through any negligence; moreover he is directed to give notice that each resident should keep water on the upper floor. He has also been assigned jurisdiction over those who take care of clothing in baths for a fee; and if while taking care of clothing they commit any fraud, he must try the case himself. **18**

The Hippodrome at Constantinople

Constantinople, capital of the Byzantine Empire, was built on seven hills on the Bosporus and surrounded by a triple wall of fortifications. It was the largest city of medieval Europe and at its height (10th century) it had some one million people. In the selection that follows French historian C. Diehl described sports activities at Constantinople's Hippodrome and their impact on the daily life and politics during Justinian's reign.

Atmeidan Place is in the heart of modern Stamboul. Down to the present day it has preserved the name and kept the form of the gigantic circus, the Byzantine Hippodrome. It was 370 meters long, and 60 to 70 meters wide. On the sides were 30 or 40 rows of marble seats, where more than 30,000 men could be seated. The broad aisles and walks were decorated with a host of statues. Some of the most dramatic scenes in the history of the empire of the East have been played in this Hippodrome; the struggles there bring out one of the most curious sides of the Byzantine civilization. Although we no longer believe, as people formerly did, that the rivalries of the circus, the famous quarrels of the Greens and the Blues, make up, together with the theological controversies, the whole empire of the East; nevertheless, we must admit that the Hippodrome represents one of the most characteristic aspects of the Byzantine world. It has been well said that at Constantinople "God had St. Sophia, the emperor had the sacred palace, and the people had the Hippodrome."

After imperial absolutism had effaced in the monarchy every trace of the ancient Roman liberties, the Hippodrome had become the true forum of Byzantium, the hearth and center of all the public life which still survived. There, in the presence of the assembled people, the most important festivals of the national life were celebrated; there, before the eyes of the Byzantine loafers, the trophies which bore witness to the victories of the basileus were exhibited. There, in honor of the successes of Belisarius, Justinian revived all the pomp of the ancient Roman triumphs. That day, for hours, the throng which filled the seats of the circus saw passing before them the spoils of conquered Africa: thrones of gold, precious vases, heaps of gems, costly plates and dishes, magnificent vestments, sumptuous carriages, a hoard of money—all the treasures which the Vandals had accumulated in a hundred years of pillage. Here, it was the insignia of the empire and the vases of Solomon, which had been seized by Gaiseric in the sack of Rome, and which, after passed until it reached the space before the imperial throne. There the Vandal king, brutally despoiled of his purple, was thrown as a suppliant at the feet of the sovereign; and while from the mouth of the conquered fell the words of Ecclesiastes, "Vanity of vanities, all is vanity," Belisarius in his turn knelt before the master. Then the pompous procession again passed on, while the victor distributed to the people the spoils of the barbarians: golden girdles, silver vases, and precious objects of every king; and a last ray of the vanished Roman glories seemed to descend upon the Hippodrome in its festal array.

It was in the Hippodrome, also, that a new emperor first came in contact with his people. There Justinian and Theodora, consecrated in St. Sophia by the hand of the patriarch, received the enthusiastic acclamations of their new subjects, when, in the midst of the pompous procession of patricians and body-guards, they came to seat themselves in the imperial box upon the golden throne and, amid the acclamations, the vows for their prosperity, and the rhythmic chants of the factions, they made, for the first time, according to the accustomed rite, the sign of the cross above the heads of the assembled multitude. There, some years later, other and more tragic scenes were enacted between the basileus and his people, when those amazing dialogues took place between the master and his subjects, in which the people questioned Justinian directly, and hooted at him and insulted him. Indeed, for the Byzantines of the sixth century, the Hippodrome was the asylum of the last public liberties. Long before, this mob, which called itself the heir of the Roman people, had abdicated most of its ancient rights. It no longer voted in the forum, it no longer elected tribunes or consuls, but it always retained in the circus the liberty of cheering, railing, hooting, and applauding, the right of addressing to the emperor its petitions and complaints; more frequently still, its sarcasms and insults. In the Hippodrome, in fact, the prince and his people met face to face—one in the pomp of his imperial splendor, surrounded by his patricians, chamberlains, and soldiers; the other in their formidable numerical power, in the fury of their strong but fickle passions; and more than once, in the presence of the clamors of the circus, the all-powerful basileus had to yield.

Lastly, the Hippodrome performed another function: it was the most admirable of museums. Upon the narrow terrace, or the *spina*, which divided the arena into two tracks, along the broad canal which ran in front of the lowest seats, upon the facade of the imperial box, in the marvelous promenade which covered the upper terraces, and from which there was a splendid view over the whole city and beyond the Bosphorus as far as the distant mountains and the green trees on the Asiatic coast, under the colonnaded porticos—everywhere, there was placed a multitude of statues. They were the masterpieces of ancient art, which Asia, Greece, and Rome had been compelled to give up for the embellishment of the new capital of the empire. By the wolf of Romulus stood the Hercules of Lysippus, and that admirable statue of Helen, whose "mouth half open like the calyx of a flower, whose enchanting smile, liquid eyes, and charming figure" were destined to leave the rude companions of Villehardouin unmoved. Above the imperial box stood the four horses of gilded bronze which were carried in the fifth century from Chios to Byzantium, and at the present day adorn the facade of St. Mark's at Venice. In the Hippodrome were all the glories and all the works of art, torn from the shade of their sanctuaries; some of these inspired the superstitious Byzantines with strange and formidable terrors. But, above all else, the Hippodrome was for the people of Byzantium the usual scene of their amusements, the place where their favorite tastes and most ardent passions found satisfaction.

Never did any people, unless it was the Roman people, take a greater interest in the pleasures of the circus than did the Byzantines of the sixth century. A contemporary wrote: "At this spectacle more than any other the ardor which enflames the soul with an unheard-of passion is prodigious. If the Green jockey gets ahead, part of the people is disconsolate; if the Blue passes him, immediately half of the city is in mourning. People who derive no profit from the affair yell frantic insults, people who have suffered no evil feel grossly injured; and thus, with no cause, they begin fighting as if it were a question of saving their native country." The grave Procopius himself, who shows in general little taste for these sports, says somewhere that without the theater and the Hippodrome life is really joyless.

With much greater reason, the common citizens of Byzantium were madly fond of these pleasures. Two anecdotes, selected from a thousand, will show how far this passion went in the days of Justinian. At the time when the emperor was building St. Sophia, one owner had refused to be forced to sell a piece of land which the architects needed. He had been offered enormous sums and had refused them all. He had been put in prison and had been obstinate in his resistance. He had been deprived of food, and had suffered hunger without complaining or yielding. The prefect of the city then had an idea: he got the emperor to announce races at the Hippodrome; it was too much for the courage of the prisoner; at the thought that he would not see the sight he let his house go at a low price. Another owner was more accommodating. He declared that he was ready to sell at once the property which was desired, but on the condition that he should have for himself, and for his heirs, a place of honor at the Hippodrome, and that people should pay to him when he entered the same honors as to the emperor. This ridiculous and vain Byzantine was a shoemaker by trade. Justinian was amused and consented to the man's demands, but with this reservation: that the imperial honors should be paid to him from behind. This is the reason why, many centuries later, the people made ironical acclamations and grotesque genuflections before the descendants of Justinian's shoemaker.

However that may be, the whole population of Constantinople was excited when there were to be games in the Hippodrome. The evening before, the whole city was in motion. In the private amphitheaters of each faction there was a final rehearsal of the troupe. In the Hippodrome the last preparations were made; over the arena they extended great awnings of silk and purple to protect the spectators from the heat of the sun; on the ground they spread fresh sand mixed with fragrant powdered cedar; they tested the barriers behind which the contestants awaited the signal to start; and through the great gates opening upon the Forum Augusteum a multitude of people was already hastening to occupy the best places. When the time came all Constantinople was assembled upon the benches which ran along the sides of the Hippodrome and around the semi-circle at the end; upon the benches nearest the arena were the official members of the factions, girded with scarfs of the rival colors, holding in their hands a short baton surmounted by a cross. Elsewhere in reserved seats were placed the ambassadors of foreign nations, and in the decorated boxes arranged along the straight side of the circus were seated generals, senators, and high dignitaries of the palace and even of the Church. There also was the imperial box, elevated several stories above the level of the arena, so that the basileus, while in the midst of his people, was not at all at their mercy. For that reason, in the Hippodrome no stairway led from the circus to the official tribune, and on the projecting terrace, slightly below, detachments of the guard were placed all ready to protect the master against the sudden pranks of the populace; for that reason, too, behind the prince's box there was a direct communication with the palace, and solid bronze doors closed the tribune against every unforeseen assault. There, among his eunuchs, courtiers, and high functionaries, the emperor came to sit upon his throne with his crown upon his forehead and his scepter in his hand. Over the bowed heads of the people he made the solemn sign of the cross, while applause, hymns, and the songs of the factions burst forth from every side. The empress did not sit in the imperial box. In this Oriental court it was contrary to etiquette that she should appear frequently in public. But, like the true Byzantine woman that she was, the empress was no less interested in the circus than her husband and his subjects. Procopius says, somewhere, that the women, although they never went to the circus, were as passionately interested as the men in the factional strifes; and how could Theodora have been indifferent to the theater of her first exploits, her first triumphs, and her first hatreds? Accordingly, she witnessed the games—invisible, but present. She sat with her court of ladies in the upper galleries of the church of St. Sophia, which overlooked the circus, and the spectacle began when the people became aware of the presence of their sovereign lady behind the grilled windows of the basilica.

When the signal was given by the basileus, four doors opened on the ground floor of the imperial box; Four chariots of the four different colors rushed forth, each one drawn by four horses. Amid cries and acclamations they raced along the track, encouraged by the applause, accompanied by the vows of the rival factions, attempting to pass one another, risking a smash-up at the difficult turn which marked the end of the *spina*. Then the passion for the races, that "mental malady," as Procopius called it, took complete possession of the whole people. They forgot everything,—relatives, friends, laws divine and human,—and thought only of the triumph of the faction. Then were the perils of the State and the cares of private life forgotten; each one would have given joyfully his fortune, his very life, to secure the victory to the jockey of his party. Leaning forward, panting for breath, the spectators followed the fortunes of the race with a fierceness which was still more exasperated by the sight of the rival faction triumphing over its opponent's defeat, replying by insults or jeers to its uneasiness of grief. Then from one side to the other they shot glances charged with hatred; they challenged one another; they dared one another with voice and gesture; they exchanged sarcasms and insults; and if the guards, with their batons in their hands, had not kept the spectators back, more than one of these excitable people would have leaped into the arena, without exactly knowing why, as a contemporary said, and would have gone to punch the heads of the men in the other party. At last the race was finished, and the winner proclaimed; afterward, the same spectacle was repeated three times in the leveled arena. The first part of the program was over.

Then was the time for the interludes—pantomimes, exhibitions of strange animals, feats of acrobats, and tricks of the clowns. We know the way in which, according to report, Theodora, in her youth, charmed the crowd during this part of the show. On other occasions the show, though less piquant, was no less amusing to the people. A trick dog, yellow, and blind in one eye, was in the time of Justinian, the particular favorite of the amphitheater. It was a very remarkable animal! It could classify the medals of the emperor as well as a professional numismatist; when rings were mixed up in a vase, it carried each one back to its rightful owner; in a circle of spectators it could designate without error the most miserly person, the most generous, and the most vicious; it could even pick out women who behaved badly; and the witty loungers of Byzantium said that this dog certainly had in his body the prophetic spirit of a witch.

Thus the morning passed. Then the emperor retired with the high officials to the dining-room of the palace of Kathisma, near the imperial box. The people got out their own provisions, unless the prince, in order to do the thing handsomely, gave his subjects this meal. Generally, it was very modest; the fare was made up of vegetables, fruit, and salt fish; but these were enough to make the people happy. The emperor, however, had to be as moderate as his subjects. If he sat too long at table the crowd very soon became impatient. One day, when the emperor Phocas, a successor of Justinian, took too long in dining, the crowd began to sing, respectfully at first: "Rise, O imperial sun, rise and appear." But as the basileus kept them waiting, the cries soon became more lively and the tone more insolent: "You have kissed the bottle too often; you will get into more trouble!"

Generally, the emperor did not have to be called to order. Of his own accord, he returned to give the signal for more races. As in the morning, there were four in the afternoon. But when the show ended, the passions which had been excited did not cool down. Then they went out, the victors marched, proudly waving the winning colors in the midst of the crowd. The defeated were pursued with jokes and insults. Accordingly, rows were frequent, and these often became bloody battles, which the imperial guard did not always succeed in stopping.

Sunday, January 11, 532, the races were taking place, as usual, in the Hippodrome. The emperor was present in great pomp; but that day the crowd was very boisterous. Upon the benches where the Greens sat, the racket was incessant and the hooting continuous; the faction believed that they had reason to complain of an official of the palace, the grand chamberlain Calopodios, and at every opportunity they gave vent to their bad humor. At last, Justinian became impatient, and ordered a herald to speak to the people. Then between the spokesman of the Greens and the emperor's herald there was a most astonishing dialogue, in which the complaints were at first respectful, but very soon changed into violent invectives, and anger mingled with irony. This debate must be quoted almost completely, as it is so characteristic of the Byzantine manners, in the sixth century.

The Greens: "Long live Emperor Justinian! May he be ever victorious! But, O best of Princes, we are suffering all kinds of injustice. God knows we cannot stand it any longer. Yet we are afraid to name our persecutor, from fear that he may become more angry and that we shall incur still greater dangers."

Herald: "I do not know of whom you are speaking."

Greens: "Our oppressor, O thrice August! lives in the shoemakers' quarter."

Herald: "No one is doing you any injury."

Greens: "A single man persecutes us. O Mother of God, protect us!"

Herald: "I do not know this man'."

Greens: "Oh, yes, you do! You know very well, thrice August, who is our executioner at present."

Herald: "If any one is persecuting you, I do not know who it is."

Greens: "Well, Master of the World, it is Calopodios."

Herald: "Calopodios has nothing to do with you."

Greens: "Whoever it is will suffer the fate of Judas, and God will very soon punish him for his injustice."

Herald: "You didn't come here to see the show, but only to insult the officials."

Greens: "Yes, if any one annoys us he will suffer the fate of Judas."

Herald: "Shut up, you Jews, Manicheans, Samaritans!"

Greens: "You call us Jews and Samaritans; may the Mother of God protect us all equally!"

Herald: "I want you to get baptized."

Greens: "All right, we'll get baptized."

Herald: "I tell you, if you don't shut up, I'll have your heads cut off."

Greens: "Each one seeks to have power, in order to be safe. If our remarks hurt you, we hope that you will not be at all irritated. He who is divine ought to bear everything patiently. But, while we are talking, we shall call a spade a spade. We no longer know, thrice August, where the palace is or the government; the only way we know the city now is when we pass through it on an ass's back. And that is unjust, thrice August."

Herald: "Every freeman can appear publicly wherever he likes, without danger."

Greens: "We know very well we are free, but we are not allowed to use our liberty. And if any freeman is suspected of being a Green, he is always punished by public authority."

Herald: "Jail-birds, don't you fear for your souls?"

Greens: "Let the color which we wear be suppressed, and the courts will be out of a job. You allow us to be assassinated, and, in addition, you order us to be punished. You are the source of life, and you kill whomsoever you choose. Truly, human nature cannot endure these two opposites. Ah! Would to heaven that your father, Sabbatios, had never been born! He would not have begotten an assassin. Just now a sixth murder took place in the Zeugma; yesterday, the man was alive, and in the evening, Master of all things, he was dead."

Blues: "All the murderers in the Stadium belong to your party."

Greens: "You do the killing, and you escape punishment."

Blues: "You do the killing, and you keep on talking; all the assassins in the Stadium belong to your faction."

Greens: "O Emperor Justinian! They complain, and yet no one is killing them. Come, let's discuss it; who killed the dealer in wood in the Zeugma?"

Herald: "You did."

Greens: "And the son of Epagathos, who killed him, O Emperor?"

Herald: "You did that, too, and you accuse the Blues of it."

Greens: "That will do. May the Lord have mercy on us! Truth is getting the worst of it. If it is true that God governs the world, where do so many calamities come from?"

Herald: "God is a stranger to evil."

Greens: "God is a stranger to evil! Then why are we persecuted? Let a philosopher or a hermit come to solve the dilemma."

Herald: "Blasphemers, enemies of God, will you not keep still?"

Greens: "If your Majesty orders us we shall keep still, thrice August, but it will be against our will. We know all about it, but we are silent. Adieu. Justice, thou dost not exist any longer. We are going away; we'll become Jews. God knows, it is better to be a pagan than a Blue."

Blues: "Oh, horrors! we don't want to see them any longer; such hatred frightens us."

Greens: "We hope the boxes of the spectators will be thrown into the sewer some day."

With these words the Green faction left the Hippodrome in a body; it was the worst insult they could inflict upon the emperor.

While the exasperated mob went out of the circus and spread through the streets, Justinian returned to the palace thinking that as usual the rivalry of the Blues would very quickly allay the fury of the other party. Unfortunately, a troublesome accident united the two parties. The prefect of the city had been too zealous; he had had several rioters arrested and condemned to death. But the executioner bungled his job; twice the rope broke under the weight of the condemned. Then the mob got angry and rescued the victims, whom the monks of St. Conon received into a neighboring church. Now, by chance, one of the prisoners was a Blue and the other a Green; thus the two fractions found themselves brought together by a common danger. Two days later, January 13, it was very evident in the Hippodrome; again there was a violent uproar, and instead of the loyalist cry, "Victory to the Emperor Justinian!" they shouted on all sides, "Long live the Greens and the Blues, united for mercy!" and with the cry of *Nika* (victory)—from this rallying-cry the insurrection got the name by which it is handed down in history—the rioters rushed through the city. They attacked the prefecture, demanding the release of the guilty who were still in prison; the guards were massacred; the prefect's palace was burned, and during the whole night the seething mob filled all the streets in the capital. With the union of the two parties, the riot assumed a more serious form. The next day, January 14, the flood of people was beating against the palace gates, demanding the dismissal of the grand chamberlain and of the prefect of the city, and in addition the discharge of the two detested ministers, Tribonian and John of Cappadocia. Justinian yielded, but already it was too late. The emperor's yielding merely encouraged a furious mob; the revolt became a revolution.

Up to that time, however, the sane portion of the people had taken no part in these events and all was not lost. Justinian believed that he could take vigorous action; on the fifteenth, he let loose upon the insurgents his barbarian soldiers, with Belisarius at their head. Unfortunately, in the conflict these mercenaries maltreated the priests of St. Sophia, who had brought out the sacred relics and had intervened to separate the combatants. Then there was a general row. From the windows and the terraced roofs a hail of tiles and stones fell upon the sacrilegious, and the women, who were particularly enraged, engaged actively in the battle. Before this tempest the disconcerted soldiers had to beat a retreat to the palace, and to hasten their flight the victorious people set fire to the public buildings in the neighborhood. The senate-house and the approaches to the pal became the prey of the flames; for three days the fire, driven by strong wind, continued its ravages, destroying, in succession, St. Sophia, the approaches to the Augusteum, the baths of Zeuxippus, St. Irene, the Xenodochion of Ebulus, the great hospital of Sampson with all its patients, a large number of palaces and private houses, and the whole quarter, one of the most beautiful in the city, which extended from the sacred palace to the Forum of Constantine.

"The city," said an eye-witness, "was left a mass of blackened mounds; as at Lipari or Vesuvius, it was full of smoke and cinders; the smell of the burning spreading everywhere made it uninhabitable, and the sight filled a spectator with mingled terror and pity."

Justinian was frightened. He had shut himself up in the palace, with those who stood by him; means of defense were almost entirely wanting. The guard was a body of ornamental troops, intended to be shown off in ceremonies, and he was not sure that he could trust them. The barbarian troops of Belisarius and Mundus were the only ones that he had confidence in, and they were not very numerous. So the basileus was very uneasy, thinking that he already saw conspirators and assassins all around him, and he became more and more excited and confused. The nephews of Anastasius had come to the palace to protest that they were loyal; he commanded them, in spite of their prayers, to return home, without realizing that he was thus furnishing for the insurrection the leaders which as yet it lacked.

January 18, the sixth day of the riot, Justinian made a last attempt. He appeared in the Hippodrome, holding the Gospel in his hand, and addressed the assembled people: "I swear by this sacred book that I pardon all your offences. I will have no one of you arrested, provided that all trouble ceases. You are not at all responsible for what has happened. I am the sole cause of everything. My sins led me to refuse what you demanded in the Hippodrome." These words were received with a little scattered applause, but from all sides they responded to the prince: "You lie, ass; you are swearing a false oath." And this time Theodora does not appear to have escaped the insults. So Justinian, without waiting for anything more, went back very hastily to the palace.

What might have been expected, happened. The people, in a hurry to give themselves a new master, went to find Hypatius, the nephew of Anastasius, whom they had been applauding on every occasion for several days. In spite of his own unwillingness and the tears of his wife, they dragged him to the Forum of Anastasius, raised him on a shield, placed a golden chain on his forehead in place of a diadem, and gave him the insignia of the empire and the imperial robe, which they had carried off from the part of the palace which they had invaded. Then the crowd hastened to the Hippodrome; they hoisted the new sovereign into the imperial box, and the chiefs of the rebellion began to discuss the best way of storming the residence, which they said Justinian had just left in great haste.

It was the afternoon of January 18. The insurrection, which now included all the discontented and also a considerable number of senators and nobles, assumed more and more the form of a political movement. Events were moving rapidly, and the decisive moment had come. "The empire itself," as Lydus said, "seemed on the eve of its fall." Justinian, without resources, and without hope was thinking of abandoning everything, when Theodora's energy aroused the courage of the emperor and his counselors. At last they took some measures to defend themselves, while Narses attempted to detach the Blues from the revolt, and succeeded in doing so by bribery; and while, because of this division, discord arose among the insurgents, and some loyalists were again heard shouting, "Long live Justinian! O Lord, protect Justinian and Theodora!" Belisarius and Mundus were preparing for a decisive attack upon the Hippodrome. Belisarius succeeded, with some difficulty, in penetrating through the burning débris into the arena, while the soldiers of Mundus broke in at the opposite gate, called the Gate of the Dead, and from the lofty promenades of the amphitheater the imperial troops poured upon the crowd a hail of arrows. Then in the multitude crowded in the circus there was a frightful panic, which became greater when the soldiers pushed mercilessly across the arena, giving no quarter. All who came in their way were massacred without pity, and at night, when the slaughter ceased, more than thirty thousand corpses, according to some,—according to others, nearly fifty thousand,—were strewn on the bloody soil of the Hippodrome.

Hypatius was arrested, with his cousin Pompeius, and brought before Justinian. Both threw themselves on their knees, imploring mercy, swearing that they were innocent, and that they had been forced to do what they did. They added that in getting all the rebels together in the Hippodrome, they had planned to deliver them defenseless to the blows of the emperor. And it was the truth; but unfortunately for Hypatius, amid the disorder of the palace the message which he had sent to Justinian had not reached the basileus. The latter, accordingly, having now recovered his *sang froid,* responded to the suppliants with cruel irony: "Very good; but since you had so much authority over these men, you ought to have exerted it before they burned my city." And early the next morning he had them both executed. Justinian, as Gibbon said, "had been too much terrified to forgive."

Moreover, some senators compromised in the uprising were executed or exiled, and, to justify the severity, an official account of the event was made public, stating that Hypatius and his cousin had planned, and voluntarily carried on, the rebellion to which the imperial authority had almost succumbed.

The frightful bloodshed which terminated this six days' battle calmed the factions of the Hippodrome, and completed the foundation of the imperial absolutism. Justinian was able, without protest, to restrict, and even for some years to suppress almost entirely, the games of the circus. Undoubtedly the parties regained their courage later in his reign; factional disputes and struggles again appeared in the amphiheater; outcries and insults against the emperor were again herd, and Justinian resented these the more deeply because a foreign ambassador was present at this inglorious episode; and more than once, as in 532, Constantinople again witnessed tumult and battle in her streets and flames swept away her public buildings. But the imperial authority was stronger, and always repressed these seditious manifestations promptly and energetically; and, becoming more equitable, it was not afraid even to punish the Blues when, on several occasions, confiding in the protection of the prince, they gave the signal for riots. "Thanks to this timely severity," says a contemporary, "order was restored in the city, every one enjoyed freedom from this time on, and all could go about their business or pleasure without fear." Although the capital was sometimes disturbed, these riots were really of little importance compared with the great uprising which, but for Theodora's energy, would have deprived Justinian of his throne.

Such were, fourteen hundred years ago, the tumultuous scenes which filled the Hippodrome and Byzantium with massacre and conflagration. But if the insurrection was put down, its traces were everywhere present. The fire had spread its ravages over the old city of Constantine; everything had to be rebuilt—churches, palaces, and public monuments. It is one of the most meritorious and striking of the tasks of Justinian, that he made his capital veritably in his own image, and attached his name indissolubly to the splendors of St. Sophia. **19**

IV. The Middle Ages

Out of the chaos of the post-imperial world, a European civilization slowly emerged. The consolidation of several centuries' building coincided with the resurrection of a moribund urbanism in many areas of the western Mediterranean and the establishment of new cities in Germanic Europe during the 11th and 12th centuries. Indeed, a new civilization, based on a revitalized urbanism had clearly taken a primary place in the world by the end of the 15th century.

The materials of this section present glimpses of the urban process in various stages of its development. Selections from secondary documentation indicate such developments as the nature of the urban revival, the communal struggles, and the search for stability which, in many areas, led to despotism. Contemporary eye-witness accounts provide an insight into the way of life of the time, and the manifestations of corporate privilege and order.

Medieval Towns in Germany

Medieval city life in Germany as described by K. Lamprecht in *Deutsche Geschicte* (1886).

> In the glorious days of the medieval towns, say in the second half of the fourteenth century, when a traveler approached a large city, its very appearance suggested to him that he had reached his journey's end. Proudly and almost boastingly the silhouette of the city rose from the horizon, with its turrets and towers, its chapels and churches. Even then, from outside, the cities showed the same elevation that is familiar to us from the great woodcuts which have come down from the first decades of the sixteenth century, although in the latter the perspective is somewhat idealized.
>
> First of all, its strong fortifications impressed the traveler. The narrow city limits included normally the old city market and often a much larger territory. All of this was embraced in the fortifica-

tion. Its boundaries were surrounded by ramparts and a wall with a ditch in front. This was often strengthened still more by so-called hedges and widely projecting watch-towers at regular intervals. Even when the ramparts were less strongly fortified, there was at least a beacon with a wide outlook. Here a guard kept watch, and by signals communicated his information to the garrison within the city. Frequently these beacons were buildings of great extent and beautiful proportions. There are still some which adorn all the country round about, like the beacon at Andernach. In the larger cities the commander of the beacon directed an extensive system of communications that extended beyond the limits of the city's territory, and at times assumed the form of a secret service.

When the stranger was admitted through the barricade at the outposts and approached the city more closely, he might well be astonished, even in the smaller cities, by the extent of the fortifications and mass of towers which surrounded the city, especially at the gates. Until well into the twelfth century the walls of even the larger cities had been simple enough. Earlier, at least on the Rhine, the old Roman walls had given sufficient protection, until they were destroyed by the assault of the enemy or sacrificed to the internal need for building-space when the city's area was enlarged. Then simple walls of earth, crowned by palisades, with fortifications at the gate, had sufficed. But since the twelfth century the larger, and since the thirteenth the smaller, cities had done more. Funds were collected everywhere "for the work of the city." Everywhere the citizen sought permission from the lord of the city to raise a special tax for building purposes; sometimes they asked the monasteries in the city to contribute. Thus they built with relatively small means, often for generations, but almost always with stubborn energy. From the old earthen wall rose arch upon arch, and these arches supported the new walls, which often reached the respectable height of twenty-five to thirty feet. And while the walls were raised, the ditches were at the same time deepened and broadened and a glacis was thrown up with the dirt which had been excavated. There were few gates in the walls, and these usually opened only upon the chief streets. They were considered the most dangerous points in the fortifications, and therefore were made especially strong. The gate was built with a pointed arch, and flanked on each side by a strong tower. Not infrequently the whole was included in a new defense extending to the city proper. There were also a drawbridge and a portcullis behind its ironbound gate. Thus a regular castle developed at the gate, especially in the north. When bricks were used it became a splendid building. For this reason the commanders of the several gates were called burggraves in most cities. Paid soldiers, often nobles from the surrounding country, but always men trained to arms whose business was war, were expressly engaged by the city council. They furnished a small garrison for the gate: the watchman who stood on the lead roof of the gate tower and in case of danger blew his horn; the gatekeepers, common soldiers, who were always present to manage affairs at the gate and under some circumstances had to help the officials who collected the tolls; lastly, as it often happened that a jail was connected with the gate, they supplied keepers for the prisoners whom the city councilors had lodged beneath the tower.

In addition to this regular garrison, which was remarkably small, there were usually, in times of peace, only a few guards posted along the city wall. These were chosen from the citizens and relieved every day. It was their duty to make the rounds of the wall regularly, especially during the night; for this service a path was made along the inner side of the wall. But it was realized that such an arrangement was very unsatisfactory. Making a path necessitated the acquisition of expensive land, and the guards could see, on their rounds, little or nothing of what went on outside the walls. The idea of placing the walk on the wall itself readily occurred to them. For this reason they either made the wall broad enough to have a path behind the battlements which crowned it, or else built a wooden walk on supports at the top of the battlements.

While they thus obtained the desired security for the watchmen on duty, careful rules were made for calling all the citizens to arms. For military purposes most cities were divided into quarters, each of which had its own place of assembly in case of alarm; gathering in these places, they hastened to defend the walls. About every hundred and twenty feet, following the old usage of the long hundred, the wall was interrupted by small towers (as, for example, at Wisby) which were open on the side toward the city and frequently had scarcely any roof; but where the path for the guards crossed them there was a vaulted chamber which contained a regular arsenal of catapults, bows and arrows, as well as covered steps leading to the top of the wall. Here the troops stationed at the different parts of the wall got their weapons, and issuing forth, appeared unexpectedly on the battlements wherever an attack was made.

In times of peace any one who looked out over the country from these battlements enjoyed a very delightful view. In the foreground of the ivy-covered walls of the city the most intensive agriculture was practised. Here plants grown for commercial purposes flourished, and cultivation with the spade took the place of the ruder plowing. In the level country beyond, the three-field system, employing only a small number of cattle, imposed almost insuperable obstacles to anything more than meager cultivation. Even the largest cities still retained some traces of cultivation in common on a large scale; everywhere there were forests belonging to the city community as a whole, as well as commons to which the cattle of the citizens were driven each morning; and there were city herdsmen and field watchmen appointed by the councilors. But as fast as individual citizens acquired a private property in the neighborhood of the city, cultivation with the spade spread more and more. Here arose vineyards and vegetable and rose gardens; hops, flax, and woad were planted. And, a thing that may at first view appear remarkable, inside the city, near the walls, there was in many parts the same prospect as outside, especially in the most important and rapidly growing cities which had extended their walls. Within the city walls there were also vineyards and cherry orchards, vegetable and flower gardens; and skirting them, broad, dirty streets, with little houses filled with the poor agriculturists, and stately manure-heaps in front.

The aspect of the cities is explained by the fact that it was not so very long since they had broken away from the system of *natural economy* which had prevailed exclusively up to that time; the traces of their earlier life, when they had been merely larger and more prosperous villages, still clung to them. Most cities were still to a very great extent engaged in agriculture; at Coblenz, in the second half of the thirteenth century, work on the city walls had to be given up during harvest-time, because of the lack of workmen; at Frankfort in the year 1387 the city employed four herdsmen and six field-guards, and even in the fifteenth century a strict law was enacted against allowing pigs to run about in the city streets. Even in the largest cities there are very many indications of the activities of a widely extended population engaged in agriculture. Cattle-breeding and gardening were actively engaged in along with manufacturing and trade; in fact, the former had their own location in the country before the gates, as well as in the parts of the city which lay nearest the walls.

Manufacturing and trade, on the contrary, were located near the center. Here the guilds often dwelt together in narrow lanes with shops opening upon the street; here by the river or some other road the merchants thronged to the warehouses; here little shops of the retail dealers were snuggled in every corner. In walking through this portion, in the very heart of the city, somewhere around the market and city hall, one often came upon a few streets shut off by wooden doors, with only a few entrances and very compactly built up; that was the Jewish quarter. Here the Jews' school, the synagogue, stood in the midst of the congregation; until the middle of the fourteenth century it was often a splendid Roman or early Gothic building, with peculiar Oriental traces of a mixed style; here the bishop of the Jews ruled with his elders and kept one of the keys with which the doors of the quarter were locked at night to protect from the rage of the populace the Jews, who were considered hostile to the citizens both in economic matters and because of their race.

It was no accident that, in the medieval towns, the kinds and locations of the citizens' activities were distributed in this way. The results of historical evolution can easily be recognized in the fact that the activities in trade and manufacturing, which are peculiarly characteristic of a city, were situated at the center; and that, on the other hand, agricultural occupations were carried on in the outer portion of the city's area. Until some time in the thirteenth century most of the cities had been small. In the west they were often surrounded by the walls of an old Roman city which had grown out of a camp; in the east, recently founded on a small spot of ground, they were scarcely more than large castles. This narrow area was almost the only scene of earnest industrial activity and extensive intercourse with foreign parts. But about this center, later known as the old city, religious societies established themselves very early and acquired widely extended possessions; sometimes there were more than a half-dozen monasteries and cloisters and a bishop's seat, too, which with their property surrounded and sometimes crossed the center of the city. When the development of city life began in the twelfth and thirteenth centuries, the old walls were destroyed; generally the area of the cities began to be extended; and usually the new fortifications were placed beyond the circle in which the clerical property was situated. Thus the rural population was brought into the city; it was a long time before they gave up their old occupations and mode of life; indeed, they were strong enough to create outside of the city walls new groups of fruit and vegetable gardens. In time, to be sure, the space, between the walls and the center of the city, which had once been covered with gardens, was filled with streets, and again the suburbs of the city began to extend beyond the gates. But the movement in this direction no longer proceeded from the lords of the old ecclesiastical property: they had fallen long before; now it was rather the business interests of the city itself which caused a new settlement at this point. Before the gates, especially in the neighborhood of a much frequented bridge, suburbs extended in long rows of streets, with low hovels, some of which were inhabited by rough people with interests which were partly rural and partly urban; these often found expression in a special government for the community. These were by no means the pleasantest portions of the city; here were the retail trades in their most humble forms and the pawnshops; here the fortune-tellers and "wise women" lived and boasted of their occupations; here the vagabonds and criminals had come when, by the extension of the city they had been driven out of their caves under the city walls, and with them all sorts of evil-livers; here, too, in the case of cities which made cloth on a large scale, the great mass of the poor weavers lived.

It was the dregs of the population that lived in a suburb. Its separation from the city, in the course of the fourteenth century, shows that from this time we can date the completion of one stage in the development of the city's population. **20**

French Towns

From Paul Lacroix's description of *Manners, Customs and Dress during the Middle Ages and during the Renaissance Period* (1874) we get a picture of the French town.

On the fall of the Roman Empire commerce was rendered insecure, and, indeed, it was almost completely put a stop to by the barbarian invasions, and all facility of communication between different nations, and even between towns of the same country was interrupted. In those times of social confusion, there were periods of which poverty and distress, that for want of money commerce was reduced to the simple exchange of the positive necessities of life. When order was a little restored, and society and the minds of people became more composed we see commerce recovering its position; and France was, perhaps, the only country in Europe in which this happy change took place. Those southern cities of Gaul, which ancient authors describe to us as so rich and so industrious, quickly recovered their former prosperity, and the friendly relations which were established between the kings of the Franks and the Levant Empire encouraged the Gallic cities in cultivating a commerce, which was at that time the most important and most extensive in the world.

Marseilles, the ancient Phoenician colony, once the rival and then the successor to Carthage, was undoubtedly at the head of the commercial cities of France. Next to her came Arles, which supplied ship-builders and seamen to the fleet of Provence; and Narbonne, which admitted into its harbour ships from Spain, Sicily, and Africa, until, in consequence of the Aude having changed its course, it was obliged to relinquish the greater part of its maritime commerce in favour of Montpellier.

Commerce maintained frequent communications with the East; it sought its supplies on the coast of Syria, and especially at Alexandria, in Egypt, which was a king of depôt for goods obtained from the rich countries lying beyond the Red Sea. The Frank navigators imported from these countries, groceries, linen, Egyptian paper, pearls, perfumes, and a thousand other rare and choice articles. In exchange they offered chiefly the precious metals in bars rather than coined, and it is probable that at this period they also exported iron, wines, oil, and wax. The agricultural produce and manufactures of Gaul had not sufficiently developed to provide anything more than what was required for the producers themselves. Industry was as yet, if not purely domestic, confined to monasteries and to the houses of the nobility; and even the kings employed women as serf workmen to manufacture the coarse stuffs with which they clothed themselves and their households. We may add, that the bad state of the roads, the little security they offered to travellers, the extortions of all kinds to which foreign merchants were subjected, and above all the iniquitous system of fines and tolls which each landowner thought right to exact, before letting merchandise pass through his domains, all created insuperable obstacles to the development of commerce.

The Frank kings on several occasions evinced a desire that communications favourable to trade should be re-established in their dominions. We find, for instance, Chilpéric making treaties with Eastern emperors in Levant of the merchants of Agde and Marseilles, Queen Brunehaut making viaducts worthy of the Romans, and which still bear her name, and Dagobert opening at St. Denis free fairs—that is to say, free, or nearly so, from all tolls and taxes— to which goods, both agricultural and manufactured, were sent from every corner of Europe and the known world, to be afterwards distributed through the towns and provinces by the enterprise of internal commerce.

After the reign of Dagobert, commerce again declined without positively ceasing, for the revolution, which transferred the power of the kings to the mayors of the palace was not of a nature to exhaust the resources of public prosperity; and a charter of 710 proves that the merchants of Saxony, England, Normandy, and even Hungary, still flocked to the fairs of St. Denis.

Under the powerful and administrative hand of Charlemagne, the roads being better kept up, and the rivers being made more navigable, commerce became safe and more general; the coasts were protected from piratical incursions; lighthouses were erected at dangerous points, to prevent shipwrecks; and treaties of commerce with foreign nations, including even the most distant, guaranteed the liberty and security of French traders abroad.

Under the weak successors of this monarch, notwithstanding their many efforts, commerce was again subjected to all sorts of injustice and extortions, and all its safeguards were rapidly destroyed. The Moors in the south, and the Normans in the north, appeared to desire to destroy everything which came in their way, and already Marseilles, in 838, was taken and pillaged by the Greeks. The constant altercations between the sons of Louis le Débonnaire and their unfortunate father, their jealousies amongst themselves, and their fratricidal wars, increased the measure of public calamity, so that soon, overrun by foreign enemies and destroyed by her own sons, France became a vast field of disorder and desolation.

The Church, which alone possessed some social influence, never ceased to use its authority in endeavouring to remedy this miserable state of things; but episcopal edicts, papal anathemas, and decrees of councils, had only a partial effect at this unhappy period. At any moment agricultural and commercial operations were liable to be interrupted, if not completely ruined, by the violence of a wild and rapacious soldiery; at every step the roads, often impassable, were intercepted by toll-bars for some due of a vexatious nature, besides being continually infested by bands of brigands, who carried off the merchandise and murdered those few merchants who were so bold as to attempt to continue their business. It was the Church, occupied as she was with the interests of civilization, who again assisted commerce to emerge from the state of annihilation into which it had fallen; and the "Peace or Truce of God," established in 1041, endeavoured to stop at least the internal wars of feudalism, and it succeeded, at any rate for a time, in arresting these disorders. This was all that could be done at this period, and the Church accomplished it, by taking the high hand; and with as much unselfishness as energy and courage, she regulated society, which had been abandoned by the civil power from sheer impotence and want of administrative capability.

At all events, thanks to ecclesiastical foresight, which increased the number of fairs and markets at the gates of abbeys and convents, the first step was made towards the general resuscitation of commerce. Indeed, the Church may be said to have largely contributed to develop the spirit of progress and liberty, whence were to spring societies and nationalities, and, in a word, modern organization.

The Eastern commerce furnished the first elements of that trading activity which showed itself on the borders of the Mediterranean, and we find the ancient towns of Provence and Languedoc springing up again by the side of the republics of Amalfi, Venice, Genoa, and Pisa, which had become the rich depôts of all maritime trade.

At first, as we have already stated, the wares of India came to Europe through the Greek port of Alexandria, or through Constantinople. The Crusades, which had facilitated the relations with Eastern countries, developed a taste in the West for their indigenous productions, gave a fresh vigour to this foreign commerce, and rendered it more productive by removing the stumbling blocks which had arrested its progress.

The conquest of Palestine by the Crusaders had first opened all the towns and harbours of this wealthy region to Western traders, and many of them were able permanently to establish themselves there, with all sorts of privileges and exemptions from taxes, which were gladly offered to them by the nobles who had transferred feudal power to Mussulman territories.

Ocean commerce assumed from the moment proportions hitherto unknown. Notwithstanding the papal bulls and decrees, which forbade Christians from having any connection with infidels, the voice of interest was more listened to than that of the church, and traders did not fear to disobey the political and religious orders which forbade them to carry arms and slaves to the enemies of the faith.

It was easy to foretell, from the very first, that the military occupation of the Holy Land would not be permanent. In consequence of this, therefore, the nearer the loss of this fine conquest seemed to be, the greater were the efforts made by the maritime towns of the West to re-establish, on a more solid and lasting basis, a commercial alliance with Egypt, the country which they selected to replace Palestine, in a mercantile point of view. Marseilles was the greatest supporter of this intercourse with Egypt; and in the twelfth and thirteenth centuries she reached a very high position, which she owed to her shipowners and traders. In the fourteenth century, however, the prices of the house of Anjou ruined her like the rest of Provence, in the great and fruitless efforts which they made to recover the kingdom of Naples; and it was not until the reign of Louis XI. that the old Phoenician city recovered its maritime and commercial prosperity.

Languedoc, depressed, and for a time nearly ruined in the thirteenth century by the effect of the wars of the Albigenses, was enabled, subsequently, to recover itself. Béziers, Agde, Narbonne, and especially Montpellier, so quickly established important trading connections with all the ports of the Mediterranean, that at the end of the fourteenth century consuls were appointed at each of these towns, in order to protect and direct their transmarine commerce. A traveller of the twelfth century, Benjamin de Tudèle, relates that in these ports, which were afterwards called the stepping stones to the Levant, every language in the world might be heard.

Toulouse was soon on a par with the towns of Lower Languedoc, and the Garonne poured into the markets, not only the produce of Guienne, and of the western parts of France, but also those of Flanders, Normandy, and England. We may observe, however, that Bordeaux, although placed in a most advantageous position, at the mouth of the river, only possessed, where under the English dominion, a very limited commerce, principally confined to the export of wines to Great Britain in exchange for corn, oil, &c.

La Rochelle, on the same coast, was much more flourishing at this period, owing to the numerous coasters which carried the wines of Aunis and Saintonge, and the salt of Brouage to Flanders, the Netherlands, and the north of Germany. Vité already had its silk manufactories in the fifteenth century, and Nantes gave promise of her future greatness as depôt of maritime commerce. It was about this time also that the fisheries became a new industry, in which Bayonne and a few villages on the sea-coast took the lead, some being especially engaged in whaling, and others in the rod and herring fisheries.

Long before this, Normandy had depended on other branches of trade for its commercial prosperity. Its fabrics of woolen stuffs, its arms and cutlery, besides the agricultural productions of its fertile and well cultivated soil, each furnished material for export on a large scale.

The towns of Rouen and Caen were especially manufacturing cities, and were very rich. This was the case with Rouen particularly, which was situated on the Seine, and was at that time an extensive depôt for provisions and other merchandise which was sent down the river for export, or was imported for future internal consumption. Already Paris, the abode of kings, and the metropolis of government, began to foreshadow the immense development which it was destined to undergo, by becoming the centre of commercial affairs, and by daily adding to its labouring and mercantile population.

It was, however, outside the walls of Paris that commerce, which needed liberty as well as protection, at first progressed most rapidly. The northern provinces had early united manufacturing industry with traffic, and this double source of local prosperity was the origin of their enormous wealth. Ghent and Bruges in the Low Countries, and Beauvaias and Arras, were celebrated for their manufacture of clothes, carpets, and serge, and Cambrai for its fine cloths. The artizans and merchants of these industrious cities then established their powerful corporations, whose unwearied energy gave rise to that commercial freedom so favourable to trade.

More important than the woollen manufactures—for the greater part of the wool used was brought from England—was the manufacture of flax, inasmuch as it encouraged agriculture, the raw material being produced in France. This first flourished in the northeast of France, and spread slowly to Picardy, to Beauvois, and Brittany. The central countries, with the exception of Bruges, whose cloth manufactories were already celebrated in the fifteenth century, remained essentially agricultural; and their principal towns were merely depôts for imported goods. The institution of fairs, however, rendered, it is true, this commerce of some of the towns as widespread as it was productive. In the Middle Ages religious feasts and ceremonials almost always gave rise to fairs, which commerce was not slow in multiplying as much as possible. The merchants naturally came to exhibit their goods where the largest concourse of people afforded the greatest promise of their readily disposing of them. As early as the first dynasty of Merovingian kings, temporary and periodical markets of this kind existed, but except at St. Denis, articles of local consumption only were brought to them. The reasons for this were, the heavy taxes which were levied by the feudal lords on all merchandise exhibited for sale, and the danger which foreign merchants ran of being plundered on their way, or even at the fair itself. These causes for a long time delayed the progress of an institution which was afterwards destined to become so useful and beneficial to all classes of the community.

We have several times mentioned the famous fair of Landit, which is supposed to have been established by Charlemagne, but which no doubt was a sort of revival of the fairs of St. Denis, founded by Dagobert, and which for a time had fallen into disuse in the midst of the general ruin which preceded that emperor's reign. This fair of Landit was renowned over the whole of Europe, and attracted merchants from all countries. It was held in the month of June, and only lasted fifteen days. Goods of all sorts, both of home and foreign manufacture, were sold, but the sale of parchment was the principal object of the fair, to purchase a supply of which the University of Paris regularly went in procession. On account of its special character, this fair was of less general importance than the six others, which from the twelfth century were held at Troyes, Provins, Lagny-sur-marne, Rheims, and Bar-sur-Aube. These infused so much commercial vitality into the province of Champagne, that the nobles for the most part shook off the prejudice which forbad their entering into any sort of trading association.

Fairs multiplied in the centre and in the south of France simultaneously. Those of Puy-en-Velay, now the capital of the Haute-Loire, are looked upon as the most ancient, and they preserved their old reputation and attracted a considerable concourse of people, which was also increased by the pilgrimages then made to Notre-Dame du Puy. These fairs, which were more of a religious than of a commercial character, were then of less importance as regards trade than those held at Beaucaire. This town rose to great repute in the thirteenth century, and, with the Lyons market, became at that time the largest centre of commerce in the southern provinces. Placed at the junction of the Saône and the Rhône, Lyons owed its commercial development to the proximity of Marseilles and the town of Italy. Its four annual fairs were always much frequented, and when the kings of France transferred to it the privileges of the fairs of Champagne, and transplanted to within its walls the silk manufactories formerly established at Tours, Lyons really became the second city of France.

Measures of length and contents often differed much from one another, although they might be similarly named, and it would require very complicated comparative tables approximately to fix their value. The *pied de re* was from ten to twelve inches, and was the least varying measure. The fathom differed much in different parts, and in the attempt to determine the relations between the innumerable measures of contents which we find recorded—a knowledge of which must have been necessary for the commerce of the period—we are stopped by a labyrinth of incomprehensible calculations, which it is impossible to determine with any degree of certainty.

The weights were more uniform and less uncertain. The pound was everywhere in use, but it was not everywhere of the same standard. For instance, at Paris it weighed sixteen ounces, whereas at Lyons it only weighed fourteen; and in weighing silk fifteen ounces to the pound was the rule. At Toulouse and in Upper Languedoc the pound was only thirteen and a half ounces; at Marseilles, thirteen ounces; and at other places it even fell to twelve ounces. There was in Paris a public scale called *poids du roi;* but this scale, though a most important means of revenue, was a great hindrance to retail trade.

In spite of these petty and irritation impediments, the commerce of France extended throughout the whole world.

The compass—known in Italy as early as the twelfth century the mercantile navy to discover new routes, and it was thus that true maritime commerce may be said regularly to have begun. The sailors of the Mediterranean, with the help of this little instrument, dared to pass the Straits of Gibraltar, and to venture on the ocean. From that moment commercial intercourse, which had previously only existed by land, and that with great difficulty, was permanently established between the northern and southern harbours of Europe.

Flanders was the central port for merchant vessels, which arrived in great numbers from the Mediterranean, and Bruges became the principal depôt. The Teutonic league, the origin of which dates from the thirteenth century, and which formed the most powerful confederacy recorded in history, also sent innumerable vessels from its harbours of Lubeck and Hamburg. These carried the merchandise of the northern countries into Flanders, and this rich province, which excelled in every branch of industry, and especially in those relating to metals and weaving, became the great market of Europe.

The commercial movement, formerly limited to the shores of the Mediterranean, extended to all parts, and gradually became universal. The northern states shared in it, and England, which for a long time kept aloof from a stage on which it was destined to play the first part, began to give indications of its future commercial greatness. The number of transactions increased as the facility for carrying them on became greater. Consumption being extended, production progressively followed, and so commerce went on gaining strength as it widened its sphere. Everything, in fact, seemed to contribute to its expansion. The downfall of the feudal system and the establishment in each country of a central power, more or less strong and respected, enabled it to extend its operations by land with a degree of security hitherto unknown; and, at the same time, international legislation came in to protect maritime trade, which was still exposed to great dangers. The sea, which was open freely to the whole human race, gave robbers comparatively easy means of following their nefarious practices, and with less fear of punishment than they could obtain on the shore of civilized countries. For this reason piracy continued its depredations long after the enactment of severe laws for its suppression.

This maritime legislation did not wait for the sixteenth century to come into existence. Maritime law was promulgated more or less in the twelfth century, but the troubles and agitations which weakened and disorganized empires during that period of the Middle Ages, deprived it of its power and efficiency. The *Code des Rhodiens* dates as far back as 1167; the *Code de la Mer*, which became a sort of recognised text-book, dates from the same period; the *Lois d'oléron* is anterior to the twelfth century, and ruled the western coasts of France, being also adopted in Flanders and in England; Venice dated her most ancient law on maritime rights from 1255, and the Statutes of Marseilles date from 1254.

The period of the establishment of commercial law and justice corresponds with that of the introduction of national and universal codes of law and consular jurisdiction. These may be said to have originated in the sixth century in the laws of the Visigoths, which empowered foreign traders to be judged by delegates from their own countries. The Venetians had consuls in the Greek empire as early as the tenth century, and we may fairly presume that the French had consuls in Palestine during the reign of Charlemagne. In the thirteenth century the towns of Italy had consular agents in France; and Marseilles had them in Savoy, in Arles, and in Genoa. Thus traders of each country were always sure of finding justice, assistance, and protection in all the centres of European commerce.

Numerous facilities for barter were added to these advantages. Merchants, who at first travelled with their merchandise, and who afterwards merely sent a factor as their representative, finally consigned it to foreign agents. Communication by correspondence in this way became more general, and paper replaced parchment as being less rare and less expensive. The introduction of Arabic figures, which were more convenient than the Roman numerals for making calculations, the establishment of banks, of which the most ancient was in operation in Venice as early as the twelfth century, the invention of bills of exchange, attributed to the Jews, and generally in use in the thirteenth century, the establishment of insurance against the risks and perils of sea and land, and lastly, the formation of trading companies, or what are now called partnerships, all tended to give expansion and activity to commerce, whereby public and private wealth was increased in spite of obstacles which routine, envy, and ill-will persistently raised against great commercial enterprises.

For a long time the French, through indolence or antipathy—for it was more to their liking to be occupied with arms and chivalry than with matters of interest and profit—took but a feeble part in the trade which was carried on so successfully on their own territory. The nobles were ashamed to mix in commerce, considering it unworthy of them, and the bourgeois, for want of liberal feeling and expansiveness in their ideas, were satisfied with appropriating merely local trade. Foreign commerce, even of the most lucrative description, was handed over to foreigners, and especially to Jews, who were often banished from the kingdom and as frequently ransomed, though universally despised and hated. Notwithstanding this, they succeeded in rising to wealth under the stigma of shame and infamy, and the immediate gains which they realised by means of usury reconciled them to, and consoled them for, the ill-treatment to which they were subjected.

At a very early period, and especially when the Jews had been absolutely expelled, the advantage of exclusively trading with and securing the rich profits from France had attracted the Italians, who were frequently only Jews in disguise, concealing themselves as to their character under the generic name of Lombards. It was under this name that the French kings gave them on different occasions various privileges, when they frequented the fairs of Champagne and came to establish themselves in the inland and seaport towns. These Italians constituted the great corporation of money-changers in Paris, and hoarded in their coffers all the coin of the kingdom, and in this way caused a perpetual variation in the value of money, by which they themselves benefited.

From 1365 to 1382 factories and warehouses were founded by Norman navigators on the western coast of Africa, in Senegal and Guinea. Numerous fleets of merchantmen, of great size for those days, were employed in transporting cloth, grain of all kinds, knives, brandy, salt, and other merchandise, which were bartered for leather, ivory, gum, amber, and gold dust. Considerable profits were realised by the shipowners and merchants, who, like Jacques Coeur, employed ships for the purpose of carrying on these large and lucrative commercial operations. These facts sufficiently testify the condition of France at this period, and prove that this, like other branches of human industry, was arrested in its expansion by the political troubles which followed in the fourteenth and fifteenth centuries Fortunately these social troubles were not universal, and it was just at the period when France was struggling and had become exhausted and impoverished that the Portuguese extended their discoveries on the same coast of Africa, and soon after succeeded in rounding the Cape of Good Hope, and opening a new maritime road to India, a country which was always attractive from the commercial advantage which it offered.

Some years after, Christopher Columbus, the Genoese, more daring and more fortunate still, guided by the compass and impelled by his own genius, discovered a new continent, the fourth continent of the world. This unexpected event, the greatest and most remarkable of the age, necessarily enlarged the field for produce as well as for consumption to an enormous extent, and naturally added, not only to the variety and quantity of exchangeable wares, but also to the production of the precious metals, and brought about a complete revolution in the laws of the whole civilised world.

Maritime commerce immediately acquired an extraordinary development, and merchants, forsaking the harbours of the Mediterranean, and even those of the Levant, which then seemed to them scarcely worthy of notice, sent their vessels by thousands upon the ocean in pursuit of the wonderful riches of the New World. The day of caravans and coasting had passed; Venice had lost its splendour; the sway of the Mediterranean was over; the commerce of the world was suddenly transferred from the active and industrious towns of that sea, which had so long monopolized it, to the Western nations, the Portuguese and Spaniards first, and then to the Dutch and English.

21

The Rise of Towns

French historians (A. Giry and A. Reville) explored the rise of towns and the rise of the urban middle class in their work on the *Emancipation of the Medieval Towns.*

> The history of the towns and of urban civilization during the first centuries of the middle ages is little known; indeed it would be truer to say that it is almost entirely unknown. The meager documents which these times have left us touch only the greater political events, the history of kings and of the more prominent characters; as to the fate of the people, the anonymous masses, they give us but rare and vague ideas. Nevertheless, though explicit statements are lacking, we may see in part what was the lot of the urban groups and of the individuals who composed them.
> The Roman Empire bequeathed to the middle ages a goodly number of towns. Of these the most important by reason of population, wealth, and rank, were the cities. There were about one hundred and twelve such towns in ancient Gaul. Other towns, called *castra,* were simply fortified places. The cities, which for a long time had enjoyed a considerable degree of freedom, possessed municipal institutions; but this régime, under oppressive action of the fisc and of an overwhelming centralization, was in full disintegration as early as the fourth century, even before the invasions had precipitated the fall of the Empire. In the anarchy which followed the arrival of the Barbarians, nothing remained standing of all this structure, for no one was interested in preserving it. The Roman municipal régime expired.
> What, then, became of the cities? In most of them a certain personage soon distinguished himself among the inhabitants and gained over them an undisputed preeminence: this was the bishop. He was no longer simply the first priest of his town, he was its lord. As early as the end of the seventh century, perhaps before, Tours was under the rule of its bishop. Thus it was that most of the old Roman cities became, in the middle ages, episcopal seigniories. This was the case with Amiens, Laon, Beauvais, and many others.

All, however, did not have the same fate. Some, in consequence of wars, or of partitions, passed into the hands of lay princes. Angers belonged to the court of Anjoy, Bordeaux to the duke of Aquitaine; Orleans and Paris were directly under the king. Elsewhere, beside the old city where the bishop ruled, there sprang up a new town, the bourg, which was under another lord, lay or ecclesiastical: thus at Marseilles the city was under the bishop, and the town under the viscount. In the same way the bourg was distinguished from the city at Arles, Narbonne, Toulouse, and Tours. Other places again, pillaged, ruined, and depopulated, lost their rank as towns and were reduced to simple villages, or were even blotted out. London, after the English invasions, was a heap of ruins, and the courses of the old Roman roads which intersected it were so completely obscured that the new streets, marked out in the same directions when the town was reviving in the middle ages, no longer coincided with them. . . .

Such are the vague ideas which we possess concerning the political changes in the Roman towns at the beginning of the middle ages: with so much the more reason do we know nothing of the history of the small towns, of the simple fortified bourgs, which were built in great numbers at the end of the Empire. All must have come to constitute seigniories, but we do not know how this transformation took place.

We might expect then to find at the dawn of the eleventh century only a small number of towns, shattered and fallen remnants of the ancient cities and bourgs surviving in a new age. But while these lived on obscurely down to the time when they were to reappear in public life, there were groups of more recent origin which had sprung up on all sides. The numerous domains into which the land had been divided under Roman domination met various fates. Although most of these domains were sparsely settled and became later simple rural parishes, others attracted immigrants who grouped themselves in large numbers under the shadow of the seigniorial castle or abbey; and on their sites future towns formed slowly. Such domains, nameless in the sixth century, had become important centers in the eleventh. Examples are numerous. In the southern provinces, Montpellier and Montauban; in the northern, Bruges, Ghent, Lille; in the central, Blois, Chateaudun, and Etampes grew up around castles. More numerous still, especially in the north, were the towns which owed their origin to the protection of an abbey. Such were Saint-Denis, Saint-Omer, Saint-Valey, Remiremont, Münster, Weissenburg, Redon, Condom, Aurillac, and many others.

It is uncertain at just what time and under what circumstances the movement of concentration was brought about; but it is probable that a variety of causes called it forth. The assurance of finding under the protection of certain seigniors a paternal government, security, impartial justice, and other similar guaranties, must certainly have attracted to their domains a host of peasants in search of better conditions, and this explains perhaps the fortune of many small ecclesiastical bourgs. "There is good living under the cross," runs an old saying. Elsewhere it was a clever expedient of the lords, like the establishing of a market, which brought strangers upon their lands, and instead of a simple castle there soon appeared a town. Such is the history of Cateau-Cambrésis. Among the most important of these causes, however were the Norman invasions, which, for a century laid waste the country, ruined the peasants, and drove them within fortified walls. The most interesting example of this cause is the origin of Saint-Omer. In the ninth century, as a simple abbey under the protection of Saint Bertin, it was devastated twice in succession, in 860 and 878, together with the region which surrounded it. Taught by experience, the monks surrounded their monastery by walls, so that when the Normans returned the third time in 891, the abbey was in position to resist them. This domain was settled so rapidly that by the tenth century the former monastery had become a town.

To-day, of more than five hundred French towns hardly eighty date back to the Gallo-Roman period; the others are for the most part fortified villages. The generic name which is given them is simply the Latin word *villa*, which means rural domain.

Care should be taken not to overestimate the importance of the urban communities during the first centuries of the middle ages. They were more numerous than important, and it is probable that they were neither very populous nor very rich. In a backward state of civilization it is impossible for towns to develop. A large city can live only by the exchange of its products for those things which it does not produce but which are brought to it. Without commerce there can be no large cities. Now, in that obscure age which extends from the fifth to the tenth century, all commerce was reduced to an indispensable minimum, except during an ephemeral renaissance in the time of Charlemagne. Only the shores of the Mediterranean continued to be frequented by merchants, and the relations between Provence, Italy, Greece, and the Orient were never entirely broken. In consequence, the cities of that privileged region preserved, it seems, a commercial class and a certain degree of prosperity. Everywhere else commerce was nearly annihilated, because there was neither the security nor the centers of exchange which it needed. Each domain lived upon itself, was almost self-sufficient; made the iron, wood, and woolen articles it needed, as well as produced its own wheat. The towns probably did the same; they were rural bourgs, and the inhabitants were peasants who worked on the surrounding land. Besides, custom did not aid in their development. Kings, nobles, Gallo-Roman and Germanic proprietors preferred to live in the country; the towns were no longer the theater of great events.

It is difficult to form a clear picture of the urban groups at that time and of the people that composed them. The new small towns huddled around the castles, abbeys, and churches. The old cities, once spacious, razed their former suburbs and restricted their limits so as to have less area to defend, as at Paris, Bordeaux, Evreaux, Poitiers, and Sens. Roman monuments are discovered to-day outside the enclosures which these towns made for themselves at the time of the invasions. All towns, whenever possible, encircled themselves with ramparts, with embattled walls surrounded by moats, and armed their counterscarps with traps, abatis, and palisades. Inside the city the population, although not numerous, must have lived crowded together, as the architecture of the houses shows. The Roman dwelling was spread out in a comfortable way, with large inner court, the atrium, and was generally low. Now the atrium was given up, filled in, and the roof rose high over a series of stories, which perhaps already were built so as to overhang, to gain still more room. As for monuments, the only ones which adorned the towns were those which the Romans had left. And sometimes even these were appropriated to strange uses, like the temple of Vesuna at Perigueux, which was changed into a tower for purposes of defense, or like the circus of Nimes, which sheltered a part of the inhabitants and formed a veritable "quarter." Sometimes, too, these monuments were destroyed that the materials might be used for other constructions, especially for fortifications.

Between the church and the seigniorial dwelling, which was usually built to one side upon a precipitous hill or upon an artificial mound, the townsman passed his monotonous life, happy when a private war or an incursion for pillage did not bring upon his house or upon him the horrors of assault. Of political rights, he had none. The lord or his officers ruled the inhabitants as master, imposed dues upon them, arrested, and judged them. The civil condition of the inhabitants must also have grown harder. It seems, indeed, that the number of freemen had noticeably diminished in the towns as well as in the country. Perhaps the cities of the south, thanks to their privileged situation, may have escaped in part this social decline; but this decline was general in the north, where only those preserved their independence who made it their business to bear arms in the following of a seignior and to live at the expense of others.

Thus from the sixth to the tenth century, townsmen did not count in society, Bishop Adalberon, in a famous poem to King Robert, considered around him only two classes: churchmen and nobles, beneath whom, but very far beneath, were the commons who worked. . . .

There came a day when the towns demanded of their lords guaranties against the arbitrary exploitation of which they were victims; when certain of them demanded and obtained a relative autonomy; when those serfs and commons that bishop Adalberon looked down upon with scorn, treated with their masters upon an equal footing. This movement of emancipation of the towns, which extended throughout western Europe from the end of the tenth century to the thirteenth, has received the name of the communal revolution. . . .

The real cause of the emancipation of the towns . . . lay in the economic and social transformation which was taking place from the tenth to the twelfth century, in the revival of labor and of production in all its forms, which was then stirring Europe. From the end of the tenth century, the feudal world was in process of organization; in the midst of the universal parceling, a relative degree of order prevailed; there was no longer the anarchy of former times, and each lord endeavored to organize and exploit his fief for his best interests: new markets were opened; relations were established between town and town. Traffickers multiplied and ventured far from the walls which protected them; men began again to exchange commodities: local commerce was reestablished. At the same time, the society which had been languishing in the villages and bourgs contracted the taste for travel and adventure, for pilgrimages even to the Holy Land; the world grew larger; the horizon of men's minds broadened; relations were opened between the north and the south, between the occident and the orient; commerce on a large scale was revived. The result upon the towns was immediately felt. Necessarily poor and weak when there was no commerce, they now grew in wealth and population. The inhabitants soon became able to resist their lords. The best proof in support of this explanation is that the path of emancipation followed exactly the great commercial currents of the time. The first towns were the cities of Italy; then came the towns of the Rhine,—that great highway of commerce which united northern Europe with the Mediterranean,—and the principal places of Flanders, Hainault, and Picardy, that is to say, the principal commercial centers of the middle ages. And it was the merchants who directed the communal revolution in each town: their associations were the cradles of the communes and often their place of meeting, their gild-hall, the cloth-hall as at Beauvais, Ypres, and Arras, was the first town hall.

But, it will be asked, how could the townspeople everywhere be organized against their lords: How could they be grouped thus in opposition to the powers over them? The reason is that everywhere the towns were suffering from the same evils. The preambles of the charters of the communes give most eloquent testimony on the subject. Louis VII confirmed the commune of Nantes "because of the excessive oppression under which the poor were groaning." The counts of Ponthieu assured liberties to the towns of Abbeville and Doullens, "to free them from the wrongs and exactions which the townspeople continued to suffer at the hands of the lords of the land." The evils which these documents signalize were without doubt of long standing; they must have called forth complaints for a long time. But when there came to be in each urban community a merchant aristocracy, wealthy, bold, and capable of consecrating its resources to the work of common emancipation, complaints led to acts, and the revolution began.

This revolution developed very early upon the shores of the Mediterranean, in Italy and in Provence. Here the old cities had never ceased to have trade relations with the Orient; their traffic, although reduced by the universal disorganization into which Europe fell at the beginning of the middle ages, does not seem to have suffered complete interruption. Even the more recent towns attracted to themselves a portion—often considerable—of this commerce. Not only did Venice, Genoa, and Amalfi send their galleys into the Byzantine Empire, but Arles, a city of less importance, sustained with Greece relations regular enough to be mentioned as early as 921. In the eleventh and twelfth centuries, when the passion for pilgrimages and crusades spread abroad, this commerce greatly increased, not only with Constantinople but especially with the Infidel. Thus the urban communities of the south were early richer and more populous than elsewhere. In them was formed an opulent burghal class, experienced in business, capable of resisting the lords, and even of triumphing over them.

This was so much more the case because these towns, different from the northern bourgs, were inhabited not simply by common people. The small nobles also lived in them. . . . Again, the southern lords, who were more civilized, more broad-minded, and more far-sighted, took an interest, not only in war and in the crusades but also in the commerce which was enriching them while it enriched their subjects. They understood more quickly, perhaps, the advantage which there was for them in freeing the working classes, who should be more prosperous according as they were more independent, and they did show toward the efforts of the communities the savage and obstinate hostility that was seen elsewhere.

Finally, the sovereigns were far away. The king of France was not likely to interfere in favor of a vassal, such as the count of Toulouse, who might be threatened by the ambitious designs of his lesser subjects. The German emperor never appeared in Provence, and made into Italy only rapid and infrequent expeditions. In short, the most diverse circumstances united to render the emancipation of the Mediterranean towns prompt, easy, and complete.

Like that of the Italian cities, and for the same reason, the emancipation of the communities of Provence, though somewhat later, was precocious. If the Italian cities obtained full liberty as early as the eleventh century, those of southern France were only beginning their transformation at that time, and this work of emancipation, less favored by circumstances, was prolonged until the year 1200 and later. It is very difficult to fix with greater precision the time when the towns of southern France succeeded in escaping from the seigniorial despotism. One must not think that they did not enjoy any independence until they were in possession of a communal charter and of a clearly organized municipal administration; these did not come until later. The oldest charters of enfranchisement granted them date from the twelfth century and do not antedate the charters of liberties given the towns of the north. Many even were not issued before the first years of the thirteenth century. But at that time these communities had long enjoyed, in fact if not in law, incontestable privileges, and some of these must have had a very remote origin. . . .

The emancipation of the towns of central and northern France, of Germany, and of England, followed closely the emancipation of the Mediterranean cities. The first manifestations were in Flanders, on the banks of the Rhine, and in the French provinces of the northeast. As early as 957 the inhabitants of Cambrai, taking advantage of the absence of their bishop, banded together and had the audacity to shut the gates of the town in his face when he returned. In 967 the abbey of Saint Arnulf of Metz granted a charter of liberties to the bourg of Morville-sur-Seille, and some years later, in 984, it granted another to the domain of Broc. In 1003 the emperor, Henry II, recognized privileges for the bourg of Cateau-Cambrésis. Nevertheless these were rare and premature cases, and more than half a century passed before other attempts came to light. Then, however, they multiplied. Saint-Quentin conquered its title of commune before 1077, and Beauvais before 1099; Arras became independent in the course of the eleventh century; Noyon emancipated itself about 1108; Valenciennes in 1114; Amiens between 1113 and 1117; Corbie about the year 1120; Soissons about 1126; Bruges, Lille, and Saint-Omer about 1127; and Ghent and Liège a few years after. This was the heroic age of the communal revolution. From this time on the movement was accentuated; the budding desire for independence spread from town to town. The freed cities became models; their successes emboldened others. The wave reached its height in the twelfth century and in the first half of the thirteenth; then it slowly receded. It had done its work in two hundred years. The cities had obtained satisfaction. The map of feudal Europe was dotted from north to south and from east to west with independent or privileged communities. The public mind was penetrated by a new idea, that of the free town; the political vocabulary was enriched by a new word, commune.

This work of emanicipation was not carried out without great difficulties. The urban communities were less populous, less rich, and less strong in the north than upon the shores of the Mediterranean. Besides, the seigniorial class was so powerful in the north that the people there seemed incapable of making way against it. Finally, the king of France, the king of England, and the German emperor were near at hand, and it seemed certain that they would sustain their vassals energetically. . . .

Like the feudal lords and for the same reasons, the French kings, in principle, refused independence to the towns of their domain. Louis VII suppressed with severity a seditious attempt at Orleans. But upon the lands of their vassals, where they intervened as suzerains, they did not have the same reasons for declaring and enforcing their opinion. Here their policy, which was not inspired by any fixed principle, lacked clearness and continuity. Tradition formerly attributed to Louis VI the honor of having "freed the communes." Such, however, was not the case. While he confirmed a number of charters granted by the lords, on the other hand he did not hesitate to aid by his own forces barons who were struggling against rebellious communities: the bishop of Noyon, and the abbots of Saint-Riquier and Corbie. In the same year, 1112, he protected the commune of Amiens and destroyed that of Laon. Very sensitive to the attractions of gain, he sometimes offered independence to towns, but, money in hand, he was ready to turn against them, if later he found it to his advantage. Upon the square of Laon, over which the bishop and the people were disputing, his support was literally bid off at auction. His successor, Louis VII, apparently saw more clearly that communes upon the lands of vassals whom he feared were natural allies of the crown in the camp of the enemy, and that it was to his interest to aid in their development. If he protected the rights of the archbishops of Rheims and of Sens, of the bishops of

Beauvais, Chalons-sur-Marne, Soissons, of the abbots of Tournus and of Corbie, on the other hand he multiplied the concessions of charters and sustained the emancipated towns against the hostility of the lords. Philip Augustus, accentuating this policy, confirmed charters granted by others, and he even freed a number of communities in the district which he united to the crown, and even in the domain. But he made them pay for his support, and he imposed upon them his protection, giving out liberties with one hand while with the other he extended royal supremacy.

This systematic benevolence was tardy, for the communal revolution was by that date drawing to a close. So it may be said, in résumé that in the beginning the towns met a universal resistance, which in some cases was never done away with but in others was weakened or transformed at the bidding of interest. . . .

In this common work of enfranchisement the lot of the towns of the Empire was peculiar. Instead of conquering their liberties all at once by force or by some adroit maneuver, and of extending them little by little by taking advantage of every favorable circumstance, as the other communities did, they were obliged to pass through two clearly separated stages to attain independence. In the twelfth century, like all the other urban agglomerations, they strove to free themselves. But the emperor, upon whom they were directly dependent after he had raised them to the rank of tenants-in-chief, held them under his powerful hand and consented to grant them only civil liberties. Each time that they desired autonomy and independence they met with his refusal. In 1161, Barbarossa subjugated the burghers of Treves, who had conspired against their archbishop. In 1163, learning that the people of Mainz had killed their lord, he hastened thither, sacked the city, and razed the ramparts. Thus in the twelfth century the towns gained only the most essential liberties: guaranties against the arbitrary power of their lords; never political independence. In the middle of the thirteenth century, however, the Swabian dynasty died out and feudal Germany enjoyed a prolonged interregnum. The towns, which now had only local sovereigns to oppose them, pressed their claims, and after a struggle in which success and failure were mingled, many of them triumphed. Metz, which had been enjoying certain liberties since the twelfth century, then attained full independence. Strassburg obtained a municipal administration distinct from the episcopal administration. Besançon organized a commune and in 1290 had its emancipation sanctioned by the new emperor, Rudolph. The second stage was passed a hundred years after the first, and it was then that the famous free towns of the Empire were constituted.

Thus all Europe presented the same spectacle from the eleventh to the thirteenth century. The urban communities, before so humble and so profoundly silent that we know almost nothing of them, were developing, were raising their voices, and were all tending toward the same end, emancipation. Everywhere, in spite of diversities of place, time, circumstances, obstacles, or aids, they reached their goal or approached it more or less closely. It was a universal current which carried all with it. . . .

As they had attained their emancipation by the most diverse ways, the towns of the middle ages were not likely to have any uniform constitution, and their independence, like their organization, varied greatly from one center to another. One commune was almost autonomous, while another had only the appearance of liberty. In some cases the source of authority resided in a general assembly of the inhabitants, in others the power was in the hands of an oligarchy formed of a few families who reserved for themselves the magistracies and the municipal offices. Thus it is impossible to characterize the situation in these towns comprehensively and precisely. And on the other hand, between the localities which were most independent and those which remained under the immediate surveillance of royal or seigniorial officials, there were so many intermediate types, . . . the transitions from one to another were so imperceptible, that it is no less difficult to find categories into which they can be grouped for systematic study. They formed a continuous hierarchy without breaks, or without periods of arrested development. Nevertheless historians are accustomed to rank them in two distinct classes: communes and towns of burgessy. Under the name of communes they designate those centers which had acquired from their lord a certain degree of political independence. In the towns of burgessy, on the contrary, the inhabitants had gained civil liberties only, guarantees against the administrative, fiscal, judicial, and military despotism of the master; they had not conquered the right to govern themselves. This division is purely arbitrary. It does not date from the middle ages and in practice it would be difficult, if not impossible, to distinguish clearly the least free of the communes from the most independent of the towns of burgessy. With this reservation we shall make use of it, because it is used and is perhaps as good as any.

Whether extended or restricted, the rights of the commune were almost always set forth in a written indenture, a contract which was entered into between the commune and the lord, a fundamental agreement which could be referred to in case of new difficulties or of disputes, and which served at the same time as a certificate of birth and as a deed of constitution. This was the communal charter. It is true that certain places, like Abbeville, are cited where emancipation was not at first sanctioned upon parchment, but these are exceptions to the rule.

Although these charters were zealously guarded in coffers, the keys of which were in possession of the municipal authorities alone, they have rarely been preserved to us in their original form; usually they are known only by more recent confirmation. They differed remarkably from each other. That of Corbie comprised only seven articles; that of Molliens-Vidame, a little place in Picardy, contained sixty. The length of the act was not in proportion to the importance of the place. They were drawn up ordinarily in the form of a seigniorial, but sometimes in an impersonal, style. The clauses were usually an enumeration without order, often ambiguous, and at times contradictory. As a rule they aimed principally to guarantee the existence of the communal bond, to regulate the relation of the commune to its suzerain, especially in the matter of justice and of imposts, and to determine the rights and privileges of the burgesses. These liberties, as they were called, concerned the limitation of the taille, taxes, corvées, tolls, banalities, chevauchée, and war, and the exercise and extent of seigniorial justice. The charters rarely described the whole municipal constitution. Generally they mentioned only the innovations and illuminated the doubtful points, while they passed in silence established usuages which were not subjects of dispute. Hence the incoherence, vagueness, in incompleteness apparent in these charters. **22**

Charter of Henry I to London in 1130

On the basis of such charters as the one granted by Henry I to London in 1130 towns of the Middle Ages regulated their liberties.

Henry, by the grace of God, king of the English, to the archbishop of Canterbury, and to the bishops and abbots, and earls and barons and justices and sheriffs, and to all his liegemen, both French and English, of the whole of England, greeting. Know that I have granted to my citizens of London that they shall hold Middlesex at 'farm' for 300 pounds 'by tale' for themselves and their heirs from me and my heirs, so that the citizens shall appoint as sheriff from themselves whomsoever they may choose, and shall appoint from among themselves as justice whomsoever they choose to look after the pleas of my crown and the pleadings which arise in connexion with them. No other shall be justice over the same men of London. And the citizens shall not plead outside the walls of the city in respect of any plea; and they shall be quit of scot and of Danegeld and the murder-fine. Nor shall any of them be compelled to offer trial by battle. And if any one of the citizens shall be impleaded in respect of the pleas of the crown, let him prove himself to be a man of London by an oath which shall be judged in the city. Let no one be billeted within the walls of the city, either of my household, or by the force of anyone else. And let all the men of London and their property be quit and free from toll and passage and lestage and from all other customs throughout all England and at the seaports. And let the churches and barons and citizens hold and have well and in peace their sokes, with all their customs, so that those who dwell in these sokes shall pay no customs except to him who possesses the soke, or the steward whom he has placed there. And a man of London shall not be fined at mercy except according to his 'were,' that is to say, up to 100 shillings: this applies to an offence which can be punished by a fine. And there shall no longer be 'miskenning' in the hustings court, nor in the folk-moot, nor in other pleas within the city. And the hustings court shall sit once a week, to wit, on Monday. I will cause my citizens to have their lands and pledges and debts within the city and outside it. And in respect of the lands about which they make claim to me, I will do them right according to the law of the city. And if anyone has taken toll or custom from the citizens of London, then the citizens of London may take from the borough or village where toll or custom has been levied as much as the man of London gave for toll, and more also may be taken for a penalty. And let all debtors to the citizens of London discharge their debts, or prove in London that they do not owe them; and if they refuse either to pay, or to come and make such proof, then the citizens to whom the debts are due take pledges within the city either from the borough or from the village or from the county in which the debtor lives. And the citizens shall have their hunting chases, as well and fully as had their predecessors, to wit, in Chiltern and Middlesex and Surrey. Witness: the bishop of Winchester; Robert, son of Richer; Hugh Bigot; Alfred of Totnes; William of Aubigny; Hubert the king's chamberlain; William of Montfique; Hagulf "de Tani"; John Belet; Robery, son of Siward. Given at Westminster. **23**

Henry II's Charter to the Weavers Gild of London in 1155

Not only did the Kings have the power to charter and grant authority to towns but they chartered such organizations as stock companies and guilds. When this charter was granted weaving was one of the most important industries of England and it was one of the bases of English trade with the European continent.

Henry, by the grace of God, king of England, duke of Normandy and Aquitaine, count of Anjou, to the bishops, justiciars, sheriffs, barons, and all his servants and liegemen of London, greeting. Know that I have granted to the weavers of London to have their gild in London with all the liberties and customs which they had in the time of King Henry, my grandfather. Let no one carry on this occupation unless by their permission, and unless he belong to their gild, within the city or in Southwark or in the other places pertaining to London, other than those who were wont to do so in the time of King Henry, my grandfather. Wherefore I will, and firmly order that they shall everywhere legally carry on their business, and that they shall have all the aforesaid things as well and peacefully and freely and honourably and entirely as ever they had them in the time of King Henry, my grandfather; provided always that for this privilege they pay me each year 2 marks of gold at Michaelmas. And I forbid anyone to do them injury or insult in respect of this on pain of 10 pounds forfeiture. Witness: Thomas of Canterbury; Warin fitz Gerold. At Winchester **24**

12th Century London

12th century London as described by William fitz Stephen, biographer of

Thomas Becket. Herein we find descriptions of housing, trade, commerce and recreation of the people in early London.

> Among the noble and celebrated cities of the world that of London, the capital of the kingdom of the English, is one which extends its glory farther than all the others and sends its wealth and merchandise more widely into distant lands, Higher than all the rest does it lift its head. It is happy in the healthiness of its air; in its observance of Christian practice; in the strength of its fortifications; in its natural situation; in the honour of its citizens; and in the modesty of its matrons. It is cheerful in its sports, and the fruitful mother of noble men. Let us look into these things in turn.
> If the mildness of the climate of this place softens the character of its inhabitants, it does not make them corrupt in following Venus, but rather prevents them from being fierce and bestial, making them liberal and kind.
> In the church of St. Paul there is the episcopal seat. Once it was metropolitan, and some think it will again become so, if the citizens return to the island, unless perhaps the archiepiscopal title of the blessed martyr, Thomas, and the presence of his body preserves that dignity for ever at Canterbury where it is at present. But as St. Thomas has made both cities illustrious, London by his rising and Canterbury by his setting, each can claim advantage of the other with justice in respect of that saint. As regards the practice of Christian worship, there are in London and its suburbs thirteen greater conventual churches and, besides these, one hundred and twenty-six lesser parish churches.
> It has on the east the Palatine castle, very great and strong: the keep and walls rise from very deep foundations and are fixed with a mortar tempered by the blood of animals. On the west there are two castles very strongly fortified, and from these there runs a high and massive wall with seven double gates and with towers along the north at regular intervals. London was once also walled and turreted on the south, but the mighty Thames, so full of fish, has with the sea's ebb and flow washed against, loosened, and thrown down those walls in the course of time. Upstream to the west there is the royal palace which is conspicuous above the river, a building

incomparable in its ramparts and bulwarks. It is about two miles from the city and joined thereto by a populous suburb.

Everywhere outside the houses of those living in the suburbs, and adjacent to them, are the spacious and beautiful gardens of the citizens, and these are planted with trees. Also there are on the north side pastures and pleasant meadow lands through which flow streams wherein the turning of mill-wheels makes a cheerful sound. Very near lies a great forest with woodland pastures in which there are the lairs of wild animals: stags, fallow deer, wild boars and bulls. The tilled lands of the city are not of barren gravel, but fat Asian plains that yield luxuriant crops and fill the tillers' barns with the sheaves of Ceres.

There are also outside London on the north side excellent suburban wells with sweet, wholesome and clear water that flows rippling over the bright stones. Among these are Holywell, Clerkenwell and St. Clement's Well, which are all famous. These are frequented by great numbers and much visited by the students from the schools and by the young men of the city, when they go out for fresh air on summer evenings. Good indeed is this city when it has a good lord!

The city is honoured by her men, glorious in its arms, and so populous that during the terrible wars of King Stephen's reign the men going forth from it to battle were reckoned as twenty thousand armed horsemen and sixty thousand foot-soldiers, all equipped for war. The citizens of London are regarded as conspicuous above all others for their polished manners, for their dress and for the good tables which they keep. The inhabitants of other towns are called citizens, but those of London are called barons. And with them a solemn pledge is sufficient to end every dispute.

The Matrons of this city are very Sabines.

In London the three principal churches (that is to say, the episcopal church of St. Paul, the church of the Holy Trinity, and the church of St. Martin) have famous schools of special privilege and by virtue of their ancient dignity. But through the favour of some magnate, or through the presence of teachers who are notable or famous in philosophy, there are also other schools. On feast-days the masters hold meetings for their pupils in the church whose festival it is. The scholars dispute, some with oratory and some with argument; some recite enthymemes; others excel in using perfect syllogisms. Some dispute for ostentation, like wrestlers with opponent; others argue in order to establish the truth in its perfection. Sophists who speak paradoxes are praised for their torrent of words, whilst others seek to overthrow their opponents by using fallacious arguments. Now and then orators use rhetoric for persuasion, being careful to omit nothing essential to their art. Boys of different schools strive against each other in verses, or contend about the principles of grammar and the rules governing past and future tenses. Others use epigrams, rhythm and metre in the old trival banter; they pull their comrades to pieces with "Fescennine Licence": mentioning no names, they dart abuse and gibes, and mock the faults of their comrades and sometimes even those of their elders, using Socratic salt and biting harder even than the tooth of Theon in daring dithyrambics. Their hearers, ready to enjoy the joke, wrinkle up their noses as they guffaw in applause.

Of the Ordering of the City

Those engaged in business of various kinds, sellers of merchandise, hirers of labour, are distributed every morning into their several localities according to their grade. Besides, there is in London on the river bank among the wines for sale in ships and in the cellars of the vintners a public cook-shop. There daily you may find food according to the season, dishes of meat, roast, fried and boiled, large and small fish, coarser meats for the poor and more delicate for the rich, such as venison and big and small birds. If any of the citizens should unexpectedly receive visitors, weary from their journey, who would fain not wait until fresh food is bought and cooked, or until the servants have brought bread or water for washing, they hasten to the river bank and there find all they need. However great the multitude of soldiers and travellers entering the city, or preparing to go out of it, at any hour of the day or night—that these may not fast too long, and those may not go out supperless—they turn aside thither, if they please, where every man can refresh himself in his own way. Those who would cater for themselves fastidiously need not search to find sturgeon or the bird of Africa or the Ionian godwit. For this is a public kitchen, very convenient to the city, and part of its amenities. Hence the dictum in the Gorgias of Plato that the art of cookery is an imitation of medicine and flatters a quarter of civic life.

Immediately outside one of the gates there is a field which is smooth both in fact and in name. On every sixth day of the week, unless it be a major feast-day, there takes place there a famous exhibition of fine horses for sale. Earls, barons and knights, who are in the town, and many citizens come out to see or to buy. It is pleasant to see the high-stepping palfreys with their gleaming coats, as they go through their paces, putting down their feet alternately on one side together. Next, one can see the horses suitable for esquires, moving faster though less smoothly, lifting and setting down, as it were, the opposite fore and hind feet: here are colts of fine breed, but not yet accustomed to the bit, stepping high with jaunty tread; there are the sumpter-horses, powerful and spirited; and after them there are the war-horses, costly, elegant of form, noble of stature, with ears quickly tremulous, necks raised and large haunches. As these show their paces, the buyers first try those of gentler gait, then those of quicker pace whereby the fore and hind feet move in pairs together. When a race is about to begin among such chargers that are so powerful to carry and so swift to run, a shout is raised, and orders are given that the inferior animals should be led apart. Three jockeys who mount these flying steeds (or at times two, as may be agreed) prepare themselves for the contest; skilled in managing them, they curb their untamed mouths with bitted bridles. To get a good start in the race is their chief concern. Their mounts also enter into the spirit of the contest as they are able; their limbs tremble, and so impatient are they of delay that they cannot keep still. When the signal is given, they stretch their limbs to the uttermost, and dash down the course with courageous speed. The riders, covetous of applause and ardent for victory, plunge their spurs into the loose-reined horses, and urge them forward with their shouts and their whips. You would agree with Heraclitus that all things are in motion! You would know Zeno to be completely wrong when he said that there was no motion and no goal to be reached!

By themselves in another part of the field stand the goods of the countryfolk: implements of husbandry, swine with long flanks, cows with full udders, oxen of immense size, and wooly sheep.

There also stand the mares fit for plough, some big with foal, and others with brisk young colts closely following them.

To this city from every nation under heaven merchants delight to bring their trade by sea. The Arabian sends gold; the Sabaean spice and incense. The Scythian brings arms, and from the rich, fat lands of Babylon comes oil of palms. The Nile sends precious stones; the men of Norway and Russia, furs and sables; nor is China absent with purple silk. The Gauls come with their wines.

London, as historians have shown, is a much older city than Rome, for though it derives from the same Trojan ancestors, it was founded by Brutus before Rome was founded by Romulus and Remus. Wherefore they still have the same laws from their common origin. This city is like Rome divided into wards; it has annual sheriffs instead of consuls; it has its senatorial order and lower magistrates; it has drains and aqueducts in its streets; it has its appointed places for the hearing of cases deliberative, demonstrative and judicial; it has its several courts, and its separate assemblies on appointed days.

I do not think there is a city with a better record for church-going, doing honour to God's ordinances, keeping feast-days, giving alms and hospitality to strangers, confirming betrothals, contracting marriages, celebrating weddings, providing feasts, entertaining guests, and also, it may be added, in care for funerals and for the burial of the dead. The only plagues of London are the immoderate drinking of fools and the frequency of fires.

To this it may be added that almost all the bishops, abbots and magnates of England are in a sense citizens and freemen of London, having their own splendid town-houses. In them they live, and spend largely, when they are summoned to great councils by the king or by their metropolitan, or drawn thither by their private affairs.

Of the Sports of London

We now come to speak of the sports of the city, for it is not fitting that a city should be merely useful and serious-minded, unless it be also pleasant and cheerful. For this cause on the seals of the supreme pontiff, down to the time of the last Pope Leo, on one side of the lead was engraved the figure of Peter the fisherman and above him a key, as it were, held out to him from heaven by the hand of God, and around it was inscribed the verse, "For me didst thou leave the ship, receive now the key." And on the other side was engraved a city with the inscription "Golden Rome". Moreover, it was said in honour of Augustus Caesar and Rome, "It rains all night, games usher in the day; Caesar, thou dost divide dominion with Jove." Instead of shows in the theatre and stage-plays, London provides plays of a more sacred character, wherein are presented the miracles worked by saintly confessors or the sufferings which made illustrious the constancy of martyrs. Furthermore, every year on the day called Carnival—to begin with the sports of boys (for we were all boys once)—scholars from the different schools bring fighting-cocks to their masters, and the whole morning is set apart to watch their cocks do battle in the schools, for the boys are given a holiday that day. After dinner all the young men of the town go out into the fields in the suburbs to play ball. The scholars of the various schools have their own ball, and almost all the followers of each occupation have theirs also. The seniors and the fathers and the wealthy magnates of the city come on horseback to watch the contests of the younger generation, and in their turn recover their lost youth; the motions of their natural heat seem to be stirred in them at the mere sight of such strenuous activity and by their participation in the joys of unbridled youth.

Every Sunday in Lent after dinner a fresh swarm of young men goes forth into the fields on war-horses, steeds foremost in the contest, each of which is skilled and schooled to run in circles. From the gates there sallies forth a host of laymen, sons of the citizens, equipped with lances and shields, the younger ones with spears forked at the top, but with the steel point removed. They make a pretence at war, carry out field-exercises and indulge in mimic combats. Thither too come many courtiers, when the king is in town, and from the households of bishops, earls and barons come youths and adolescents, not yet girt with the belt of knighthood, for the pleasure of engaging in combat with one another. Each is inflamed with the hope of victory. The fiery steeds neigh with tremulous limbs and champ their bits; impatient of delay they cannot stand still. When at last their trampling hooves ring on the ground in rapid flight, their boy riders divide their ranks; some pursue those immediately in front of them, but fail to catch up with them;

others overtake their fellows, force them to dismount and fly past them.

At the Easter festival they play at a kind of naval warfare. A shield is firmly bound to a tree in mid-stream, and a small boat, swiftly impelled by many an oar and the current of the river, carries on the stern a youth armed with a lance with which to strike the shield. If he breaks the lance by striking the shield, and yet keeps his footing, he has achieved his aim and gratified his wish, but if he strikes the shield firmly and the lance remains unbroken, he is thrown overboard into the flowing river, and the boat, impelled by its own motion, rushes past him. There are, however, two other boats moored, one on each side of the target, with several youths on board to seize hold of the striker who had been engulfed by the stream, as soon as he comes into view or when he rises on the crest of the wave for the second time. On the bridge and the terraces fronting the river stand the spectators, ready to laugh their fill.

On feast-days throughout the summer the young men indulge in the sports of archery, running, jumping, wrestling, slinging the stone, hurling the javelin beyond a mark and fighting with sword and buckler. Cythera leads the dance of maidens, and until the moon rises, the earth is shaken with flying feet.

In winter on almost every feast-day before dinner either foaming boars, armed with lightning tusks, fight for their lives "to save their bacon", or stout bulls with butting horns, or huge bears do battle with the hounds let loose upon them. When the great marsh that washes the north wall of the city is frozen over, swarms of young men issue forth to play games on the ice. Some, gaining speed in their run, with feet set well apart, slide sideways over a vast expanse of ice. Others make seats out of a large lump of ice, and whilst one sits thereon, others with linked hands run before and drag him along behind them. So swift is their sliding motion that sometimes their feet slip, and they all fall on their faces. Others, more skilled at winter sports, put on their feet the shin-bones of animals, binding them firmly round their ankles, and, holding poles shod with iron in their hands, which they strike from time to time against the ice, they are propelled swift as a bird in flight or a bolt shot from an engine of war. Sometimes, by mutual consent, two of them run against each other in this way from a great distance, and, lifting their poles, each tilts against the other. Either one or both fall, not without some bodily injury, for, as they fall, they are carried along a great way beyond each other by the impetus of their run, and wherever the ice comes in contact with their heads, it scrapes off the skin utterly. Often a leg or an arm is broken, if the victim falls with it underneath him; but theirs is an age greedy of glory, youth yearns for victory, and exercises itself in mock combats in order to carry itself more bravely in real battles.

Many of the citizens take pleasure in sporting with birds of the air, with hawks, falcons and such-like, and with hounds that hunt their prey in the woods. The citizens have the rights of the chase in Middlesex, Hertfordshire, all the Chiltern country, and in Kent as far as the river Cray. The Londoners, who were then known as Trinobantes, drove back Julius Caesar, whose delight it was to wade through paths steeped in blood. Whence Lucas writes: "To the Britons whom he had sought he turned his back in flight."

The city of London has given birth to several men who have subdued many realms and even the Roman empire to their dominion, and also many another whose valour has raised him to the gods as lord of the world, as was promised to Brutus by the oracle of Apollo: "Brutus, beyond Gaul, beneath the setting sun, there lies an isle washed by the waves of ocean. Thither direct thy course, for there shall be thy seat for ever. This shall be to thy sons a second Troy. Here from thy stem shall kings arise, and the whole world shall be subject unto them."

Afterwards in Christian times this city produced that noble emperor Constantine, son of the empress Helena, who bestowed the city of Rome and all the imperial insignia on God and St. Peter and on Sylvester, the Roman pope, to whom he dispensed the office of a groom, no longer rejoicing to be called emperor but rather the defender of the holy Roman Church; and, lest the peace of the lord pope should be disturbed by the uproar of secular strife occasioned by his presence, he himself altogether abandoned the city which he had bestowed upon the lord pope, and built for himself the city of Byzantium. And in modern times also London has given birth to illustrious and noble monarchs, the empress Maud, King "Henry III", and the blessed Archbishop Thomas, that glorious martyr of Christ, than whom she bore no purer saint nor one more dear to all good men throughout the Latin world.

25

The University of the Middle Ages

Closely associated with the growth of towns was the college or university. A town with a college had a good chance of growing in view of the commerce and activity which the school promoted. In the following selection we note the privileges and distinctions granted to university personnel and we might compare those with contemporary faculty-student demands.

The Foundations of the University at Heidelberg, 1386

a. We, Rupert the elder, by the grace of God Count Palatine of the Rhine, elector of the Holy Empire and duke of Bavaria—lest we seem to abuse the privilege conceded to us by the apostolic see of founding a place of study at Heidelberg like to that at Paris, and lest, for this reason, being subjected to the divine judgment, we should merit to be deprived of the privilege granted,—do decree with provident counsel, which decree is to be observed there unto all time, that the university of Heidelberg shall be ruled, disposed and regulated according to the modes and matters accustomed to be observed in the university of Paris. Also that, as a handmaid of the Parisian institution—a worthy one, let us hope,—the latter's steps shall be imitated in every way possible; so that, namely, there shall be four faculties in it: the first, of sacred theology or divinity; the second, of canon and civil law, which, by reason of their similarity, we think best to comprise under one faculty; the third, of medicine; the fourth, of liberal arts—of the threefold philosophy, namely, primal, natural and moral, three mutually subservient daughters. We wish this institution to be divided and marked out into four nations, as it is at Paris; and that all these faculties shall make one university, and that to it the individual students, in whichever of the said faculties they are, shall indivisibly belong like lawful sons of one mother. Likewise that that university shall be governed by one rector, and that the different masters and teachers before they are admitted to the common pursuits of our institution, shall swear to observe the statutes, laws, privileges, liberties and franchises of the same, and not reveal its secrets, to whatever grade they may rise. Also that they will uphold the honour of the rector and the rectorship of our university, and will obey the rector in all things lawful and honest, whatever be the grade to which they may afterwards happen to be promoted. Moreover that the different masters and bachelors shall read their lectures and exercise their scholastic functions and go about in caps and gowns of a uniform and similar nature, according as that has been observed at Paris up to this time in the different faculties. And we will that if any faculty, nation or person shall oppose the aforesaid regulations, or pertinaciously refuse to obey them or any one of them—which God forbid,—from that time forward that same faculty, nation or person, if it do not desist upon being warned, shall be deprived of all connection with our aforesaid institution, and shall not have the benefit of our defence or protection. Moreover we will and ordain that as the university as a whole may do for those assembled here and subject to it, so each faculty, nation or province of it may found lawful statutes and ones suitable to its needs, provided that through them or any one of them no prejudice is done to the above regulations and to our institution, and that no kind of impediment arise from them. And we will that when the separate bodies shall have passed the statutes for their own observance, they may make them perpetually binding on those subject to them and on their successors. And as in the university of Paris the different servants of the institution have the benefit of the different privileges which its masters and scholars enjoy, so in starting our institution in Heidelberg, we grant, with even greater liberality, through these presents, that all the servants, viz.: its Pedells, librarians, lower officials, preparers of parchment, scribes, illuminators and others who serve it, may each and all, without fraud, enjoy in it the same privileges, franchises, immunities and liberties with which its masters or scholars are now or shall hereafter be endowed.

b. Lest in the new community of the city of Heidelberg, their faults being unpunished, there be an incentive to the scholars of doing wrong, we ordain with provident counsel by these presents, that the bishop of Worms, as judge ordinary of the clerks of our institution, shall have and possess, now and hereafter while our institution shall last, prisons, and an office in our town of Heidelberg for the detention of criminal clerks. These things we have seen fit to grant to him and his successors, adding these conditions: that he shall permit no clerk to be arrested unless for a misdemeanour; that he shall restore any one detained for such fault or for any light offence to his master or to the rector if he asks for him, a promise having been given that the culprit will appear in court and that the rector or master will answer for him if the injured parties should go to law about the matter. Furthermore that, on being requested, he will restore a clerk arrested for a crime on slight evidence, upon receiving a sufficient pledge—sponsors if the prisoner can obtain them, otherwise an oath if he can not obtain sponsors—to the effect that he will answer in court the charges against him; and in all these things there shall be no pecuniary exactions, except that the clerk shall give satisfaction, reasonably and according to the rule of the aforementioned town, for the expenses which he incurred while in prison. And that he will detain honestly and without serious injury a criminal clerk thus arrested for a crime where the suspicion is grave and strong, until the truth can be found out concerning the deed of which he is suspected. And he shall not for any cause, moreover, take away any clerk from our aforesaid town, or permit him to be taken away, unless the proper observances have been followed, and he has been condemned by judicial sentence to perpetual imprisonment for a crime. We command our advocate and bailiff and their servants in our aforesaid town, under pain of losing their office and our favour, not to put a detaining hand on any master or scholar of our said institution, nor to arrest him nor allow him to be arrested, unless the deed be such a one that that master or scholar ought rightly to be detained. He shall be restored to his rector or master, if he is held for a slight cause, provided he will swear and promise to appear in court concerning the matter; and we decree that a slight fault is one for which a layman, if he had committed it, ought to have been condemned to a light pecuniary fine. Likewise, if the master or scholar detained be found gravely or strongly suspected of the crime, we command that he be handed over by our officials to the bishop or to his representative in our said town, to be kept in custody.

    c. By the tenor of these presents we grant to each and all the masters and scholars that, when they come to said institution, while they remain there, and also when they return from it to their homes, they may freely carry with them both coming and going, throughout all the lands subject to us, all their things which they need while pursuing their studies, and all the goods necessary for their support, without any duty, levy, imposts, tailles, gabelles, or other exactions whatever. And we wish them and each one of them, to be free from all the aforesaid imposts when purchasing corn, wines, meat, fish, clothes and all things necessary for their living and for their rank. And we decree that the scholars from their stock in hand of provisions, if there remain over one or two waggon-loads of wine without their having practised deception, may after the feast of Easter of that year sell it en gros without paying impost. We grant to them, moreover, that each day the scholars, of themselves or through their servants, may be allowed to buy in the town of Heidelberg, at the accustomed hour, freely and without impediment or hurtful delay, any eatables or other necessaries of life.

   d. Lest the masters and scholars of our institution of Heidelberg may be oppressed by the citizens, avarice inducing them, through the extortionate price of lodgings, we have seen fit to decree that henceforth each year, after Christmas, one expert from the university on the part of the scholars, and one prudent, pious and circumspect citizen on the part of the citizens, shall be deputed to fix on the price for the students' lodgings. Moreover we will and decree that the different masters and scholars shall, through our bailiff, our judge and the officials subject to us, be defended and maintained in the quiet possession of the lodgings given to them free or of those for which they pay rent. Moreover, by the tenor of these presents, we grant to the rector and the university, or to those deputed by them, entire and total jurisdiction concerning the paying of rents for the lodgings occupied by the students, concerning the making and buying of codices, and the borrowing of money for other purposes by the scholars of our institution; also concerning the payment of assessments, together with everything that arises from, depends on and is connected with these.

   —. In addition we command our officials that, when the rector requires our and their aid and assistance for carrying out his sentences against scholars who try to rebel, they shall assist our clients and servants in this matter; first, however, obtaining lawful permission to proceed against clerks from the lord bishops of Worms, or from one deputed by him for this purpose.

The Plague

Giovanni Boccaccio (1313-1375) was born in Paris and spent his life in Italy. His major work was the *Decameron* (1348-1353). Written in Italian the *Decameron* was one of the earliest humanistic works of the Renaissance. In the excerpt that follows we read of the plague which struck Florence, Italy in the 14th century and how it destroyed the people of the city.

    I say, then, that the years of the beatific incarnation of the Son of God had reached the tale of one thousand three hundred and forty-eight, when in the illustrious city of Florence, the fairest of all the cities of Italy, there made its appearance that deadly pestilence, which, whether diseminated by the influence of the celestial bodies, or sent upon us mortals by God in His just wrath by way of retribution for our iniquities, had had its origin some years before in the East, whence, after destroying an innumerable multitude of living beings, it had propagated itself without respite from place to place, and so, calamitously, had spread into the West.

    In Florence, despite all that human wisdom and forethought could devise to avert it, as the cleansing of the city from many impurities by officials appointed for the purpose, the refusal of entrance to all sick folk, and the adoption of many precautions for the preservation of health; despite also humble supplications addressed to God, and often repeated both in public procession and otherwise, by the devout; towards the beginning of the spring of the said year the doleful effects of the pestilence began to be horribly apparent by symptoms that shewed as if miraculous.

    Not such were they as in the East, where an issue of blood from the nose was a manifest sign of inevitable death; but in men and women alike it first betrayed itself by the emergence of certain tumours in the groin or the armpits, some of which grew as large as a common apple, others as an egg, some more, some less, which the common folk called gavoccioli. From the two said parts of the body this deadly gavocciolo soon began to propagate and spread itself in all directions indifferently; after which the form of the malady began to change, black spots or livid making their appearance in many cases on the arm or the thigh or elsewhere, now few and large, now minute and numerous. And as the gavocciolo had been and still was an infallible token of approaching death, such also were these spots on whomsoever they shewed themselves. Which maladies seemed to set entirely at naught both the art of the physician and the virtues of physic; indeed, whether it was that the disorder was of a nature to defy such treatment, or that the physicians were at fault—besides the qualified there was now a multitude both of men and of women who practised without having received the slightest tincture of medical science—and, being in ignorance of its source, failed to apply the proper remedies; in either case, not merely were those that recovered few, but almost all within three days from the appearance of the said symptoms, sooner or later, died, and in most cases without any fever or other attendant malady.

Moreover, the virulence of the pest was the greater by reason that intercourse was apt to convey it from the sick to the whole, just as fire devours things dry or greasy when they are brought close to it. Nay, the evil went yet further, for not merely by speech or association with the sick was the malady communicated to the healthy with consequent peril of common death; but any that touched the clothes of the sick or aught else that had been touched or used by them, seemed thereby to contract the disease.

So marvellous sounds that which I have now to relate, that, had not many, and I among them, observed it with their own eyes, I had hardly dared to credit it, much less to set it down in writing, though I had had it from the lips of a credible witness.

I say, then, that such was the energy of the contagion of the said pestilence, that it was not merely propagated from man to man, but, what is much more startling, it was frequently observed, that things which had belonged to one sick or dead of the disease, if touched by some other living creature, not of the human species, were the occasion, not merely of sickening, but of an almost instantaneous death. Whereof my own eyes (as I said a little before) had cognisance, one day among others, by the following experience. The rags of a poor man who had died of the disease being strewn about the open street, two hogs came thither, and after, as is their wont, no little trifling with their snouts, took the rags between their teeth and tossed them to and fro about their chaps; whereupon, almost immediately, they gave a few turns, and fell down dead, as if by poison, upon the rags which in an evil hour they had disturbed.

In which circumstances, not to speak of many others of a similar or ever graver complexion, divers apprehensions and imaginations were engendered in the minds of such as were left alive, inclining almost all of them to the same harsh resolution, to wit, to shun and abhor all contact with the sick and all that belonged to them, thinking thereby to make each his own health secure. Among whom there were those who thought that to live temperately and avoid all excess would count for much as a preservative against seizures of this kind. Wherefore they banded together, and, dissociating themselves from all others, formed communities in houses where there were no sick, and lived a separate and secluded life, which they regulated with the utmost care, avoiding every kind of luxury, but eating and drinking very moderately of the most delicate viands and the finest wines, holding converse with none but one another, lest tidings of sickness or death should reach them, and diverting their minds with music and such other delights as they could devise. Others, the bias of whose minds was in the opposite direction, maintained, that to drink freely, frequent places of public resort, and take their pleasure with song and revel, sparing to satisfy no appetite, and to laugh and mock at no event, was the sovereign remedy for so great an evil: and that which they affirmed they also put in practice, so far as they were able, resorting day and night, now to this tavern, now to that, drinking with an entire disregard of rule or measure, and by preference making the houses of others, as it were, their inns, if they but saw in them aught that was particularly to their taste or liking; which they were readily able to do, because the owners, seeing death imminent, had become as reckless of their property as of their lives; so that most of the houses were open to all comers, and no distinction was observed between the stranger who presented himself and the rightful lord. Thus, adhering ever to their inhuman determination to shun the sick, as far as possible, they ordered their life. In this extremity of our city's suffering and tribulation the venerable authority of laws, human and divine, was abased and all but totally dissolved, for lack of those who should have administered and enforced them, most of whom, like the rest of the citizens, were either dead or sick, or so hard bested for servants that they were unable to execute any office; whereby every man was free to do what was right in his own eyes.

Not a few there were who belonged to neither of the two said parties, but kept a middle course between them, neither laying the same restraint upon their diet as the former, nor allowing themselves the same license in drinking and other dissipations as the latter, but living with a degree of freedom sufficient to satisfy their appetites, and not as recluses. They therefore walked abroad, carrying in their hands flowers or fragrant herbs or divers sorts of spices, which they frequently raised to their noses, deeming it an excellent thing thus to comfort the brain with such perfumes, because the air seemed to be everywhere laden and reeking with the stench emitted by the dead and the dying, and the odours of drugs.

Some again, the most sound, perhaps, in judgment, as they were also the most harsh in temper, of all, affirmed that there was no medicine for the disease superior or equal in efficacy to flight; following which prescription a multitude of men and women, negligent of all but themselves, deserted their city, their houses, their estates, their kinsfolk, their goods, and went into voluntary exile, or migrated to the country parts, as if God in visiting men with this pestilence in requital of their iniquities would not pursue them with His wrath wherever they might be, but intended the destruction of such alone as remained within the circuit of the walls of the city; or deeming, perchance, that it was now time for all to flee from it, and that its last hour was come.

Of the adherents of these divers opinions not all died, neither did all escape; but rather there were, of each sort and in every place, many that sickened, and by those who retained their health were treated after the example which they themselves, while whole, had set, being everywhere left to languish in almost total neglect. Tedious were it to recount, how citizen avoided citizen, how among neighbours was scarce found any that shewed fellow-feeling for another, how kinsfolk held aloof, and never met, or but rarely; enough that this sore afflication entered so deep into the minds of men and women, that in the horror thereof brother was forsaken by brother, nephew by uncle, brother by sister, and oftentimes husband by wife; nay, what is more, and scarcely to be believed, fathers and mothers were found to abandon their own children, untended, unvisited, to their fate, as if they had been strangers. Wherefore the sick of both sexes, whose number could not be estimated, were left without resource but in the charity of friends (and few such there were), or the interest of servants, who were hardly to be had at high rates and on unseemly terms, and being, moreover, one and all, men and women of gross understanding, and for the most part unused to such offices, concerned themselves no further than to supply the immediate and expressed wants of the sick, and to watch them die; in which service they themselves not seldom perished with their gains. In consequence of which dearth of servants and dereliction of the sick by neighbours, kinsfolk and friends, it came to pass—a thing, perhaps, never before heard of—that no woman, however dainty, fair or well-born she might be, shrank, when stricken with the disease, from the ministrations of a man, no matter whether he were young or no, or scrupled to expose to him every part of her body, with no more shame than if he had been a woman, submitting of necessity to that which her malady required; wherefrom, perchance, there resulted in after time some loss of modesty in such as recovered. Besides which many succumbed, who with proper attendance, would, perhaps, have escaped death; so that, what with the virulence of the plague and the lack of due tendance of the sick, the multitude of the deaths, that daily and nightly took place in the city, was such that those who heard the tale—not to say witnessed the fact—were struck dumb with amazement. Whereby, practices contrary to the former habits of the citizens could hardly fail to grow up among the survivors.

It has been, as to-day it still is, the custom for the women that were neighbours and of kin to the deceased to gather in his house with the women that were most closely connected with him, to wail with them in common, while on the other hand his male kinsfolk and neighbours, with not a few of the other citizens, and a due proportion of the clergy according to his quality, assembled without, in front of the house, to receive the corpse; and so the dead man was borne on the shoulders of his peers, with funeral pomp of taper and dirge, to the church selected by him before his death. Which rites, as the pestilence waxed in fury, were either in whole or in great part disused, and gave way to others of a novel order. For not only did no crowd of women surround the bed of the dying, but many passed from this life unregarded, and few indeed were they to whom were accorded the lamentations and bitter tears of sorrowing relations; nay, for the most part, their place was taken by the laugh, the jest, the festal gathering; observances which the women, domestic piety in large measure set aside, had adopted with very great advantage to their health. Few also there were whose bodies were attended to the church by more than ten or twelve of their neighbours, and those not the honourable and respected citizens; but a sort of corpse-carriers drawn from the baser ranks, who called themselves becchini and performed such offices for hire, would shoulder the bier, and with hurried steps carry it, not to the church of the dead man's choice, but to that which was nearest at hand, with four or six priests in front and a candle or two, or, perhaps, none; nor did the priests distress themselves with too long and solemn an office, but with the aid of the becchini hastily consigned the corpse to the first tomb which they found untenanted. The condition of the lower, and, perhaps, in great measure of the middle ranks, of the people shewed even worse and more deplorable; for, deluded by hope or constrained by poverty, they stayed in their quarters, in their houses, where they sickened by thousands a day, and, being without service or help of any kind, were, so to speak, irredeemably devoted to the death which overtook them. Many died daily or nightly in the public streets; of many others, who died at home, the departure was hardly observed by their neighbours, until the stench of their putrefying bodies carried the tidings; and what with their corpses and the corpses of others who died on every hand the whole place was a sepulchre.

It was the common practice of most of the neighbours, moved no less by fear of contamination by the putrefying bodies than by charity towards the deceased, to drag the corpses out of the houses with their own hands, aided, perhaps, by a porter, if a porter was to be had, and to lay them in front of the doors, where any one who made the round might have seen, especially in the morning, more of them than he could count; afterwards they would have biers brought up, or, in default, planks, whereon they laid them. Nor was it once or twice only that one and the same bier carried two or three corpses at once; but quite a considerable number of such cases occurred, one bier sufficing for husband and wife, two or three brothers, father and son, and so forth. And times without number it happened, that, as two priests, bearing the cross, were on their way to perform the last office for some one, three or four biers were brought up by the porters in rear of them, so that, whereas the priests supposed that they had but one corpse to bury, they discovered that there were six or eight, or sometimes more. Nor, for all their number, were their obsequies honoured by either tears or lights or crowds of mourners; rather, it was come to this, that a dead man was then of no more account than a dead goat would be to-day. From all which it is abundantly manifest, that that lesson of patient resignation, which the sages were never able to learn from the slight and infrequent mishaps which occur in the natural course of events, was now brought home even to the minds of the simple by the magnitude of their disasters, so that they became indifferent to them.

As consecrated ground there was not in extent sufficient to provide tombs for the vast multitude of corpses which day and night, and almost every hour, were brought in eager haste to the churches for interment, least of all, if ancient custom were to be observed and a separate resting-place assigned to each, they dug, for each graveyard, as soon as it was full, a huge trench, in which they laid the corpses as they arrived by hundreds at a time, piling them up as merchandise is stowed in the hold of a ship, tier upon tier, each covered with a little earth, until the trench would hold no more. But I spare to rehearse with minute particularity each of the woes that came upon our city, and say in brief, that, harsh as was the tenor of her fortunes, the surrounding country knew no mitigation; for there—not to speak of the castles, each, as it were, a little city in itself—in sequestered village, or on the open champaign, by the wayside, on the farm, in the homestead, the poor hapless husbandmen and their families, forlorn of physicians' care or servants' tendance, perished day and night alike, not as men, but rather as beasts. Wherefore, they too, like the citizens, abandoned all rule of life, all habit of industry, all counsel of prudence; nay, one and all, as if expecting each day to be their last, not merely ceased to aid Nature to yield her fruit in due season of their beasts and their lands and their past labours, but left no means unused, which ingenuity could devise, to waste their accumulated store; denying shelter to their oxen, asses, sheep, goats, pigs, fowls, nay, even to their dogs, man's most faithful companions, and driving them out into the fields to roam at large amid the unsheaved, nay unreaped corn. Many of which, as if endowed with reason, took their fill during the day, and returned home at night without any guidance of herdsman. But enough of the country! **26**

V. The Renaissance City

It was the city and its multifarious activities that helped give birth to the Renaissance in Italy. With the city's burgeoning activities there grew a secularization of life which enabled the genius of such giants as Michelangelo and da Vinci to flourish.

There was a reawakening. There grew an awareness towards the value of man. During this period we have the discoveries of Copernicus, Galileo, Bruno and Newton; the art of Michelangelo, da Vinci and Raphael; the philosophies of Machiavelli, Erasmus, Brandt, Luther and Calvin, but mankind had not reached utopia. As we can see by examining Burckhardt's description of The *Civilization of the Renaissance in Italy* and Vasari's *Lives of the Painters* and Michelangelo's own writings humankind had not achieved perfection by any means. With all its greatness the Renaissance city still had its superstitions, inequities, crime, congestion, and misfortunes.

The City as Burckhardt Saw It

Jacob Christoph Burckhardt (1818-1897) Swiss born historian helped found the study of cultural history by writing such works as *The Civilization of the Renaissance in Italy* (1860). In the following selection from that work Burckhardt portrayed the streets and houses as well as the mores and customs of the Italian Renaissance city.

Equalization of Classes

Every period of civilization which forms a complete and consistent whole manifests itself not only in political life, in religion, art, and science, but also sets its characteristic stamp on social life. Thus the Middle Ages had their courtly and aristocratic manners and etiquette, differing but little in the various countries of Europe, as well as their peculiar forms of middle-class life.

Italian customs at the time of the Renaissance offer in these respects the sharpest contrast to medievalism. The foundation on which they rest is wholly different. Social intercourse in its highest and most perfect form now ignored all distinctions of caste, and was based simply on the existence of an educated class as we now understand the word. Birth and origin were without influence, unless combined with leisure and inherited wealth. Yet this assertion must not be taken in an absolute and unqualified sense, since medieval distinctions still sometimes made themselves felt to a greater or less degree, if only as a means of maintaining equality with the aristocratic pretensions of the less advanced countries of Europe. But the main current of the time went steadily toward the fusion of classes in the modern sense of the phrase.

The fact was of vital importance that, from certainly the twelfth century onward, the nobles and the burghers dwelt together within the walls of the cities. The interests and pleasures of both classes were thus identified, and the feudal lord learned to look at society from another point of view than that of his mountain-castle. The Church too in Italy never suffered itself, as in Northern countries, to be used as a means of providing for the younger sons of noble families. Bishoprics, abbacies, and canonries were often given from the most unworthy motives, but still not according to the pedigrees of the applicants; and if the bishops in Italy were more numerous, poorer, and, as a rule, destitute of all sovereign rights, they still lived in the cities where their cathedrals stood, and formed, together with their chapters, an important element in the cultivated society of the place. In the age of despots and absolute princes which followed the nobility in most of the cities had the motives and the leisure to give themselves up to a private life free from political danger and adorned with all that was elegant and enjoyable, but at the same time hardly distinguishable from that of the wealthy burgher. And after the time of Dante, when the new poetry and literature were in the hands of all Italy, when to this was added the revival of ancient culture and the new interest in man as such, when the successful *condottiere* became a prince, and not only good birth, but legitimate birth, ceased to be indispensable for a throne, it might well seem that the age of equality had dawned, and the belief in nobility vanished for ever.

From a theoretical point of view, when the appeal was made to antiquity the conception of nobility could be both justified and condemned from Aristotle alone. Dante, for example, adapts from the Aristotelian definition, "Nobility rests on excellence and inherited wealth," his own saying, "Nobility rests on personal excellence or on that of predecessors." But elsewhere he is not satisfied with this conclusion. He blames himself, because even in Paradise, while talking with his ancestor Cacciaguida, he made mention of his noble origin, which is but as a mantle from which time is ever cutting something away, unless we ourselves add daily fresh worth to it. And in the *Convivio* he disconnects *nobile* and *nobiltà* from every condition of birth, and identifies the idea with the capacity for moral and intellectual eminence, laying a special stress on high culture by calling *nobiltà* the sister of *filosofia*.

And as time went on the greater the influence of humanism on the Italian mind, the firmer and more widespread became the conviction that birth decides nothing as to the goodness or badness of a man. In the fifteenth century this was the prevailing opinion. Poggio, in his dialogue *On Nobility,* agrees with his interlocutors— Niccolo Niccoli and Lorenzo de' Medici, brother of the great Cosimo—that there is no other nobility than that of personal merit. The keenest shafts of his ridicule are directed against much of what vulgar prejudice thinks indispensable to an aristocratic life.

> A man is all the farther removed from true nobility the longer his forefathers have plied the trade of brigands. The taste for hawking and hunting savours no more of nobility than the nests and lairs of the hunted creatures of spikenard. The cultivation of the soil, as practised by the ancients, would be much nobler than this senseless wandering through the hills and woods, by which men make themselves liker to the brutes than to the reasonable creatures. It may serve well enough as a recreation, but not as the business of a lifetime.

The life of the English and French chivalry in the country or in the woody fastnesses seems to him thoroughly ignoble, and worst of all the doings of the robber-knights of Germany. Lorenzo here begins to take the part of the nobility, not—which is characteristic—appealing to any natural sentiment in its favour, but because Aristotle in the fifth book of the *Politics* recognizes the nobility as existent, and defines it as resting on excellence and inherited wealth. To this

Niccoli retorts that Aristotle gives this not as his own conviction, but as the popular impression; in his *Ethics,* where he speaks as he thinks, he calls him noble who strives after that which is truly good. Lorenzo urges upon him vainly that the Greek word for nobility means good birth; Niccoli thinks the Roman word *nobilis*— *i.e.,* remarkable—a better one, since it makes nobility depend on a man's deeds. Together with these discussions we find a sketch of the condition of the nobles in various parts of Italy. In Naples they will not work, and busy themselves neither with their own estates nor with trade and commerce, which they hold to be discreditable; they either loiter at home or ride about on horseback. The Roman nobility also despise trade, but farm their own property; the cultivation of the land even opens the way to a title; "it is a respectable but boorish nobility." In Lombardy the nobles live upon the rent of their inherited estates; descent and the abstinence from any regular calling constitute nobility. In Venice the *nobili,* the ruling caste, were all merchants. Similarly in Genoa the nobles and non-nobles were alike merchants and sailors, and separated only by their birth; some few of the former, it is true, still lurked as brigands in their mountain-castles. In Florence a part of the old nobility had devoted themselves to trade; another and certainly by far the smaller part enjoyed the satisfaction of their titles and spent their time either in doing nothing at all or else in hunting and hawking.

The decisive fact was that nearly everywhere in Italy even those who might be disposed to pride themselves on their birth could not make good the claims against the power of culture and of wealth, and that their privileges in politics and at Court were not sufficient to encourage any strong feeling of caste. Venice offers only an apparent exception to this rule, for there the *nobili* led the same life as their fellow-citizens, and were distinguished by few honorary privileges. The case was certainly different at Naples, which the strict isolation and the ostentatious vanity of its nobility excluded, above all other causes, from the spiritual movement of the Renaissance. The traditions of medieval Lombardy and Normandy, and the French aristocratic influences which followed, all tended in this direction; and the Aragonese Government, which was established by the middle of the fifteenth century, completed the work, and accomplished in Naples what followed a hundred years later in the rest of Italy—a social transformation in obedience to Spanish ideas, of which the chief features were the contempt for work and the passion for titles. The effect of this new influence was evident, even in the smaller towns, before the year 1500. We hear complaints from La Cava that the place had been proverbially rich as long as it was filled with masons and weavers; while now, since instead of looms and trowels nothing but spurs, stirrups, and gilded belts was to be seen, since everybody was trying to become Doctor of Laws or of Medicine, notary, officer, or knight, the most intolerable poverty prevailed. In Florence an analogous change appears to have taken place by the time of Cosimo, the first Grand Duke; he is thanked for adopting the young people, who now despise trade and commerce, as knights of his Order of St. Stephen. This goes straight in the teeth of the good old Florentine custom, by which fathers left property to their children on the condition that they should have some occupation. But a mania for title of a curious and ludicrous sort sometimes crossed and thwarted, especially among the Florentines, the levelling influence of art and culture. This was the passion for knighthood, which became one of the most striking follies of the day, at a time when the dignity itself had lost every shadow of significance.

Toward the end of the fourteenth century Franco Sacchetti writes:

> A few years ago everybody saw how all the workpeople down to the bakers, how all the wool-carders, usurers, money-changers, and blackguards of all descriptions became knights. Why should an official need knighthood when he goes to preside over some little provincial town? What has this title to do with any ordinary bread-winning pursuit? How art thou sunken, unhappy dignity! Of all the long list of knightly duties what single one do these knights of ours discharge? I wished to speak of these things that the reader might see that knighthood is dead. And as we have gone so far as to confer the honour upon dead men, why not upon figures of wood and stone, and why not upon an ox?

The stories which Sacchetti tells by way of illustration speak plainly enough. There we read how Bernabo Visconti knighted the victor in a drunken brawl, and then did the same derisively to the vanquished; how German knights with their decorated helmets and devices were ridiculed—and more of the same kind. At a later period Poggio makes merry over the many knights of his day without a horse and without military training. Those who wished to assert the privilege of the order and ride out with lance and colours found in Florence that they might have to face the Government as well as the jokers.

On considering the matter more closely we shall find that this belated chivalry, independent of all nobility of birth, though partly the fruit of an insane passion for title, had nevertheless another and better side. Tournaments had not yet ceased to be practised, and no one could take part in them who was not a knight. But the combat in the lists, and especially the difficult and perilous tilting with the lance, offered a favourable opportunity for the display of strength, skill, and courage, which no one, whatever might be his origin, would willingly neglect in an age which laid such stress on personal merit. They were without noble blood in their veins—that the society which surrounded them was in no respects inferior to a Court. Even under Cosimo and afterward under the elder Pietro, brilliant tournaments were held at Florence. The younger Pietro neglected the duties of government for these amusements, and would never suffer himself to be painted except clad in armour. The same practice prevailed at the Court of Alexander VI, and when the Cardinal Ascanio Sforza asked the Turkish Prince Djem how he liked the spectacle the barbarian replied with much discretion that such combats in his country only took place among slaves, since then, in the case of accident, nobody was the worse for it. The Oriental was unconsciously in accord with the old Romans in condemning the manners of the Middle Ages.

Apart, however, from this particular prop of knighthood, we find here and there in Italy—for example, at Ferrara—orders of Court service whose members had a right to the title.

But great as were individual ambitions and the vanities of nobles and knights, it remains a fact that the Italian nobility took its place in the centre of social life, and not at the extremity. We find it habitually mixing with other classes on a footing of perfect equality, and seeking its natural allies in culture and intelligence. It is true that for the courtier a certain rank of nobility was required, but this exigence is expressly declared to be caused by a prejudice rooted in the public mind—"per l'oppenion universale"—and never was held to imply the belief that the personal worth of one who was not of noble blood was in any degree lessened thereby, nor did it follow from this rule that the prince was limited to the nobility for his society. It was meant simply that the perfect man—the true courtier—should not be wanting in any conceivable advantage, and therefore not in this. If in all the relations of life he was specially bound to maintain a dignified and reserved demeanour the reason was not found in the blood which flowed in his veins, but in the perfection of manner which was demanded from him. We are here in the presence of a modern distinction, based on culture and on wealth, but on the latter solely because it enables men to devote their lives to the former, and effectually to promote its interests and advancement.

The Outward Refinements of Life

But in proportion as distinctions of birth ceased to confer any special privilege was the individual himself compelled to make the most of his personal qualities, and society to find its worth and charm in itself. The demeanour of individuals and all the higher forms of social intercourse became ends pursued with a deliberate and artistic purpose.

Even the outward appearance of men and women and the habits of daily life were more perfect, more beautiful, and more polished than among the other nations of Europe. The dwellings of the upper classes fall rather within the province of the history of art; but we may note how far the castle and the city mansion in Italy surpassed in comfort, order, and harmony the dwellings of the Northern noble. The style of dress varied so continually that it is impossible to make any complete comparison with the fashions of other countries, all the more because since the close of the fifteenth century limitations of the latter were frequent. The costumes of the time, as given us by the Italian painters, are the most convenient and the most pleasing to the eye which were then to be found in Europe; but we cannot be sure if they represent the prevalent fashion, or if they are faithfully reproduced by the artist. It is nevertheless beyond a doubt that nowhere was so much importance attached to dress as in Italy. The people was, and is, vain; and even serious men among it looked on a handsome and becoming costume as an element in the perfection of the individual. At Florence, indeed, there was a brief period when dress was a purely personal matter, and every man set the fashion for himself, and till far into the sixteenth century there were exceptional people who still had the courage to do so; and the majority at all events showed themselves capable of varying the fashion according to their individual tastes. It is a symptom of decline when Giovanni della Casa warns his readers not to be singular or to depart from existing fashions. Our own age, which, in men's dress at any rate, treats uniformity as the supreme law, gives up by so doing far more than it is itself aware of. But it saves itself much time, and this, according to our notions of business, outweighs all other disadvantages.

In Venice and Florence at the time of the Renaissance there were rules and regulations prescribing the dress of the men and restraining the luxury of the women. Where the fashions were less free, as in Naples, the moralists confess with regret that no difference can be observed between noble and burgher. They further deplore the rapid changes of fashion, and—if we rightly understand their words—the senseless idolatry of whatever comes from France, though in many cases the fashions which were received back from the French were originally Italian. It does not further concern us how far these frequent changes and the adoption of French and Spanish ways contributed to the national passion for external display; but we find in them additional evidence of the rapid movement of life in Italy in the decades before and after the year 1500. The occupation of different parts of Italy by foreigners caused the inhabitants not only to adopt foreign fashions, but sometimes to abandon all luxury in matters of dress. Such a change in public feeling at Milan is recorded by Landi. But the differences in costume, he tells us, continued to exist, Naples distinguishing itself by splendour, and Florence, to the eye of the writer, by absurdity.

We may note in particular the efforts of the women to alter their appearance by all the means which the toilette could afford. In no country of Europe since the fall of the Roman Empire was so much trouble taken to modify the face, the colour of skin, and the growth of the hair as in Italy at this time. All tended to the formation of a conventional type, at the cost of the most striking and transparent deceptions. Leaving out of account costume in general, which in the fourteenth century was in the highest degree varied in colour and loaded with ornament, and at a later period assumed a character of more harmonious richness, we here limit ourselves more particularly to the toilette in the narrower sense.

No sort of ornament was more in use than false hair, often made of white or yellow silk. The law denounced and forbade it in vain, till some preacher of repentance touched the worldly minds of the wearers. Then was seen, in the middle of the public square, a lofty pyre on which, beside lutes, dice-boxes, masks, magical charms, song-books, and other vanities lay masses of false hair, which the purging fires soon turned into a heap of ashes. The ideal colour sought for both in natural and artificial hair was blond. And as the sun was supposed to have the power of making the hair of this colour many ladies would pass their whole time in the open air on sunshiny days. Dyes and other mixtures were also used freely for the same purpose. Besides all these we meet with an endless list of beautifying waters, plasters, and paints for every single part of the face—even for the teeth and eyelids—of which in our day we can form no conception. The ridicule of the poets, the invectives of the preachers, and the experience of the baneful effects of these cosmetics on the skin were powerless to hinder women from giving their faces an unnatural form and colour. It is possible that the frequent and splendid representations of mysteries, at which hundreds of people appeared painted and masked, helped to further this practice in daily life. It is certain that it was widely spread, and that the countrywomen vied in this respect with their sisters in the towns. It was vain to preach that such decorations were the mark of the courtesan; the most honourable matrons, who all the year round never touched paint, used it nevertheless on holidays when they showed themselves in public. But whether we look on this bad habit as a remnant of barbarism, to which the painting of savages is a parallel, or as a consequence of the desire for perfect youthful beauty in features and in colour, as the art and complexity of the toilette would lead us to think—in either case there was no lack of good advice on the part of the men.

The use of perfumes too went beyond all reasonable limits. They were applied to everything with which human beings came into contact. At festivals even the mules were treated with scents and ointments. Pietro Aretino thanks Cosimo I for a perfumed roll of money.

The Italians of that day lived in the belief that they were more cleanly than other nations. There are, in fact, general reasons which speak rather for than against this claim. Cleanliness is indispensable to our modern notion of social perfection, which was developed in Italy earlier than elsewhere. That the Italians were one of the richest of existing peoples is another presumption in their favour. Proof either for or against these pretensions can, of course, never be forthcoming, and if the question were one of priority in establishing rules of cleanliness the chivalrous poetry of the Middle Ages is perhaps in advance of anything that Italy can produce. It is nevertheless certain that the singular neatness and cleanliness of some distinguished representatives of the Renaissance, especially in their behaviour at meals, was noticed expressly, and that 'German' was the synonym in Italy for all that was filthy. The dirty habits which Massimiliano Sforza picked up in the course of his German education, and the notice they attracted on his return to Italy, are recorded by Giovio. It is at the same time very curious that, at least in the fifteenth century, the inns and hotels were left chiefly in the hands of Germans, who probably, however, made their profit mostly out of the pilgrims journeying to Rome. Yet the statements on this point may refer rather to the country districts since it is notorious that in the great cities Italian hotels held the first place. The want of decent inns in the country may also be explained by the general insecurity of life and property.

To the first half of the sixteenth century belongs the manual of politeness which Giovanni della Casa, a Florentine by birth, published under the title *Il Galateo*. Not only cleanliness in the strict sense of the word, but the dropping of all the tricks and habits which we consider unbecoming, is here prescribed with the same unfailing tact with which the moralist discerns the highest ethical truths. In the literature of other countries the same lessons are taught, though less systematically, by the indirect influence of repulsive descriptions.

In other respects also the *Galateo* is a graceful and intelligent guide to good manners—a school of tact and delicacy. Even now it may be read with no small profit by people of all classes, and the politeness of European nations is not likely to outgrow its precepts. So far as tact is an affair of the heart, it has been inborn in some men from the dawn of civilization, and acquired through force of will by others; but the Italian first recognized it as a universal social duty and a mark of culture and education. And Italy itself had altered much in the course of two centuries.

Violence

When in the course of the sixteenth century Italian life fell more and more under Spanish influence the violence of the means to which jealousy had recourse perhaps increased. But this new phase must be distinguished from the punishment of infidelity which existed before, and which was founded in the spirit of the Renaissance itself. As the influence of Spain declined these excesses of jealousy declined also, till toward the close of the seventeenth century they had wholly disappeared, and their place was taken by that indifference which regarded the *cicisbeo* as an indispensable figure in every household, and took no offence at one or two supernumerary lovers (*patiti*).

But who can undertake to compare the vast sum of wickedness which all these facts imply with what happened in other countries? Was the marriage-tie, for instance, really more sacred in France during the fifteenth century than in Italy? The *fabliaux* and farces would lead us to doubt it, and rather incline us to think that unfaithfulness was equally common, though its tragic consequences were less frequent, because the individual was less developed and his claims were less consciously felt than in Italy. More evidence, however, in favour of the Germanic peoples lies in the fact of the social freedom enjoyed among them by girls and women, which impressed Italian travellers so pleasantly in England and in the Netherlands. And yet we must not attach too much importance to this fact. Unfaithfulness was doubtless very frequent, and in certain cases led to a sanguinary vengeance. We have only to remember how the Northern princes of that time dealt with their wives on the first suspicion of infidelity.

But it was not merely the sensual desire, not merely the vulgar appetite of the ordinary man, which trespassed upon forbidden ground among the Italians of that day, but also the passion of the best and noblest; and this not only because the unmarried girl did not appear in society, but also because the man, in proportion to the completeness of his own nature, felt himself most strongly attracted by the woman whom marriage had developed. These are the men who struck the loftiest notes of lyrical poetry, and who have attempted in their treatises and dialogues to give us an idealized image of the devouring passion—*l'amor divino*. When they complain of the cruelty of the winged god they are not only thinking of the coyness or hard-heartedness of the beloved one, but also of the unlawfulness of the passion itself. They seek to raise themselves above this painful consciousness by that spiritualization of love which found a support in the Platonic doctrine of the soul and of which Pietro Bembo is the most famous representative. His thoughts on this subject are set forth by himself in the third book of the *Asolani*, and indirectly by Castiglione, who puts in his mouth the splendid speech with which the fourth book of the *Cortigiano* concludes; neither of these writers was a Stoic in his conduct, but at that time it meant something to be at once a famous and a good man, and this praise must be accorded to both of them; their contemporaries took what these men said to be a true expression of their feeling, and we have not the right to despise it as affectation. Those who take the trouble to study the speech in the *Cortigiano* will see how poor an idea of it can be given by an extract. There were then living in Italy several distinguished women who owed their celebrity chiefly to relations of this kind, such as Giulia Gonzaga, Veronica da Coreggio, and, avove all, Vittoria Colonna. The land of profligates and scoffers respected these women and this sort of love—and what more can be said in their favour? We cannot tell how far vanity had to do with the matter, how far Vittoria was flattered to hear round her the sublimated utterances of hopeless love from the most famous men in Italy. If the thing was here and there a fashion, it was still no trifling praise for Vittoria that she, at least, never went out of fashion, and in her latest years produced the most profound impressions. It was long before other countries had anything similar to show.

In the imagination, then, which governed the people more than any other, lies one general reason why the course of every passion was violent, and why the means used for the gratification of passion were often criminal. There is a violence which cannot control itself because it is born of weakness; but in Italy what we find is the corruption of powerful natures. Sometimes this corruption assumed a colossal shape, and crime seems to acquire almost a personal existence of its own.

The restraints of which men were conscious were but few. Each individual, even among the lowest of the people, felt himself inwardly emancipated from the control of the State and its police, whose title to respect was illegitimate, and itself founded on violence; and no man believed any longer in the justice of the law. When a murder was committed the sympathies of the people, before the circumstances of the case were known, ranged themselves instinctively on the side of the murderer. A proud, manly bearing before and at the execution excited such admiration that the narrator often forgets to tell us for what offence the criminal was put to death. But when we add to this inward contempt of law and to the countless grudges and enmities which called for satisfaction the impunity which crime enjoyed during times of political disturbance we can only wonder that the State and society were not utterly dissolved. Crises of this kind occurred at Naples during the transition from the Aragonese to the French and Spanish rule, and at Milan on the repeated expulsions and returns of the Sforzas; at such times those men who have never in their hearts recognized the bonds of law and society come forward and give free play to their instincts of murder and rapine. Let us take, by way of example, a picture drawn from a humbler sphere.

When the Duchy of Milan was suffering from the disorders which follows the death of Giangaleazzo Sforza, about the year 1480 all safety came to an end in the provincial cities. This was the case in Parma, where the Milanese Governor, terrified by threats of murder, and after vainly offering rewards for the discovery of the offenders, consented to throw open the gaols and let loose the most abandoned criminals. Burglary, the demolition of houses, shameless offences against decency, public assassination and murders, especially of Jews, were events of everyday occurrence. At first the authors of these deeds prowled about singly and masked; soon large gangs of armed men went to work every night without disguise. Threatening letters, satires, and scandalous jests circulated freely; and a sonnet in ridicule of the Government seems to have roused its indignation far more than the frightful condition of the city. In many churches the sacred vessels with the Host were stolen, and this fact is characteristic of the temper which prompted these outrages. It is impossible to say what would happen now in any country of the world if the Government and police ceased to act, and yet hindered by their presence the establishment of a provisional authority; but what then occurred in Italy wears a character of its own through the great share which personal hatred and revenge had in it. The impression, indeed, which Italy at this period makes on us is that even in quiet times great crimes were commoner than in other countries. We may, it is true, be misled by the fact that we have far fuller details on such matters here than elsewhere, and that the same force of imagination which gives a special character to crimes actually committed causes much to be invented which never really happened. The amount of violence was perhaps as great elsewhere. It is hard to say for certain whether in 1500 men were any safer, whether human life was after all better protected, in powerful, wealthy Germany, with its robber-knights, extortionate beggars, and daring highwaymen. But one thing is certain, that premeditated crimes, committed professionally and for hire by third parties, occurred in Italy with great and appalling frequency.

So far as regards brigandage, Italy, especially in the more fortunate provinces, such as Tuscany, was certainly not more, and probably less, troubled than the countries of the North. But the figures which do meet us are characteristic of the country. It would be hard, for instance, to find elsewhere the case of a priest gradually driven by passion from one excess to another, till at last he came to head a band of robbers. That age offers us this example among others. On August 12, 1495, the priest Don Niccolo de' Pelegati of Figarolo was shut up in an iron cage outside the tower of S. Giuliano at Ferrara. He had twice celebrated his first Mass; the first time he had the same day committed murder, but afterward received absolution at Rome; he then killed four people and married two wives, with whom he travelled about. He afterward took part in many assassinations, violated women, carried others away by force, plundered far and wide, and infested the territory of Ferrara with a band of followers in uniform, extorting food and shelter by every sort of violence. When we think of what all this implies, the mass of guilt on the head of this one man is something tremendous. The clergy and monks had many privileges and little supervision, and among them were doubtless plenty of murderers and other malefactors—but hardly a second Pelegati. It is another matter, though by no means creditable, when ruined characters sheltered themselves in the cowl in order to escape the arm of the law, like the corsair whom Massuccio knew in a convent in Naples. What the real truth was with regard to Pope John XXIII in this respect is not known with certainty.

The age of the famous brigand chief did not begin till later, in the seventeenth centry, when the political strife of Guelph and Ghibelline, of Frenchman and Spaniard, no longer agitated the country. The robber then took place of the partisan.

In certain districts of Italy where civilization had made little progress the country people were disposed to murder any stranger who fell into their hands. This was especially the case in the more remote parts of the kingdom of Naples, where the barbarism dated probably from the days of the Roman *latifundia,* and when the stranger and the enemy (*hospes* and *hostis*) were in all good faith held to be one and the same. These people were far from being irreligious. A herdsman once appeared in great trouble at the confessional, avowing that while making cheese during Lent a few drops of milk had found their way into his mouth. The confessor, skilled in the customs of the country, discovered in the course of his examination that the penitent and his friends were in the practice of robbing and murdering travellers, but that, through the force of habit, this usage gave rise to no twinges of conscience within them. We have already mentioned to what a degree of barbarism the peasants elsewhere could sink in times of political confusion.

A worse symptom than brigandage of the morality of that time was the frequency of paid assassination. In that respect Naples was admitted to stand at the head of all the cities of Italy. "Nothing," says Pontano, "is cheaper here than human life." But other districts could also show a terrible list of these crimes. It is hard, of course, to classify them according to the motives by which they were prompted, since political expediency, personal hatred, fear, and revenge all play into one another. It is no small honour to the Florentines, the most highly developed people of Italy, that offences of this kind occurred more rarely among them than anywhere else, perhaps because there was a justice at hand for legitimate grievances which was recognized by all, or because the higher culture of the individual gave him different views as to the right of men to interfere with the decrees of Fate. In Florence, if anywhere, men were able to feel the incalculable consequences of a deed of blood, and to understand how insecure the author of a so-called profitable crime is of any true and lasting gain. After the fall of Florentine liberty assassination, especially by hired agents, seems to have rapidly increased, and continued till the government of Cosimo I had attained such strength that the police were at last able to repress it.

Elsewhere in Italy paid crimes were probably more or less frequent in proportion to the existence of powerful and solvent buyers. It is impossible to make any statistical estimate of their number, but if only a fraction of the deaths which public report attributed to violence were really murders the crime must have been terribly frequent. The worst example of all was set by princes and Governments, who without the faintest scruple reckoned murder as one of the instruments of their power. And this without being in the same category with Cesare borgia. The Sforzas, the Aragonese monarchs, the Republic of Venice, and, later on, the agents of Charles V resorted to it whenever it suited their purpose. The imagination of the people at last became so accustomed to facts of this kind that the death of any powerful man was seldom or never attributed to natural causes. There were certainly absurd notions current with regard to the effects of various poisons. There may be some truth in the story of that terrible white powder used by the Borgias, which did its work at the end of a definite period, and it is possible that it was really a *velenum atterminatum* which the Prince of Salerno handed to the Cardinal of Aragon with the words: "In a few days you will die, because your father, King Ferrante, wished to trample upon us all." But the poisoned letter which Caterina Riario sent to Pope Alexander VI would hardly have caused his death even if he had read it; and when Alfonso the Great was warned by his physicians not to read in the Livy which Cosimo de' Medici had presented to him he told them with justice not to talk like fools. Nor can that poison with which the secretary of Piccinino wished to anoint the Sedan chair of Pius II have affected any other organ than the imagination. The proportion which mineral and vegetable poisons bore to one another cannot be ascertained precisely. The poison with which the painter Rosso Fiorentino destroyed himself was evidently a powerful acid, which it would have been impossible to administer to another person without his knowledge. The secret use of weapons, especially of the dagger, in the service of powerful individuals was habitual in Milan, Naples, and other cities. Indeed, among the crowds of armed retainers who were necessary for the personal safety of the great, and who lived in idleness, it was natural that outbreaks of this mania for blood should from time to time occur. Many a deed of horror would never have been committed had not the master known that he needed but to give a sign to one or other of his followers.

Among the means used for the secret destruction of others—so far, that is, as the intention goes—we find magic, practised, however, sparingly. Where *maleficii, malie,* and so forth are mentioned they appear rather as a means of heaping up additional terror on the head of some hated enemy. At the Courts of France and England in the fourteenth and fifteenth centuries magic, practiced with a view to the death of an opponent, plays a far more important part than in Italy.

In this country, finally, where individuality of every sort attained its highest development we find instances of that ideal and absolute wickedness which delights in crimes for their own sake, and not as means to an end, or at any rate as means to ends for which our psychology has no measure.

Superstitions

The belief in omens seems a much more innocent matter than astrology. The Middle Ages had everywhere inherited them in abundance from the various pagan religions; and Italy did not differ in this respect from other countries. What is characteristic of Italy is the support lent by humanism to the popular superstition. The pagan inheritance was here backed up by a pagan literary development.

The popular superstition of the Italians rested largely on premonitions and inferences drawn from ominous occurrences, with which a good deal of magic, mostly of an innocent sort, was connected. There was, however, no lack of learned humanists who boldly ridiculed these delusions, and to whose attacks we partly owe the knowledge of them. Gioviano Pontano, the author of the great astrological work already mentioned, enumerates with pity in his *Charon* a long string of Neapolitan superstitions—the grief of the women when a fowl or a goose caught the pip; the deep anxiety of the nobility if a hunting falcon did not come home, or if a horse sprained his foot; the magical formulae of the Apulian peasants, recited on three Saturday evenings, when mad dogs were at large. The animal kingdom, as in antiquity, was regarded as specially significant in this respect, and the behaviour of the lions, leopards, and other beasts kept by the State gave the people all the more food for reflection, because they had come to be considered as living symbols of the State. During the siege of Florence, in 1529, an eagle which had been shot at fled into the city, and the Signoria gave the bearer four ducats, because the omen was good. Certain times and places were favourable or unfavourable, or even decisive one way or the other, for certain actions. The Florentines, so Varchi tells us, held Saturday to be the fateful day on which all important events, good as well as bad, commonly happened. Their prejudice against marching out to war through a particular street has been already mentioned. At Perugia one of the gates, the Porta Eburnea, was thought lucky, and the Baglioni always went out to fight through it. Meteors and the appearance of the heavens were as significant in Italy as elsewhere in the Middle Ages, and the popular imagination saw warring armies in an unusual formation of clouds, and heard the clash of their collision high in the air. The superstition became a more serious matter when it attached itself to sacred things, when figures of the Virgin wept or moved the eyes, or when public calamities were associated with some alleged act of impiety, for which the people demanded expiation. In 1478, when Piacenza was visited with a violent and prolonged rainfall, it was said that there would be no dry weather till a certain usurer, who has been lately buried at S. Francesco, had ceased to rest in consecrated earth. As the bishop was not obliging enough to have the corpse dug up, the young fellows of the town took it by force, dragged it round the streets amid frightful confusion, offered it to be insulted and maltreated by former creditors, and at last threw it into the Po. Even Politian accepted this point of view in speaking of Giacomo Pazzi, one of the leaders of the conspiracy of 1478 in Florence which is called after his name. When he was put to death he devoted his soul to Satan with fearful words. Here, too, rain followed and threatened to ruin the harvest; here, too, a party of men, mostly peasants dug up the body in the church, and immediately the clouds departed and the sun shone—"so gracious was fortune in the opinion of the people," adds the great scholar. The corpse was first cast into unhallowed ground, the next day again dug up, and after a horrible procession through the city thrown into the Arno.

These facts and the like bear a popular character, and might have occurred in the tenth just as well as in the sixteenth century. But now comes the literary influence of antiquity. We know positively that the humanists were peculiarly susceptible to prodigies and auguries, and instances of this have been already quoted. If further evidence were needed it would be found in Poggio. The same radical thinker who denied the rights of noble birth and the inequality of men not only believed in all the medieval stories of ghosts and devils, but also in prodigies after the ancient pattern, like those said to have occurred on the last visit of Eugenius IV to Florence.

> Near Como there was seen one evening four thousand dogs, who took the road to Germany; these were followed by a great herd of cattle, and these by an army on foot and horseback, some with no heads and some with almost invisible heads, and then a gigantic horseman with another herd of cattle behind him.

/ / /

The popular faith in what is called the spirit-world was nearly the same in Italy as elsewhere in Europe. In Italy, as elsewhere, there were ghosts—that is, reappearances of deceased persons; and if the view taken of them differed in any respect from that which prevailed in the North the difference betrayed itself only in the ancient name *ombra*. Nowadays if such a shade presents itself a couple of Masses are said for its repose. That the spirits of bad men appear in a dreadful shape is a matter of course, but along with this we find the notion that the ghosts of the departed are universally malicious. The dead, says the priest in Bandello, kill the little children. It seems as if a certain shade was here thought of as separate from the soul, since the latter suffers in Purgatory, and when it appears does nothing but wail and pray. To lay the ghost the tomb was opened, the corpse pulled to pieces, the heart burned, and the ashes scattered to the four winds. At other times what appears is not the ghost of a man, but of an event—of a past condition of things. So the neighbours explained the diabolical appearances in the old palace of the Visconti near S. Giovanni in Conca, at Milan, since here it was that Bernabo Visconti had caused countless victims of his tyranny to be tortured and strangled, and no wonder if there were strange things to be seen. One evening a swarm of poor people with candles in their hands appeared to a dishonest guardian of the poor at Perugia, and danced round about him; a great figure spoke in threatening tones on their bahalf—it was St Alo, the patron saint of the poor-house. These modes of belief were so much a matter of course that the poets could make use of them as something which every reader would understand. The appearance of the slain Lodovico Pico under the walls of the besieged Mirandola is finely represented by Castiglione. It is true that poetry made the freest use of these conceptions when the poet himself had outgrown them.

Italy, too, shared the belief in daemons with the other nations of the Middle Ages. Men were convinced that God sometimes allowed bad spirits of every class to exercise a destructive influence on parts of the world and of human life. The only reservation made was that the man to whom the Evil One came as a tempter could use his free will to resist. In Italy the daemonic influence, especially as shown in natural events, easily assumed a character of poetical greatness. In the night before the great inundation of the Val d'Arno in 1333 a pious hermit above Vallombrosa heard a diabolical tumult in his cell, crossed himself, stepped to the door, and saw a crowd of black and terrible knights gallop by in armour. When conjured to stand one of them said: "We go to drown the city of Florence on account of its sins, if God will let us." With this the nearly contemporary vision at Venice (1340) may be compared, out of which a great master of the Venetian school, probably Giorgione, made the marvellous picture of a galley full of daemons, which speeds with the swiftness of a bird over the stormy lagoon to destroy the sinful island-city, till the three saints, who have stepped unobserved into a poor boatman's skiff, exorcized the fiends and sent them and their vessel to the bottom of the waters.

To this belief the illusion was now added that by means of magical arts it was possible to enter into relations with the Evil Ones, and use their help to further the purposes of greed, ambition, and sensuality. Many persons were probably accused of doing so before the time when it was actually attempted by many; but when the so-called magicians and witches began to be burned the deliberate practice of the black art became more frequent. With the smoke of the fires in which the suspected victims were sacrificed were spread the narcotic fumes by which numbers of ruined characters were drugged into magic; and with them many calculating impostors became associated.

The primitive and popular form in which the superstition had probably lived on uninterruptedly from the time of the Romans was the art of the witch (*strega*). The witch, so long as she limited herself to mere divination, might be innocent enough, were it not that the transition from prophecy to active help could easily, though often imperceptibly, be a fatal downward step. She was credited in such a case not only with the power of exciting love or hatred between man and woman, but also with purely destructive and malignant arts, and was especially charged with the sickness of little children, even when the malady obviously came from the neglect and stupidity of the parents. It is still questionable how far she was supposed to act by mere magical ceremonies and formulae, or by a conscious alliance with the fiends, apart from the poisons and drugs which she administered with a full knowledge of their effect.

The more innocent form of the superstition, in which the mendicant friar could venture to appear as the competitor of the witch, is shown in the case of the witch of Gaeta, whom we read of in Pontano. His traveller Suppatius reaches her dwelling while she is giving audience to a girl and a servant-maid, who come to her with a black hen, nine eggs laid on a Friday, a duck, and some white thread—for it is the third day since the new moon. They are then sent away, and bidden to come again at twilight. It is to be hoped that nothing worse than divination is intended. The mistress of the servant-maid is pregnant by a monk; the girl's lover has proved untrue and has gone into a monastery. The witch complains:

> "Since my husband's death I support myself in this way, and should make a good thing of it, since the Gaetan women have plenty of faith, were it not that the monks baulk me of my

> gains by explaining dreams, appeasing the anger of the saints for money, promising husbands to the girls, men-children to the pregnant women, offspring to the barren, and besides all this visiting the women at night when their husbands are away fishing, in accordance with the assignations made in daytime at church."

Suppatius warns her against the envy of the monastery, but she has no fear, since the guardian of it is an old acquaintance of hers.

But the superstition further gave rise to a worse sort of witches—namely, those who deprived men of their health and life. In these cases the mischief, when not sufficiently accounted for by the evil eye and the like, was naturally attributed to the aid of powerful spirits. The punishment, as we have seen in the case of Finicella, was the stake; and yet a compromise with fanaticism was sometimes practicable. According to the laws of Perugia, for example, a witch could settle the affair by paying down four hundred pounds. The matter was not then treated with the seriousness and consistency of later times. In the territories of the Church, at Norcia (Nursia), the home of St Benedict, in the upper Apennines, there was a perfect nest of witches and sorcerers, and no secret was made of it. It is spoken of in one of the most remarkable letters of Aeneas Sylvius, belonging to his earlier period. He writes to his brother:

> The bearer of this came to me to ask if I knew of a Mount of Venus in Italy, for in such a place magical arts were taught, and his master, a Saxon and a great astronomer, was anxious to learn them. I told him that I knew of a Porto Venere not far from Carrara, on the rocky coast of Liguria, where I spent three nights on the way to Basel; I also found that there was a mountain called Eryx in Sicily, which was dedicated to Venus, but I did not know whether magic was taught there. But it came into my mind while talking that in Umbria, in the old Duchy [Spoleto], near the town of Nursia, there is a cave beneath a steep rock, in which water flows. There, as I remember to have heard, are witches [*striges*], daemons, and nightly shades, and he that has the courage can see and speak to ghosts [*spiritus*], and learn magical arts. I have not seen it, nor taken any trouble about it, for that which is learned with sin is better not learned at all.

/ / /

We learn something more about the neighbourhood of Norcia through the necromancer who tried to get Benvenuto Cellini into his power. A new book of magic was to be consecrated, and the best place for the ceremony was among the mountains in that district. The master of the magician had once, it is true, done the same thing near the Abbey of Farfa, but had there found difficulties which did not present themselves at Norcia; further, the peasants in the latter neighbourhood were trustworthy people who had practice in the matter, and who could afford considerable help in case of need. The expedition did not take place, else Benvenuto would probably have been able to tell us something of the impostor's assistants. The whole neighbourhood was then proverbial. Aretino says somewhere of an enchanted well, "there dwell the sisters of the sibyl of Norcia and the aunt of the Fata Morgana." And about the same time Trissino could still celebrate the place in his great epic with all the resources of poetry and allegory as the home of authentic prophecy.

After the famous Bull of Innocent VIII (1484) witchcraft and the persecution of witches grew into a great and revolting system. The chief representatives of this system of persecution were German Dominicans; and Germany and, curiously enough, those parts of Italy nearest Germany were the countries most afflicted by this plague. The Bulls and injunctions of the Popes themselves refer, for example, to the Dominican province of Lombardy, to Cremona, to the dioceses of Brescia and Bergamo. We learn from Sprenger's famous theoretico-practical guide, the *Malleus Maleficarum*, that forty-one witches were burnt at Como in the first year after the publication of the Bull; crowds of Italian women took refuge in the territory of the Archduke Sigismund, where they believed themselves to be still safe. Witchcraft ended by taking firm root in a few unlucky Alpine valleys, especially in the Val Camonica; the system of persecution had succeeded in permanently infecting with the delusion those populations which were in any way predisposed for it. This essentially German form of witchcraft is that we should think of when reading the stories and novels of Milan or Bologna. That it did not make further progress in Italy is probably due to the fact that elsewhere a highly developed *streghe-*

ria was already in existence, resting on a different set of ideas. The Italian witch practised a trade, and needed for it money and, above all, sense. We find nothing about her of the hysterical dreams of the Northern witch, of marvellous journeys through the air, of Incubus and Succubus; the business of the *strega* was to provide for other people's pleasure. If she was credited with the power of assuming different shapes, or of transporting herself suddenly to distant places, she was so far content to accept this reputation, as her influence was thereby increased; on the other hand, it was perilous for her when the fear of her malice and vengeance, and especially of her power for enchanting children, cattle, and crops, became general. Inquisitors and magistrates were then thoroughly in accord with popular wishes if they burnt her.

By far the most important field for the activity of the *strega* lay, as has been said, in love affairs, and included the stirring up of love and of hatred, the producing of abortion, the pretended murder of the unfaithful man or woman by magical arts, and even the manufacture of poisons. Owing to the unwillingness of many persons to have to do with these women, a class of occasional practitioners arose who secretly learned from them some one or other of their arts, and then used this knowledge on their own account. The Roman prostitutes, for example, tried to enhance their personal attractions by charms of another description, in the style of Horatian Canidia. Aretino may not only have known, but have also told the truth about them in this particular. He gives a list of the loathsome messes which were to be found in their boxes—hair, skulls, ribs, teeth, dead men's eyes, human skin, the navels of little children, the soles of shoes and pieces of clothing from tombs. They even went themselves to the graveyard and fetched bits of rotten flesh, which they slily gave their lovers to eat—with more that is still worse. Pieces of the hair and nails of the lover were boiled in soil stolen from the ever-burning lamps in the church. The most innocuous of their charms was to make a heart of glowing ashes, and then to pierce it while singing:

> Prima che 'l fuoco spenghi,
> Fa ch' a mia porta venghi;
> Tal ti punga mio amore
> Quale io fo questo cuore.

There were other charms practised by moonshine, with drawings on the ground, and figures of wax or bronze, which doubtless represented the lover, and were treated according to circumstances.

These things were so customary that a woman who, without youth and beauty, nevertheless exercised a powerful charm on men, naturally became suspected of witchcraft. The mother of Sanga, secretary to Clement VII, poisoned her son's mistress, who was a woman of this kind. Unfortunately the son died too, as well as a party of friends who had eaten of the poisoned salad.

Next comes, not as helper but as competitor to the witch, the magician or enchanter—*incantatore*— was still more familiar with the most perilous business of the craft. Sometimes he was as much or more of an astrologer than of a magician; he probably often gave himself out as an astrologer in order not to be prosecuted as a magician, and a certain astrology was essential in order to find out the favourable hour for a magical process. But since many spirits are good or indifferent, the magician could sometimes maintain a very tolerable reputation, and Sixtus IV in 1474 had to proceed expressly against some Bolognese Carmelites, who asserted in the pulpit that there was no harm in seeking information from the daemons. Very many people believed in the possibility of the thing itself; an indirect proof of this lies in the fact that the most pious men believed that by prayer they could obtain visions of good spirits. Savonarola's mind was filled with these things; the Florentine Platonists speak of a mystic union with God; and Marcellus Palingenius gives us to understand clearly enough that he had to do with consecrated spirits. The same writer is convinced of the existence of a whole hierarchy of bad daemons, who have their seat from the moon downward, and are ever on the watch to do some mischief to nature and human life. He even tells of his own personal acquaintance with some of them, and as the scope of the present work does not allow of a systematic exposition of the then prevalent belief in spirits the narrative of Palingenius may be given as one instance out of many.

27

Moses
Holding the Tablets of the Law under his right arm Michelangelo's Moses is about to destroy the Tablets as he sees his people worshipping the Golden Calf.

Life and Times of Michelangelo

From Giorgio Vasari (1511-1574) Italian painter whose best work was *Lives of the Painters* we learn about the life and times of Michelangelo's Renaissance cities.

> On the death of Lorenzo, Michelagnolo returned to his father's house in great sorrow for his loss; here he bought a large piece of marble from which he made a Hercules, four braccia high, which was much admired, and after having remained for some years in the Strozzi Palace, was sent to France, in the year of the siege, by Giovan Battista della Palla. It is said that Piero de' Medici, the heir of Lorenzo, who had been long intimate with Michelagnolo, often sent for him when about to purchase cameos or other antiques; and that, one winter, when much snow fell in Florence, he caused Michelagnolo to make in his court a Statue of Snow, which was exceedingly beautiful. His father, seeing him thus honoured for his abilities, and beginning to perceive that he was esteemed by the great, now began to clothe him in a more stately manner than he had before done.

St. Peter's
Michelangelo was appointed its chief architect in 1546. He designed and finished part of the dome. His successors continued its construction following his designs.

For the Church of Santa Spirito, in Florence, Michelagnolo made a Crucifix in wood, which is placed over the lunette of the High Altar. This he did to please the Prior, who had given him a room wherein he dissected many dead bodies, and, zealously studying anatomy, began to give evidence of that perfection to which he afterwards brought his design. Some weeks before the Medici were driven from Florence, Michelagnolo had gone to Bolgona, and thence to Venice, having remarked the insolence and bad government of Piero, and fearing that some evil would happen to himself, as a servant of the Medici: but finding no means of existence in Venice, he returned to Bologna, where he had the misfortune to neglect the counter-sign, which it was needful to take at the gate, if one desired to go out again; Messer Giovanni Bentivogli having then commanded that all strangers, who had not this protection, should be fined fifty Bolgonese lira. This fine Michelagnolo had no means of paying, but he having, by chance, been seen by Messer Giovan Francesco Aldovrandi, one of the sixteen members of the government, the latter, making him tell his story, delivered him

View of Florence

from that peril, and kept him in his own house for more than a year. One day, Aldovrandi took him to see the Tomb of San Domenico, which is said to have been executed by the old sculptors, Giovanni Pisano and Maestro Niccolo dell' Arca: here, as it was found that two figures, of a braccio high, a San Petronio, and an Angel holding a candlestick namely, were wanting, Aldovrandi asked Michelagnolo if he had courage to undertake them, when he replied that he had; and having selected a piece of marble, he completed them in such sort that they are the best figures of the work, and he received thirty ducats for the two. He remained, as we have said, a year with Aldovrandi, and to have obliged him would have remained longer, the latter being pleased with his ability in design, and also with his Tuscan pronunciation in reading, listening with pleasure while Michelagnolo read the works of Dante, Petrarch, Boccaccio, and other Tuscan authors. But our artist, knowing that he was losing time at Bologna, returned to Florence, where he executed a San Giovanni in marble for Lorenzo di Pier Francesco de' Medici; after which he commenced a Sleeping Cupid, also in marble and the size of life. This being finished was shown as a fine work, by means of Baldassare del Milanese to Pier-Francesco, who having declared it beautiful, Baldassare then said to Michelagnolo, "I am certain that, if you bury this Statue for a time, and then send it to Rome so treated, that it may look old, you may get much more for it than could be obtained here" and this Michelagnolo is said to have done, as indeed he very easily could, that or more, but others declare that it was Milanese who, having taken this Cupid to Rome, there buried it, and afterwards sold it as an antique to the Cardinal San Giorgio for two hundred crowns. Others again affirm that the one sold to San Giorgio was made by Michelagnolo for Milanese who wrote to beg that Pier-Francesco would give Michelagnolo thirty crowns, declaring that sum to be all he had obtained for it, thus deceiving both him and Michelagnolo.

Cardinal San Giorgio had, meanwhile, discovered that the Cupid had been made in Florence, and having ascertained the whole truth, he compelled Milanese to return the money and take back the Statue, which, having fallen into the hands of the Duke Valentino, was presented by him to the Marchioness of Mantua, who took it to that city, where it is still to be seen. San Giorgio, meanwhile, incurred no small ridicule and even censure in the matter, he not having been able to appreciate the merit of the work; for this consisted in its absolute perfection, wherein, if a modern work be equal to the ancient, wherefore not value it as highly? for is it not a mere vanity to think more of the name than the fact? But men who regard the appearance more than the reality, are to be found in all times. The reputation of Michelagnolo increased greatly from this circumstance, and he was invited to Rome, where he was engaged by the Cardinal San Giorgio, with whom he remained nearly a year, but that Prelate, not understanding matters of art, did nothing for him.

At that time a Barber of the Cardinal, who had been a painter, and worked tolerably in fresco, but had no power of design, formed an acquaintance with Michelagnolo, who made him a Cartoon of St. Francis receiving the Stigmata, and this was painted by the Barber very carefully; it is now in the first Chapel of the Church of San Pietro, in Montorio. The ability of Michelagnolo, was, however, clearly perceived by Messer Jacopo Galli, a Roman gentleman of much judgment, who commissioned him to make a

Cupid, the size of life, with a Bacchus of ten palms high; the latter holds a Tazza in the right hand, and in the left he has the skin of a Tiger, with a bunch of grapes which a little Satyr is trying to nibble away from him. In this figure the artist has evidently brought to mingle beauties of a varied kind, labouring to exhibit the bold bearing of the youth united to the fulness and roundness of the female form; and herein did he prove himself to be capable of surpassing the statues of all other modern masters.

During his abode in Rome, Michelagnolo made so much progress in art, that the elevation of thought he displayed, with the facility with which he executed works in the most difficult manner, was considered extraordinary, by persons practised in the examination of the same, as well as by those unaccustomed to such marvels, all other works appearing as nothing in the comparison with those of Michelagnolo. These things caused the Cardinal Saint Denis, a Frenchman, called Rovano, to form the desire of leaving in that renowned city some memorial of himself by the hand of so famous an artist. He therefore commissioned Michelagnolo to execute a Pietà of marble in full relief; and this when finished, was placed in San Pietro, in the Chapel of Santa Maria della Febbre namely, at the Temple of Mars. To this work I think no sculptor, however distinguished an artist, could add a single grace, or improve it by whatever pains he might take, whether in elegance and delicacy or force, and the careful perforation of the marble, nor could any surpass the art which Michelagnolo has here exhibited.

Among other fine things may be remembered—to say nothing of the admirable draperies—that the body of the Dead Christ exhibits the very perfection of research in every muscle, vein, and nerve, nor could any corpse more completely resemble the dead than does this. There is besides a most exquisite expression in the countenance, and the limbs are affixed to the trunk in a manner that is truly perfect; the veins and pulses, moreover, are indicated with so much exactitude, that one cannot but marvel how the hand of the artist should in a short time have produced such a work, or how a stone which just before was without form or shape, should all at once display such perfection as Nature can but rarely produce in the flesh. The love and care which Michelagnolo had given to this group were such that he there left his name—a thing he never did again for any work—on the cincture which girdles the robe of Our

Lady; for it happened one day that Michelagnolo, entering the place where it was erected, found a large assemblage of strangers from Lombardy there, who were praising it highly; one of these asking who had done it, was told "Our Hunchback of Milan;" hearing which, Michelagnolo remained silent, although surprised that his work should be attributed to another. But one night he repaired to Saint Peter's with a light and his chisels, to engrave his name as we have said on the figure, which seems to breathe a spirit as perfect as her form and countenance, speaking as one might think in the following words:

> Beauty and goodness, piety and grief,
> Dead in the living marble. Weep not thus;
> Be comforted, time shall awake the dead.
> Cease then to weep with these unmeasured tears,
> Our Lord, and thine, thy father, son, and spouse,
> His daughter, thou his mother and sole bride.

From this work then Michelagnolo acquired great fame; certain dullards do indeed affirm that he has made Our Lady too young, but that is because they fail to perceive the fact that unspotted maidens long preserve the youthfulness of their aspect, while persons afflicted as Christ was do the contrary; the youth of the Madonna, therefore, does but add to the credit of the master.

Michelagnolo now received letters from friends in Florence advising him to return, since he might thus obtain that piece of marble which Pier Soderini, then Gonfaloniere the city, had talked of giving to Leonardo da Vinci, but was now preparing to present to Andrea dal Monte Sansavino, an excellent sculptor who was making many efforts to obtain it. It was difficult to get a statue out of it without the addition of several pieces, and no one, Michelagnolo excepted, had the courage to attempt it; but he, who had long wished for the block, no sooner arrived in Florence than he made every effort to secure the same. This piece of marble was nine braccia high, and unluckily, a certain Maestro Simone da Fiesole had commenced a colossal figure thereon; but the work had been so grievously injured that the Superintendents had suffered it to remain in the House of Works at Santa Maria del Fiore for many years, without thinking of having it finished, and there it seemed likely to continue.

Michelagnolo measured the mass anew to ascertain what sort of figure he could draw from it, and accommodating himself to the attitude demanded by the injuries which Maestro Simone had inflicted on it, he begged it from the Superintendents and Soderini, by whom it was given to him as a uselsss thing, they thinking that whatever he might make of it must needs be preferable to the state in which it then lay, and wherein it was totally useless to the fabric. Michelagnolo then made a model in wax, representing a young David, with the sling in his hand, as the ensigns of the Palace, and to intimate that, as he had defended his people and governed justly, so they who were then ruling that city should defend it with courage and govern it uprightly. He commenced his labours in the House of Works, at Santa Maria del Fiore, where he formed an enclosure of planks and masonry, which surrounded the perfection. The marble having been much injured by Simone, did not entirely suffice to the wishes of Michelagnolo, who therefore permitted some of the traces of Simone's chisel to remain; these may be still perceived, and certainly it was all but a miracle that Michelagnolo performed, when he thus resuscitated one who was dead.

When the Statue was set up, it chanced that Soderini, whom it greatly pleased, came to look at it while Michelagnolo was retouching it at certain points, and told the artist that he thought the nose too short. Michelagnolo perceived that Soderini was in such a position beneath the figure that he could not see it conveniently, yet to satisfy him, he mounted the scaffold with his chisel and a little powder gathered from the floor in his hand, when striking lightly with the chisel, but without altering the nose, he suffered a little of the powder to fall, and then said to the Gonfaloniere who stood below, "Look at it now." "I like it better now," replied Piero; "you have given it life." Michelagnolo then descended, not without compassion for those who desire to appear good judges of matters whereof they know nothing. The work fully completed, Michelagnolo gave it to view, and truly may we affirm that this Statue surpasses all others whether ancient or modern, Greek or Latin: neither the Marforio at Rome, the Tiber and the Nile in the Belvedere, nor the Giants of Monte Cavallo, can be compared with it, to such perfection of beauty and excellence did our artist bring his work.

The outline of the lower limbs is most beautiful. The connexion of each limb with the trunk is faultless, and the spirit of the whole form is divine: never since has there been produced so fine an attitude, so perfect a grace, such beauty of head, feet, and hands; every part is replete with excellence; nor is so much harmony and admirable art to be found in any other work. He that has seen this, therefore, need not care to see any production besides, whether of our own times or those preceding it. For this Statue, Michelagnolo received from Soderini the sum of four hundred crowns; it was placed on its pedestal in the year 1504, and the glory resulting to the artist therefrom became such as to induce the Gonfaloniere to order a David in bronze, which, when Michelagnolo had completed, was sent to France.

About this time Michelagnolo cast a Madonna in bronze for certain Flemish merchants called Moscheroni, persons of much account in their own land, and who paid him a hundred crowns for his work, which they sent into Flanders. The Florentine citizen, Agnolo Doni, likewise desired to have some production from the hand of Michelagnolo, who was his friend, and he being, as we have before said, a great lover of fine works in art, whether ancient or modern; wherefore Michelagnolo began a circular painting of Our Lady for him; she is kneeling, and presents the Divine Child, which she holds in her arms, to Joseph, who receives him to his bosom. Here the artist has finely expressed the perfection of delight with which the mother regards the beauty of her Son, and which is clearly manifest in the turn of her head and fixedness of her gaze: equally obvious is her wish that this contentment shall be shared by the pious old man who receives the babe with infinite tenderness and reverence. Nor did this suffice to Michelagnolo, since the better to display his art, he has assembled numerous undraped figures in the back-ground of his picture, some upright, some half recumbent, and others seated. The whole work is, besides, executed with so much care and finish, that of all his pictures, which indeed are but few, this is considered the best.

When the picture was completed, Michelagnolo sent it, still uncovered, to Agnolo Doni's house, with a note demanding for it a payment of sixty ducats. But Agnolo, who was a frugal person, declared that a large sum to give for a picture, although he knew it was worth more, and told the messenger that forty ducats which he gave him was enough. Hearing this, Michelagnolo sent back his man to say that Agnolo must now send a hundred ducats or give the picture back; whereupon Doni, who was pleased with the work, at once offered the sixty first demanded. But Michelagnolo, offended by the want of confidence exhibited by Doni, now declared that if he desired to have the picture, he must pay a hundred and forty ducats for the same, thus compelling him to give more than double the sum first required.

The Moses, in marble, five braccia high, was also completed by Michelagnolo, and never will any modern work approach the beauty of this statue; nay, one might with equal justice affirm, that of the ancient statues none is equal to this.

Seated in an attitude of imposing dignity, the Lawgiver rests one arm on the Tables, and with the other restrains the flowing beard, that, descending softly, is so treated as to exhibit the hair (which presents so great a difficulty in sculpture) soft, downy, and separated, hair from hair, in such sort, as might appear to be impossible, unless the chisel had become a pencil. The countenance is of the most sublime beauty, and may be described as that of a truly sacred and most mighty prince; but to say nothing of this, while you look at it, you would almost believe the figure to be on the point of demanding a veil wherewith to conceal that face, the beaming splendour of which is so dazzling to mortal gaze. So well at a word, has the artist rendered the divinity which the Almighty had imparted to the most holy countenance of that great Lawgiver The draperies also are most effectively raised from the marble ground, and are finished with beautiful foldings of the edges: the muscles of the arms, with the anatomical development and nerve of the hands, are exhibited to the utmost perfection; and the sam may be said of the lower limbs, which, with the knees and feet, ar clothed in admirably appropriate vestments. At a word, the sculp tor has completed his work in such sort that Moses may be trul affirmed more than ever now to merit his name of the friend c God. Nay, the Jews are to be seen every Saturday, or on their Sal bath, hurrying like a flight of swallows, men and women, to vis and worship this figure, not as a work of the human hand, but ; something divine.

Having at length made all his preparations, and approached tl conclusion of the same, Michelagnolo erected one portion of tl

Tomb, the shorter sides namely, at San Pietro in Vincola. It is said that while he was employed on that operation, a certain part of the marbles arrived from Carrara, where they had been suffered to remain, and as it was necessary to pay those who had delivered them, our artist repaired to the Pope, as was his custom. But finding His Holiness engaged with important intelligence just received from Bologna, he returned home, and paid with his own money, expecting to receive the order for it from the Pontiff immediately. He went to the palace a few days after therefore, but was again desired to wait and take patience, by a groom of the chambers, who affirmed that he was forbidden to admit him. A Bishop who stood near observed to the attendant that he was perhaps unacquainted with the person of the man whom he refused to admit; but the groom replied that he knew him only too well. "I, however," he added, "am here to do as my superiors command, and to obey the orders of the Pope." Displeased with this reply, the master departed, bidding the attendant tell his Holiness when next he should inquire for Michelagnolo, that he had gone elsewhere. He then returned to his dwelling, and ordering two of his servants to sell all his moveables to the Jews, and then follow him to Florence, he took post-horses that same night, and left Rome.

Arrived at Poggibonsi, a town on the road to the first-named city, in the Florentine territory, and consequently in a place of safety, the master made a halt; five couriers followed him one after another with letters from the Pope, and orders to convey him back, but no entreaty and no threat of the disgrace that would await him in case of refusal, would induce him to return. He was, however, finally prevailed on to write in reply, when he declared that His Holiness must excuse his returning to his presence, which he was resolved not to do, seeing that he, Julius, had driven him forth like a worthless person, which was a mode of treatment that his faithful service had not merited; he added that the Holy Father might seek elsewhere for some one who should serve him better.

Having reached Florence, Michelagnolo set himself to complete the Cartoon for the Great Hall, at which he worked during the three months of his stay in the city, Piero Soderini, the Gonfaloniere, being anxious to see it finished. The Signoria meanwhile received three Briefs, with the request that Michelagnolo might be sent back to Rome, but the latter, doubting what this eagerness of the Pope might portend, entertained, as it is said, some intention of going to Constantinople, there to serve the Grand Seigneur, who sought to engage him, by means of certain Franciscan Monks, for the purpose of constructing a bridge to connect Constantinople with Pera. But the Gonfaloniere labouring to induce Michelagnolo to repair to the Pope instead, and the master still refusing, Sodernini at length prevailed on him to do so by investing him with the character of Ambassador from the Florentine Republic, and recommending him also to the care of his brother, the Cardinal Soderini, whom he charged to introduce Michelagnolo to His Holiness; he then sent the artist to Bologna, in which city Pope Julius had already arrived from Rome.

Michelagnolo found his chief pleasure in the labours of art; all that he attempted, however difficult, proving successful, because nature had imparted to him the most admirable genius, and his application to those excellent studies of design was unremitting. For the greater exactitude, he made numerous dissections of the human frame, examining the anatomy of each part, the articulations of the joints, the various muscles, the nerves, the veins, and all the different minutiae of the human form. Nor of this only, but of animals, and more particularly of horses, which he much delighted in, and kept for his pleasure, examining them so minutely in all their relations to art, that he knew more of them than do many whose sole business is the care of those animals. These labours enabled him to complete his works, whether of the pencil or chisel, with inimitable perfection, and to give them a grace, a beauty, and an animation, wherein (be it said without offence to any) he has surpassed even the antique. In his works he has overcome the difficulties of art, with so much facility, that no trace of labour appears in them, however great may be that which those who copy them find in the imitation of the same.

The genius of Michelagnolo was acknowledged in his lifetime, and not as happens in many cases, after his death only; and he was favoured, as we have seen, by Julius II., Leo X., Clement VII., Paul III., Julius III., Paul IV., and Pius IV.; these Pontiffs having always desired to keep him near them, as indeed would Soliman, Emperor of the Turks, Francis, King of France, the Emperor Charles V., the Signoria of Venice, and lastly Duke Cosimo de' Medici: all very gladly have done, each of those monarchs and potentates having offered him the most honourable appointments, for the love of his great abilities. These things do not happen to any except men of the highest distinction, but in him all the three arts were found in such perfection, as God hath vouchsafed to no other master, ancient or modern, in all the many years that the sun has been turning round.

His powers of imagination were such that he was frequently compelled to abandon his purpose, because he could not express by the hand those grand and sublime ideas, which he had conceived in his mind, nay, he has spoiled and destroyed many works for this cause; and I know too that some short time before his death he burnt a large number of his designs, sketches, and cartoons, that none might see the labours he had endured, and the trials to which he had subjected his spirit, in his resolve not to fall short of perfection. I have myself secured some drawings by his hand, which were found in Florence, and are now in my book of designs and these, although they give evidence of his great genius, yet prove also that the hammer of Vulcan was necessary to bring Minerva from the head of Jupiter. He would make his figures of nine, ten, and even twelve heads long, for no other purpose than the research of a certain grace in putting the parts together which is not to be found in the natural form, and would say that the artist must have his measuring tools, not in the hand but in the eye, because the hands do but operate, it is the eye that judges; he pursued the same idea in architecture also.

None will marvel that Michelagnolo should be a lover of solitude, devoted as he was to Art, which demands the whole man, with all his thoughts, for herself. He who resigns his life to her may well disregard society, seeing that he is never alone nor without food for contemplation; and whoever shall attribute this love of solitude to caprice or eccentricity, does wrong; the man who would produce works of merit should be free from cares and anxieties, seeing that Art demands earnest consideration, loneliness, and quietude; she cannot permit wandering of the mind. Our artist did nevertheless greatly prize the friendship of distinguished and learned men, he enjoyed the society of such at all convenient seasons, maintaining close intercourse with them, more especially with the illustrious Cardinal Ippolito de' Medici, who loved him greatly. Having heard that an Arab horse which he possessed was much admired for its beauty by Michelagnolo, the Cardinal sent it to him as a present, with ten mules, all laden with corn, and a servant to take care of those animals, which the master accepted very willingly. The most illustrious Cardinal Pole was also a very intimate friend of Michelagnolo, who delighted in the talents and virtues of that Prelate. The Cardinals Farnese and Santa Croce, the latter afterwards Pope Marcellus, with the Cardinals Ridolfi and Maffeo, Monsignore Bembo, Carpi, and many other Cardinals and Prelates, were in like manner among his associates, but need not all be named here. Monsignore Claudio Tolomei was one of his intimates, and the Magnificent Messer Ottaviano de' Medici was his gossip, Michelagnolo having been godfather to one of his sons. Another of his friends was Messer Bindo Altoviti, to whom he gave that cartoon of the Chapel, wherein Noah is represented as inebriated and derided by one of his sons, while the other two compassionately seek to veil the degradation of their father.

Michelagnolo loved the society of artists, and held much intercourse with many among them, as, for example, with Jacopo Sansovino, Il Rosso, Pontormo, Daniello da Volterra, and the Aretine Giorgio Vasari, to whom he showed infinite kindness. It was by him indeed that Vasari was led to the study of architecture, Michelagnolo intending some day to make use of his services, and gladly conferring with him on matters connected with art. Those who affirm that he was not willing to instruct others are wrong, he would assist all with whom he was intimate or who asked his counsels. I have been present many times when this has happened, but I say no more, not desiring to proclaim the defects of others. It is true that he was not fortunate with those whom he took into his house, having chanced upon disciples wholly incapable of imitating their master. The Pistolese, Pietro Urbino, had ability but would never give himself the trouble to work. Antonio Mini was sufficiently willing, but had not quickness of perception, and when the wax is hard it does not take a good impression. Ascanio della Ripa took great pains, but no results have been displayed, whether in designs or finished works; he spent several years over a picture of which Michelagnolo had given him the cartoon, and, at a word, the hopes conceived of him have vanished in smoke. I remember that Michelagnolo, having compassion on Ripa's hard labours, would sometimes help him with his own hand, but it was all to little purpose.

Had he found a disciple to his mind, he would have made studies of anatomy, and written a treatise on that subject, even in his old age, as he often said to me, desiring to do this for the benefit of artists, who are frequently misled by want of knowledge in anatomy. But he distrusted his power of doing justice to his conceptions with the pen, having little practice in speaking, although in his letters he expressed his thoughts well and in few words. He delighted in the reading of our Italian poets, more especially of Dante, whom he honoured greatly and imitated in his thoughts as well as copied in his inventions. Like Petrarch also, he was fond of writing madrigals and making sonnets, many of which are very serious, and have since been made subjects of commentary.

Michelagnolo sent a large number of these verses to the most illustrious Marchesana di Pescara, receiving replies both in verse and prose from that lady, of whose genius he was as much enamoured as she of his. She went more than once from Viterbo to Rome to see him, and Michelagnolo designed for her a Pietà, with two Angels of infinite beauty; an admirable work, as is also a figure of Christ on the Cross, raising his head to heaven, and commending his spirit to his Father, and one of Our Saviour at the Well with the Woman of Samaria, both executed for the Marchesana. He delighted in the reading of scripture, like a good Christian as he was, and greatly honoured the writings of Fra Girolamo Savonarola, whom he had heard in the pulpit. He was an ardent admirer of beauty for the purposes of art; and from the beautiful he knew how to select the most beautiful, a quality without which no master can produce perfection; but he was not liable to the undue influence of beauty, as his whole life has proved. In all things Michelagnolo was exceedingly moderate; ever intent upon his work during the period of youth, he contented himself with a little bread and wine, and at a later period, until he had finished the Chapel namely, it was his habit to take but a frugal refreshment at the close of his day's work; although rich, he lived like a poor man; rarely did any friend or other person eat at his table, and he would accept no presents, considering that he would be bound to any one who offered him such: his temperance kept him in constant activity, and he slept very little, frequently rising in the night because he could not sleep, and resuming his labours with the chisel.

For these occasions he had made himself a cap of pasteboard, in the centre of which he placed his candle, which thus gave him light without encumbering his hands. Vasari had often seen this cap; and, remarking that Michelagnolo did not use wax-lights, but candles made of unmixed goat's tallow, which are excellent, he sent the master four packets of the same, weighing forty pounds. His own servant presented them respectfully in the evening, but Michelagnolo refused to accept them; whereupon the man replied: "Messere, I have nearly broken my arms in bringing them from the bridge hither, and have no mind to carry them back; now, there is a heap of mud before your door which is thick enough to hold them upright, so I'll e'en stick them up there, and set them all a-light." But, hearing that, the master bade him lay down the candles, declaring that no such pranks should be played before his house.

He has told me that, in his youth, he frequently slept in his clothes, being wearied with his labours he had no mind to undress merely that he might have to dress again. Many have accused him of being avaricious, but they are mistaken; he has proved himself the contrary, whether as regards his works in art or other possessions. He presented rich productions of various kind, as we have seen, to Messer Tommaso de' Cavalieri and Messer Bindo, with designs of considerable value to Fra Bastiano: while to his disciple, Antonio Mini, he gave designs, cartoons, the picture of the Leda, and all the models in clay or wax that ever he had made, but which were left in France as we have said. To Gherardo Perini, a Florentine gentleman and his friend, he gave three plates of most beautiful heads, which have fallen since his death into the hands of the most illustrious Don Francesco, Prince of Florence, by whom they are kept as the gems which they truly are. For Bartolommeo Bellini he made the Cartoon of a Cupid kissing his mother Venus; a beautiful thing, now at Florence, in the possession of Bellini's heirs. For the Marquis del Vasto, moreover, he made the Cartoon of a *Noli me tangere;* and these two last-mentioned works were admirably painted by Pontormo, as we have before related. The two Captives he gave to Signor Ruberto Strozzi; and the Pietà, in marble, which he had broken, to Antonio, his servant, and Francesco Bandini.

Who is it then that shall tax this master with avarice, seeing that the gifts he thus made were of things for which he might have obtained thousands of crowns; to say nothing of a fact which I well know, that he has made innumerable designs, and inspected buildings in great numbers, without ever gaining one scudo for the same? But to come to the money which he did gain: this was made, not by offices nor yet by trafficking or exchanges, but by the labour and thought of the master. I ask also, can he be called avaricious who assisted the poor as he did, who secretly paid the dowry of so many poor girls, and enriched those who served him? As witness Urbino, whom he rendered very rich; this man, having been long his disciple, had served him many years when Michelagnolo one day said to him, "When I die what will thou do?" "Serve some one else," replied Urbino. "Thou poor creature!" returned Michelagnolo, "I must save thee from that;" whereupon he gave him two thousand crowns at one time, a mode of proceeding befitting the Caesars and high Princes of the world. To his nephew also, he has more than once given three and four thousand crowns at a time, and has finally left him ten thousand crowns, besides the property in Rome.

He proved himself resentful, but with good reason, against those who had done him wrong, yet he never sought to avenge himself by any act of injury or violence; very orderly in all his proceedings, modest in his deportment, prudent and reasonable in discourse, usually earnest and serious, yet sometimes amusing, ingenious, and quick in reply; many of his remarks have been remembered and well merit to be repeated here, but I will add only a few of these recollections. A friend once speaking to him of death, remarked that Michelagnolo's constant labours for art, leaving him no repose, must needs make him think of it with great regret. "By no means," replied Michelagnolo, "for if life be a pleasure, yet, since death also is sent by the hand of the same master, neither should that displease us." To a citizen who observed him standing at Or San Michele, to look at the San Marco of Donato, and who inquired what he thought of that statue, he replied, that he had never seen a face looking more like that of a good man; adding, "If St. Mark looked thus we may safely believe what he has written." Being once shown the drawing of a boy who was recommended to his favour, and told, by way of excuse for defects, that he had not been long learning, he answered, "It is easy to perceive that." A similar remark escaped him when a painter who had depicted a Pietà was found to have succeeded badly; "It is indeed a pity," observed the master.

When Michelagnolo heard that Sebastiano Veniziano was to paint a Monk in the Chapel of San Pietro a Montorio, he declared that this would spoil the work; and being asked wherefore, replied, that "as the monks had spoiled the world, which was so large, it could not be surpising that they should spoil that Chapel which was so small." A painter had executed a work with great labour, and spent much time over it, but acquired a good sum when it was finished; being asked what he thought of the artist, Michelagnolo replied, "While he is labouring to become a rich man, he will always continue a poor painter." A friend of his who had taken orders, arrived in Rome, wearing the garb of a pilgrim, and meeting Michelagnolo, saluted him, but the latter pretended not to know him, compelling the monk to tell his name at length, when Michelagnolo, feigning surprise at his dress, remarked, "Oh, you really have a fine aspect; if you were but as good within as you seem without, it would be well for your soul." The same monk had recommended a friend of his own to Michelagnolo, who had given him a statue to execute, and the monk then begged him to give something more; this also our artist good-naturedly did, but it was now found that the pretended friend had made these requests only in the certainty that they would not be granted, and suffered his disappointment to be seen; whereupon Michelagnolo declared that such gutter-minded men were his abhorrence; and, continuing to take his metaphors from architecture, he added, "channels that have two mouths rarely act well."

Being asked his opinion of an artist who, having copied the most renowned antique marble statues and imitated the same, then boasted that he had surpassed the ancients, he made answer to this effect:—"He who walks on the traces of another is but little likely to get before him; and an artist who cannot do good of himself, is but poorly able to make good use of the works of others." A certain painter, I know not who, had produced a picture wherin there was an ox that was better than all besides, when, being asked why the artist had made that animal more life-like than the rest, Michelagnolo replied, "Every painter draws himself well." Passing one day by San Giovanni, in Florence, he was asked his opinion of the doors, and said, "They are so beautiful that they deserve to be used as the gates of Paradise." Seeing a prince who changed his plans daily, and was never in one mind, he remarked to a friend, "The head of this Signore is like a weather-cock; it turns around with every wind that touches it." Going to see a work in sculpture which was about to be fixed in its place, the sculptor took great pains to arrange the lights, that the work might be seen well, when Michelagnolo said:—"Do not trouble yourself; the principal question is, how it will bear the light of the Piazza,"—meaning to imply that when a work is given to public view, the people judge it, whether good or bad. There was a great prince in Rome who desired to pass for a good architect, and had caused certain niches to be made wherein he meant to place figures; each recess was three times the height of its depth, with a ring at the summit, and here the prince had various statues placed, but they did not turn out well. He then asked Michelagnolo what he could put into the niches. "Hang a bunch of eels in that Ring," replied the master.

With the Commissioners of San Pietro there was associated a gentleman who professed to understand Vitruvius, and to criticize the works accomplished. "You have now a man in the building who has great genius," remarked some one to Michelagnolo; "True," replied our artist, "but he has a bad judgment." A painter had executed a story, for which he had taken so many parts from drawings and other pictures, that there was nothing in it which was not copied: this being shown to Michelagnolo, and his opinion requested, he made answer, "It is very well; but at the day of Judgment, when every body shall retake its own limbs, what will this Story do, for then it will have nothing remaining?"—a warning to those who would practise art that they should do something for themselves. Passing once through Modena, he saw many beautiful figures which the Modanese sculptor, Maestro Antonio Bigarino, had made of terra-cotta, coloured to look like marble, which appeared to him to be most excellent productions; and as that sculptor did not know how to work in marble, he said, "If this earth were to become marble, woe to the antiques."

Michelagnolo was told that he ought to resent the perpetual competition of Nanni di Baccio Bigio, to which he replied: "He who strives with those who have nothing gains but little." A priest, who was his friend, said to him, "'Tis a pity that you have not married, that you might have left children to inherit the fruit of these honourable toils;" when Michelagnolo replied, "I have only too much of a wife in my art, and she has given me trouble enough; as to my children, they are the works that I shall leave; and if they are not worth much, they will at least live for some time. Woe to Lorenzo Ghiberti, if he had not made the gates of San Giovanni; for his children and grandchildren have sold or squandered all that he left; but the gates are still in their place." Vasari was sent one night by Pope Julius III. to the house of Michelagnolo for a design, and the master was then working at the Pietà in marble which he afterwards broke, knowing by the knock, who stood at the door, he descended with a lamp in his hand, and having ascertained what Vasari wanted, he sent Urbino for the drawing, and fell into conversation on other matters. Vasari meanwhile turned his eyes on a Leg of the Christ on which Michelagnolo was working and endeavouring to alter it; but to prevent Vasari from seeing this, he suffered the lamp to fall from his hand, and they remained in darkness. He then called to Urbino to bring a light, and stepping beyond the enclosure in which was the work, he remarked: "I am so old that death often pulls me by the cape, and bids me go with him; some day I shall fall myself, like this lamp, and the light of life will be extinguished."

With all this he took pleasure in the society of men like Menighella, a rude person and common-place painter of Valdarno, but a pleasant fellow; he came sometimes to see Michelagnolo, who made him a design of San Rocco and Sant' Antonio, which he had to paint for the country people; and this master, who would not work for kings without entreaty, often laid aside all other occupation to make designs of some simple matter for Menighella, "dressed after his own mind and fashion," as the latter would say. Among other things Menighella received from him the model of a Crucifix, which was most beautiful; he formed a mould from this also, whence Menighella made copies in various substances, and went about the country selling them. This man would sometimes make Michelagnolo laugh till he cried, more especially when he related the adventures he met with; as, for example, how a peasant, who had ordered the figure of San Francesco, made complaints that the painter had given him a grey dress, he desiring to have a finer colour, when Menighella put a pluvial of brocade on the back of the Saint, which gladdened the peasant to his heart.

He favoured, in like manner, the stone-cutter Topolino, who imagined himself an excellent sculptor, although, in fact, a very poor creature. He passed much time at the quarries of Carrara, sending marbles to Michelagnolo, nor did he ever despatch a cargo without adding three or four little figures from his own hand, at the sight of which Michelagnolo would almost die of laughing. At length, and after his return, he had rough-hewn a figure of Mercury in marble, which he was on the point of finishing, when he begged Michelagnolo to go and see it, insisting earnestly that he should give his true opinion of the work. "Thou art a fool to attempt figures, Topolino," said the master; "for dost thou not see that, from the knee to the foot, this Mercury of thine wants a full third of a braccio of its due length? and thou hast made him a dwarf and a cripple?" "Oh, that is nothing," replied Topolino, "if it has no other fault I shall find a remedy for that, never fear me." The master laughed again at his simplicity and departed; when Topolino, sawing his Mercury in two below the knee, fastened a piece of marble nicely between the parts, and having thus added the length required, he gave the figure a pair of buskins, the fastenings of which passed beyond the junctures. He then summoned the master once more; and Michelagnolo could not but wonder as well as laugh, when he saw the resolutions of which those untaught persons are capable, when driven by their needs, and which would certainly never be taken by the best of masters.

While Michelagnolo was concluding the Tomb of Julius II., he permitted a stone-cutter to execute a terminal figure, which he desired to put up in San Pietro in Vincola, directing him meanwhile by telling him daily, "Cut away here,"—"level there,"—"chisel this,"—"polish that," until the stone-cutter had made a figure before he was aware of it; but when he saw what was done, he stood lost in admiration of his work. "What dost thou think of it?" inquired Michelagnolo. "I think it very beautiful," returned the other, "and am much obliged to you." "And for what?" demanded the artist. "For having been the means of making known to me a talent which I did not think I possessed."

But now, to bring the matter to a conclusion, I will only add, that Michelagnolo had an excellent constitution, a spare form, and strong nerves. He was not robust as a child, and as a man he had two serious attacks of illness, but he was subject to no disease, and could endure much fatigue. It is true that infirmities assailed him in his old age, but for these he was carefully treated by his friend and physician, Messer Realdo Colombo. He was of middle height, the shoulders broad, and the whole form well-proportioned. In his latter years he constantly wore stockings of dog-skin for months together, and when these were removed, the skin of the leg sometimes came with them. Over his stockings he had boots of Cordovan leather, as a protection against the swelling of those limbs, to which he then became liable. His face was round, the brow square and ample, with seven direct lines in it; the temples projected much beyond the ears, which were somewhat large, and stood a little off from the cheeks; the nose was rather flattened, having been broken with a blow of the fist by Torrigiano, as we have related in the Life of that artist; the eyes were rather small than large, of a dark colour, mingled with blue and yellowish points; the eye-brows had but few hairs; the lips were thin, the lower somewhat the larger, and slightly projecting; the chin well-formed, and in fair proportion to the rest of the face; the hair black, mingled with grey, as was the beard, which was divided in the middle, and neither very thick nor very long.

This master, as I said at the beginning, was certainly sent on the earth by God as an example for the men of our arts, to the end that they might profit by his walk in life, as well as learn from his works what a true and excellent artist ought to be. I, who have to thank God for an infinite amount of happiness, such as is rarely granted to those of our vocation, account it among the greatest of my blessings that I was born while Michelagnolo still lived, was found worthy to have him for my master, and being trusted by him, obtained him for my friend, as every one knows, and as the letters which he has written to me clearly prove. To his kindness for me I owe it that I have been able to write many things concerning him, which others could not have related, but which, being true, shall be recorded. Another privilege, and one of which he often reminded me, is, that I have been in the service of Duke Cosimo. "Thank God for this, Giorgio," has Michelagnolo said to me; "for to enable thee to build and paint, in execution of his thoughts and designs, he spares no expense, and this, as thou seest well, by the Lives thou has written, is a thing which few artists have experienced."

Michelagnolo was followed to his tomb by a concourse of all the artists, and by his numerous friends, receiving the most honourable sepulture from the Florentine nation, in the Church of Sant' Apostolo, within a sepulchre of which church he was laid, in the presence of all Rome, His Holiness expressing an intention to command that a monument should be erected to his memory in St. Peter's.

28

From Michelangelo's own pen we learn how difficult life really was. He could not recall having had one hour of well being in fifteen years.

> Dearest father—One must have faith and ask for God's mercy and repent of his sins; for such adversities stem from nothing else, and especially from pride and ingratitude. I never dealt with more ungrateful or more proud people than the Florentines. Therefore, if justice is coming, there is a good reason. I shall write a couple of verses for Giuliano de' Medici, and I shall enclose them in this letter: read them, and if you should like to take them to him, do so. If they will be of no avail, give some thought to whether we can sell what we own, and go to live elsewhere. However, if they should treat our equals the way they treat you, have patience and trust in God.
>
> You say that you have taken care of thirty ducats; take an additional thirty from mine, and send me the rest here. Take care of yourself and of your daily needs, and if you cannot have the same considerations as the other citizens of Florence, be satisfied with your daily bread, and live in the grace of God and poorly as I do here. I myself live miserably and do not care about honors and other wordly things; I live in the midst of the greatest hardships and of countless anxieties. I have been leading this sort of existence for about fifteen years, and I have not known one hour of well-being. I have done all I could to help you, and you have never acknowledged it or believed it. May the Lord forgive us all. I am prepared to continue doing what I have done as long as I live, provided I can.

THE CITY IN WESTERN CIVILIZATION

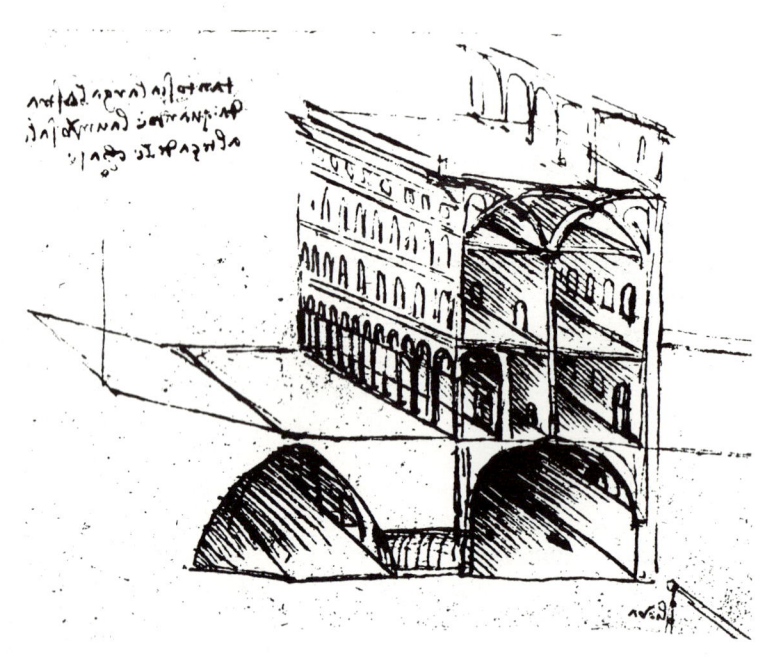

Leonardo's Transportation plan
In this drawing done by Leonardo we can see that he envisioned various levels of transportation—canals, roadways for heavy vehicles and still others for pedestrian movement.

THE RENAISSANCE CITY

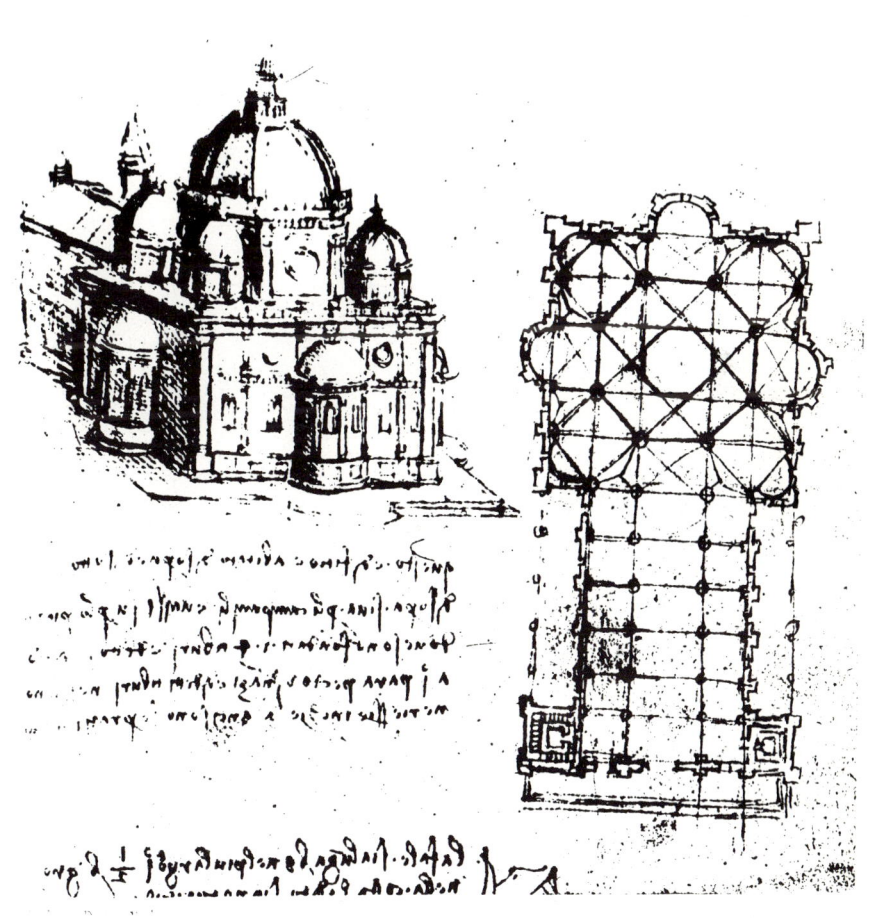

Here's one of several church plans designed by Leonardo

*Florence—Palazzo Vecchio, and the
Rape of the Sabine*

St Mark's Square in Venice

VI. 17th Century Cities

In the 17th century London and Paris—cities that would in various ways dominate European life for hundreds of years—were undergoing changes that brought them out of their medieval molds into the settings for some of the most significant economic, social and political developments of the modern world.

The changes in London were largely the result of fire and pestilence which necessitated new structures and arrangements in the name of the creation of a city that could better withstand human and natural ravages. In Paris the changes were largely the result of Louis XIV's ministers and architects who wished to make France's first city a new Rome in the name of Louis XIV—"The Sun King."

In neither case, however, did the alterations appreciably assist the growing urban poor—the majority—in their daily struggles for survival in societies which regarded them as creatures of marginal worth. The hardships and dangers of their existence could not be changed by Christopher Wren's churches, Edward Jerman' Royal Exchange, Colbert's arches of triumph or Louvois' *Place des Victoires*.

Herein we present a picture of the greatness and the depravity of 17th century cities.

Thomas Babington Macaulay (1800-1859) English historian, member of Parliament and officer of the British Crown in India. His major work *The History of England from the Accession of James* was published from 1849 to 1861 in five volumes, and therein he presented the history of England in a colorful and dramatic fashion as we can see from this selection describing English towns in the 17th century.

> Great as has been the change in the rural life of England since the Revolution, the change which has come to pass in the cities is still more amazing. At present above a sixth part of the nation is crowded into provincial towns of more than thirty thousand inhabitants. In the reign of Charles the Second no provincial town in the

kingdom contained thirty thousand inhabitants; and only four provincial towns contained so many as ten thousand inhabitants.

Bristol

Next to the capital, but next at an immense distance, stood Bristol, then the first English seaport, and Norwich, then the first English manufacturing town. Both have since that time been far outstripped by younger rivals; yet both have made great positive advances. The population of Bristol has quadrupled. The population of Norwich has more than doubled.

Pepys, who visited Bristol eight years after the Restoration, was struck by the splendor of the city. But his standard was not high; for he noted down as a wonder the circumstance that, in Bristol, a man might look round him and see nothing but houses. It seems that in no other place with which he was acquainted, except London, did the buildings completely shut out the woods and fields. Large as Bristol might then appear, it occupied but a very small portion of the area on which it now stands. A few churches of eminent beauty rose out of a labyrinth of narrow lanes built upon vaults of no great solidity. If a coach or a cart entered those alleys, there was danger that it would be wedged between the houses, and danger also that it would break in the cellars. Goods were therefore conveyed about the town almost exclusively in trucks drawn by dogs; and the richest inhabitants exhibited their wealth, not by riding in gilded carriages, but by walking the streets with trains of servants in rich liveries, and by keeping tables loaded with good cheer. The pomp of the christenings and burials far exceeded what was seen at any other place in England. The hospitality of the city was widely renowned, and especially the collations with which the sugar refiners regaled their visitors. The repast was dressed in the furnace, and was accompanied by a rich beverage made of the best Spanish wine, and celebrated over the whole kingdom as Bristol milk. This luxury was supported by a thriving trade with the North American plantations and with the West Indies. The passion for Colonial traffic was so strong that there was scarcely a small shopkeeper in Bristol who had not a venture on board of some ship bound for Virginia or the Antilles. Some of these ventures indeed were not of the most honorable kind. There was, in the transatlantic possessions of the crown, a great demand for labor, and this demand was partly supplied by a system of crimping and kidnapping at the principal English seaports. Nowhere was this system in such active and extensive operation as at Bristol. Even the first magistrates of that city were not ashamed to enrich themselves by so odious a commerce. The number of houses appears, from the returns of the hearth money, to have been in the year 1685, just five thousand three hundred. We can hardly suppose the number of persons in a house to have been greater than in the city of London; and in the city of London we learn from the best authority that there were then fifty-five persons to ten houses. The population of Bristol must therefore have been about twenty-nine thousand souls.

Norwich

Norwich was the capital of a large and fruitful province. It was the residence of a Bishop and of a Chapter. It was the chief seat of the chief manufacturer of the realm. Some men distinguished by learning and science had recently dwelt there; and no place in the kingdom, except the capital and the Universities, had more attraction for the curious. The library, the museum, the aviary, and the botanical garden of Sir Thomas Browne, were thought by Fellows of the Royal Society well worthy of a long pilgrimage. Norwich had also a court in miniature. In the heart of the city stood an old palace of the Dukes of Norfolk, said to be the largest town house in the kingdom out of London. In this mansion, to which were annexed a tennis court, a bowling green, and a wilderness stretching along the banks of the Wansum, the noble family of Howard frequently resided, and kept a state resembling that of petty sovereigns. Drink was served to guests in goblets of pure gold. The very tongs and shovels were of silver. Pictures by Italian masters adorned the walls. The cabinets were filled with a fine collection of gems purchased by that Earl of Arundel, whose marbles are now among the ornaments of Oxford. Here, in the year 1671, Charles and his court were sumptuously entertained. Here, too, all comers were annually welcomed, from Christmas to Twelfth Night. Ale flowed in oceans for the populace. Three coaches, one of which had been built at a cost of five hundred pounds to contain fourteen persons, were sent every afternoon round the city to bring ladies to the festivities; and the dances were always followed by a luxurious banquet. When the Duke of Norfolk came to Norwich, he was greeted like a king returning to his capital. The bells of the Cathedral and of St. Peter Mancroft were rung: the guns of the castle were fired; and the Mayor and Aldermen waited on their illustrious fellow citizen with complimentary addresses. In the year 1693 the population of Norwich was found by actual enumeration, to be between twenty-eight and twenty-nine thousand souls.

Far below Norwich, but still high in dignity and importance, were some other ancient capitals of shires. In that age it was seldom that a country gentleman went up with his family to London. The county town was his metropolis. He sometimes made it his residence during part of the year. At all events, he was often attracted thither by business and pleasure, by assizes, quarter sessions, elections musters of militia, festivals and races. There were the halls where the judges, robed in scarlet and escorted by javelins and trumpets, opened the King's commission twice a year. There were the markets at which the corn, the cattle, the wood, and the hops of the surrounding country were exposed to sale. There were the great fairs to which merchants came down from London, and where the rural dealer laid in his annual stores of sugar, stationery, cutlery and muslin. There were the shops at which the best families of the neighborhood bought grocery and millinery. Some of these places derived dignity from interesting historical recollections, from cathedrals decorated by all the art and magnificence of the middle ages, from palaces where a long succession of prelates had dwelt, from closes surrounded by the venerable abodes of deans and canons, and from castles which had in the old time repelled the Nevilles or de Veres, and which bore more recent traces of the vengeance of Rupert or of Cromwell.

Conspicuous amongst these interesting cities were York, the capital of the north, and Exeter, the capital of the west. Neither can have contained much more than ten thousand inhabitants. Worcester, the queen of the cider land, had but eight thousand; Nottingham probably as many. Gloucester, renowned for that resolute defence which had been fatal to Charles the First, had certainly between four and five thousand; Derby not quite four thousand. Shrewsbury was the chief place of an extensive and fertile district. The Court of the Marches of Wales were held there. In the language of the gentry many miles round the Wrekin, to go to Shrewsbury was to go to town. The provincial wits and beauties imitated, as well as they could, the fashions of St. Jame's Park, in the walks along the side of the Severn. The inhabitants were about seven thousand.

The population of every one of these places has, since the Revolution, much more than doubled. The population of some has multiplied seven fold. The streets have been almost entirely rebuilt. Slate has succeeded to thatch, and brick to timber. The pavements and the lamps, the display of wealth in the principal shops, and the luxurious neatness of the dwellings occupied by the gentry would, in the seventeenth century, have seemed miraculous. Yet is the relative importance of the old capitals of counties by no means what it was. Younger towns, towns which are rarely or never mentioned in our early history and which sent no representatives to our early Parliaments, have, within the memory of persons still living, grown to a greatness which this generation contemplates with wonder and pride, not unaccompanied by awe and anxiety.

Manchester

The most eminent of these towns were indeed known in the seventeenth century as respectable seats of industry. Nay, their rapid progress and their vast opulence were then sometimes described in language which seems ludicrous to a man who has been their present grandeur. One of the most populous and prosperous among them was Manchester. Manchester had been required by the Protector to send one representative to his Parliament, and was mentioned by writers of the time of Charles the Second as a busy and opulent place. Cotton had, during half a century, been brought thither from Cyprus and Smyrna; but the manufacture was in its infancy. Whitney had not yet taught how the raw material might be furnished in quantities almost fabulous. Arkwright had not yet taught how it might be worked up with a speed and precision which seem magical. The whole annual import did not, at the end of the seventeenth century, amount to two millions of pounds, a quantity which would now hardly supply the demand of forty-eight hours. That wonderful emporium, which in population and wealth far surpasses capitals so much as Berlin, Madrid, and Lisbon, was then a mean and ill built market town containing under six thousand people. It then had not a single press. It now supports a hundred printing establishments. It then had not a single coach. It now supports twenty coachmakers.

Leeds

Leeds was already the chief seat of the woolen manufacturers of Yorkshire; but the elderly inhabitants could still remember the time when the first brick house, then and long after called the Red House, was built. They boasted loudly of their increasing wealth, and of the immense sales of the cloth which took place in the open air on the birdge. Hundreds, nay thousands of pounds had been paid down in the course of one busy market day. The rising importance of Leeds had attracted the notice of successive governments. Charles the First had granted municipal privileges to the town. Oliver had invited it to send one member to the House of Commons. But from the returns of the hearth money it seems certain that the whole population of the borough, an extensive district which contains many hamlets, did not, in the reign of Charles the Second, exceed seven thousand souls. In 1841 there were more than a hundred and fifty thousand.

About a day's journey south of Leeds, on the verge of a wild moorland tract, lay an ancient manor, now rich with cultivation, then barren and unenclosed, which was known by the name of Hallamshire. Iron abounded there; and, from a very early period, the rude whittles fabricated there had been sold all over the kingdom. They had, indeed, been mentioned by Jeoffrey Chaucer in one of his Canterbury Tales. But the manufacture appears to have made little progress during the three centuries which followed his time. This languor may, perhaps, be explained by the fact that the trade was during almost the whole of this long period, subject to such regulations as the lord and his court leet thought fit to impose. The more delicate kinds of cutlery were either made in the capital or brought from the Continent. Indeed, it was not till the reign of George the First that the English surgeons ceased to import from France those exquisitely fine blades which are required for operations on the human frame. Most of the Hallamshire forges were collected in a market town which had sprung up near the castle of the proprietor, and which, in the reign of James the First, had been a singularly miserable place, containing about two thousand inhabitants, of whom a third were half starved and half-naked beggars. It seems certain, from the parochial registers, that the population did not amount to four thousand at the end of the reign of Charles the Second. The effects of a species of toil singularly unfavorable to the health and vigor of the human frame were at once discerned by every traveller. A large proportion of the people had distorted limbs. This is that Sheffield which now, with its dependencies, contains a hundred and twenty thousand souls, and which sends forth its admirable knives, razors, and lancets to the farthest ends of the world.

Birmingham

Birmingham had not been thought of sufficient importance to return a member to Oliver's Parliament. Yet the manufacturers of Birmingham were already a busy and thriving race. They boasted that their hardware was highly esteemed, not indeed as now, at Pekin and Lima, at Bokhara, and Timbuctoo, but in London, and even as far off as Ireland. They had acquired a less honorable renown as coiners of bad money. In allusion to their spurious groats, some Tory wit had fixed on demagogues, who hypocritically affected zeal against Popery, the nickname of Birminghams. Yet in 1685 the population, which is now little less than two hundred thousand, did not amount to four thousand. Birmingham buttons were just beginning to be known: of Birmingham guns nobody had yet heard; and the place whence, two generations later, the magnificent editions of Baskerville went forth to astonish all the librarians of Europe, did not contain a single regular shop where a Bible or an almanac could be bought. On Market days a bookseller named Michael Johnson, the father of the great Samuel Johnson, came over from Lichfield, and opened a stall during a few hours. This supply of literature was long found equal to the demand.

These four chief seats of our great manufactures deserve especial mention. It would be tedious to enumerate all the populous and opulaent hives of industry which, a hundred and fifty years ago, were hamlets without parish churches, or desolate moors, inhabited only by grouse and wild deer. Nor has the change been less signal in those outlets by which the products of the English looms and forges are poured forth over the whole world. At present Liverpool contains more than three hundred thousand inhabitants. The shipping registered at her port amounts to between four and five hundred thousand tons. Into her custom house has been repeatedly paid in one year a sum more than thrice as great as the whole income of the English crown in 1685. The receipts of her post office, even since the great reduction of the duty, exceed the sum which the postage of the whole kingdom yielded to the Duke of York. Her endless docks, quays, and warehouses are among the wonders of the world. Yet even those docks and quays and warehouses seem hardly to suffice for the gigantic trade of the Mersey; and already a rival city is growing fast on the opposite shore. In the days of Charles the Second Liverpool was described as a rising town which had recently made great advances, and which maintained a profitable intercourse with Ireland and with the sugar colonies. The customs had multiplied eight-fold within sixteen years, and amounted to what was then considered as the immense sum of fifteen thousand pounds annually. But the population can hardly have exceeded four thousand: the shipping was about fourteen hundred tons, less than the tonnage of a single modern Indiaman of the first class; and the whole number of seamen belonging to the port cannot be estimated at more than two hundred.

Such has been the progress of those towns where wealth is created and accumulated. Not less rapid has been the progress of towns of a very different kind, towns in which wealth, created and accumulated elsewhere, is expended for purposes of health and recreation. Some of the most remarkable of these gay places have sprung into existance since the time of the Stuarts. Cheltenham is now a greater city than any which the kingdom contained in the seventeenth century, London alone excepted. But in the seventeenth century, and at the beginning of the eighteenth, Cheltenham was mentioned by local historians merely as a rural parish lying under the Cotswold Hills, and affording good ground both for tillage and pasture. Corn grew and cattle browsed over the space now covered by that long succession of streets and villas. Brighton was described as a place which had once been thriving, which had possessed many small fishing barks, and which had, when at the height of prosperity, contained above two thousand inhabitants, but which was sinking fast into decay. The sea was gradually gaining on the buildings, which at length almost entirely disappeared. Ninety years ago the ruins of an old fort were to be seen lying among the pebbles and seaweed on the beach; and ancient men could still point out the traces of foundations on a spot where a street of more than a hundred huts had been swallowed up by the waves. So desolate was the place after this calamity, that the vicarage was thought scarcely worth having. A few poor fishermen, however, still continued to dry their nets on those cliffs, on which now a town, more than twice as large and populous as the Bristol of the Stuarts, presents, mile after mile, its gay and fantastic front to the sea.

Bath

But at the head of the English watering places, without a rival, was Bath. The springs of that city had been renowned from the days of the Romans. It had been, during many centuries, the seat of a Bishop. The sick repaired thither from every part of the realm. The King sometimes held his court there. Nevertheless, Bath was then a maze of only four or five hundred houses, crowded within an old wall in the vicinity of the Avon. Pictures of what were considered as the finest of those houses are still extant, and greatly resemble the lowest rag shops and pot-houses of Ratcliffe Highway. Travellers, indeed, complained loudly of the narrowness and meanness of the streets. That beautiful city which charms even eyes familiar with the masterpieces of Bramante and Palladio, and which the genius of Anstey and of Smollet, of Frances Burney, and of Jane Austen, has made classic ground, had not begun to exist. Milsom street itself was an open field lying far beyond the walls; and hedgerows intersected the space which is now covered by the Crescent and the Circus. The poor patients to whom the waters had been recommended lay on straw in a place which, to use the language of a contemporary physician, was a covert rather than a lodging. As to the comforts and luxuries which were to be found in the interior of the houses of Bath by the fashionable visitors who resorted thither in search of health or amusement, we possess information more complete and minute than can generally be obtained on such subjects. A writer who published an account of that city about sixty years after the Revolution has accurately described the changes which had taken place within his own recollection. He assures us that, in his younger days, the gentlemen who visited the springs slept in rooms hardly as good as the garrets which he lived to see occupied by footmen. The floors of the dining rooms were uncarpeted, and were colored brown with a wash made of soot and small beer, in order to hide the dirt. Not a wainscot was painted. Not a hearth or a chimmeypiece was of marble. A slab of common free-stone and fire irons which had cost from three to four shillings were thought sufficient for any fireplace. The best apartments were hung with course woolen stuff, and were furnished with rushbottomed chairs. Readers who take an interest in the progress of civilization and of the useful arts will be grateful to the humble topographer who has recorded these facts, and will perhaps wish that historians of far higher pretensions had sometime spared a few pages from military evolutions and political intrigues, for the purpose of letting us know how the parlors and bedchambers of our ancestors looked.

London

The position of London, relatively to the other towns of the empire, was, in the time of Charles the Second, far higher than at present. For at present the population of London is little more than six time the population of Manchester or of Liverpool. In the days of Charles the Second the population of London was more than seventeen times the population of Bristol or of Norwich. It may be doubted whether any other instance can be mentioned of a great kingdom in which the first city was more than seventeen times as large as the second. There is reason to believe that, in 1685, London had been, during about half a century, the most populous capital in Europe. The inhabitants, who are now at lease nineteen hundred thousand, were then probably little more than half a million. London had in the world only one commercial rival, now long ago outstripped, the mighty and opulent Amsterdam. English writers boasted of the forests of masts and yardarms which covered the river from the Bridge to the Tower, and of the stupendous sums which were collected at the Custom House in Thames Street. There is, indeed, no doubt that the trade of the metropolis then bore a far greater proportion than at present to the whole trade of the country; yet to our generation the honest vaunting of our ancestors must appear almost ludicrous. The shipping which they thought incredibly great appears not to have exceeded seventy thousand tons. This was, indeed, then more than a third of the whole tonnage of the kingdom, but is now less than a fourth of the tonnage of Newcastle, and is nearly equalled by the tonnage of the steam vessels of the Thames. The customs of London amounted, in 1685, to about three hundred and thirty thousand pounds a year. In our time the net duty paid annually, at the same place, exceeds ten millions.

Whoever examines the maps of London which were published towards the close of the reign of Charles the Second will see that only the nucleus of the present capital then existed. The town did not, as now, fade by imperceptible degrees into the country. No long avenues of villas, embowered in lilacs and laburnums, extended from the great centre of wealth and civilization almost to the boundaries of Middlesex and far into the heart of Kent and Surrey. In the east, no part of the immense line of warehouses and artificial lakes which now stretches from the Tower to Blackwall had even been projected. On the west, scarcely one of those stately piles of building which are inhabited by the noble and wealthy was in existence; and Chelsea, which is now peopled by more than forty thousand human beings, was a quiet country village with about a thousand inhabitants. On the north, cattle fed, and sportsmen wandered with dogs and guns, over the site of the borough of Marylebone, and over far the greater part of the space now covered by the boroughs of Finsbury and of the Tower Hamlets. Islington was almost a solitude; and poets loved to contrast its silence and repose with the din and turmoil of the monster London. On the south the capital is now connected with its suburb by several bridges, not inferior in magnificence and solidity to the noblest works of the Ceasars. In 1685, a single line of irregular arches, overhung by piles of mean and crazy houses, and garnished, after a fashion worthy of the naked barbarians of Dahomy, with scores of mouldering heads, impeded the navigation of the river.

Of the metropolis, the City properly so called, was the most important division. At the time of the Restoration it had been built, for the most part, of wood and plaster; the few bricks that were used were ill baked; the booths where goods were exposed to sale projected far into the streets, and were overhung by the upper stories. A few specimens of this architecture may still be seen in those districts which were not reached by the great fire. That fire had, in a few days, covered a space of little less than a square mile with the ruins of eighty-nine churches and of thirteen thousand houses. But the City had risen again with a celerity which had excited the admiration of neighboring countries. Unfortunately, the old lines of the streets had been to a great extent preserved; and those lines, originally traced in an age when even princesses performed their journeys on horseback, were often too narrow to allow wheeled carriages to pass each other with ease, and were therefore ill adapted for the residence of wealthy persons in an age when a coach and six was a fashionable luxury. The style of building was, however, far superior to that of the City which had perished. The ordinary material was brick, of much better quality than had formerly been used. On the sites of the ancient parish churches had arisen a multitude of new domes, towers, and spires which bore the mark of the fertile genius of Wren. In every place save one the traces of the great devastation had been completely effaced. But the crowds of workmen, the scaffolds, and the masses of hewn stone were still to be seen where the noblest of Protestant temples was slowly rising on the ruins of the Old Cathedral of Saint Paul.

The whole character of the City has, since that time, undergone a complete change. At present the bankers, the merchants, and the chief shopkeepers repair thither on six mornings of every week for the transaction of business; but they reside in other quarters of the metropolis, or at suburban country seats surrounded by shrubberies and flower gardens. This revolution in private habits has produced a political revolution of no small importance. The City is no longer regarded by the wealthiest traders with that attachment which every man naturally feels for his home. It is no longer associated in their minds with domestic affections and endearments. The fireside, the nursery, the social table, the quiet bed are not there. Lombard Street and Threadneedle Street are merely places where men toil and accumulate. They go elsewhere to enjoy and to expend. On a Sunday, or in an evening after the hours of business, some courts and alleys, which a few hours before had been alive with hurrying feet and anxious faces, are as silent as the glades of a forest. The chiefs of the mercantile interest are no longer citizens. They avoid, they almost contemn, municipal honors and duties. Those honors and duties are abandoned to men who, though useful and highly respectable, seldom belong to the princely commercial houses of which the names are renowned throughout the world.

London's Merchant's Residence

In the Seventeenth century the City was the merchant's residence. Those mansions of the great old burghers which still exist have been turned into counting-houses and warehouses: but it is evident that they were originally not inferior in magnificence to the dwellings which were then inhabited by the nobility. They sometimes stand in retired and gloomy courts, and are accessible only by inconvenient passages: but their dimensions are ample, and their aspect stately. The entrances are decorated with richly carved pillars and canopies. The staircases and landing places are not wanting in grandeur. The floors are sometimes of wood tessellated after the fashion of France. The palace of Sir Robert Clayton, in the Old Jewry, contained a superb banqueting room wainscoted with cedar, and adorned place to an edifice more magnificent still.

Nearer to the Court, on a space called St. James's Fields, had just been built St. James's Square and Jermyn Street. St. James's Church had recently been opened for the accommodation of the inhabitants of this new quarter. Golden Square, which was in the next generation inhabited by lords and ministers of state, had not yet been begun. Indeed the only dwellings to be seen on the north of Piccadilly were three or four isolated and almost rural mansions, of which the most celebrated was the costly pile erected by Clarendon, and nicknamed Dunkirk House. It has been purchased after its founder's downfall by the Duke of Albemarle. The Clarendon Hotel and Albemarle Street still preserve the memory of the site.

He who then rambled to what is now the gayest and most crowded part of Regent Street found himself in a solitude and was sometimes so fortunate as to have a shot at a woodcock. On the north the Oxford road ran between hedges. Three or four hundred yards to the south were the garden walls of a few great houses which were considered as quite out of town. On the west was a meadow renowned for a spring from which, long afterwards Conduit Street was named. On the east was a field not to be passed without a shudder by any Londoner of that age. There, as in a place farm from the haunts of man, had been dug, twenty years before, when the great plague was raging, a pit into which the dead carts had nightly shot corpses by scores. It was popularly believed that the earth was deeply tainted with infection, and could not be disturbed without imminent risk to human life. No foundations were laid there till two generations had passed without any return of the pestilence, and till the ghastly spot had long been surrounded by buildings.

We should greatly err if we were to suppose that any of the streets and squares then bore the same aspect as at present. The great majority of the houses, indeed, have, since that time, been wholly, or in great part, rebuilt. If the most fashionable parts of the capital could be placed before us such as they then were, we should be disgusted by their squalid appearance, and poisoned by their noisome atmosphere.

The Market

In Convent Garden a filthy and noisy market was held close to the dwellings of the great. Fruit women screamed, carters fought, cabbage stalks and rotten apples accumulated in heaps at the thresholds of the Countess of Berkshire and of the Bishop of Durham.

The center of Lincoln's Inn Fields was an open space where the rabble congregated every evening, within a few yards of Cardigan House and Winchester House, to hear mountebanks harangue, to see bears dance, and to set dogs at oxen. Rubbish was shot in every part of the area. Horses were exercised there. The beggars were as noisy and importunate as in the worst governed cities of the Continent. A Lincoln's Inn mumper was a proverb. The whole fraternity knew the arms and liveries of every charitably disposed grandee in the neighborhood, and as soon as his lordship's coach and six appeared, came hopping and crawling in crowds to persecute him. These disorders lasted, in spite of many accidents, and of some legal proceedings, till, in the reign of George the Second, Sir Joseph Jekyll, Master of the Rolls, was knocked down and nearly killed in the middle of the Square. Then at length palisades were set up, and a pleasant garden laid out.

Saint James's Square was a receptacle for all the offal and cinders, for all the dead cats and dead dogs of Westminster. At one time a cudgel player kept the ring there. At another an impudent squatter settled himself there, and built a shed for rubbish under the windows of the gilded saloons in which the first magnates of the realm, Norfolk, Ormond, Kent, and Pembroke, gave banquets and balls. It was not till these nuisances had lasted through a whole generation, and till much had been written about them, that the inhabitants applied to Parliament for permission to put up rails, and to plant trees.

When such was the state of the region inhabited by the most luxurious portion of society, we may easily believe that the great body of the population suffered what would now be considered as insupportable grievances. The pavement was detestable: all foreigners cried shame upon it. The drainage was so bad that in rainy weather the gutters soon became torrents. Several facetious poets have commemorated the fury with which these black rivulets roared down Snow Hill and Ludgate Hill, bearing to Fleet Ditch a vast tribute of animal and vegetable filth from the stalls of butchers and green grocers. This flood was profusely thrown to right and left by coaches and carts. To keep as far from the carriage road as possible was therefore the wish of every pedestrian. The mild and timid gave the wall. The bold and athletic took it. If two roisterers met, they cocked their hats in each other's faces, and pushed each other about till the weaker was shoved towards the kennel. If he was a mere bully he sneaked off, muttering that he should find a time. If he was pugnacious, the encounter probably ended in a duel behind Montague House.

The houses were not numbered. There would, indeed, have been little advantage in numbering them; for of the coachmen, chairmen, porters, and errand boys of London, a very small proportion could read. It was necessary to use marks which the most ignorant could understand. The shops were therefore distinguished by painted or sculptured signs, which gave a gay and grotesque aspect to the streets. The walk from Charing Cross to Whitechapel lay through an endless succession of Saracens' Heads, Royal Oaks, Blue Bears, and Golden Lambs, which disappeared when they were no longer required for the direction of the common people.

Danger in the Streets

When the evening closed in, the difficulty and danger of walking about London became serious, indeed. The garret windows were opened, and pails were emptied, with little regard to those who were passing below. Falls, bruises, and broken bones were of constant occurrence. For, till the last year of the reign of Charles the Second, most of the streets were left in profound darkness. Thieves and robbers plied their trade with impunity: yet they were hardly so terrible to peaceable citizens as another class of ruffians. It was a favorite amusement of dissolute young gentlemen to swagger by night about the town, breaking windows, upsetting sedans, beating quiet men, and offering rude caresses to pretty women. Several dynasties of these tyrants had, since the Restoration, domineered over the streets. The Muns and Tityre Tus had given place to the Hectors, and the Hectors had been recently succeeded by the Scourers. At a later period arose the Nicker, the Hawcubite, and the yet more dreaded name of Mohawk. The machinery for keeping the peace was utterly contemptible. There was an Act of Common Council which provided that more than a thousand watchmen should be constantly on the alert in the city, from sunset to sunrise, and that every inhabitant should take his turn of duty. But this Act was negligently executed. Few of those who were summoned left their homes; and those few generally found it more agreeable to tipple in alehouses than to pace the streets.

It ought to be noticed that, in the last year of the reign of Charles the Second began a great change in the police of London, a change which has, perhaps, added as much to the happiness of the body of the people as revolutions of much greater fame. An ingenious projector, named Edward Heming, obtained letters patent conveying to him, for a term of years, the exclusive right of lighting up London. He undertook, for a moderate consideration, to place a light before every tenth door, on moonless nights, from Michaelmas to Lady Day, and from six to twelve of the clock. Those who now see the capital all the year round, from dusk to dawn, blazing with a splendor beside which the illuminations of La Hogue and Blenheim would have looked pale, may, perhaps, smile to think of Heming's lanterns, which glimmered feebly before one house in ten during a small part of one night in three. But such was not the feeling of his contemporaries. His scheme was enthusiastically applauded, and furiously attacked. The friends of improvement extolled him as the greatest of all the benefactors of his city. What, they asked, were the boasted inventions of Archimedes, when compared with the achievement of the man who had turned the nocturnal shades into noon-day? In spite of these eloquent eulogies the cause of darkness was not left undefended. There were fools in that age who opposed the introduction of what was called the new light as strenuously as fools in our age have opposed the introduction of vaccination and railroads, as strenuously as the fools of an age anterior to the dawn of history, doubtless, opposed the introduction of the plough and of alphabetical writing. Many years after the date of Heming's patent there were extensive districts in which no lamp was seen.

We may easily imagine what, in such times, must have been the state of the quarters of London which were peopled by the outcasts of society. Among those quarters one had attained a scandalous pre-eminence. On the confines of the City and the Temple had been founded, in the thirteenth century, a House of Carmelite Friars, distinguished by their white hoods. The precinct of this house had, before the Reformation, been a sanctuary for criminals, and still retained the privilege of protecting debtors from arrest. Insolvents consequently were to be found in every dwelling, from cellar to garret. Of these a large proportion were knaves and libertines, and were followed to their asylum by women more abandoned than themselves. The civil power was unable to keep order in a district swarming with such inhabitants; and thus Whitefriars became the favorite resort of all who wished to be emancipated from the restraints of the law. Though the immunities legally belonging to the place extended only to cases of debt, cheats, false witnesses, forgers and highwaymen found refuge there. For amidst a rabble so desperate no peace officer's life was in safety. At the cry of "Rescue," bullies with swords and cudgels, and termagant hags with spits and broomsticks, poured forth by hundreds; and the intruder was fortunate if he escaped back into Fleet street, hustled, stripped, and pumped upon. Even the warrant of the Chief Justice of England could not be executed without the help of a company of musketeers. Such relics of the barbarism of the darkest ages were to be found within a short walk of the chambers where Somers was studying history and law, of the chapel where Tillotson was preaching, of the coffee house where Dryden was passing judgment on poems and plays, and of the hall where the Royal Society was examining the astronomical system of Isaac Newton.

The Coffee Houses

The coffee house must not be dismissed with a cursory mention. It might indeed at that time have been not improperly called a most important political institution. No Parliament had sat for years. The municipal council of the City had ceased to speak the sense of the citizens. Public meetings, harangues, resolutions, and the rest of the modern machinery of agitation had not yet come into fashion. In such circumstances the coffee houses were the chief organs through which the public opinion of the metropolis vented itself.

The first of these establishments had been set up by a Turkey merchant, who had acquired among the Mahometans a taste for their favorite beverage. The convenience of being able to make appointments in any part of the town, and of being able to pass evenings socially at a very small charge, was so great that the fashion spread fast. Every man of the upper or middle class went daily to his coffee house to learn the news and to discuss it. Every coffee house had one or more orators to whose eloquence the crowd listened with admiration, and who soon became, what the journalists of our time have been called, a fourth Estate of the realm. The Court had long seen with uneasiness the growth of this new power in the state. An attempt had been made, during Danby's administration, to close the coffee houses. But men of all parties missed their usual places of resort so much that there was an universal outcry. The government did not venture, in opposition to a feeling so strong and general, to enforce a regulation of which the legality might well be questioned. Since that time ten years had elapsed, and during those years the number and influence of the coffee houses had been constantly increasing. Foreigners remarked that the coffee house was that which especially distinguished London from all other cities; that the coffee house was the Londoner's home, and that those who wished to find a gentleman commonly asked, not whether he lived in Fleet Street or Chancery Lane, but whether he frequented the Grecian or the Rainbow. Nobody was excluded from these places who laid down his penny at the bar. Yet every rank and profession and every shade of religious and politcal opinion, had its own head quarters. There were houses near Saint Jame's Park where flops congregated, their heads and shoulders covered with black or flaxen wigs, not less ample than those which are now worn by the Chancellor and by the Speaker of the House of Commons. The wig came from Paris and so did the rest of the fine gentleman's ornaments, his embroidered coat, his fringed gloves, and the tassel which upheld his pantaloons. The conversation was in that dialect which, long after it had ceased to be spoken in fashionable circles, continued, in the mouth of Lord Foppington, to excite the mirth of theatres. The atmosphere was like that of a perfumer's shop. Tobacco in any other form than that of richly scented snuff was held in abomination. If any clown, ignorant of the usages of the house, called for a pipe, the sneers of the whole assembly and the short answers of the waiters soon convinced him that he had better go somewhere else. Nor, indeed, would he have had far to go. For, in general the coffee rooms reeked with tobacco like a guard room: and strangers sometimes expressed their surprise that so many people should leave their own firesides to sit in the midst of external fog and stench. Nowhere was the smoking more constant than at Will's. That celebrated house, situated between Covent Garden and Bow Street, was sacred to polite letters. There the talk was about poetical justice and the unities of place and time. There was a faction for Perrault and the moderns, a faction for Boileau and the ancients. One group debated whether Paradise Lost ought to have been hooted from the stage. Under no roof was a greater variety of figures to be seen. There were Earls in stars and garters, clergymen in cassocks and bands, pert Templars, sheepish lads from the Universities, translators and index makers in regged coats of frieze. The great press was to get near the chair where John Dryden sate. In winter that chair was always in the warmest nook by the fire; in summer it stoood in the balcony. To bow to the Laureate, and to hear his opinion of Racine's last tragedy or of Bossu's treatise on epic poetry, was thought a privilege. A pinch from his snuff box was an honor sufficient to turn the head of a young enthusiast. There were coffee houses where the first medical men might be consulted. Doctor John Radcliffe, who, in the year 1685, rose to the largest practice in London, came daily, at the hour when the Exchange was full, from his house in Bow Street, then a fashionable part of the capital, to Garraway's, and was to be found, surrounded by surgeons and apothecaries, at a particular table. There were Puritan coffee houses, where no oath was heard, and where lank-haired men discussed election and reprobation through their noses; Jew coffee houses where dark-eyed money changers from Venice and Amsterdam greeted each other; and Popish coffee houses, where, as good Protestants believe, Jesuits planned, over their cups, another great fire, and cast silver bullets to shoot the king.

These gregarious habits had no small share in forming the character of the Londoner of that age. He was, indeed, a different being from the rustic Englishman. There was not then the intercourse that now exists between the two classes. Only very great men were in the habit of dividing the year between town and country. Few esquires came to the capital thrice in their lives. Nor was it yet the practice of all citizens in easy circumstances to breathe the fresh air of the fields and woods during some weeks of every summer. A cockney, in a rural village, was stared at as much as if he had intruded into a Kraal of Hottentots. On the other hand, when the Lord of a Lincolnshire or Shropshire man appeared in Fleet Street, he was as easily distinguished from the resident population as a Turk or a Lascar. His dress, his gait, his accent, the manner in which he gazed at the shops, stumbled into the gutters, ran against the porters, and stood under the waterspouts, marked him out as an excellent subject for the operations of swindlers and banterers. Bullies jostled him into the kennel. Hackney coachmen splashed him from head to foot. Thieves explored with perfect security the huge pockets of his horseman's coat, while he stood entranced by the splendor of the Lord Mayor's show. Money droppers, sore from the cart's tail, introduced themselves to him, and appeared to him the most honest friendly gentlemen that he had ever seen. Painted women, the refuse of Lewkner Lane and Whitestone Park, passed themselves on him for countesses and maids of honor. If he asked his way to St. Jame's, his informant sent him to Mile End. If he went into a shop, he was instantly discerned to be a fit purchaser of everything that nobody else would buy, of secondhand embroidery, copper rings and watches that would not go. If he rambled into any fashionable coffee house, he became a mark for the insolent derision of fops and the grave waggery of Templars. Enraged and mortified, he soon returned to his mansion, and there, in the homage of his tenants and the conversation of his boon companions, found consolation for the vexations and humiliations which he had undergone. There he was once more a great man, and saw nothing above himself, except when at the assizes he took his seat on the bench near the Judge, or when at the muster of the militia he saluted the Lord Lieutenant.

Transportation

The chief cause which made the fusion of the different elements of society so imperfect was the extreme difficulty which our ancestors found in passing from place to place. Of all inventions, the alphabet and the printing press alone excepted, those inventions which abridge distance have done most for the civilization of our species. Every improvement of the means of locomotion benefits mankind morally and intellectually as well as materially, and not only facilitates the interchange of the various productions of nature and art, but tends to remove national and provincial antipathies, and to bind together all the branches of the great human family. In the seventeenth century the inhabitants of London were, for almost every practical purpose, further from Reading than they now are from Edinburgh, and farther from Edinburgh than they are from Vienna.

The subjects of Charles the Second were not, it is true, quite unacquainted with the principle which has, in our own time, produced an unprecedented revolution in human affairs, which has enabled navies to advance in face of wind and tide, and brigades of troops, attended by all their baggage and artillery, to traverse kingdoms at a pace equal to that of the fleetest race horse. The Marquess of Worcester had recently observed the expansive power of moisture rarefied by heat. After many experiments he had succeeded in constructing a rude steam engine, which he called a fire water work, and which he pronounced to be an admirable and most forcible instrument of propulsion. But the Marquess was suspected to be a madman, and known to be a Papist. His interventions, therefore, found no favorable reception. His fire water work might, perhaps, furnish matter for conversation at a meeting of the Royal Society, but was not applied to any practical purpose. There were no railways, except a few made of timber, on which coals were carred from the mouths of the Northumbrian pits to the banks of the Tyne. There was very little internal communication by water. A few attempts had been made to deepen and embank the natural streams, but with slender success. Hardly a single navigable canal has been even projected. The English of that day were in the habit of talking with mingled admiration and despair of the immense trench by which Lewis the Fourteenth had made a junction between the Atlantic and the Mediterranean. They little thought that their country would, in the course of a few generations, be intersected, at the cost of private adventurers, by artificial rivers making up more than four times the length of the Thames, the Severn, and the Trent together.

It was by the highways that both travellers and goods generally passed from place to place; and those highways appear to have been far worse than might have been expected from the degree of wealth and civilization which the nation had even then attained.

It was only in fine weather that the whole breadth of the road was available for wheeled vehicles. Often the mud lay deep on the right and the left; and only a narrow track of firm ground rose above the quagmire. At such times obstructions and quarrels were frequent, and the path was sometimes blocked up during a long time by carriers, neither of whom would break the way. It happened, almost every day, that coaches stuck fast, until a team of cattle could be procured from some neighboring farm, to tug them out of the slough. But in bad seasons the traveller had to encounter inconveniences still more serious.

One chief cause of the badness of the roads seems to have been the defective state of the law. Every parish was bound to repair the highways which passed through it. The peasantry were forced to give their gratuitous labor six days in the year. If this was not sufficient, hired labor was employed, and the expense was met by a parochial rate. That a route connecting two great towns, which have a large and thriving trade with each other, should be maintained at the cost of the rural population scattered between them is obviously unjust; and this injustice was peculiarly glaring in the case of the great North road, which traversed very poor and thinly inhabited districts, and joined very rich and populous districts. Indeed it was not in the power of the parishes of Huntingdonshire to mend a highway worn by the constant traffic between the West Riding of Yorkshire and London. Soon after the Restoration this grievance attracted the notice of Parliament; and an act, the first of our many turnpike acts, was passed, imposing a small toll on travellers and goods, for the purpose of keeping some parts of this important line of communciation in good repair. This innovation, however, excited many murmurs; and the other great avenues to the capital were long left under the old system. A change was at length effected, but not without much difficulty. For unjust and absurd taxation to which men are accustomed is often borne far more willingly than the most reasonable impost which is new. It was not till many toll bars had been violently pulled down, till the troops had, in many districts been forced to act against the people, and till much blood had been shed, that a good system was introduced. By slow degrees reason triumphed over prejudice; and our island is now crossed in every direction by near thirty thousand miles of turnpike road.

On the best highways heavy articles were, in the time of Charles the Second, generally conveyed from place to place by stage wagons. In the straw of these vehicles nestled a crowd of passengers, who could not afford to travel by coach or on horseback, and who were prevented by infirmity, or by the weight of their luggage, from going on foot. The expense of transmitting heavy goods in this way was enormous. From London to Birmingham the charge was seven pounds a ton; from London to Exeter twelve pounds a ton. This was about fifteen pence a ton for every mile, more by a third than was afterwards charged on turnpike roads, and fifteen times what is now demanded by railway companies. The cost of conveyance amounted to a prohibitory tax on many useful articles. Coal in particular was never seen except in the districts where it was produced, or in the districts to which it could be carried by sea, and was indeed always known in the south of England by the name of sea coal.

A coach and six is in our time never seen, except as part of some pageant. The frequennt mention therefore of such equipages in old books is likely to mislead us. We attribute to magnificence what was really the effect of a very disagreeable necessity. People, in the time of Charles the Second, travelled with six horses, because with a smaller number there was great danger of sticking fast in the mire. Nor were even six horses always sufficient. Vanbrugh, in the succeeding generation, described with great humor the way in which a country gentleman, newly chosen a member of Parliament, went up to London. On that occasion all the exertions of six beasts, two of which had been taken from the plough, could not save the family coach from being embedded in a quagmire.

Public carriages had recently been much improved. During the years which immediately followed the Restoration, a diligence ran between London and Oxford in two days. The passengers slept at Beaconsfield. At length, in the spring of 1669, a great and daring innovation was attempted. It was announced that a vehicle, described as the Flying Coach, would perform the whole journey between sunrise and sunset. This spirited undertaking was solemnly considered and sanctioned by the Heads of the University, and appears to have excited the same sort of interest which is excited in our own time by the opening of a new railway. The Vicechancellor, by a notice affixed in all public places, prescribed the hour and place of departure. The success of the experiment was complete. At six in the morning the carriage began to move from before the ancient front of All Souls College; and at seven in the evening the adventurous gentlemen who had run the first risk were safely deposited at their inn in London. The emulation of the sister University was moved; and soon a diligence was set up to the capital. At the close of the reign of Charles the Second, flying carriages ran thrice a week from London to the chief towns. But no stage coach, indeed no stage waggon, appears to have proceeded further north than York, or further west than Exeter. The ordinary day's journey of a flying coach was about fifty miles in the summer; but in winter, when the ways were bad and the nights long, little more than thirty. The Chester coach, the York coach, and the Exeter coach generally reached London in four days during the fine season, but at Christmas not till the sixth day. The passengers, six in number, were all seated in the carriage. For accidents were so frequent that it would have been most perilous to mount the roof. The ordinary fare was about twopence halfpenny a mile in summer, and somewhat more in winter.

This mode of travelling, which by Englishmen of the present day would be regarded as insufferably slow, seemed to our ancestors wonderfully and indeed alarmingly rapid. In a work published a few months before the death of Charles the Second, the flying coaches are extolled as far superior to any similar vehicles ever known in the world. Their velocity is the subject of special commendation, and is triumphantly contrasted with the sluggish pace of the continental posts. But with boasts like these was mingled the sound of complaint and invective. The interests of large classes had been unfavorably affected by the establishment of the new diligences; and, as usual, many persons were, from mere stupidity and obstinacy, disposed to clamor against the innovation, simply because it was an innovation. It was vehemently argued that this mode of conveyance would be fatal to the breed of horses, and to the noble art of horsemanship; that the Thames, which had long been an important nursery of seamen, would cease to be the chief thoroughfare from London up to Windsor and down to Gravesend; that saddlers and spurriers would be ruined by hundreds; that numerous inns, at which mounted travellers had been in the habit of stopping, would be deserted, and would no longer pay any rent; that the new carriages were too hot in summer and too cold in winter; that the passengers were greviously annoyed by invalids and crying children; that the coach sometimes reached the inn so late that it was impossible to get supper, and sometimes started so early that it was impossible to get breakfast. On these grounds it was gravely recommended that no public coach should be permitted to have more than four horses, to start oftener than once a week, or to go more than thirty miles a day. It was hoped that if this regulation were adopted, all except the sick and the lame would return to the old mode of travelling. Petitions embodying such opinions as these were presented to the King in Council from several companies of the City of London, from several provincial towns, and from the justices of several counties. We smile at these things. It is not impossible that our descendants, when they read the history of the opposition offered by cupidity and prejudice to the improvements of the nineteenth century, may smile in their turn.

In spite of the attractions of the flying coaches, it was still usual for men who enjoyed health and vigor, and who were not encumbered by much baggage, to perform long journeys on horseback. If the traveller wished to move expeditiously he rode post. Fresh saddle horses and guides were to be procured at convenient distances

17th century cities

along all the great lines of road. The charge was threepence a mile for each horse, and fourpence a stage for the guide. In this manner, when the ways were good, it was possible to travel, for a considerable time, as rapidly as by any conveyance known in England, till vehicles were propelled by steam. There were as yet no post chaises; nor could those who rode in their own coaches ordinarily procure a change of horses. The King, however, and the great officers of state were able to command relays. Thus Charles commonly went in one day from Whitehall to Newmarket, a distance of about fifty-five miles through a level country; and this was thought by his subjects a proof of great activity. Evelyn performed the same journey in company with the Lord Treasurer Clifford. The coach was drawn by six horses, which were changed at Bishop Stortford and again at Chesterford. The travellers reached Newmarket at night. Such a mode of conveyance seems to have been considered as a rare luxury confined to princes and ministers.

Whatever might be the way in which a journey was performed, the travellers, unless they were numerous and well armed, ran considerable risk at being stopped and plundered. The mounted highwayman, a marauder known to our generation only from books, was to be found on every main road. The waste tracts which lay on the great routes near London were especially haunted by plunderers of this class. Hounslow Heath, on the Great Western Road, and Finchley Common, on the Great Northern Road, were perhaps the most celebrated of these spots. The Cambridge scholars trembled when they approached Epping Forest, even in broad daylight. Seamen who had just been paid off at Chatham were often compelled to deliver their purses on Gadshill, celebrated near a hundred years earlier by the greatest of poets as the scene of the depredations of Falstaff. The public authorities seem to have been often at a loss how to deal with the plunderers. At one time it was announced in the Gazette, that several persons who were strongly suspected of being highwaymen, but against whom there was not sufficient evidence, would be paraded at Newgate in riding dresses: there horses would also be shown; and all gentlemen who had been robbed were invited to inspect this singular exhibition. On another occasion a pardon was publicly offered to a robber if he would give up some rough diamonds, of immense value, which he had taken when he stopped the Harwich mail. A short time after appeared another proclamation, warning the innkeepers that the eye of the government was upon them. Their criminal connivance, it was affirmed, enabled banditti to infest the roads with impunity. That these suspicions were not without foundation, is proved by the dying speeches of some penitent robbers of that age, who appear to have received from the innkeepers services much resembling those which Farquhar's Boniface rendered to Gibbet.

It was necessary to the success and even to the safety of the highwayman that he should be a bold and skilful rider, and that his manners and appearance should be such as suited the master of a fine horse. He therefore held an aristocratical position in the community of thieves, appeared at fashionable coffee houses and gaming houses, and betted with men of quality on the race ground. Sometimes, indeed, he was a man of good family and education. A romantic interest therefore attached, and perhaps still attaches, to the names of reebooters of this class. The vulgar eagerly drank in tales of their ferocity and audacity, of their occasional acts of generosity and good nature, of their amours, of their miraculous escapes, of their desperate struggles, and of their manly bearing at the bar and in the cart. Thus it was related of William Nevison, the great robber of Yorkshire, that he levied a quarterly tribute on all the northern drovers, and, in return, not only spared them himself, but protected them against all other thieves; that he demanded purses in the most courteous manner; that he gave largely to the poor what he had taken from the rich; that his life was once spared by the royal clemency, but that he again tempted his fate, and at length died, in 1685, on the gallows of York. It was related how Claude Duval, the French page of the Duke of Richmond, took to the road, became captain of a formidable gang, and had the honor to be named first in a royal proclamation against notorious offenders; how at the head of his troop he stopped a lady's coach, in which there was a booty of four hundred pounds; how he took only one hundred, and suffered the fair owner to ransom the rest by dancing a coranto with him on the heath; how his vivacious gallantry stole away the hearts of all women; how his dexterity at sword and pistol made him a terror to all men; how, at length, in the year 1670, he was seized when overcome by wine; how dames of high rank visited him in prision, and with tears interceded for his life; how the king would have granted a pardon, but for the interference of Judge Morton, the terror of highwaymen, who threatened to resign his office unless the law were carried into full effect; and how, after the execution, the corpse lay in state with all the pomp of scutcheons, wax lights, black hangings and mutes, till the same cruel judge, who had intercepted the mercy of the crown, sent officers to disturb the obsequies. In these anecdotes there is doubtless a large mixture of fable; but they are not on that account unworthy of being recorded; for it is both an authentic and an important fact that such tales, whether false or true, were heard by our ancestors with eagerness and faith.

Mail Service

The mode in which correspondence was carried on between distant places may excite the scorn of the present generation; yet it was such as might have moved the admiration and envy of the polished nations of antiquity, or of the contemporaries of Raleigh and Cecil. A rude and imperfect establishment of posts for the conveyance of letters had been set up by Charles the First, and had been swept away by the civil war. Under the Commonwealth the design was resumed. At the Restoration the proceeds of the Post Office, after all expenses had been paid, were settled on the Duke of York. On most lines of road the mails went out and came in only on the alternative days. In Cornwall, in the fens of Lincolnshire, and among the hills and lakes of Cumberland, letters were received only once a week. During a royal progress a daily post was despatched from the capital to the place where the court sojourned. There was also daily communication between London and the Downs; and the same privilege was sometimes extended to Tunbridge Wells and Bath at the seasons when those places were crowded by the great. The bags were carried on horseback day and night at the rate of about five miles an hour.

The revenue of this establishment was not derived solely from the charge for the transmission of letters. The Post Office alone was entitled to furnish post horses; and, from the care with which this monopoly was guarded, we may infer that it was found profitable. If, indeed, a traveller had waited half an hour without being supplied, he might hire a horse wherever he could.

To facilitate correspondence between one part of London and

another was not originally one of the objects of the Post Office. But, in the reign of Charles the Second, an enterprising citizen of London, William Dockwray, set up, at great expense, a penny post, which delivered letters and parcels six or eight times a day in the busy and crowded streets near the Exchange, and four times a day in the outskirts of the captial. This improvement was, as usual, strenuously resisted. The porters complained that their interests were attacked, and tore down the placards in which the scheme was announced to the public. The excitement caused by Godfrey's death, and by the discovery of Coleman's papers, was then at the height. A cry was therefore raised that the penny post was a Popish contrivance. The great Dr. Oates, it was affirmed, had hinted a suspicion that the Jesuits were at the bottom of the scheme, and that the bags, if examined, would be found full of treason. The utility of the enterprise was, however, so great and obvious that all opposition proved fruitless. As soon as it became clear that the speculation would be lucrative, the Duke of York complained of it as an infraction of his monopoly; and the courts of law decided in his favor.

Newspapers

No part of the load which the old mails carried out was more important than the newsletters. In 1685 nothing like the London daily paper of our time existed, or could exist. Neither the necessary capital nor the necessary skill was to be found. Freedom too was wanting, a want as fatal as that of either capital or skill. The press was not indeed at that moment under a general censorship. The licensing act, which had been passed soon after the restoration, had expired in 1679. Any person might therefore print, at his own risk, a history, a sermon, or a poem, without the previous approbation of any officer; but the Judges were unanimously of opinion that this liberty did not extend to Gazettes, and that, by the common law of England, no man, not authorized by the crown, had a right to publish political news. While the Whig party was still formidable, the government thought it expedient occasionally to connive at the violation of this rule. During the great Battle of the Exclusion Bill, many newspapers were suffered to appear, the Protestant Intelligence, the Current Intelligence, the Domestic Intelligence, the True News, the London Mercury. None of these was published oftener than twice a week. None exceeded in size a single small leaf. The quantity of matter which one of them contained in a year was not more than is often found in two numbers of the Times. After the defeat of the Whigs it was no longer necessary for the King to be sparing in the use of that which all his Judges had pronounced to be his undoubted prerogative. At the close of his reign no newspaper was suffered to appear without his allowance: and his allowance was given exclusively to the London Gazette. The London Gazette came out only on Mondays and Thursdays. The contents generally were a royal proclamation, two or three Tory addresses, notices of two or three promotions, an account of a skirmish between the imperial troops and the Janissaries on the Danube, a description of a highwayman, an announcement of a grand cockfight between two persons of honor, and an advertisement offering a reward for a strayed dog. The whole made up two pages of moderate size. Whatever was communicated respecting matters of the highest moment was communicated in the most meagre and formal style. Sometimes, indeed, when the government was disposed to gratify the public curiosity respecting an important transaction, a broadside was put forth giving fuller details than could be found in the Gazette: but neither the Gazette nor any supplementary broadside printed by authority ever contained any intelligence which it did not suit the purposes of the Court to publish. The most important parliamentary debates, the most important state trials recorded in our history, were passed over in profound silence. In the capital the coffee houses supplied in some measure the place of a journal. Thither the Londoners flocked, as the Athenians of old flocked to the market place, to hear whether there was any news. There men might learn how brutally a Whig had been treated the day before in Westminister Hall, what horrible accounts the letters from Edinburgh gave of the torturing of Covenanters, how grossly the Navy Board had cheated the crown in the victualling of the fleet, and what grave charges the Lord Privy Seal had brought against the Treasury in the matter of the hearth money. But people who lived at a distance from the great theatre of political contention could be kept regularly informed of what was passing there only by means of newsletters. To prepare such letters became a calling in London, as it now is among the natives of India. The newswriter rambled from coffee room to coffee room, collecting reports, squeezed himself into the sessions House at the Old Bailey if there was an interesting trial, nay perhaps obtained admission to the gallery of Whitehall, and noticed how the King and Duke looked. In this way he gathered materials for weekly epistles destined to enlighten some county town or some bench of rustic magistrates. Such were the sources from which the inhabitants of the largest provincial cities, and the great body of the gentry and clergy, learned almost all that they knew of the history of their own time. We must suppose that at Cambridge there were as many persons curious to know what was passing in the world as at almost any place in the kingdom, out of London. Yet at Cambridge, during a great part of the reign of Charles the Second, the Doctors of Laws and the Masters of Arts had no regular supply of news except through the London Gazette. At length the services of one of the collectors of intelligence in the capital were employed. That was a memorable day on which the first newsletter from London was laid on the table of the only coffee-room in Cambridge. At the seat of a man of fortune in the country the newsletter was impatiently expected. Within a week after it had arrived it had been thumbed by twenty families. It furnished the neighboring squires with matter for talk over their October, and the neighboring rectors with topics for sharp sermons against Whiggery or Popery. Many of these curious journals might doubtless still be detected by a diligent search in the archives of old families. Some are to be found in our public libraries; and one series, which is not the least valuable part of the literary treasures collected by Sir James McIntosh, will be occasionally quoted in the course of this work.

It is scarcely necessary to say that there were then no provincial newspapers. Indeed, except in the capital and at the two Universities, there was scarcely a printer in the kingdom. The only press in England north of Trent appears to have been at York.

It was not only by means of the London Gazette that the government undertook to furnish political instruction to the people. That journal contained a scanty supply of news without comment. Another journal, published under the patronage of the court, consisted of comment without news. This paper, called the Observator, was edited by an old Tory pamphleteer named Roger Lestrange. Lestrange was by no means deficient in readiness and shrewdness; and his diction, though coarse, and disfigured by a mean and flippant jargon which then passed for wit in the green room and the tavern, was not without keenness and vigor. But his nature, at once ferocious and ignoble, showed itself in every line that he penned. When the first Observators appeared there was some excuse for his acrimony. The Whigs were then powerful; and he had to contend against numerous adversaries, whose unscrupulous violence might seem to justify unsparing retaliation. But in 1685 all the opposition had been crushed. A generous spirit would have disdained to insult a party which could not reply, and to aggravate the misery of prisoners, of exiles, of bereaved families: but from the malice of Lestrange the grave was no hiding place, and the house of mourning no sanctuary. In the last month of the reign of Charles the Second, William Jenkyn, an aged dissenting pastor of great note, who had been cruelly persecuted for no crime but that of worshipping God according to the fashion generally followed throughout Protestant Europe, died of hardships and privations at Newgate. The outbreak of popular sympathy could not be repressed.

Books

Literature which could be carried by the post bag then formed the greater part of the intellectual nutriment ruminated by the country divines and country justices. The difficulty and expense of conveying large packets from place to place was so great, that an extensive work was longer in making its way from Paternoster Row to Devonshire or Lancashire than it now is in reaching Kentucky. How scantily a rural parsonage was then furnished, even with books the most necessary to a theologian, has already been remarked. The houses of the gentry were not more plentifully supplied. Few knights of the shire had libraries so good as may now perpetually be found in a servants' hall or in the back parlor of a small shopkeeper. An esquire passed among his neighbors for a great scholar, if Hudibras and Baker's Chronicle, Tarleton's Jests, and the Seven Champions of Christendom, lay in his hall window among the fishing rods and fowling pieces. No circulating library, no book society, then existed even in the capital: but in the capital those students who could not afford to purchase largely had a resource. The shops of the great booksellers, near St. Paul's churchyard, were crowded every day and all day long with readers; and a known customer was often permitted to carry a volume home. In the country there was no such accomodation; and every man was under the necessity of buying whatever he wished to read.

The sale of books was so small that a man of the greatest name could hardly expect more than a pittance for the copyright of the best performance. There cannot be a stronger instance than the fate of Dryden's last production, the Fables. That volume was published when he was universally admitted to be the chief of living English poets.

It contains about twelve thousand lines. The versification is admirable, the narratives and descriptions full of life. To this day Palamon and Arcite, Cymon and Iphigenia, Theodore and Honoria are the delight both of critics and of schoolboys. The collection includes Alexander's Feast, the noblest ode in our language. For the copyright Dryden received two hundred and fifty pounds, less than in our days has sometimes been paid for two articles in a review. Nor does the bargain seem to have been a hard one. For the book went off slowly; and the second edition was not required till the author had been ten years in his grave. By writing for the theatre it was possible to earn a much larger sum with much less trouble. Southern made seven hundred pounds by one play. Otway was raised from beggary to temporary influence by the success of his Don Carlos. Shadwell cleared a hundred and thirty pounds by a single representation of the Squire of Alsatia. The consequence was that every man who had to live by his wit wrote plays, whether he had any internal vocation to write plays or not. It was thus with Dryden. As a satirist he has rivelled Juvenal. As a didactic poet he perhaps might, with care and meditation, have rivalled Lucretius. Of lyric poets he is, if not the most sublime, the most brilliant and spirit-stirring. But nature, profuse to him of many rare gifts, had withheld from him the dramatic faculty. Nevertheless all the energies of his best years were wasted on dramatic composition. He had too much judgment not to be aware that in the power of exhibiting character by means of dialogue he was deficient. That deficiency he did his best to conceal, sometimes by surprising and amusing incidents, sometimes by stately declamation, sometimes by harmonious numbers, sometimes by ribaldry but too well suited to the taste of a profane and licentious pit. Yet he never obtained any theatrical success equal to that which rewarded the exertions of some men far inferior to him in general powers. He thought himself fortunate if he cleared a hundred guineas by a play; a scanty remuneration, yet apparently larger than he could have earned in any other way by the same quantity of labor.

The recompense which the wits of that age could obtain from the public was so small, that they were under the necessity of eking out their incomes by levying contributions on the great. Every rich and goodnatured lord was pestered by authors with a mendicancy so importunate, and a flattery so abject, as may in our time seem incredible. The patron to whom a work was inscribed was expected to reward the writer with a purse of gold. The fee paid for the dedication of a book was often much larger than the sum which any publisher would give for the copyright. Books were therefore frequently printed merely that they might be dedicated. This traffic in praise produced the effect which might have been expected. Adulation pushed to the verge sometimes of nonsense, and sometimes of impiety, was not thought to disgrace a poet. Independence, veracity, selfrespect, were things not required by the world from him. In truth, he was in morals something between a pandar and a beggar.

To the other vices which degraded the literary character was added, towards the close of the reign of Charles the Second, the most savage intemperance of party spirit. The wits, as a class, had been impelled by their old hatred of Puritanism to take the side of the court, and had been found useful allies. Dryden, in particular, had done good service to the government. His Absalom and Achitophel, the greatest satire of modern times, had amazed the town, had made its way with unprecedented rapidity even into rural districts, and had, wherever it appeared, bitterly annoyed the Exclusionists, and raised the courage of the Tories. But we must not, in the admiration which we naturally feel for noble diction and versification, forget the great distinctions of good and evil. The spirit by which Dryden and several of his compeers were at this time animated against the Whigs deserves to be called fiendish. The servile Judges and Sheriffs of those evil days could not shed blood as fast as the poets cried out for it. Calls for more victims, hideous jests on hanging, bitter taunts on those who, having stood by the king in the hour of danger, now advised him to deal mercifully and generously by his vanquished enemies, were publicly recited on the stage, and, that nothing might be wanting to the guilt and the shame, were recited by women, who, having long been taught to discard all modesty, were now taught to discard all compassion.

It is a remarkable fact that, while the lighter literature of England was thus becoming a nuisance and a national disgrace, the English genius was effecting in science a revolution which will, to the end of time, be reckoned among the highest achievements of the human intellect. Bacon had sown the good seed in a sluggish soil and an ungenial season. He had not expected an early crop, and in his last testament had solemnly bequeathed his fame to the next age. During a whole generation his philosophy had, amidst tumults, wars, and proscriptions, been slowly ripening in a few well constituted minds. While factions were struggling for dominion over each other, a small body of sages had turned away with benevolent disdain from the conflict, and had devoted themselves to the nobler work of extending the dominion of man over matter. As soon as tranquility was restored, these teachers easily found attentive audience. For the discipline through which the nation had passed had brought the public mind to a temper well fitted for the reception of the Verulamian doctrine. The civil troubles had stimulated the faculties of the educated classes, and had called forth a restless activity and an insatiable curiosity, such as had not before been known among us. Yet the effect of those troubles was that schemes of political and religious reform were generally regarded with suspicion and contempt.

Science

The year 1660, the era of the restoration of the old constitution, is also the era from which dates the ascendency of the new philosophy. In that year the Royal Society, destined to be a chief agent in a long series of glorious and salutary reforms, began to exist. In a few months experimental science became all the mode. The transfusion of blood, the ponderation of air, the fixation of mercury, succeeded to that place in the public mind which had been lately occupied by the controversies of the Rota. Dreams of perfect forms of government made way for dreams of wings with which men were to fly from the Tower to the Abbey, and of doublekeeled ships which were never to founder in the fiercest storm. All classes were hurried along by the prevailing sentiment. Cavalier and Roundhead, Churchman and Puritan, were for once allied. Divines, jurists, statesmen, nobles, princes, swelled the triumph of the Baconian philosophy. Poets sang with emulous fervor the approach of the golden age. Cowley, in lines weighty with thought and resplendent with wit, urged the chosen seed to take possession of the promised land flowing with milk and honey, that land which their great deliverer and lawgiver had seen, as from the summit of Pisgah, but had not been permitted to enter. Dryden, with more zeal than knowledge, joined voice to the general acclamation to enter, and foretold things which neither he nor anybody else understood. The Royal Society, he predicted, would soon lead us to the extreme verge of the globe, and there delight us with a better view of the moon.

Two able and aspiring prelates, Ward, Bishop of Salisbury and Wilkins, Bishop of Chester, were conspicuous among the leaders of the movement. Its history was eloquently written by a younger divine, who was rising to high distinction in his profession, Thomas Sprat, afterwards Bishop of Rochester. Both Chief Justice Hale and Lord Keeper Guildford stole some hours from the business of their courts to write on hydrostatics. Indeed it was under the immediate direction of Guildford that the first barometers ever exposed to sale in London were constructed. Chemistry divided, for a time, with wine and love, with the stage and the gaming table, with the intrigues of a courtier and the intrigues of a demogogue, the attention of the fickle Buckingham. Rupert has the credit of having invented mezzotinto; from him is named that curious bubble of glass which has long amused children and puzzled philosophers. Charles himself had a laboratory at Whitehall, and was far more active and attentive there than at the council board. It was almost necessary to the character of a fine gentleman to have something to say about air pumps and telescopes; and even fine ladies, now and then, thought it becoming to affect a taste for science, went in coaches and six to visit the Gresham curiosities, and broke forth into cries of delight at finding that a magnet really attracted a needle, and that a microscope really made a fly look as large as a sparrow.

In this, as in every great stir of the human mind, there was doubtless something which might well move a smile. It is the universal law that whatever pursuit, whatever doctrine, becomes fashionable, shall lose a portion of that dignity which it had possessed while it was confined to a small but earnest minority, and was loved for its own sake alone. It is true that the follies of some persons who, without any real aptitude for science, professed a passion for it, furnished matter of contemptuous mirth to a few malignant satirists who belonged to the preceding generation, and were not disposed to unlearn the lore of their youth. But it is not less true that the great work of interpreting nature was performed by the English of that age as it had never before been performed in any age by any nation. The spirit of Francis Bacon was abroad, a spirit admirably compounded of audacity and sobriety. There was a strong persuasion that the whole world was full of secrets of high moment to the happiness of man, and that man had, by his Maker, been entrusted with the key, which, rightly used, would give access to them. There was at the same time a conviction that in physics it was impossible to arrive at the knowledge of general laws except by the careful observation of particular facts. Deeply impressed with these great truths, the professors of the new philosophy applied themselves to their task, and, before a quarter of a century had expired, they had given ample earnest of what has since been achieved. Already a reform of agriculture had been commenced. New vegetables were cultivated. New implements of husbandry were employed. New manures were applied to the soil. Evelyn had, under the formal sanction of the Royal Society, given instruction to his countrymen in planting. Temple, in his intervals of leisure, had tried many experiments in horticulture and had proved that many delicate fruits, the natives of more favored climates, might, with the help of art, be grown on English ground. Medicine, which in France was still in abject bondage, and afforded an inexhaustible subject of just ridicule to Moliere, had in England become an experimental and progressive science, and every day made some new advance in defiance of Hipocrates and Galen.

The attention of speculative men had been, for the first time, directed to the important subject of sanitary police. The great plague of 1665 induced them to consider with care the defective architecture, draining, and ventilation of the capital. The great fire of 1666 afforded an opportunity for effecting extensive improvements. The whole matter was diligently examined by the Royal Society; and to the suggestions of that body must be partly attributed the changes which, though far short of what the public welfare required, yet made a wide difference between the new and the old London, and probably put a final close to the ravages of pestilence in our country. At the same time one of the founders of the Society, Sir William Petty, created the science of political arithmetic, the humble but indispensable handmaid of political philosophy. No kingdom of nature was left unexplored. To that period belong the chemical discoveries of Boyle, and the earliest botanical researches of Sloane. It was then that Ray made a new classification of birds and fishes, and that the attention of Woodward was first drawn towards fossils and shells. One after another phantoms which haunted the world through ages of darkness fled before the light. Astrology and Alchymy became jests. Soon there was scarcely a county in which some of the old Quorum did not smile contemptuously when an old woman was brought before them for riding on broomsticks or giving cattle the murrain. But it was in those noblest and most arduous departments of knowledge in which induction and mathematical demonstration co-operate for the discovery of truth that the English genius won in that age the most memorable triumphs. John Wallis placed the whole system of statics on a new foundation. Edmund Halley investigated the properties of the atmosphere, the ebb and flow of the sea, the laws of magnetism, and the course of the comets; nor did he shrink from toil, peril and exile in the cause of science. While he, on the rock of Saint Helena, mapped the constellations of the southern hemisphere, our national observatory was rising at Greenwich; and John Flamsteed, the first Astronomer Royal, was commencing that long series of observations which is never mentioned without respect and gratitude in any part of the globe.

29

The Plague of London

Samuel Pepys (1633-1703) has left us many intimate details of Lond in his *Diary* (1825). Here Pepys described the Plague of 1665.

/ / /

THE CITY IN WESTERN CIVILIZATION

Buckingham Palace
A *bird's eye view of Buckingham Palace, St. James Park and Horse Guard Parade.*

17TH CENTURY CITIES

Lord Mayor's Show at Law Courts

House of Parliament

Aug. 31st. Thus this month ends with great sadness upon the publick, through the greatness of the plague every where through the kingdom almost. Every day sadder and sadder news of its encrease. In the City died this week 7496, and of them 6102 of the plague. But it is feared that the true number of the dead this week is near 10,000; partly from the poor that cannot be taken notice of, through the greatness of the number, and partly from the Quakers and others that will not have any bell ring for them. Our fleet gone out to find the Dutch, we having about 100 sail in our fleet, and in them the Soveraigne one; so that it is a better fleet than the former with which the Duke was. All our fear is that the Dutch should be got in before them; which would be a very great sorrow to the publick, and to me particularly, for my Lord Sandwich's sake. A great deal of money being spent, and the kingdom not in a condition to spare, nor a parliament without much difficulty to meet to give more. And to that; to have it said, what hath been done by our late fleets? As to myself I am very well, only in fear of the plague, and as much of an ague by being forced to go early and late to Woolwich, and my family to lie their continually. My late gettings have been very great to my great content, and am likely to have yet a few more profitable jobbs in a little while; for which Tangier and Sir W. Warren I am wholly obliged to.

Sept. 3 (Lord's day). Up; and put on my coloured silk suit very fine, and my new periwigg, bought a good while since, but durst not wear, because the plague was in Westminister when I bought it; and it is a wonder what will be the fashion after the plague is done, as to periwiggs, for nobody will dare to buy any haire, for fear of the infection, that it had been cut off the heads of people dead of the plague. My Lord Brouncker, Sir J. Minnes, and I up to the Vestry at the desire of the Justices of the Peace, in order to the doing something for the keeping of the plague from growing; but Lord! to consider the madness of people of the town, who will (because they are forbid) come in crowds along with the dead corpses to see them buried; but we agreed on some orders for the prevention thereof. Among other stories, one was very passionate, methought, of a complaint brought against a man in the town for taking a child from London from an infected house. Alderman Hooker told us it was the child of a very able citizen in Gracious Street, a saddler, who had buried all the rest of his children of the plague, and himself and wife now being shut up and in despair of escaping, did desire only to save the life of this little child; and so prevailed to have it received stark-naked into the arms of a friend, who brought it (having put it into new fresh clothes) to Greenwich; where upon hearing the story, we did agree it should be permitted to be received and kept in the town.

4th. Walked home, my Lord Brouncker giving me a very neat cane to walk with; but it troubled me to pass by Coome farme where about twenty-one people have died of the Plague.

5th. After dinner comes Colonel Blunt in his new chariot made with springs; as that was of wicker, wherein a while since we rode at his house. And he hath rode, he says, now his journey, many miles in it with one horse, and out-drives any coach, and out-goes any horse, and so easy, he says. So for curiosity I went into it to try it, and up the hill to the heath, and over the cart-ruts and found it pretty well, but not so easy as he pretends.

6th. To London, to pack up more things; and there I saw fires burning in the streets, as it is through the whole City, by the Lord Mayor's order. Thence by water to the Duke of Albemarle's: all the way fires on each side of the Thames, and strange to see in broad daylight two or three burials upon the Bankside, one at the very heels of another: doubtless all of the plague; and yet at least forty or fifty people going along with every one of them. The Duke mightly pleasant with me; telling me that he is certainly informed that the Dutch were not come home upon the 1st instant, and so he hopes our fleet may meet with them.

7th. To the Tower and there sent for the Weekly Bill, and find 8252 dead in all, and of them 6978 of the plague; which is a most dreadful number, and shows reason to fear that the plague hath got that hold that it will yet continue among us. **30**

The Fire of 1666

In his *Diary* (1818) John Evelyn (1620-1706) furnished much information to posterity on the fire of 1666 which seemed to consume all of London.

2nd September. This fatal night, about ten, began the deplorable fire, near Fish-street, in London.

3rd. I had public prayers at home. The fire continuing, after dinner, I took coach with my wife and son, and went to the Bankside in Southwark, where we beheld that dismal spectacle, the whole city in dreadful flames near the waterside; all the houses from the Bridge, all Thames-street, and upwards towards Cheapside, down to the Three Cranes, were now consumed; and so returned, exceeding astonished what would become of the rest.

The fire having continued all this night (if I may call that night which was light as day for ten miles round about, after a dreadful manner), when conspiring with a fierce eastern wind in a very dry season, I went on foot to the same place; and saw the whole south part of the City burning from Cheapside to the Thames, and all along Cornhill (for it likewise kindled back against the wind as well as forward), Tower-street, Fenchurch-street, Gracious-street, and so along to Baynard's Castle, and was now taking hold of St. Pauls church, to which the scaffolds contributed exceedingly. The conflagration was so universal, and the people so astonished, that, from the beginning, I know not by what despondency, or fate, they hardly stirred to quench it; so that there was nothing heard, or seen, but crying out and lamentation, running about like distracted creatures, without at all attempting to save even their goods; such a strange consternation there was upon them, so as it burned both in breadth and length, the churches, public halls, Exchange, hospitals, monuments, and ornaments; leaping after a prodigious manner, from house to house, and street to street, at great distances one from the other. For the heat, with a long set of fair and warm weather, had even ignited the air, and prepared the materials to conceive the fire, which devoured, after an incredible manner, houses, furniture, and every thing. Here, we saw the Thames covered with good floating, all the barges and boats laden with what some had time and courage to save, as, on the other side, the carts, &c., carrying out to the fields, which for many miles were strewed with moveables of all sorts, and tents erecting to shelter both people and what goods they could get away. Oh, the miserable and calamitous spectacle! such as haply the world had not seen since the foundation of it, nor can be outdone till the universal conflagration thereof. All the sky was of a fiery aspect, like the top of a burning oven, and the light seen above forty miles round-about for many nights. God grant mine eyes may never behold the like, who now saw above 10,000 houses all in one flame! The noise and cracking and thunder of the impetuous flames, the shrieking of women and children, the hurry of people, the fall of towers, houses and churches, was like a hideous storm; and the air all about so hot and inflamed, that at the last one was not able to approach it, so that they were forced to stand still, and let the flames burn on, which they did, for near two miles in length and one in breadth. The clouds also of smoke were dismal, and reached, upon computation, near fifty miles in length. Thus, I left it this afternoon burning, a resemblance of Sodom or the last day. It forcibly called to my mind that passage—*non enim hic habemus stabilem civitatem:* the ruins resembling the picture of Troy. London was, but is no more! Thus, I returned.

4th September. The burning still rages, and it is now gotten as far as the Inner Temple. All Fleet-street, the Old Bailey, Ludgate-hill, Warwick-lane, Newgate, Paul's-chain, Watling-street, now flaming, and most of it reduced to ashes; the stones of Paul's flew like grenados, the melting lead running down the streets in a stream, and the very pavements glowing with fiery redness, so as no horse, nor man, was able to tread on them, and the demolition had stopped all the passages, so that no help could be applied. The eastern wind still more impetuously driving the flames forward. Nothing but the Almighty power of God was able to stop them; for vain was the help of man.

5th September. It crossed towards Whitehall; but oh! the confusion there was then at that Court! It pleased his Majesty to command me, among the rest, to look after the quenching of Fetter-lane end to preserve (if possible) that part of Holborn, whilst the rest of the gentlemen took their several posts, some at one part, and some at another (for now they began to bestir themselves, and not till now, who hitherto had stood as men intoxicated, with their hands across), and began to consider that nothing was likely to put a stop but the blowing up of so many houses as might make a wider gape than any had yet been made by the ordinary method of pulling them down with engines. This some stout seamen proposed early enough to have saved near the whole City, but this some tenacious and avaricious men, aldermen, &c., would not permit, because their houses must have been of the first. It was, therefore, now commended to be practised; and my concern being particularly for the Hospital of St. Bartholomew, near Smithfield, where I had many wounded and sick men, made me the more diligent to promote it; nor was my care for the Savoy less. It now pleased God, by abating the wind, and by the industry of the people, when almost all was lost infusing a new spirit into them, that the fury of it began sensibly to abate about noon, so as it came no farther than the Temple westward, nor than the entrance of Smithfield, north: but continued all this day and night so impetuous towards Cripplegate and the Tower, as made us all despair. It also brake out again in the Temple; but the courage of the multitude persisting, and many houses being blown up, such gaps and desolations were soon made, as, with the former three days' consumption, the back fire did not so vehemently urge upon the rest as formerly. There was yet no standing near the burning and glowing ruins by near a furlong's space.

The coal and wood-wharfs, and magazines of oil, rosin, &c., did infinite mischief, so as the invective which a little before I had dedicated to his Majesty and published, giving warning what probably might be the issue of suffering those shops to be in the City was looked upon as a prophecy.

The poor inhabitants were dispersed about St. George's Fields, and Moorfields, as far as Highgate, and several miles in circle, some under tents, some under miserable huts and hovels, many without a rag, or any necessary utensils, bed or board, who from delicateness, riches, and easy accommodations in stately and well-furnished houses, were now reduced to extremest misery and poverty.

In this calamitous condition, I returned with a sad heart to my house, blessing and adoring the distinguishing mercy of God to me and mine, who, in the midst of all this ruin, was like Lot, in my little Zoar, safe and sound.

6th September. Thursday. I represented to his Majesty the case of the French prisoners at war in my custody, and besought him that there might be still the same care of watching at all places contiguous to unseized houses. It is not indeed imaginable how extraordinary the vigilance and activity of the King and the Duke was, even labouring in person, and being present to command, order, reward, or encourage workmen; by which he showed his affection to his people, and gained theirs. Having, then, disposed of some under cure at the Savoy, I returned to Whitehall, where I dined at Mr. Offley's, the groom-porter, who was my relation.

7th. I went this morning on foot from Whitehall as far as London Bridge, through the late Fleet-street, Ludgate-hill by St. Paul's, Cheapside, Exchange, Bishopsgate, Aldersgate, and out to Moorefields, thence through Cornhill, &c., with extraordinary difficulty, clambering over heaps of yet smoking rubbish, and frequently mistaking where I was: the ground under my feet so hot, that it even burnt the soles of my shoes. In the meantime, his Majesty got to the Tower by water, to demolish the houses about the graff, which, being built entirely about it, had they taken fire and attacked the White Tower, where the magazine of powder lay, would undoubtedly not only have beaten down and destroyed all the bridge, but sunk and torn the vessels in the river, and rendered the demolition beyond all expression for several miles about the country.

At my return, I was infinitely concerned to find that goodly Church, St. Paul's—now a sad ruin, and that beautiful portico (for structure comparable to any in Europe, as not long before repaired by the late King) now rent in pieces, flakes of large stones split asunder and nothing remaining entire but the inscription in the architrave, showing by whom it was built, which had not one letter of it defaced! It was astonishing to see what immense stones the heat had in a manner calcined, so that all the ornaments, columns, friezes, capitals, and projectures of massy Portland stone, flew off, even to the very roof, where a sheet of lead covering a great space (no less than six acres by measure) was totally melted. The ruins of the vaulted roof falling, broke into St. Faith's, which being filled with the magazines of books belonging to the Stationers and carried thither for safety, they were all consumed, burning for a week following. It is also observable that the lead over the altar at the east end was untouched, and among the divers monuments the body of one bishop remained entire. Thus lay in ashes that most venerable church, one of the most ancient pieces of early piety in the Christian world, besides near one hundred more. The lead, iron-work, bells, plate, &c., melted, the exquisitely wrought Mercer's Chapel, the sumptuous Exchange, the august fabric of Christ Church, all the rest of the Companies' Halls, splendid buildings, arches, entries, all in dust; the fountains dried up and ruined, whilst the very waters remained boiling; the voragos of subterranean cellars, wells, and dungeons, formerly warehouses, still burning in stench and dark clouds of smoke; so that in five or six miles traversing about I did not see one load of timber unconsumed, nor many stones but what were calcined white as snow.

   The people, who now walked about the ruins, appeared like men in some dismal desert, or rather, in some great city laid waste by a cruel enemy; to which was added the stench that came from some poor creatures' bodies, beds, and other combustible goods. Sir Thomas Gresham's statue, though fallen from its niche in the Royal Exchange, remained entire, when all those of the Kings since the Conquest were broken to pieces. Also the standard in Cornhill, and Queen Elizabeth's effigies, with some arms on Ludgate, continued with but little detriment, whilst the vast iron chains of the City-streets, hinges, bars, and gates of prisons, were many of them melted and reduced to cinders by the vehement heat. Nor was I yet able to pass through any of the narrow streets, but kept the widest; the ground and air, smoke and fiery vapour, continued so intense, that my hair was almost singed, and my feet unsufferably surbated. The by-lanes and narrow streets were quite filled up with rubbish; nor could one have possibly known where he was, but by the ruins of some Church, or Hall, that had some remarkable tower, or pinnacle remaining.

   I then went towards Islington and Highgate, where one might have seen 200,000 people of all ranks and degrees dispersed, and lying along by their heaps of what they could save from the fire, deploring their loss; and, though ready to perish for hunger and destitution, yet not asking one penny for relief, which to me appeared a stranger sight than any I had yet beheld. His Majesty and Council indeed took all imaginable care for their relief, by proclamation for the country to come in, and refresh them with provisions.

   In the midst of all this calamity and confusion, there was I know not how, an alarm begun that the French and Dutch with whom we were now in hostility, were not only landed but even entering the City. There was, in truth, some days before, great suspicion of those two nations joining; and now that they had been the occasion of firing the town. This report did so terrify, that on a sudden there was such an uproar and tumult that they run from their goods, and taking what weapons they could come at, they could not be stopped from falling on some of those nations whom they casually met, without sense or reason. The clamour and peril grew so excessive, that it made the whole Court amazed and they did with infinite pains and great difficulty, reduce and appease the people, sending troops of soldiers and guards, to cause them to retire into the fields again, when they were watched all this night. I left them pretty quiet and came home sufficiently weary and broken. Their spirits thus a little calmed, and the affright abated, they now began to repair into the suburbs about the City, where such as had friends, or opportunity, got shelter for the present; to which his Majesty's proclamation also invited them.

Still, the plague continuing in our parish, I could not, with danger, adventure to our church.

10*th September*. I went again to the ruins; for it was now no longer a city.

John Evelyn described the Great Frost of 1683-1684

1683-4. 1*st January*. The weather continuing intolerably severe, streets of booths were set upon the Thames; the air was so very cold and thick, as of many years there had not been the like. The small-pox was very mortal.

2*nd*. I dined at Sir Stephen Fox's: after dinner came a fellow who eat live charcoal, glowingly ignited, quenching them in his mouth, and then champing and swallowing them down. There was a dog also which seemed to do many rational actions.

6*th*. The river quite frozen.

9*th*. I went across the Thames on the ice, now become so thick as to bear not only streets of booths, in which they roasted meat, and had divers shops of wares, quite across as in a town, but coaches, carts, and horses passed over. So I went from Westminster-stairs to Lambeth, and dined with the Archbishop: where I met my Lord Bruce, Sir George Wheeler, Colonel Cooke, and several divines. After dinner and discourse with his Grace till evening prayers, Sir George Wheeler and I walked over the ice from Lambeth-stairs to the Horse-ferry.

10*th*. I visited Sir Robert Reading, where after supper we had music, but not comparable to that which Mr. Bridgeman made us on the guitar with such extraordinary skill and dexterity.

16th January. The Thames was filled with people and tents, selling all sorts of wares as in the City.

24th. The frost continuing more and more severe, the Thames before London was still planted with booths in formal streets, all sorts of trades and shops furnished, and full of commodities, even to a printing-press, where the people and ladies took a fancy to have their names printed, and the day and year set down when printed on the Thames: this humour took so universally, that it was estimated the printer gained £5 a day, for printing a line only, at sixpence a name, besides what he got by ballads, &c. Coaches plied from Westminister to the Temple, and from several other stairs to and fro, as in the streets, sleds, sliding with skates, a bull-baiting, horse and coach-races, puppet-plays and interludes, cooks, tippling, and other lewd places, so that it seemed to be a bacchanalian triumph, or carnival on the water, whilst it was a severe judgment on the land, the trees not only splitting as if lightning-struck, but men and cattle perishing in divers places, and the very seas so locked up with ice, that no vessels could stir out or come in. The fowls, fish, and birds, and all our exotic plants and greens, universally perishing. Many parks of deer were destroyed, and all sorts of fuel so dear, that there were great contributions to preserve the poor alive. Nor was this severe weather much less intense in most parts of Europe, even as far as Spain and the most southern tracts. London, by reason of the excessive coldness of the air hindering the ascent of the smoke, was so filled with the fuliginous steam of the sea-coal, that hardly could one see across the streets, and this filling the lungs with its gross particles, exceedingly obstructed the breast, so as one could scarcely breathe. Here was no water to be had from the pipes and engines, nor could the brewers and divers other tradesmen work, and every moment was full of disastrous accidents.

4th February. I went to Sayes Court to see how the frost had dealt with my garden, where I found many of the greens and rare plants utterly destroyed. The oranges and myrtles very sick, the rosemary and Laurels dead to all appearance, but the cypress likely to endure it.

5th. It began to thaw, but froze again. My coach crossed from Lambeth to the Horse-ferry at Milbank, Westminster. The booths were almost all taken down; but there was first a map or landscape cut in copper representing all the manner of the camp, and the several actions, sports, and pastimes thereon, in memory of so signal a frost. **31**

Paris

Paris, France—a city of great contrasts. One could see extraordinary wealth and luxury side by side with dire poverty and misery. Saint Simon (1675-1755) French courtier, utopian philosopher and author of *Memoirs* told of the grandeur and brilliance of Versailles while Martin Lister, a 17th century traveler, wrote of life in Paris. There's quite a contrast between the two accounts as there is in almost every big city.

Hotel des Invalides
Constructed by order of Louis XIV in the 1670's it was a hospital for those who had fought in his many costly wars.

Notre Dame

Saint Simon's Paris

So much for the reign of this vainglorious monarch.

Let me touch now upon some other incidents in his career, and upon some points in his character.

He early showed a disinclination for Paris. The troubles that had taken place there during the minority made him regard the place as dangerous; he wished, too, to render himself venerable by hiding himself from the eyes of the multitude; all these considerations fixed him at St. Germains soon after the death of the Queen, his mother. It was to that place he began to attract the world by *fetes* and gallantries, and by making it felt that he wished to be often seen.

His love for Madame de la Vallière, which was at first kept secret, occasioned frequent excursions to Versailles, then a little card castle, which had been built by Louis XIII.—annoyed, and to his suite still more so, at being frequently obliged to sleep in a wretched inn there, after he had been out hunting in the forest of Saint Leger. That monarch rarely slept at Versailles more than one night, and then from necessity; the King, his son, slept there, so that he might be more in private with his mistress, pleasures unknown to the hero and just man, worthy son of Saint Louis, who built the little *chateau*.

These excursions of Louis XIV. by degrees gave birth to those immense buildings he erected at Versailles; and their convenience for a numerous court, so different from the apartments at St. Germains, led him to take up his abode there entirely shortly after the death of the Queen. He built an infinite number of apartments, which were asked for by those who wished to pay their court to him; whereas at St. Germains nearly everybody was obliged to lodge in the town, and the few who found accommodation at the *chateau* were strangely inconvenienced.

The frequent *fetes,* the private promenades at Versailles, the journeys, were means on which the King seized in order to distinguish or mortify the courtiers, and thus render them more assiduous in pleasing him. He felt that of real favors he had not enough to bestow; in order to keep up the spirit of devotion, he therefore unceasingly invented all sorts of ideal ones, little preferences and petty distinctions, which answered his purpose as well.

He was exceedingly jealous of the attention paid him. Not only did he notice the presence of the most distinguished courtiers, but those of inferior degree also. He looked to the right and to the left, not only upon rising but upon going to bed, at his meals, in passing through his apartments, or his gardens of Versailles, where alone the courtiers were allowed to follow him; he saw and noticed everybody; not one escaped him, not even those who hoped to remain unnoticed. He marked well all absentees from the Court, found out the reason of their absence, and never lost an opportunity of acting toward them as the occasion might seem to justify. With some of the courtiers (the most distinguished), it was a demerit not to make the Court their ordinary abode; with others it was a fault to come but rarely; for those who never or scarcely ever came it was certain disgrace. When their names were in any way mentioned, "I do not know them," the King would reply haughtily. Those who presented themselves but seldom were thus characterized: "They are people I never see"; these decrees were irrevocable. He could not bear people who liked Paris.

Louis XIV. took great pains to be well informed of all that passed everywhere; in the public places, in the private houses, in society, and familiar intercourse. His spies and tell-tales were infinite. He had them of all species; many who were ignorant that their information reached him; others who knew it; others who wrote to him direct, sending their letters through channels he indicated; and all these letters were seen by him alone, and always before everything else; others who sometimes spoke to him secretly in his cabinet, entering by the back stairs. These unknown means ruined an infinite number of people of all classes, who never could discover the cause; often ruined them very unjustly; for the King, once prejudiced, never altered his opinion, or so rarely, that nothing was more rare. He had, too, another fault, very dangerous for others and often for himself, since it deprived him of good subjects. He had an excellent memory; in this way, that if he saw a man who, twenty years before, perhaps, had in some manner offended him, he did not forget the man, though he might forget the offense. This was enough, however, to exclude the person from all favor. The representations of a minister, of a general, of his confessor even, could not move the King. He would not yield.

The most cruel means by which the King was informed of what was passing—for many years before anybody knew it—was that of opening letters. The promptitude and dexterity with which they were opened passes understanding. He saw extracts from all the letters in which there were passages that the chiefs of the post-office, and then the minister who governed it, thought ought to go before him; entire letters, too, were sent to him, when their contents seemed to justify the sending. Thus the chiefs of the post, nay, the principal clerks, were in a position to suppose what they pleased and against whom they pleased. A word of contempt against the King or the Government, a joke, a detached phrase, was enough. It is incredible how many people, justly or unjustly were more or less ruined, always without resource, without trial, and without knowing why. The secret was impenetrable; for nothing ever cost the king less than profound silence and dissimulation.

This last talent he pushed almost to falsehood, but never to deceit, pluming himself upon keeping his word,—therefore he scarcely ever gave it. The secrets of others he kept as religious as his own. He was even flattered by certain confessions and certain confidences; and there was no mistress, minister, or favorite, who could have wormed them out, even though the secret regarded themselves.

We know, among many others, the famous story of a woman of quality, who, after having been separated a year from her husband, found herself in the family way just as he was on the point of returning from the army, and who, not knowing what else to do; in the most urgent manner begged a private interview of the King. She obtained it, and confided to him her position, as to the worthiest man in the realm, as she said. The King counseled her to profit by her distress, and live more wisely for the future, and immediately promised to retain her husband on the frontier as long as was necessary, and to forbid his return under any pretext, and in fact he gave orders the same day to Louvois, and prohibited the husband not only all leave of absence, but forbade him to quit for a single day the post he was to command all the winter. The officer who was distinguished, and who had neither wished nor asked to be employed all the winter upon the frontier, and Louvois, who had in no way thought of it, were equally surprised and vexed. They were obliged, however, to obey to the letter, and without asking why; and the King never mentioned the circumstance until many years afterward, when he was quite sure nobody could find out either husband or wife, as in fact they never could, or even obtain the most vague or the most uncertain suspicion. **32**

Paris as Martin Lister Saw It

City Planning

The houses are built of hewn stone intirely, or whited over with plaister: some indeed in the beginning of this age are of brick with free-stone, as the Place-Royal, Place-Dauphin, &c. but that is wholly left off now; and the white plaister is in some few places only coloured after the fashion of brick, as part of the abbay of St. Germain. The houses every where are high and stately; the churches numerous, but not very big; the towers and steeples are but few in proportion to the churches, yet that noble way of steeple, the domes or cupolas, have a marvellous effect in prospect; though they are not many, as that of Val de Grace, des Invalides, College Mazaria, de l'Assumption, the Grand Jesuits, la Sorbonne, and some few others.

All the houses of persons of distinction are built with porte-cocheres, that is, wide gates to drive in a coach, and consequently have courts within; and mostly remises to set them up. There are reckoned above 700 of these great gates; and very many of these are after the most noble patterns of ancient architecture.

The lower windows of all houses are grated with strong bars of iron; which must be a vast expense.

As the houses are magnificent without, so the finishing within-side and furniture answer in riches and neatness; as hangings or rich tapestry, raised with gold and silver threads, crimson damask and velvet beds or of gold and silver tissue. Cabinets and bureaus of ivory inlaid with tortoiseshell, and gold and silver plates in a 100 different manners: branches and candlesticks of crystal: but above all most rare pictures. The gildings, carvings and paintings of the roofs are admirable.

These things are in this city and the country about, to such a variety and excess, that you can come into no private house of any man of substance, but you see something of them; and they are observed frequently to ruin themselves in these expenses. Every one, that has any thing to spare, covets to have some good picture or sculpture of the best artist; the like in the ornaments of their Gardens, so that, it is incredible what pleasure that vast quantity of fine things give the curious stranger. Here as soon as ever a man gets any thing by fortune or inheritance, he lays it out in some such was as now named.

Yet, after all, many utensils and conveniences of life are wanting here, which we in England have. This makes me remember what Monsieur Justell, a Parisian formerly, told me here, that he had made a catalogue of near threescore things of this nature which they wanted in Paris.

The pavements of the streets is all of square stone, of about eight or ten inches thick; that is, as deep in the ground as they are broad at top; the gutters shallow, and laid round without edges, which makes the coaches glide easily over them.

However, it must needs be said, the streets are very narrow, and the passengers a-foot no ways secured from the hurry and danger of coaches, which always passing the streets with an air of haste, and a full trot upon broad flat stones, betwixt high and large resounding houses, makes a sort of music which should seem very agreeable to the Parisians.

The royal palaces are surprisingly stately; as the Louvre and Tuilleries, Palais Luxembourg, Palais Royal.

The convents are great, and numerous, and well built; as Val de Grace, St. Germains, St. Victor, St. Genevieve, the Grand Jesuits, &c.

The squares are few in Paris, but very beautiful; as the Place Royal, Place Victior, Place Dauphine, none of the largest, except the Places Vendosme, not yet finished.

The gardens within the walls, open to the public, are vastly great, and very beautiful, as the Tuilleries, Palais Royal, Luxembourg, the Royal Physic Garden, of the arsenal, and many belonging to convents.

But that which makes the dwelling in this city very diverting for people of quality, is the facility of going out with their coaches into the fields on every side; it lying round, and the avenues to it so well paved; and the places of airing so clean, open, or shady, as you please, or the season of the year and time of the day require: as the Cour de la Reyne, Bois de Bologne, Bois de Vincennes, les Sables de Vaugerarde, &c.

But to descend to a more particular review of this great city, I think it not amiss to speak first of the streets and public places, and what may be seen in them; next of the houses of note; and what curiosities of nature or art, also of men and libraries, I met with: next of their diet and recreations; next of the gardens, and their furniture and ornaments; and of the air and health. We shall conclude the whole with the present state of physic and pharmacy here.

To begin with the coaches, where are very numerous here and very fine in gilding: but these are but few, and those only of the great nobility, which are large, and have two seats. But what they want in the largeness, beauty, and neatness of ours in London, they have infinitely in the easiness of carriage, and the ready turning in the narrowest streets. For this purpose, they are all crane-necked, and the wheels before very low; not above two feet and a half diameter; which makes them easy to get into, and brings down the coach box low, that you have a much better prospect out of the foremost glass, our high seated coachmen being ever in the point of view. Again, they are most, even fiacres or hackneys, hung with double springs at the four corners, which insensibly breaks all jolts.

This I never was so sensible of, as after having practised the Paris coaches for four months. I once rid in the easiest chariot of my lord's, which came from England; but not a jolt but what affected a man: so as to be tired more in one hour in that, than in six in these.

Besides the great number of coaches of the gentry, here are also coaches de Remise, by the month, which are very well gilt, neat harness, and good horses: and these all strangers hire by the day or month, at about three crowns English a day. 'Tis this sort that spoils the hackneys and chairs, which here are the most nasty and miserable voiture that can be; and yet near as dear again as in London, and but very few of them neither.

Recreation

As for their recreation and walks, there are no people more fond of coming together to see and to be seen. This conversation without doubt takes up a great part of their time: and for this purpose, the Cour de la Reyne is frequented by all people of quality. It is a treble walk of trees of a great length, near the river side, the middle walk having above double the breadth to the two side ones; and will hold eight files of coaches, and in the middle a great open circle to turn, with fine gates at both ends. Those that would have better and freer air, go further, and drive into the Bois de Bologne, others out of other parts of the town to Bois de Vincennes, scarce any side amiss. In like manner these persons light and walk in the Tuilleries, Luxembourg, and other gardens, belonging to the crown and princes, (all which are very spacious) and are made convenient, with many seats for the entertainment of all people; the lacquies and mob excepted.

The Streets

/ / /

'Tis pretty to observe, how the king disciplines this great city, by small instances of obedience. He caused them to take down all their signs at once, and not to advance them above a foot or two from the wall, nor to exceed such a small measure of square; which was readily done: so that the signs obscure not the streets at all, and

Versailles—Hall of Mirrors

make little or no figure, as though there were none; being placed very high and little.

There are great number of hostels in Paris, by which word is meant public inns, where lodgings are let; and also the noblemen and gentlemen's houses are so called, mostly with titles over the gate in letters of gold on a black marble. This seems as it were, to denote that they came at first to Paris as strangers only, and inned publicly; but at length built them inns or houses of their own. It is certain, a great and wealthy city cannot be without people of quality; nor such a court as that of France without the daily inspection of what such people do. But whether the country can spare them or not, I question. The people of England seem to have less manners and less religion, where the gentry have left them wholly to themselves; and the taxes are raised with more difficulty, inequality, and injustice, than when the landlords live upon the desmaines.

It may very well be, that Paris is in a manner a new city within this forty years. It is certain since this king came to the crown, it is so much altered for the better, that it is quite another thing; and if it be true what the workmen told me, that a common house, built of rough stone and plaistered over, would not last above twenty-five years, the greatest part of the city has been lately rebuilt. In this age certainly most of the great Hostels are built, or re-edified; in like manner the convents, the bridges and churches, the gates of the city; add the great alteration of the streets, the keys upon the river, the pavements; all these have had great additions, or are quite new.

In the river amongst the bridges, both above and below, are a vast number of boats, of wood, hay, charcoal, corn, and wine, and other commodities. But when a sudden thaw comes, they are often in danger of being split and crushed to pieces upon the bridges; which also are sometimes damaged by them. There have been great losses to the owners of such boats and goods.

It has been proposed to dig near the city a large basin for a winter harbour; but this had not had the face of profit to the government; so they are still left to execute their own project. There are no laws or projects so effectual here, as what bring profit to the government. Farming is admirably well understood here.

The great multitude of poor wretches in all parts of this city is such, that a man in a coach, a-foot, in the shop, is not able to do any business for the numbers and importunities of beggars; and to hear their miseries is very lamentable; and if you give to one, you immediately bring a whole swarm upon you. These, I say, are true monks, if you will, of God Almighty's making, offering you their prayers for a farthing, that find the evil of the day sufficient for the day, and that the miseries of this life are not to be courted, or made a mock of. These worship, much against their will, all rich men, and make saints of the rest of mankind for a morsel of bread.

But let these men alone with their mistaken zeal; it is certainly god's good providence which orders all things in this world. And the flesh-eaters will ever defend themselves, if not beat the Lenten men; good and wholesome food, and plenty of it, gives men naturally great courage. Again, a nation will sooner be peopled by the free marriage of all sorts of people, than by the additional stealth of a few starved monks, supposing them at any time to break their vow. This limiting of marriage to a certain people only is a deduction and an abatement of mankind, not less in a papist country than a constant war. Again, this lessens also the number of God's worshippers, instead of multiplying them as the stars in the firmament, or the sand upon the sea shore; these men wilfully cut off their posterity, and reduce God's congregation for the future.

There is very little noise in this city of public cries of things to be sold, or any disturbance from pamphlets and hawkers. One thing I wondered at, that I heard of nothing lost, or any public advertisement, till I was shewed printed papers upon the corners of streets, wherein were in great letters, *Un, Deux, Cinq, Dix jusq; a Cinquante Louis à c gagner,* that is, from one to fifty louis to be got; and then underneath an account of what was lost. This sure is a good and quiet way; for by this means without noise you often find your goods again; every body that has found them repairing in a day or two to such places. The Gazettes come out but once a week, and but few people buy them.

The streets are lighted alike all the winter long, as well when the moon shines, as at other times of the month; which I remember the rather, because of the impertinent usage of our people at London, to take away the lights for half of the month, as though the moon was certain to shine and light the streets, and that there could be no cloudy weather in winter. The lanthorns here hang down in the very middle of all the streets, about twenty paces distance, and twenty foot high. They are made of a square of glass about two tended to be preserved by it. For whether boiled from the inland salt-pits, or the sea water, it is little less than quicklime, and burns and reeses all it touches; so that it is pity to see so much good fish, as is caught upon the northern line of coast, particularly the cod and ling, and herring, now of little value, which were formerly the most esteemed commodities of England. It is certain, there is no making good salt by fierce and vehement boiling, as is usual; but it must be kerned either by the heat of the sun, as in France; or by a full and over-weighty brine, as at Milthrope in the Washes of Lancashire; for in no other place in England I ever saw it right made; but yet that is not there understood to purpose; for they also boil the brine, which possibly by some slight artifice might be brought to give its salt without stress of fire.

In lent the common people feed much on white kidney beans, and white or pale lentils, of which there are great provisions made in all the markets, and to be had ready boiled. I was well pleased with this lentil; which is a sort of pulse we have none of in England. There are two sorts of white lentils sold here, one small one from Burgandy, by the cut of Briare; and another bigger, as broad again, from Chartres; a third also much larger, is sometimes to be had from Languedoc. Those excepted, our seed shops far exceed theirs, and consequently our gardens in the pulse-kind for variety; both pea and bean.

The roots differ much from ours. There are here no round turnips, but all long ones and small; but excellently well tasted, and are of a much greater use, being proper for soups also; for which purpose ours are too strong: we have indeed of late got them into England; but our gardeners understand not the managing of them. They sow them here late after midsummer; and at martinmas or sooner, before the frost begin, they dig them up, cut off the tops, and put them into sand in their cellars, where they will keep good till after Easter. The sandy plains of Vaugerard near Paris are famous for this sort of most excellent root. After the same manner they keep their carrots.

After we had been two or three days' journey in France, we found no other turnips, but the navet; and still the nearer Paris the better. These as I said, are small long turnips, not bigger than a knife-hast, and most excellent in soups, and with boiled and stewed mutton. I think it very strange that the seed should so much improve in England, as to produce roots of the same kind six or ten times as big as there; for I make no question but the long turnips, of late only in our markets are the same.

The potatoe is scarce to be found in their markets, which are so great a relief to the people of England, and very nourishing and wholesome roots; but there are stores of Jerusalem artichokes.

They delight not so much in cabbage as I expected, at least at the season, while we were there, from December to Midsummer. I never saw in all the markets once sprouts, that is, the tender shoots of cabbages; nor in their public gardens any reserves of old stalks. The red cabbage is esteemed here. . . .

But to make amends for this, they abound in vast quantities of large red onions and garlick. And the long and sweet white onion of Languedoc are to be had also here. Also leeks, rockhamboy, and shallots are here in great use.

The southern people are pleased with the onion kind, for the same reason, for that the great heats meliorate them, but give a rankness to the cabbage. The leeks are here much smaller, than with us; but to recompense this, they are blanched here with more care and art, and are three times as long in the white part, which is by sinking them early so deep in mellow earth. There is no plant of the onion kind so hardy as this, and so proper for the cold mountains, witness the use the Welsh have made of them from all ages; and indeed it is excellent against spitting of blood, and all diseases of the throat and lungs.

Though the lettuce be the great and universal sallad, yet I did not find they came near our people, for the largeness and hardness of them; indeed, about a week before we left Paris, the long Roman lettuce filled their markets, which was incomparable. . . .

April and May the markets were served with vast quantities of white beets, an herb rarely used with us, and never that I know of, in that manner for soups. The leaves grow long and large, and are tied up, as we do our Silesian or Roman lettuce to blanch, and then cut by the root. The stalks are very broad and tender, and they only are used, stripped of the green leaves. They cook those stalks in different manners.

The asparagus here are in great plenty, but for the first month they were very bitter and unpleasant; from whence that proceeded I cannot guess; afterwards I did not much perceive it.

They are so great lovers of Sorrel, that I have seen whole acres of it planted in the fields; and they are to be commended for it; for nothing is more wholesome, and it is good to supply the place of lemons against the scurvy, or any ill habit of the body.

But after all, the French delight in nothing so much as mushrooms, of which they have daily, and all the winter long, store of fresh and new gathered in the markets. This surprised me; nor could I guess, where they had them, till I found they raised them on hot beds in their gardens.

Of forced mushrooms they have many crops in a year; but for the months of August, September, October, when they naturally grow in the fields, they prepare no artificial beds.

They make in the fields and gardens out of the bar of Vaugerard (which I saw) long narrow trenches, and fill those trenches with horse dung two or three feet thick, on which they throw up the common earth of the place, and cover the dung with it, like the ridge of a house, high pitched; and over all they put long straw or long horse litter. Out of this earth springs the champignons, after rain; and if rain comes not, they water the beds every day, even in winter.

They are six days after their springing or first appearance, before they pull them up for the market.

On some beds they have plenty, on others but few, which demonstrate they come of feed in the ground; for all the beds are alike.

A gardner told me, he had the other year near an acre of ground ordered in this manner, but he lost a hundred crowns by it; but mostly they turn to as good profit as any thing they can plant.

They destroy their old beds in summer, and dung their grounds with them.

They prepare their new beds the latter end of August, and have plentiful crops of mushrooms towards christmas, and all the spring, till after March.

I saw in the markets the beginning of April, fresh gathered moriglios, the first of that kind of mushroom, that I remember ever to have seen: though formerly I had been very curious and inquisitive about this kind of plant, and had distinguished and described thirty species of them growing in England; yet I do not remember ever to have found this species with us; it is blackish, and becomes much blacker when boiled, whence probably it had its name; but there are some few of them that are yellow. They are always of a round pyramidal figure, upon a short thick foot-stalk. The foot-stalk is smooth, but the outside of the mushroom is all deeply plated and wrinkled like the inside of a beasts maw. The moriglio split in two from top to bottom is all hollow and smooth, foot, stalk, and all. In this hollowness is sometimes contained dangerous insects. The taste raw, is not ungrateful, and very tender. This mushroom seems to me to be produced of the tree kind.

This sort of mushroom is much esteemed in France, and is mostly gathered in woods at the foot of the oaks. There were some of them as big as turkey eggs. They are found in great quantities in the woods in Champagne, about Reims, and Nostre Dame de Liesse.

They string them, and dry them; and they seem to me to have a far better relish than the Champignons.

The city is well served with carp, of which there is an incredible quantity spent in the lent. They are not large, and I think are the better for it, but they are very clean of mud, and well tasted.

They have a particular way of bringing fresh oysters to town, which I never saw with us; to put them up in straw baskets of a peck, suppose, cut from the shell, and without the liquor. They are thus very good for stewing, and all other manner of dressing.

There is such plenty of macreuse, a sort of sea ducks, in the markets all lent, that I admire, where they got so many; but these are reckoned and esteemed as fish, and therefore they take them with great industry. They have a rank fishy taste, yet for want of other flesh were very welcome. I remember we had at our treat at the king's charge at Versailles, a macreuse pie near two feet diameter, for it was in lent; which being high seasoned, did go down very well with rare burgundy. There is a better argument in Leewenhoeke for birds participating something of the nature of fish, though their blood is hot, then any the council of Trent could think of, and that is, that the Globuli of the blood of birds are oval, as those of fishes are; but this will take in all the bird kind: which also in time those gentlemen may think fit to grant.

As for their flesh, mutton, and beef, if they are good in their kind, they come little short of ours, I cannot say they exceed them. But their veal is not to be compared with ours, being red and course; and I believe no country in Europe understands the management of that sort of food like the English.

Parisians' Health

The air of Paris is drier than that of England, notwithstanding the greatest part of the city is placed in a dirty miry level; the muddy banks of the river Seine witness this; also the old Latin name of Paris, *Lutetia;* but some of them are unwilling to derive it from *Lutum,* though there are several other towns in France, formerly more considerable than it, of that very name; but from the Greek original, as *Tolon, Tolousa,* which in that language signify black dirt. We have an undoubted experiment of the different temper of the air in our Philosophic Transactions; where it is demonstrated, that there falls twice as much rain in England, as at Paris; registers of both having carefully been kept, for so many years, both here and in France.

From this quantity of rain with us, our fields are much greener; and it was a pleasing surprise to me at my return, sailing up the river of Thames, to see our green fields and pastures on every side; but we pay dearly for it, in agues and coughs, and rheumatic distempers.

The winter was very rude and fierce, as was ever known in the memory of man; the cold winds very piercing; and the common people walk the streets all in muffs, and multitudes had little brass kettles of small-coal kindled, hanging on their arms; and yet you should scarce hear any one cough.

I never saw a mist at Paris in the six months I staid there, but one; though a very broad river runs through the middle of the city, nor any very strong winds; but this may be accidental, and the temper of some one year by chance.

We were very sensible by the 20th of February our style, though the nights were cold, and the white frosts great in the mornings, that the sun at noon had a much stronger force and heat, than with us, at that time of the year.

Another argument of the dryness of the air at Paris, we had from the alteration of health; such as were thick breathed, and coughed and spit much, soon recovered; and the insensible perspiration of the skin was so clear and free, that the kidneys had little to do; so that it was observed by most, that though we drank pretty freely of the thin wines of Champagne and Burgundy, yet they never broke our sleep to get shut of them; and that very little passed that way in the morning.

Lastly, a sign of the dryness and great goodness of the air of Paris is, the vast number of iron bars all over the city; which yet are mostly intire, and the least decayed with rust, I ever saw in any place; whereas ours in London are all in a few years all over rusty, and miserably eaten.

We were sufficiently alarmed at our first coming to Paris, with the unwholesomeness of the river water, and cautioned against drinking it; and yet it was almost impossible to avoid the bad effects of it; for within the month two thirds of the family fell into fluxes, some into dysenteries, and some very ill of it. The French that come out of other remote countries suffer as well as the strangers. We were told boiling it was a good remedy to prevent its griping quality; but that is a mere notion, for we know mineral waters boiled have a stronger effect, and this quality can proceed from nothing less.

The well waters here are much worse than the river waters, because more mineral. But our safety was in the water brought from the *Maison des Eaux,* where the aqueduct of Arcueil empties itself to serve the great palaces and city fountains.

The disease of the dysentery being one of the most common in Paris, the most celebrated drug for its cure is now the ipecacuanha; though I never once made use of it to any of our people, but cured them all as soon, and as well with our usual remedies. Indeed they have great need of it here, for the poorer sort of people, through ill diet, this water, and herbs, are very subject to it; this root is said to cure it with as much certainty, and as readily, as the jesuits powder an ague; of this most of the physicians and apothecaries agreed. They give it in powder from ten grains to forty, which is the largest dose. It most commonly vomits, and sometimes purges, but both gently. It is sold here from twenty to fifty crowns a pound. They divide it into four sorts, according to its goodness.

The pox here is the great business of the town; a disease which in some measure hath contributed to the ruin of physic here, as in London. This secret service hath introduced little contemptible animals of all sorts into business, and hath given them occasion to insult families, after they had once the knowledge of these misfortunes. And it is for this reason the quacks here, as with us, do thrive vastly into great riches beyond any of the physicians, by treating privately these calamities.

It was a pleasant diversion to me to read upon the walls every where about the town, but more particularly in the Fauxbourgh of St. Germain, the quacks' bills printed in great uncial letters.

By these bills it is evident, there is yet a certain modesty and decorum left in the concealing this disease, even amongst the French: they would be cured secretly, and as though nothing were doing; which those wretches highly promise. But this is that handle which gives those mean people an occasion to insult their reputation, and injure them in their health for ever.

Every body here puts their helping hand, and meddles with the cure of this disease, as apothecaries, barbers, women, and monks; yet I did not find by all the inquiry I could make, that they had other remedies than we. Nay, there is something practised in the cure of this distemper in England, which they at Paris know nothing of. . . .

The apothecaries' shops are neat enough, if they were but as well stored with medicines; and some are very finely adorned, and have an air of greatness, as that of Monsieur Geofferie, who has been provost des merchands, in the Rue Burtebur, where the entry to the Baffe Cour is a port-cochier, with vasas of copper in the niches of the windows; within are rooms adorned with huge vasas and mortars of brass, as well for fight, as for use. The drugs and compositions are kept in cabinets disposed around the room. Also laboratories backwards in great perfection and neatness. I must needs commend this gentleman for his civility towards me; and for his care in educating his son. . . .

It is here as with us. Some practise out of mere vanity, others to make a penny any way to get bread. The cause of all this is, I think, the great confidence people have of their own skill, an arrogance without thinking. To pass a judgment upon cures, and the good and evil practice of physic, without doubt is one of the nicest things, even to men of the faculty; but a jury, that is, the very ordinary men in England, are suffered now to undertake the question; when I may truly say, that I have ever found, no disparagement to them, the most learned men of the nation, the most mistaken in these matters; and can it be otherwise in so conjectural an art, when we ourselves scarce know, when we have done ill or well.

Another cause of the low esteem of physic here, are the sorry fees that are given to physicians; which makes that science not worth the application and study. The king indeed is very liberal, as in all things else, in his pensions to his chief physician, and gives his children good preferments.

Men are apt to prescribe to their physician, before he can possibly tell what he shall in his judgment think fitting to give; it is well if this was in negatives only; but they are prejudiced by the impertinence of the age, and our men, who ought to converse with the patient and his relations with prognostics only, which are the honour of physic; and not play the philosopher by fanciful and precarious interpretations of the natures of diseases and medicines, to gain a sort of credit with the ignorant; and such certainly are all those that have not studied physic thoroughly, and in earnest. **33**

VII. The City and the American Revolution

The Europeans planted their cities and civilization in the new world. In time the people of such cities as Boston rebelled against their oppressors. This movement toward freedom by the people would help inspire similar movements in the cities of the 19th and 20th centuries.

William V. Wells who wrote *The Life of Samuel Adams* (1865) described the Boston Massacre and the Boston Tea Party by means of firsthand accounts and contemporary documentation.

The USS Constitution
Now docked next to Charlestown Naval Shipyard gate was made with pines from Maine and Paul Revere was reputed to have made the copper sheathing for its bottom.

Raul Revere's House
One of the oldest wooden structures in Boston, Revere's house dates back to 1677.

Boston Massacre

. . . blood might thus have been prevented, but a lack of care on both sides hastened the event. The first affair of any importance occurred on Friday, the second day of March. There now remained the Fourteenth and Twenty-ninth Regiments in the town, the latter of whom had been stationed near Gray's and Mr. Neill's ropewalks, where the workmen were generally high-spirited young men, and ready at all times for a brush. The proximity of the barracks to this place soon brought the hands and the troops into hostile positions. Two of the soldiers had previously encountered one of the ropewalk men near the foot of King Street, where he knocked them down for some insult. Several of the soldiers armed themselves with clubs and swords, and proceeded to Gray's ropewalk, vowing revenge. The result of their visit is given in the affidavits taken several days later to trace the origin of the massacre which soon after occurred.

Bunker Hill
Not far from the USS Constitution *is Bunker Hill. An obelisk commemorates the famous battle of the American Revolution.*

(No. 5.)

"I, Nicholas Feriter, of lawful age, testify that on Friday, the 2d instant, about half after eleven o'clock, A.M., a soldier of the 29th Regiment came to Mr. John Gray's ropewalks, and, looking into one of the windows, said, *"By God, I'll have satisfaction!"* with many other oaths; at the last he said, he was not afraid of any one in the ropewalks. I stepped out of the window and speedily knocked up his heels. On falling, his coat flew open, and a naked sword appeared; which one John Wilson, following me out, took from him, and brought into the ropewalks. The soldier then went to Green's barrack, and in about twenty minutes returned with eight or nine more soldiers armed with clubs, and began, as I was told, with three or four men in Mr. Gray's warehouse, asking them why they had abused the soldier aforesaid? These men in the warehouse passed the word down the walk for the hands to come up, which they did, and soon beat them off. In a few minutes the soldiers appeared again at the same place, reinforced to the number of thirty or forty, armed with clubs and cutlasses, and headed by a tall negro drummer with a cutlass chained to his body, with which, at first rencounter, I received a cut on the head; but being immediately supported by nine or ten more of the ropemakers, armed with their wouldring-sticks, we again beat them off. And further I say not."

(No. 6.)

"I, Jeffrey Richardson, of lawful age, testify and say that on Friday, the 2d instant, about eleven o'clock, A.M., eight or ten soldiers of the Twenty-ninth Regiment, armed with clubs, came to Mr. John Gray's ropewalks, and challenged all the ropemakers to come out and fight them. All the hands then present, to the number of thirteen or fourteen, turned out with the wouldring-sticks, and beat them off directly. They very speedily returned to the ropewalk, reinforced to the number of thirty or forty, and headed by a tall negro drummer, again challenged them out; which the same hands accepting, again beat them off with considerable bruises. And further I say not."

(No. 8.)

"I, John Hill, aged sixty-nine, testify that in the forenoon of Friday, the 2d of March current, I was at a house, the corner of a passage-way leading from Atkinson's Street to Mr. John Gray's ropewalks, near Green's Barracks, so called, when I saw eight or ten soldiers pass the window with clubs. I immediately got up and went to the door, and found them returning from the ropewalks to the barracks; whence they again very speedily reappeared, now increased to the number of thirty or forty, armed with clubs and other weapons. In this latter company was a tall negro drummer, to whom I called, 'You black rascal, what have you to do with white people's quarrels?' He answered, 'I suppose I may look on,' and went forward. I went out directly, and commanded the peace, telling them I was in commission. But they, not regarding me, knocked down a ropemaker in my presence; and two or three of them beating him with clubs, I endeavored to relieve him; but on approaching the fellows who were mauling him, one of them with a great club struck at me with such violence, that had I not happily avoided, it might have been fatal to me. The party last mentioned rushed in towards the ropewalks, and attacked the ropemakers nigh the tar-kettle, but were soon beat off, drove out of the passage-way by which they entered, and were followed by the ropemakers, whom I persuaded to go back, and they readily obeyed. And further I say not."

In Dock Square, "a tall gentleman in a large white wig and red cloak" appeared, and, standing in the midst of the people, spoke to them briefly, so that "they were whist for some time." It has never been ascertained who he was, nor did those who listened to his speech ever give any clew afterwards to its purport. The loyalists subsequently endeavored to show that his remarks and actions were of an incendiary character; and Judge Oliver in his charge to the jury, at the trial, made "the tall man with the red cloak and white wig" the special subject of his animadversion. If the people knew him, their secret died with them. The Tories generally believed it to have been Samuel Adams; and one of their writers, in a controversy with him during the trial, pointedly threatens to bring out facts to prove who the person was, if he desired it; which Mr. Adams, in his reply as "Vindex," invites him to do, because it had been injuriously asserted that, owing to the peculiarity of his dress, he must have been one "holding office in the town." The red cloak was frequently worn at this time by gentlemen of the Province; and Copley's painting of Adams, taken soon after this time, represents him in red clothing; but Samuel Adams was not a tall man, but of about medium stature. Hancock and he were both then "in office," as members of the Legislature, and Hancock was the taller of the two. One of the lieutenants of the Fourteenth, in conversation with Joseph Allen, pointed to Molineux as the real author of the troubles, but gave no reason for the opinion. Mr. Adams says, in reply to a loyalist write on the subject, "As it is not known what *the tall gentleman with the red cloak said to the people,* whether he gave them good or ill advice, or any advice at all, we may probably form some conjecture concerning it when his person is ascertained." The writer leaves no chance to fix the identity upon himself or others. Whoever he was, the influence of this mysterious personage was exerted to disperse the people and restore peace, and not to excite the populace as has been represented. None of the crown witnesses were able to give the slightest hint as to the tenor of his remarks, except that they were followed by a space of quiet. There is testimony to prove that a prominent citizen urged the officers to order their soldiers into the barracks, and upon their promise to do so, the same person advised the people to disperse, upon which the cry of "Home! home!" was raised; but others shouted, "Hurrah for the main guard! there is the nest!" and some started in that direction at the head of King Street.

A sentinel was stationed at the door of the custom-house, situated at what is now the corner of State and Exchange Streets. A party of mischievous boys gathered round, and pelted him with snowballs, and pushed each other towards him, fully believing that he would not dare to fire without the civil authority. Even while he loaded and primed his musket, and knocked the breech upon the stone steps to settle the charge, they shouted, "Fire, and be damned!" "The Lobster dare not fire!" laughing, huzzaing, and piping the boatswain's whistle through their fingers. "If you come near me," said he, "I will blow your brains out; stand off"; and he called for the main guard to turn out, while a servant ran to the guard-house near by, and said, "They are killing the sentinel, turn out the guard."

Preston, who was captain of the day, at once detached seven or eight men of the Twenty-ninth Regiment, headed by a corporal, and followed himself with a drawn sword. They went down upon the run, swinging their guns and rushing through the people with fixed bayonets, pushing to and fro, cursing and shouting, "Make way, damn you, make way." As the people stood aside to let them pass, Fosdick remained and faced them. "Damn you, stand out of the way," said the soldiers. "I will move for no man under heaven," was the sturdy response; "I have offended no one." And they passed by him, and, arriving at the sentry-box, formed in a semicircle around it. As they hurried on, a gentleman who knew Preston said, "For God's sake, keep your men in order, and mind what you are about." The Captain, without replying, commanded his men to prime and load, and, afterwards going before them, put up their levelled pieces to an upright posture. Not more than two hundred persons were in the street as the soldiers charged by; and, at their appearance, this number had so far dispersed that not more than fifty or sixty remained in King Street, some standing on the door-sills of the opposite houses.

"I took Captain Preston by the coat," are the words of Henry Knox in his affidavit, "and told him for God's sake to take his men back again; for if they fired, his life must answer for the consequence. He replied he was sensible of it, or knew what he was about, or words to that purpose, and seemed in great haste and much agitated." Richard Palmes, seeing the muskets breast high, with bayonets fixed, approached Preston, and asked him if they were loaded. His answer was that they were, with powder and ball. "I hope," continued Palmes, "you do not intend to fire on the inhabitants." "By no means," replied Preston.

After the arrival of the troops at the sentry-box, the people had remained quiet until they saw the loading of the muskets, when a number of them, mostly boys, gave three cheers, and calling the soldiers "cowardly rascals" for "bringing arms against naked men," passed along in front, some of them striking the muskets as they went by, and daring the soldiers as "bloody backs" and "lobster scoundrels" to fire. "Lay aside your guns, and we are ready for you; fire if you dare!" "You dare not fire!" The boys laughed, shouted, whistled, and hurrahed, and a few snowballs were thrown at the soldiers. Among these were Montgomery and Kilroy, who had been of the part beaten by the ropewalk-hands on the previous Friday. A stick was thrown, striking the gun of the former, when the order to present was given, and Simpson, who knew what the next word was likely to be, stooped low to avoid the discharge. Then a voice, believed by some to be Preston's, though the fact was never proved, cried, "Fire!" and, stepping aside, Montgomery discharged his gun, and shot Attucks, a negro, who had until recently been a slave in an interior town, and was particularly noisy during the evening. The order to fire was repeated in a loud voice, "Damn your blood, fire! be the consequence what it will." A shot from Kilroy quickly succeeded, though Langford, the watchman, who looked him full in the face, besought him to hold. The soldier pointed his piece, and fired directly for the head of Samuel Gray, who was passing towards where Attucks had fallen; and Gray, after struggling, turned round upon his heel and fell dead. The remainder of the squad fired in succession upon the people,—one aiming at a boy who was running for safety. In all, three persons were killed, and eight wounded; and of the eleven but one had taken any part in the disturbance.

"I hear," wrote the Lieutenant-Governor, "of but one of the dead or wounded who attacked or insulted the soldiers. The rest seem to be innocent passengers or spectators. It's a great wonder many more were not killed."

The soldiers immediately reloaded their muskets, and now, infuriated with the sight of blood, were preparing to fire again, when checked by their commanding officer. The Twenty-ninth Regiment marched into King Street, and formed in three divisions,—the front one as for platoon firing. Soldiers of the Fourteenth at Green's Barracks, on hearing the firing, gave three cheers, and ran with their muskets to King Street, some of them saying, "This is all that we want," "This is our time." "Dogs were never so greedy for their prey." "I wish," said the surgeon of the Fourteenth, "that, instead of five or six, they had killed five hundred." "Damn you," said one of the soldiers, "I would kill a thousand of them." The snow lay nearly a foot deep, and was "crimson" with the blood of the slain. Several ran forward to the assistance of the wounded; and, as they stooped to remove them, the troops prepared to fire again, but were restrained.

Instantly the alarm was sounded. The town drums beat, and the bells in the churches were rung. "The soldiers are rising! to arms! to arms!" was the cry. "Turn out with your guns," "Town-born, turn out!"—"Language," said Warren, two years later, as he described the scene, "is too feeble to paint the emotion of our souls when our streets were stained with the blood of our brethren,—when our ears were wounded with the groans of the dying, and our eyes were tormented with the sight of the mangled bodies of the dead. . . . . Our hearts beat to arms; we snatched our weapons, almost resolved by one decisive stroke to avenge the deaths of our slaughtered brethren."

Upon the fearful clangor of bells and drums the population rushed forth, and the usual stillness of the night was converted into a tumultuous confusion as they pressed towards the scene of slaughter. Artisans from the ship-yards, shopmen, ropewalk-hands, gentlemen, sailors, men of all classes and avocations, goaded to madness, ran through the snow-clogged, frozen streets, ready for the conflict. But the character of Boston vindicated itself even in that awful hour. "Propitious Heaven," continues Warren, "forbade the bloody carnage." Patriots stood firm and self-possessed, and still turned for justice to the law before adopting sterner measures. The Lieutenant-Governor was called, and repairing to the Council Chamber, from the balcony he desired the surging throng to hear him speak. He requested them to disperse, promising to inquire into the affair in the morning; that "the law should take its course"; that he would "live and die by the law." He was requested to order the troops to their barracks. "It is not in my power," answered Hutchinson; "I have no command over the troops. It is with Colonel Dalrymple, and not with me." A gentleman asked him to look out of the window facing the main guard, to see the position of the soldiers, who were drawn up, apparently ready to fire again on the people.

The Tea Party

Still the great meeting remained, and awaited the coming of Rotch with the Governor's final decision. The dim light of the church added to the impressive solemnity of the occasion. All were convinced, as the cold night darkened without, that the last scene was about to be enacted. Everything was arranged and in readiness, yet only a few could have known what was intended. Should the Governor give the clearance, the ships would be at once sent to sea, and stout arms from among a nautical people were willing to assist in working them down the harbor. In case of refusal, it would be impossible to pass the guns of the Castle and Admiral Montagu's ships at the Narrows, and there remained but one alternative to prevent the landing of the accursed freight. At a quarter past six o'clock Rotch appeared and reported that he had entered his protest in accordance with the directions of the meeting of Tuesday, and that he had waited on the Governor for a pass, but "his Excellency told him he could not, consistently with his duty, grant it until his vessel was qualified." The proceedings which followed showed how perfectly systematic were the plans of the Committee of Correspondence. As soon as Rotch had made his report, Samuel Adams stood up and gave the word: "This meeting can do nothing more to save the country!"

Instantly a shout was heard at a door of the church from those who had been intently listening for the voice of Adams. The war-whoop resounded. Forty or fifty men disguised as Indians, who must have been concealed near by, appeared and passed by the church entrance, and, encouraged by Adams, Hancock, and others, hurried along to Griffin's, now Liverpool Wharf, near the foot of Pearl Street. The accounts of this event are such as were guardedly given at the time of its occurrence; and posterity can only imagine the scene of the thousands pouring out of the church portals into the wintry night, and making their way towards the harbor. In accordance with the arrangements, guards were posted to prevent the intrusion of spies, when the "Mohawks" and some others, not so disguised, sprang aboard the ships, and three hundred and forty-two chests of tea were emptied into the Bay "without the least injury to the vessels or any other property." "Nothing was destroyed but the tea, and this was not done with noise and tumult, little or nothing being said either by the agents or the multitude who looked on. The impression was that of solemnity, rather than of riot and confusion"; and a looker-on from a small eminence about fifty yards from the nearest ship, observed that the people on board were disguised. He could hear them cut open the tea chests, when they had brought them upon the deck, so noiselessly were the proceedings conducted. Three hours were occupied in the destruction, and by the end of that time it was estimated that at least one hundred and forty persons were engaged, accessions having been constantly made to the original number. The moon shone from a clear sky during the evening, and the British squadron lay but a short distance off, yet no interruption was experienced either from fleet or troops. When the last chest had been emptied, and the Mohawks and their assistants had gained the wharf, they marched homewards through the town with fife and drum, passing the house of a Loyalist, where Admiral Montagu was visiting, and the Admiral bandied some words with them as they went by. The work had not been accomplished an hour too soon; for the next morning the tea would have been placed under the protection of the Castle. People from towns twenty miles from Boston had attended the meeting that day at the Old South, and some of them the same night carried the news back to their villages. Boston subsided at once into its usual quiet. The next day the tea was found heaped up in windrows upon the Dorchester beach, were the wind and tide had carried it. The vessels from which the tea was thrown were the Dartmouth, the Eleanor, and the Beaver. A fourth, a brig from London, having fifty-eight chests on board, had already been cast away "on the back of Cape Cod," where the "Cape Indians" probably gave a good account of "the detested tea."

The closest secrecy was preserved as to the authors of this scheme and the actors in its accomplishment until after the War of Independence, when the names of a number were obtained. In 1836, eleven survived who had been mere lads at the time. Lendall, Pitts, and Adam Colson were probably the leading actors. Early in the present century, a resident of Boston who had conversed with the men of the Revolution on this subject, wrote: "Mr. Samuel Adams is thought to have been in the counselling of this exploit, and many other men who were leaders in the political affairs of the times; and the hall of council is said to have been in the back room of Edes and Gill's printing-office, at the corner of the alley leading to Brattle Street Church from Court Street." Others of the survivors of that intrepid band, as well as eminent men of the last century, have repeatedly mentioned Adams as one of the prime movers in the Tea-Party. That he was the guiding spirit in the public transactions between the arrival of the news that the tea had been shipped and its destruction, we have already seen. Only three days before the first public measures against the landing of the tea, Hutchinson had written to the Ministry describing Samuel Adams as the "chief manager on this side the water"; and his letter to Lord Dartmouth, pointing out Adams as the leader and "director of the town of Boston and the Assembly," had been sent less than three weeks before. Adams had hinted to Arthur Lee, in November, that his next letter would probably be upon no trifling matter. By the next vessel he sent his friend a full account of the great event.

> "You cannot imagine," he writes, "the height of joy that sparkles in the eyes and animates the countenances as well as the hearts of all we meet on this occasion, excepting the disappointed, disconcerted Hutchinson and his tools. I repeat what I wrote you in my last,—if Lord Dartmouth has prepared his plan, let him produce it speedily; but his Lordship must know that it must be such a plan as will not barely amuse, much less further irritate, but conciliate the affection of the inhabitants."

The Committee of Correspondence held a meeting the next day, and appointed Samuel Adams and four others to prepare an account of the last night's proceedings; and Paul Revere rode express to Philadelphia with the news, which was received there on the 26th with the ringing of bells and every sign of joy and universal approbation; and the next day, at a public meeting, it was indorsed. . . . **34**

VIII. Paris in Revolt

The ideals of the Enlightenment, the successes of the American Revolution and the conditions of France all helped to inspire a revolution against the establishment of France in 1789. Gouverneur Morris—U.S. representative to Paris and an anti-revolutionary—recorded his impressions of the revolt in his Diary.

Sunday 12.—This Morning I begin to take Bark by itself and the Stomach is no longer out of Humour. Write all the Morning. Dine

Conciergerie
One of the earliest palaces of the French kings. Marie Antoinette was kept there during her trial.

Royal Palace
Cardinal Richelieu had this palace built for himself in the late 1630's. It was from the grounds of the Royal Palace that Camille Desmoulins incited the people to march on the Bastille on July 14, 1789.

with the Maréchal de Castries who enquires very kindly the State of my Business. I tell him that I am about to conclude an indirect Agreement for 10,000 h_{ds} at 31, instead of 20,000 at 36, because *un mauvais Accomodement vaut mieux qu'un bon Procés*. He agrees in this Sentiment and is glad that my Voyage has not been wholly fruitless. He tells me that he is in Town for a few Days which he devotes to Business & therefore enquires how mine goes on. As I am going away he takes me aside and informs me that M_r Neckar is no longer in Place. He is much affected at this Intelligence, and indeed so am I. Urge him to go immediately to Versailles. He says he will not; that they have undoubtedly taken all their Measures before this Movement and therefore he must be too late. I tell him that it is not too late to warn the King of his Danger which is infinitely greater than he imagines. That his Army will not fight against the Nation, and that if he listens to violent Counsels the Nation will undoubtedly be against him. That the Sword has fallen imperceptibly from his Hand, and that the Sovereignty of this Nation is in the Assemblée Nationale. He makes no precise Answer to

Hotel des Invalides
Constructed by order of Louis XIV in the 1670's it was a hospital for those who had fought in his many costly wars. Today it serves as a military museum. On the grounds is the church of St. Louis des Invalides and the Tomb of Napoleon.

this but is very deeply affected. He tells me that if he stays longer in Town he will inform me, that we may see each other again. Call on Madame de La Suze who is not at Home, and then on Madame de Puisignieu who is just going out of Town; as He did not intend to depart untill ToMorrow Evening I presume that he has received Orders in Consequence of the new Arrangements. Call agreably to my Promise on Madame de Flahaut. Learn that the whole Administration is routed and M̲r̲ Neckar banished. Much Alarm here. Paris begins to be in Commotion, and from the Invalid Guard of the Louvre a few of the Nobility take a Drum and beat to Arms. Monsr̲ de Narbonne, the friend of Madame de Stahl, considers a civil War as inevitable and is about to join his Regiment, being as he says in a Conflict between the Dictates of his Duty and of his Conscience. I tell him that I know of no Duty but that which Conscience dictates. I presume that his Conscience will dictate to join the strongest Side. The little humpbacked Abbé Bertrand, after sallying out in a Fiacre, returns frightened because of a large Mob in the Rue S̲t̲ Honoré, and presently comes in another Abbé who is of the Parliament and who, rejoicing inwardly at the Change, is confoundedly frightened at the Commotions. I calm the Fears of Madame, whose Husband is mad and in a printed List, it seems, of the furious Aristocrats. Offer to conduct the Abbés safely Home, which Offer Bertrand accepts of. His Terror as we go along is truly diverting. As we approach the Rue S$_t$ Honoré his Imagination magnifies the ordinary Passengers into a vast Mob, and I can scarcely perswade him to trust his Eyes instead of his Fears. Having set him down, I depart for M$_r$ Jefferson's; in riding along the Boulevards, all at once the Carriages, Horses and Foot Passengers turn about and pass rapidly. Presently after we meet a Body of Cavalry with their Sabres drawn, and coming Half Speed. After they have passed us a little Way they stop. When we come to the Place Louis Quinze observe the People, to the Number of perhaps an hundred, picking up Stones, and on looking back find that the Cavalry are returning. Stop at the Angle to see the Fray, if any. The People take Post among the Stone which lies scattered about the whole Place, being there hewn for the Bridge now building. The Officer at the Head of this Party is saluted by a Stone and immediately turns his Horse in a menacing Manner towards the Assailant. But his Adversaries are posted in Ground where the Cavalry cannot act. He pursues his Route therefore and the Pace is soon encreased to a Gallop amid a Shower of Stones. One of the Soldiers is either knocked from his Horse or the Horse falls under him. He is taken Prisoner and at first ill treated. They had fired several Pistols but without Effect, probably they were not even charged with Ball. A Party of the Swiss Guards are posted in the Champs Elisées with Cannon. Proceed to M$_r$ Jefferson's. He tells me that M$_r$ Neckar received Yesterday about Noon a Letter from the King, by the Hands of Monsieur de La Luzerne, in which he orders him to leave the Kingdom, and at the same Time Mons$_r$ de La Luzerne is desired to exact a Promise that he will not mention the Matter to any Body. M$_r$ Neckar dines, and proposes to his Wife a Visit to a female friend in the Neighbourhood. On the Route he communicates the Intelligence and they go to a Country Seat, make the needful Arrangements and depart. M$_r$ de Montmorin immediately resigned, and is now in Paris. In returning from M$_r$ Jefferson's I am turned off to the left by the Vidette posted on the Road to the Place Louis Quinze. Go to Club. A Gentleman just arrived from Versailles gives us an Account of the new Administration. The people are employed in breaking open the Armorers' Shops, and presently a large Body of the Gardes Françoises appear with Bayonets fixed, in the Garden, mingled with the Mob, some of whom are also armed. These poor Fellows have passed the Rubicon with a Witness. Success or a Halter must now be their Motto. I think the Court will again recede, and if they do, all farther Efforts will be idle. If they do not, a Civil War is among the Events most probable. If the Representatives of the Tiers have formed a just Estimate of their Constituents, in ten Days all France will be in Commotion. The little Affray which I have witnessed will probably be magnified into a bloody Battle before it reaches the Frontiers, and in that Case an infinity of Corps Bourgeois will march to the Relief of the Capital. They had better gather in the Harvest. Return Home. This has been a pleasant Day and the Evening is cool.

In Effect, the little City of Paris is in as fine a Tumult as any one could wish. They are getting Arms wherever they can find any. Seize sixty Barrils of Powder in a Boat on the Seine. Break into the Monastery of S$_t$ Lazar and find a Store of Grain which the holy Brotherhood had laid in. Immediately it is put into Carts and sent to the Market, and on every Cart a Friar. The Gardemeuble du Roy is attacked and the Arms are delivered up, to prevent worse Consequences. These however are more curious than useful. But the Detail of the Variety of this Day's Deeds would be endless. Dine at Home and La Caze dines with me. After Dinner dress and walk to the Louvre, having previously ornamented my Hat with a green Bow in Honor of the Tier, for this is the Fashion of the Day which every Body is obliged to comply with who means to march in Peace. It is somewhat whimsical that this Day of Violence and Tumult is the only one in which I have dared to walk the Streets, but as no Carriages are abroad but the Fiacres I do not hazard being crushed, and I apprehend nothing from the Populace. Madame de Flahaut is under great Apprehension, which I endeavor to appease. Capellis comes in, and when we about to set off for the Palais royal we meet on the Stairs Mons$_r$ de — from Versailles, who tells us the News there. Go to Club and sit awhile chatting on the State of Public Affairs. Mons$_r$ de Moreton tells us that the present Ministers are a Set of Rascals & Tyrants; that he knows them perfectly well; and one of them it seems is his Relation, for whom however he exhibits no Partiality. After a while Mons.r de — arrives from Versailles and tells us that the fashion at Court this Day is to believe that the Disturbances at Paris are very trifling. The Assemblée Nationale have addressed the King to recall the former Ministry, and to permit the Assembly to send a Deputation to Paris to recommend the forming des Corps Bourgeois for the Maintenance of Order in the City. To the first he replied that the Executive Power is his and he will appoint who he pleases to be his Ministers, and he disapproves of the second Measure. In Consequence of this the Assembly make some sharp Resolutions, whose Purport seems to be the devoting to public Infamy the present Administration and declaring his Majesty's Advisers to be guilty of high Treason. Thus the Court and popular Party are already pitted against each other. In ten Days I think it will be decided whether the Retreat of the Monarch will be immediate and only ruin his Counsellors, or whether it will be remote and his own Ruin involved in that of his Ministers. Some horses are brought into the Garden of the Palais Royal. We go to see what they are, but cannot learn. We are told however by one of the Orators, that they have received a Deputation from the two Regiments quartered at St Denis, offering to join the Tiers if they will come out and receive them. My Companions urge them by all Means to go, but this Manoeuvre must at least be deferred till ToMorrow. The Leaders here I think err in not bringing about immediately some pretty severe Action between the foreign and National Troops. The Consequences would, in my Opinion, be decisive. Return Home. The Weather has been cool and pleasant toDay but this Evening it approaches toward cold. Martin gives me another Note from M.r Nesbitt who wants more Money than I can spare. Indeed his Wants surprize me, for he has lived now for three Months on what I have advanced so that he appears to have made no Provision whatever for his Existence in this Country, or else his Friends are so kind as to neglect him entirely and leave the Weight of his Support upon my Shoulders.

While sitting here a Person comes in and announces the taking of the Bastile, the Governor of which is beheaded and the Prevost des Marchands is killed and also beheaded; they are carrying the Heads in Triumph thro the City. The carrying of this Citadel is among the most extraordinary Things that I have met with; it cost the Assailants sixty Men it is said. The Hôtel Royal des Invalides was forced this Morning and the Cannon and small Arms &c$_a$, &c$_a$ brought off. The Citizens are by these Means well armed; at least there are the Materials for about thirty thousand to be equipped with, and that is a sufficient Army. I find that the Information received last Night as to the Arreté of the Assemblée Nationale is not just. They have only declared that the last Administration carry with them the Regret of the Chamber, that they will persist in insisting on the Removal of the Troops and that his Majesty's Advisers, whatever their Rank and Station, are guilty of all the Consequences which may ensue. Yesterday it was the Fashion at Versailles not to believe that there were any disturbances at Paris. I presume that this Day's Transactions will induce a Conviction that all is not perfectly quiet. From M$_r$ Le Couteulx's go to visit Madame de Flahaut who is in much Anxiety. Her Husband, she tells me, is foolhardy, and she apprehends much for his Safety.

Am stopped near the Pont Royale and obliged to turn into the Rue S$_t$ Honoré. Stopped again at the Church S$_t$ Roch, and a Number of foolish Questions asked. Col$_o$ Gardner comes to me; is very happy to be in Paris at the present Moment, So am I. Considers, as I do, the Capture of the Bastile to be an Instance of great Intrepidity. A few Paces from the Church I am again stopped & a vast Deal of Self Sufficiency in the Officer brings on an Altercation with my Coachman. As every Thing is turned into this Street and Interruptions of the Kind I experience are so frequent the *Embarras* is very great. I therefore turn back and come to the Hotel to dine. While I am at Dinner La Caze comes in. He contradicts his News of this Morning but says a Deputy is just arrived from the States General who brings an Account that the King has retreated &c$_a$, &c$_a$, &c$_a$. This I expected. We shall see. After Dinner go to M$_r$ Jefferson's; meet with no Difficulty. Ask him for a Passport for M$_r$ Nesbitt which he refuses, as I expected he would; however, having asked & even urged it I have done all which was in my Power. Go according to my Promise to Madame de Flahaut's. With her Nephew and the Abbeé Bertrand we proceed along the Quai to the Tuilleries. Walk a little and sit some Time. She wants to see the Deputies of the Assemblée Nationale come to Town, owns that it is foolish but says that all Women have the like Folly. There is much *Réjouissance* in Town. After placing Madame at Home her Nephew and I go to Club. I send away my Carriage and presently after receive a Message from her desiring the Loan of it. Send the Servants after the Coachman but it is too late; his Horses are put up and he is patroling as one of the Gardes Bourgeoises. The Duc D'Aiguillon and Baron de Menou are at Club, both of them Deputies of the Noblesse. I learn thro and from them the secret History of the Resolution of this Day. Yesterday Evening an Address was presented by the Assembly, to which his Majesty returned an Answer by no Means satisfactory. The Queen, Count D'Artois and Dutchess de Polignac had been all Day tampering with two Regiments who were made almost drunk and every Officer was presented to the King, who was induced to give Promises, Money, &ca, &ca, to these Regiments. They shouted Vive la Reine! Vive le Comte D'Artois! Vive la Dutchesse de Polignac! and their Music came and played under her Majesty's Window. In the mean Time the Maréchal de Broglio was tampering in Person with the Artillery. The Plan was to reduce Paris by Famine and to take two hundred Members of the National Assembly Prisoners. But they found that the Troops would not serve against their Country, of Course these Plans could not be carried into Effect. They took Care however not to inform the King of all the Mischiefs. At two o'Clock in the Morning the Duc de Liancourt went into his Bed Chamber and waked him. Told him all. Told him that he pawned his Life on the Truth of his Narration and that unless he changed his Measures speedily all was lost. The King took his Determination, the Bishop D'Autun (they say) was called on to prepare *un Discours,* which he did. The Orders were given for dispersing the Troops; and at the Meeting of the Assembly the King, accompanied by his two Brothers and the Captain of his Guard, came in and made his Speech. This produced very enthusiastic Emotions of Joy, and he was reconducted to the Chateau by the whole Assembly and by all the Inhabitants of Versailles. They tell me that the Baron de Bezenvald is dénoncé by the *Assemblée Nationale,* which Appellation the King recognizes in his Discours; that they will pursue the present Ministry &ca, &ca. I give my Opinion that after what is passed the Count D'Artois should not be suffered to stay in France. In this they agree. They say that they will *faire le Procés* of the Maréchal de Broglio & probably of the Baron de Breteuil. Sup with them, and the Claret being better than any I have tasted in France, I give them as a Toast the Liberty of the French Nation and then the City of Paris, which are drank with very good Will. This has been a very fine Day. It is said that the King is to be in Town at Eleven o'Clock ToMorrow. But for what?—Bon Mot: the Baron de Bezenval is *dénoncé* on Account of some Letters he had written which were intercepted. The Duke de La Rochefoucault, appointed one of the Deputies from the Assemblée Nationale to the City of Paris, meets the Baron coming out of the King's Cabinet. *'Eh bien! Monsieur le Baron, avez vous encore des Orders à donner pour Paris?'* The Baron takes it as a *Politesse*. *'Non, Monsieur le Duc, excepté qu'on M'envoie ma Voiture.'*—*'Aparemment c'est une Voiture de Poste, Monsieur le Baron.'*—Another. In the Procession Yesterday the King and Count D'Artois, walking together, were much crowded. One of the Deputies said to another: *'Voyez comme on presse le Roi et Monsieur le Comte D'Artois.'* The other answered: *'Il y a cette Différence pourtant, que le Roi est pressé par l'Amour de ses Peuples.'* To which the King, perhaps not hearing more than the last Words of the Conversation, replied in turning round: *"Oui, c'est juste.'*

Thursday 16. — This Morning La Caze calls and tells me it has been impossible to do any Thing Yesterday, the Farmers being out of Town, but as soon as they return it will be accomplished. Time however wears away. The King, who was to have been in Town this Day, does not come till ToMorrow, being sick. Write to M$_r$ Nesbitt. Dine at Home and after Dinner visit at the Marquis de La Fayette's. Thence go to Doctor M$_c$Donald and Madame de La Suze's. Neither of the Three at Home. Call on Madame de Flahaut and thence go to Club. Nothing new. No Certainty as to the Administration. Sup, and drink Claret as a Remedy for by febrile Complaints. This has been a fine Day.

Friday 17. — This Morning my Coachman tells me that there are Placarts up forbidding any Carriages to run, as the King is to be in Town this Day between ten and eleven. Here then is another Day in which Nothing will be done. Dress immediately and go out. Get at a Window (thro the Aid of Madame de Flahaut) in the Rue S$_t$ Honoré, thro which the Procession is to pass. In squeezing thro the Crowd my Pocket is picked of a Handkerchief which I value far beyond what the Thief will get for it and I would willingly pay him for his Dexterity, could I retrieve it. We wait from eleven till four. It seems that his Majesty was escorted by the Militia of Versailles to the Point de Jour, where he entered the double File of Parisian Militia which extends from thence to the Hôtel de Ville; each Line composed of three Ranks, consequently it is a Body six deep extending that Distance. The Assemblée Nationale walk promiscuously together in the Procession. The King's Horse Guards, some of the Gardes de Corps, and all those who attend him have the Cockades of the City, viz: Red and Blue. It is a magnificent Procession in every Respect. After it is over, go to Dinner at the Traiteur's and get to a Beef Steak and bottle of Claret. A Deputy from Bretagne, whom I met with formerly at a Table d'hôte at Versailles, comes in and we seat him at our little Table. He tells me that the King Yesterday sent the Assembly a Letter of Recall for M$_r$ Neckar. That the Ministers have all resigned except the Baron de Breteuil, who says he never accepted. That the Count D'Artois, the Duke and Dutchess of Polignac, Mons$_r$ de Vaudreuil, and in short the whole Committee Polignac, have decamped last Night in Despair. I tell him that travelling may be useful to the Count D'Artois and therefore it would be well if he visited foreign Countries. We have a Conversation on the Commerce of their Islands in which I state to him what I conceive to be the true Principle on which their System should be founded. He desires farther Conversation when that Matter shall be agitated. Tell him I am going to London; he desires to have my Address that he may write to me. I promise to let him have it. He mentions Something which interests my Friend the Comtesse de Flahaut. I tell him sundry Truths, the Communication of which will be useful to her, and omit certain others which might prove injurious and thus make an Impression different from what he had received, but I fear the Folly of her Husband and the Madness of his Brother will ruin them both. It is impossible to help those who will not help themselves. I call on her and communicate what has passed, for her Government. Sit awhile with her and the Abbé Bertrand and then go to Club. The King this Day confirmed the Choice made of a Mayor, [Bailly.] Gave his Approbation of the Regiment of City Guards &c$_a$, &c$_a$. He put in his Hat a large Cockade of the Red and blue Ribbands and then, and not till then, received the general Shouts of Vive le Roi! This Day I think will prove an useful Lesson to him for the Rest of his Life, but he is so weak that unless he be kept out of bad Company it is impossible that he should not act wrongly. Sup at Club and drink Claret, from which within this two Days I have derived much Benefit. The Weather is fine.

Sunday 19. — La Caze calls this Morning and tells me all will be finished next Tuesday. I fret a great Deal and shew a great Deal of Humor, partly from what I feel but principally to render him urgent with Le N_d. Go to M_r Jefferson's towards noon (ie) about two o'Clock, and tell him I shall send my Servant with my Letters on Tuesday or Wednesday next and desire him to make out a Passport. Thence to Madame de Flahaut's to Dinner. Our Company the Abbé Bertrand, Duc de Biron and Éveque D'Autun. A very agreable Party. After Dinner visit a Painter and see three Pieces, in one of which the actual Execution of Perspective goes beyond my Power of Imagination, Particularly in the right Hand of the principal Figure which stands out so compleatly from the Canvass that one absolutely sees all round it, A thing scarce credible but which is not the less true. The Subject is Love escaped from his Cage and leaving by his Flight the Ladies in Anguish and Despair. The expression does not come up to my Ideas of the Power of this Art, but the Light and Shade are distributed thro the whole Piece in a most astonishing Perfection. He shews us a Piece he is now about for the King, taken from the Eneid; Venus restraining the Arm which is raised in the Temple of the Vestals to shed the Blood of Helen. I tell him he had better paint the Storm of the Bastile, it will be a more fashionable Picture, & that one Trait will admit of a fine Effect. It is one of the Gardes Françaises who, having got Hold of The Gate and unable to bring it down, cries to his Comrades of the Populace to pull by his Legs, and the Man has the Force and Courage to hold while a dozen of them pull him like a Rope and bring down the Gate, so that he actually sustains the Rack. To represent him drawn out of Joint with his Head turned round, encouraging them to draw still harder, must I think have a fine Effect. L'Éveque D'Autun agrees with me entirely in this Sentiment. Returning we find Monsieur de Rouillé, who I find is writing a History of the present Revolution. He promises to meet me at Club and give me the News from M_r Neckar. Take the Abbé Home and then go to Club. Mons_r de Rouillé tells me they have yet no News from M_r Neckar but expect an Express ToNight, and that if he is not yet farther than Bruxelles he will be in ToMorrow Night. Recommend a Subscription to collect the various Papers found in the Bastile and then to employ an able Hand in writing the Annals of that diabolical Castle from the Beginning of Louis the fourteenth's Reign to the present Moment. Something of this Sort will I believe be done. Give the Hint also of forming the Gardes Françaises into a City Guard with very high Pay, and to keep up the Corps by putting into it all those who by good Conduct shall have merited something more than the Rank of a common Soldier without being qualified for that of a Serjeant. They know not what to do at present with this Corps. Sup and take my Pint of Claret which does me much Good. A fine Day.

Monday 20. — This Morning writing. At noon go out to visit M$_r$ Le N$_d$; meet La Caze on the Way, who has the Agreement drawn fair to be signed. Take him in and visit L. Le Couteulx, who signs and desires me to call on him this Afternoon. Go thence to the Hôtel de Ville and with much Difficulty find out the Marquis de La Fayette, who is exhausted by a Variety of Attentions. Tell him I will send his Letters to America, and he must give me a Passport to visit the Bastile. Agree to dine with him on Condition that I may bring my own Wine. Return Home; write, and ab$_t$ four go to the Hôtel de La Fayette. Find there Madame, the Duc de La Rochefoucault &c$_a$. Dine. He [La Fayette] gives me my Passport. Suggest to him my Plan respecting the Gardes Françaises, which he likes. Advise him to have a compleat Plan for the Militia prepared and to submit it to the Committee. Ask him if he can think of any Steps which may be taken to induce the King to confer on him the Government of the Isle of France. He tells me that he would prefer that of Paris simply. That he has had the utmost Power his Heart could wish and is grown tired of it. That he has commanded absolutely an hundred thousand Men, has marched his Sovereign about the Streets as he pleased, prescribed the Degree of Applause which he should receive, and could have detained him Prisoner had he thought proper. He wishes therefore as soon as possible to return to private Life. In this last Expression he deceives himself or wishes to deceive me; a little of both perhaps. But in Fact he is the Lover of Freedom from Ambition, of which there are two Kinds, the one born of Pride, the other of Vanity and his partakes most of the latter. Go from hence to Monsieur Le Couteulx's; he is just going out but is discussing a Point with M$_r$ Delaville which will I am afraid do Mischief. He insists that Le N$_d$ agreed on the Part of the Farm that the Tob₀ now at Bourdeaux should be received according to the real Taxe. This is not true. It was to be left on the Footing of Le Couteulx's Agreement with Delaville. I take him aside and shew him the Folly of what he is about & that he will only alarm the Committee of the Farm &c$_a$. At length he sends after Delaville to settle the Matter but he is gone and L—t promises to write as soon as he comes home but he will I dare say neglect it. He tells me he has examined my Plan. That as to any Advantage to them in it he is quite indifferent, but with a View to serve M$_r$ Morris he will consent provided his Cousin agrees, and he wishes to consult him. All this I understand thoroughly. He tells me that M$_r$ Morris has drawn for the Freight of the *Alliance* on the House at Cadiz. I express my Surprize, which is unfeigned. Assure him that I do not comprehend it. That he has not mentioned the Matter to me and that I consider it as a Measure taken to reimburse Mess$_{rs}$ Bourdicu for their Advance &c$_a$. He says if that is the Case he shall have a better Opinion of it, but that he should feel much less 100,000 in a Train of Business than 20,000 as a dead Advance, and that had he received 40,-000 he should have gone with Pleasure into the Advance of 120,-000 . I feel too much the Force of all these Observations to reply otherwise than by assenting. I press nothing and leave my Plan to the Impression which I think it has already made. Go to Madame de Flahaut's. Make a long Visit; at first tete à tete. Give her some Verses and with infinite Coolness and Seriousness tell her that I cannot consent to be only a Friend,...that I know myself too well. That at present I am perfectly my own Master with respect to her, but that it would not long be the Case. That having No Idea of inspiring her with a Passion I have no Idea either of subjecting myself to one. That besides, I am timid to a Fault. That I know it to be wrong but cannot help it. She thinks it a very strange Conversation, and indeed so it is, but I am much mistaken if it does not make an Impression much greater on Reflection than at the first Moment. Nous verrons. Go to Club. Stay a very few Minutes. The Duke of Orleans is there. I am as cold with Respect to him as an Englishman. A thousand to one that we are never acquainted but if we are he must make au moins la Moitié du Chemin. Return Home early to meet La Caze who was to see me this Evening; find that he has been gone Half an Hour. Sit and write awhile. This has been a very fine Day.

Tuesday 21. — This Morning writing. At half past one call on Madame de Flahaut who exprest yesterday a Wish to accompany me to the Bastile. Capellis and the Abbé Bertrand are waiting. Presently after, Madame appears with Mademoiselle Duplessis. We get all together into the Coach of Capellis and go to the Bastile. Some Difficulty in getting thro the Guards notwithstanding my Passport. We meet in the Architect employed in the Demolition an old Acquaintance of the Abbé, who is glad to be useful. He shews us every Thing. More than I wish to see, as it stinks horribly. The storming of this Castle was a bold Enterprize. Return. I bring back the Ladies and leave them at Home. Go to Club and dine. We drink freely and I prevail on the Frenchmen to toast, which in their large Glasses and with very generous Bourdeaux, flushes them finely. Go thence to Le Couteulx's. He has heard nothing yet of Le Normand but at my Instigation writes him a Note. Cantellux is not yet come to Town. Laurent is to write me Tomorrow the Result of a Conference with his Cousin but I dare say he will neglect it. Being thus no farther advanced than I was before, I go and spend the Evening with Madame de Flahaut instead of writing, as I should otherwise have done. This Day has been warm but pleasant.

Wednesday 22$_d$ — This Morning write. La Caze comes in and tells me he has gained his Cause. After a while Le N$_d$ comes in and tells me that the Farm will not agree to the Form of the Contract but insist that the Tobacco shall be delivered on the same footing with that taken from the Merchants. As Delaville was with me this Morning and told me he had not received the Letter which L. Le Couteulx promised to write, I see at once how this Disappointment has happened. I tell Le N$_d$ the Story and I tell him that I am determined to agree with the Farm on their Terms if they insist, but I will write a Letter to him complaining of this Conduct &c$_a$ &c$_a$. Sit down to write this Letter instead of reading those which I have just received from America. M$_r$ Jefferson comes in. Finding me very busy he makes a very short Visit. At three I go to Club to meet the Gentlemen with whom I engaged to dine at a Table d'Hôte. We go thither and have a good Dinner for 3 ; Coffee &c$_a$, &c$_a$, included the Price of the Dinner is 48$_s$. After Dinner walk a little under the Arcade of the Palais Royal waiting for my Carriage. In this Period the Head and Body of M$_r$ de Foulon are introduced in Triumph. The Head on a Pike, the Body dragged naked on the Earth. Afterwards this horrible Exhibition is carried thro the different Streets. His Crime is to have accepted a Place in the Ministry. This mutilated Form of an old Man of seventy five is shewn to Bertier, his Son in Law, the Intend$_t$ of Paris, and afterwards he also is put to Death and cut to Pieces, the Populace carrying about the mangled Fragments with a Savage Joy. Gracious God what a People! From the Palais Royal I go to Mess$_{rs}$ Le Couteulx. Speak pretty sharply to Laurent, accusing him for what has happened this Day at the Farm; he tries to defend himself but I put an End to the Conversation and tell him my Determination. Shew the Letter I have written. He wishes to make Alterations, upon which I desire him to make a Draft. He does so, which I alter and put in my Pocket. He tells me that Cantellux also agrees to my Plan of a Circulation but makes some disagreable Observations on the Reasons why I desire it. Call for a Moment on Madame de Flahaut according to Promise but she is abroad and Monsieur presses me to return. Come Home and sit down to write. Make up my Letter to Le N$_d$ and send it. Servant from Madame de Flahaut. She is come Home and wishes to see me. Go thither and after a few Minutes return and sit down to write. Fine weather. **35**

References

1. Thucydides, *History of the Peloponnesian War* (Bangs Brothers, New York, 1855).
2. *Ibid.*
3. *Ibid.*
4. *Xenophon's Minor Works* (Henry G. Bohn, London, 1857).
5. *Ibid.*
6. *The Politics of Aristotle* (Henry G. Bohn, London, 1953).
7. *Ibid.*
8. Theocritus, *Idyl.*
9. Plutarch, *Parallel Lives* (George Bell and Sons, London, 1889).
10. Titus Livius, *Roman History* (D. Appleton and Co., New York, 1898).
11. *Ibid.*
12. Cicero, *On Duties.*
13. Sallust, *History of the Conspiracy of Catiline* (Longman, Brown, Green, London, 1845).
14. Cicero, *Laws.*
15. Suetonius, *The History of Twelve Ceasars* (David Nutt, London, 1899).
16. Tacitus, *Annals* (John Murray, London, 1909).
17. Juvenal, *Satires* (T. Ward, London, 1825).
18. Justinian, *The Digest* (Cambridge University Press, London, 1879-1881).
19. C. Diehl, *The Hippodrome at Constantinople* in D.C. Munro and George C. Sellery, *Medieval Civilization* (Century Co., New York, 1907).
20. *Ibid.*
21. Paul Lacroix, *Manners, Customs and Dress During the Middle Ages and During the Renaissance Period* (Chapman and Hall, London, 1874).
22. A. Giry and A. Reville, *Emancipation of the Medieval Towns* in *Historical Miscellany* edited by E.W. Dow (Holt, New York, 1907).
23. *English Historical Documents* (Oxford University Press) Vol. II.
24. *Ibid.*
25. *Ibid.*
26. G. Boccaccio, *Decameron* (London, 1895).
27. Jacob C. Burckhardt, *The Civilization of the Renaissance in Italy* (S. Sonneschein and Co., London, 1892).
28. Girogio Vasari, *Lives of the Painters* (London, 1852).
29. Thomas B. Macaulay, *The History of England from the Accession of James II* (Harper and Row, New York, 1849-1861).
30. *The Diary of Samuel Pepys, 1659-1669* (Frederick Warne and Co., London, 1887).

REFERENCES

31. *Diary and Correspondence of John Evelyn* (Henry G. Bohn, London, 1859).
32. *Memoirs of the Duke of Saint Simon* (M.W. Dunne, London, 1901).
33. Martin Lister, *Travels* in *A General Collection of the Best and Most Interesting Voyages and Travels in All Parts of the World* edited by John Pinkerton (London, 1809) Vol. IV.
34. William V. Wells, *Life of Samuel Adams* (Little Brown, Boston, 1865).
35. Gouverneur Morris, *A Diary of the French Revolution* (Boston, 1939), 142-159.

INDEX

Abbeville, 199, 205
Adams, Samuel, 349, 353-359
Africa, 163, 183, 193
Agis, 104-110
Agrippa, 152
Alexander VI, 242
Alexandria, 101-103, 183-185
American Revolution, 349-361
Amiens, 194
Antillea, 279
Aristotle, 68-101, 229
Arles, 191
Arno River, 245
Arras, 199, 201
Athens, 24-101
Attucks, 355
Augustus, 145-150
Aurillac, 196
Aquitaine, 195

Babel, 1-2
Babylonia, 1, 81
Bacon, Francis, 314
Bastile, 365-371
Bath, 286-287, 305
Beauvais, 194, 203
Berlin, 282
Birmingham, 284-286, 300
Blois, 195
Boccaccio, Giovanni, 219-226, 254
Bologna, 253, 261
Bordeaux, 195, 197
Boston, 349-360
Boston Massacre, 350-357
Boston Tea Party, 349, 357-360
Brighton, 285
Bristol, 279-280, 287

Broc, 201
Browne, Thomas, 280
Bruges, 188, 190, 195, 201
Bruno,G., 227
Burckhardt, Jacob Christoph, 227-251
Caen, 187
Caesar, Julius, 215
Calvin, 227
Cambrai, 201
Cambridge, 308
Canterbury Tales, 283
Capitoline Hill, 133
Carthage, 183
Catalina, 140-142
Cateau-Cambresis, 196
Cavaliers, 312
Cellini, B., 249
Champs Elisees, 364
Charlemagne, 184, 188, 191, 197
Charles I, 281, 305
Charles II, 278, 282, 285, 287, 298, 300, 301-309, 311
Charles V, 242
Cheltenham, 285
China, 215
Cicero, 138-140, 142-145
Clement VII, 251, 262
Coblenz, 180
Coffee houses of London, 295-298
Colbert, 278
Columbus, Christopher, 193
Committee of Correspondence, 357-360
Commons, 283
Copernicus, N., 227
Condom, 196
Constantinople, 162-176, 200
Corinth, 33-35

Cornwall, 305
Covent Garden, 291, 296
Crete, 76
Cromwell, Oliver, 284
Crusaders, 186
Cyprus, 1, 282
Cyrus, King, 1

Dante, A., 228, 254
Dartmouth, 358
David, King, 1-4
da Vinci, L., 227
Decameron, 219-226
de Stahl, Madame, 363
Devonshire, 309
Diocletian, 157
Dock Square, 353
Dorchester, 358
Dryden, 294, 296, 310, 311, 313

Edinburgh, 298
Egypt, 1, 5, 43, 76, 77, 101, 102, 183
Elizabeth I, 325
England, 187, 190, 195, 202-216, 278-328
Etampes, 195
Evelyn, John, 314, 320-328
Exeter, 300, 301

Feriter, Nicholas, 351
fitz Stephen, William, 208
Flanders, 199
Florence, 220, 234, 251, 252, 253, 255, 261, 273
France, 182,-197, 216, 219, 252, 290, 328-348, 361-376
Frankfort, 180

Galen, 314
Galileo, 227
Gaul, 183
Genesis, 2
Genoa, 185, 200, 230
George II, 291
Germany 177-182

Ghent, 195
Ghibelline, 241
Ghiberti, Lorenzo, 270
Gibraltar, 190
Giry, A., 194
Gray, John, 351
Gray, Samuel, 355
Great Hall, 261
Greece, 24-115, 165, 230
Green Barracks, 352
Guelph, 241

Halley, Edmund, 315
Hamburg, 190
Hancock, John, 353
Hebron, 213
Heidelberg, 216-219
Henning, Edward, 293
Henry I, 205
Henry II, 201, 207
Henry III, 215
Hippocrates, 314
Hippodrome, 162-176
Hiram, 3
Homer, 86
Hotel de Ville, 372
Hutchinson, Gov. Thomas, 357-359

Idyl, 101-103
India, 278
Ireland, 284, 285
Israel, 1-23
Italy, 191, 197, 227-278

James I, 284
Jebusites, 1
Jefferson, Thomas, 364, 371, 374
Jenkyn, William, 309
Jeremiah, 12-14
Jericho, 1
Jerman, Edward, 278
Jerusalem, 1-23
Jews, 1-23, 181, 192, 239, 260, 261, 290, 297
Johnson, Michael, 284
Johnson, Samuel, 284

Index

Jupiter, 152
Julius II, 262, 271
Justinian, 157-162, 169, 173, 174, 175, 176
Juvenal, 154-157, 310

Kent, 288, 292
Kilroy, 355
Kleomenes, 110-115

Lacroix, Paul, 182-194
La Fayette, Marquis de, 272
Lamprecht, K., 177
Lancashire, 309
Laon, 194
Lebanon, 4
Leeds, 283
Leo X, 262
Leonidas, 105-106, 108, 109
Libya, 43
Liege, 201
Lille, 195, 201
Lima, 284
Lincolnshire, 305
Lisbon, 282-283
Lister, Martin, 328, 332-348
Liverpool, 285
Livy, 116-138, 242
London, 195, 205-216, 278, 279, 280, 287-328
London Gazette, 308
Louis VI, 202
Louis VII, 199, 202
Louis VIII, 329
Louis XIV, 278, 330
Louis XV, 364
Loyalists, 358
Lubeck, 190
Luther, 227
Luxembourg, 334
Lykurgus, 104, 108

Macaulay, Thomas B., 278-315
Madrid, 282
Mainz, 203, 282-283
Manchester, 287

Marseilles, 183, 184, 190
Medici, 229-236, 252, 254, 262, 263, 264, 272, 273
Mediterranean, 1, 186, 193, 200
Michelangelo, 227, 252-272
Middle Ages, 177-226
Middlesex, 288
Milan, 239, 243
Minos, 77
Mohawk Indian,
Moliere, 314
Montpellier, 186, 195
Mount Moriah, 1
Morris, Gouverneur, 361-376
Moses, 12, 260
Munster, 196

Nantes, 199
Naples, 186, 230, 234, 239, 241, 243
Narbonne, 186, 195
Nebuchadnesser, 1
Nehemiah, 1, 14-18
Nero, 150-154
Newcastle, 288
Newgate, 303
Newton, 227
Nile, 215, 258
Norway, 212
Norwich, 280-282, 287

Old Bailey, 332
Orleans, 195
Ostia, 153
Oxford, 280, 290, 301

Palais Royal, 334, 365
Palestine, 186
'Parallel Lives,' 104
Paris, 187, 189-190, 195, 197, 216, 219, 278, 328-348, 361-376
Paul III, 262
Peloponnesian War, 24-33
Pepys, Samuel, 279, 315, 319-320
Pericles, 24
Perugia, 244

Petrarch, 254
Phoenicians, 183
Philadelphia, 360
Picardy, 199, 205
Piccadilly, 290
Pieta, 267-268, 270
Pisa, 185
Pius IV, 262
Place des Victoires, 278
Place Royal, 332
Place Vendosme, 340
Plato, 68, 83, 84, 85
Plutarch, 104-115
Preston, Captain, 355

Quakers, 319

Raphael, 227
Rhine, 178,
Rouen, 187
Red Sea, 183
Redon, 196
Renaissance, 227-277
Remiremont, 196
Revere, Paul 360
Reville, A., 194
Rheims, 202
Rhine, 199
Rome, 116-176, 181, 182, 197, 215, 256, 258, 278
Roundheads, 312-313
Royal Society, 280, 298, 312-315
Rubicon, 365
Russia, 212

Saint-Denis, 184
Saint Germain, 329, 332, 347
Saint Mark's, 165
Saint-Omer, 196, 201
Saint Paul, 209, 289, 324
Saint Peters, 261, 273
Saint Sophia, 163, 176
Saint Quentin, 201
Saint Simon, 328-332

Saint Valey, 196
Sallust, 140-142
Samaritans, 1
Saul, King, 2
Savoy, 191
Seine, 345
Senegal, 193
Sens, 202
Sicily, 183
Silver mining, 58-65
Socrates, 49-54
Sodom, 322
Soissons, 201
Solomon, King, 3-12, 163
Sorbonne, 332
Spain, 183, 237, 238-239
Sparta, 24, 104-115
Suetonius, 145-150
'Sun King', 278
Syria, 183

Tacitus, 151-154
Becket, Thomas,
Thames, 208, 287-288, 321, 345
Theocritus, 101-103
Thucydides, 24-49
Tiber, 258
Toulouse, 190, 195
Tours, 195
Trent, 308
Treves, 203
Troy, 322
Tuilleries, 334, 367
Tyre, 3, 8

Valenciennes, 201
Vasari, Giorgio, 252-273
Venice, 165, 185, 191, 192, 193, 230, 234, 242, 246, 253, 262, 297
Versailles, 328, 330, 362, 364-365, 369
Vitruvius, 269
Virginia, 279

Index

Weavers Gild, 207
Weissenburg, 196
Wells, William V., 349
West Indies, 279
Westiminster, 292,
Westminster Hall, 307
Wheeler, Sir George, 326

Wilson, John, 351
Wren, Christopher, 278

Xenophon, 24, 49-67

York, 281, 308
Yorkshire, 304
Ypres, 199